JOHN MA

CW00944269

THE SEDUCTION
OF THE GULLIBLE

THE CURIOUS HISTORY OF THE
BRITISH "VIDEO NASTIES"
PHENOMENON

PROCRUSTES PRESS

NOTTINGHAM · ROME

1997

FURY AT 'SNUFF' MOVIE FOR KIDS

A SICKENING "snuff" movie showing a man having his head chopped off has been seized at a kids' comic fair.

Horrified trading watchdogs also found banned videos featuring cannibalism, torture and mutilation.

They were discovered among pirate copies of Disney family favourites on sale at the fair in a Birmingham hotel.

A stallholder from Yorkshire was quizzed by trading standards officers but he has not been charged.

One of the videos, *Cannibal Holocaust*, showed a white man being

Daily Sport 6th April 1993

Nasties seized in comic fair swoop

hacked to death by a tribe of half-naked Amazonian Indians.

The doomed "actor" is thought to have been drugged before being decapitated and disembowelled with a jungle knife.

The city's trading standards chairman, Dr. Mike Hilburn, said: "I have never seen anything like it. And I have no doubt the scenes were genuine."

He added: "It is beyond belief that anyone could film actual scenes of humans being butchered."

Other illegal "nasties" on sale to youngsters included the notorious *Killer Driller* and gory copies of *Cannibal Feroz* and *Hellraiser*.

They were offered at £10 a time alongside cartoons and children's adventure stories.

The swoop was organised after an anonymous tip-off. But the videos had been on sale for two hours before the officers arrived.

Said Dr. Hilburn: "It is possible some of them had already been bought by children who didn't realise what they were."

His men seized more than 100 films, most of them crude imported copies with foreign sub-titles.

The sale was held at Birmingham's Midland Hotel.

A spokesman for the hotel refused to comment yesterday.

But Edgbaston MP, Dame Jill Knight, said: "It is outrageous that this appalling material was offered for sale at a function intended for children."

HORRIFIED: Trading standards boss Peter Mawdsley with some of the sick videos

SNUFFED OUT
Cops swoop to seize 3,000 sick killer videos

EVIL: A still from one of the videos

UNDERCOVER investigators have smashed a sickening international racket in depraved videos.

Police seized 3,000 nauseating tapes showing torture, mutilation and cannibalism in a series of raids.

The haul includes several "snuff" movies, in which actual murders are filmed.

Officers infiltrated the ring, which worked mainly by mail-order. On Wednesday night they swooped on houses in Liverpool, Leicester, Cardiff, Redruth, Solihull, Kettering and Rochester.

Inquiries also took them to Scotland and North Wales.

Scalped

Film titles seized included Cannibal Holocaust, Human Experiments, Blood Bath, Carnage, Blood Sucking Freaks, Weasels Rip My Flesh and A Lizard In A Woman's Skin.

In one depraved scene from Anthropophagus — the Beast, a man guts a pregnant woman, then eats the foetus. Other sick

FLASHBACK: July 27, 1990

10 KIDS DIE ON VIDEOS
Porn beasts film tortures of innocent

By GEORGE HILL

ening films show people being scalped and having their eyes removed, tongues cut out, and limbs hacked off.

Some of the videos claim to show post-mortems.

They were being sold for between £12 and £90.

Children as young as 12 were involved in copying and peddling the tapes.

Ten people were helping police inquiries yesterday. They are likely to be charged under the Video Recordings or Obscene Publications Acts.

Police have alerted Interpol to check out links with the ring in Germany, Finland and the Republic of Ireland.

Gruesome

Liverpool trading standards boss Peter Mawdsley, who co-ordinated the operation, said: "We believe most of the tapes were imported, then copied and distributed.

"The material is gruesome and horrifying — so sickening that the officers cataloguing the tapes can only watch them for short periods at a time.

"I am certain we have cracked a major network in this vile trade.

"And I can only question the mentality of people involved in it and those who watch this kind of stuff for enjoyment."

Councillor Robbie Quinn, chairman of Liverpool's consumer protection committee, added: "Some of the films are unwatchable."

Tragic young victims of evil

By FRANK CURRAN

● SICKENED police believe that up to 20 children have been murdered in snuff movies.

The Daily Star revealed two years ago how schoolboy Jason Swift's horrific slaughter was captured on film by paedophile perverts.

● Jason, 14, was abducted, gang-raped, tortured and strangled in an East London flat in 1985.

Four men were caged for life after being convicted of his manslaughter.

● They were members of a gang which detectives believe tortured and murdered 20 kids aged between six and 16.

Following Jason's death, police set up Operation Orchid to smash the paedophile network.

● They have since questioned the men serving life for Jason's murder about other horrors.

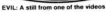

Daily Star 8th May 1992

THE SEDUCTION OF THE GULLIBLE: THE CURIOUS HISTORY OF THE BRITISH "VIDEO NASTIES" PHENOMENON by JOHN MARTIN

ISBN: 0-9522-510-1-9
(A catalogue record for this volume is available from the British Library)

Book and jacket design by John Martin
Front cover: THE HOUSE BY THE CEMETERY

The author gratefully acknowledges the following sources: THE VIDEO NASTIES by Martin Barker (Pluto Press) and WHAT THE CENSOR SAW by John Trevelyan (Michael Joseph).

The author would like to extend special thanks to Ramsey Campbell (who could have killed this project stone dead by telling me how truly awful an early version was... but didn't), Pete Atkins (for constant encouragement), Gordon Finlayson (who's digested more information about Italian zombies and cannibals than they've had hot dinners), Lucio Fulci ("Call no man happy until he is dead"), Dario Argento, Antonio Margheriti, Aristide Massaccesi, Donatella Donati, Sergio Martino, Umberto Lenzi, Fabrizio De Angelis, Giovanni Lombardo Radice, the late and irreplaceable David Warbeck, Catriona MacColl, Shaun Hutson (because I always get a name check in his books), Bill Barnes (without whom the rest of my life would not have been possible), the BBFC's Guy Phelps, Bill Lawrence, the much missed Scala Cinema Club in King's Cross, Nick Cairns (for his truly unbelievable efforts on behalf of the first edition), John Williamson, David Flint, Glyn Williams, Darrell Buxton, Dr Julian Petley, David McGillivray, Arthur Read, Nigel Wingrove, Marc Morris and the other good folks at The Redemption Centre, Peter Blumenstock, Christian Kessler, Mike Lebbing, Erik Sulev, Dennis Capicik, my Mum and Dad (who should never have let me watch all those Hammer horror films) and mostly to my divine wife Catherine, for all her loving support.

This edition is dedicated to my sister Maria... no, she's not the girl in the red barn!

Box 134
West PDO
Nottingham
NG7 7BW
England

"This royal throne of kings, this scepter'd isle,
This earth of majesty, this seat of Mars,
This other Eden, demi-paradise,
This fortress built by Nature for herself
Against infection and the hand of war
This happy breed of men, this little world,
This precious stone set in the silver sea,
Which serves it in the office of a wall
Or as a moat defensive to a house
Against the envy of less happier lands,
This blessed plot, this earth, this realm, this *England*".

RICHARD II, ACT 2 SCENE 1
William Shakespeare

THE SEDUCTION OF THE GULLIBLE

I hoped, while putting together the first, small press, limited edition of this book, that by now it would be seen as no more than an interesting time-capsule of a bygone period when Britain was temporarily in the grip of a grim, collective insanity. Given the cyclical nature of media panics, as described in the book's introductory section, any such "Some day we'll look back on all this and laugh..." expectation was always going to be a triumph of optimism over experience. Indeed, after a short period when "nasties" hysteria seemed to have gone into a welcome remission, that first edition came back from the printers the very morning after Mr Justice Morland made his infamous, out-of-left-field comments about the supposed influence of "violent videos" on the child killers of Liverpool toddler James Bulger.

British judges have a long, dishonourable track record of going off like loose cannons, of coming out with the most outrageous pronouncements about "sexually provocative 8 year-old girls", rapists who can "make amends by paying for their victims to take a little holiday", and so on. Such obnoxious utterances are usually given deservedly short shrift in the popular British press. But in this instance, what the judge said about "video nasties" tallied with the agenda of one powerful group of British newspapers, those owned by Rupert Murdoch, which have their own long, dishonourable track record of whipping up hysteria against anything that is in competition, in the leisure market, with Murdoch's satellite TV operation (only the mentally negligible could fail to note the significance of Kelvin Mackenzie's move from editorship of Murdoch's "nasty"-bashing tabloid THE SUN to a senior position in the Dirty Digger's BSkyB outfit in January 1994). Even the phone-sex lines that are advertised in non-Murdoch tabloids came under the censorious scrutiny of his hacks at one time (as if their own famous "Page 3 Girls" aren't baring their breasts to elicit exactly the same onanistic response!), but home video was always the prime target (you can almost hear the gnashing of teeth occasioned by the line "guaranteed TV holdback" in a new video's promotional blurb). Rival trash-press barons couldn't let Murdoch steal a march in the ongoing circulation war, nor were failed politicians slow to clutch at another "law and order" straw.

In the process they've managed to expand the definition of "video nasty" to encompass just about any horror film made since the heydays of Karloff and Lugosi. In this edition the reviewed "nasties" remain those identified on the Director of Public Prosecution's pre-Video Recordings Act hit-list, because any attempt to add analyses of all those subsequently saddled with this puerile term could only result in a tome beside which Gibbon's DECLINE AND FALL OF THE ROMAN EMPIRE would seem like a slim pamphlet. Ironically, the Frankenstein monster that Murdoch created would eventually turn around and come right back after him, with BSkyB being criticised for its own satellite output of films, a split from the BBFC - whose classifications they had been using - and then the ultimate embarrassment, the realisation that Sky Movies had already screened CHILD'S PLAY 3, the "video nasty" that THE SUN, THE NEWS OF THE WORLD, TODAY and THE TIMES were citing as a virtual incitement to murder. But the damage was already done and the scene set for yet another shattering blow to the British video industry, and indeed the whole British film industry (whose perenially poor condition we're all supposed to be so concerned about). Anyone who, appalled by this unmitigated cocktail of ignorance, opportunism and hypocrisy, is lulled into the facile belief that "things can only get better" for the long-suffering British video consumer, should think again. True, the electorate has finally sent the Tories packing, but consider the prominent role played by Labour leader and new Prime Minister Tony Blair in the David Alton fiasco. It's still possible that the very worst is yet to come!

John Martin, Nottingham, 1997.

THE SEDUCTION OF THE GULLIBLE

WESTERN CIVILISATION AS WE KNOW IT... UNDER THREAT? YOU BET!

Plus ca change, plus ca meme chose ... those ZOMBIE FLESH EATERS are at the door again ("They're coming in... aaargh!"), and tumescent penises rear their ugly heads in the approved "educational context", but THE EXORCIST is still refused video certification by the BBFC and, even more alarmingly, the likes of CANNIBAL HOLOCAUST and even ANTHROPOPHAGOUS BEAST are cited in the media as "snuff movies". The increasingly ludicrous misapplication of this ever more elastic term (THE MAIL ON SUNDAY even dubbed Phillip Kaufman's Sean Connery-starring RISING SUN "a particularly vile snuff movie"!) probably developed because theold term had been worn out by similarly implausible application and rampant over-use... what did they use to call films like ANTHROPOPHAGOUS BEAST and CANNIBAL HOLOCAUST? Ah yes ... "video nasties". Significantly, the re-emergence of these bogey-films under a different name has occured under circumstances of renewed economic recession. Seems we've been here before...

Taking as their pretext the "Winter of Discontent" which swept them to power, Margaret Thatcher's government of avowed right-wing idealogues began in 1979 to dismantle the whole post-War consensus of British social and political philosophy. Public spending was decimated and welfare provisions sacrificed on the altar of free-market economics, in an attempt to unshackle the entrepreneurial spirit of the British people (many of Thatcher's brave new entrepreneurs set up their own video businesses, where their enterprise was to meet with an ironic reward). Wealth was redistributed in the opposite direction to that favoured by Robin Hood, on the dubious principle that rich people needed to be given more money to motivate them, whereas those who already had precious little could only be motivated by giving them even less. In other words, despite pious utterances from the Prime Minister's crackpot economic advisers about "expanded wealth-generation trickling down to those at the bottom of the pile", what actually happened was the familiar story of the rich getting richer and the poor getting poorer (both in spades) and although promises to reduce unemployment had been a central plank of the Tories' Election campaign, the jobless figures were disappearing off the topof the graph.

This seeming injustice came all wrapped up in a pretty moral package, for Thatcher had a team of moral gurus who were every bit as crack-pot as the economic ones. By taking away people's sense of responsibility for their own lives, they argued, the accursed socialists had made them irresponsible. If "the nanny state" was taken off the backs of the people, the people would become not only more industrious and productive, but also more virtuous. Those who didn't buy this preposterous mystical clap-trap were not at all reassured by the P.M.'s constant eulogising of "Victorian Values" and oft-stated admiration for a period when Britannia ruled the waves by relentlessly exploiting its colonial subjects while at home child-labour and prostitution, destitution and widespread opium addiction were the order of the day. Hardly a promising model for a society on the verge of the 21st Century.

With the New Right tugging so relentlessly at the social fabric, it was only a matter of time before it broke, and the Summer of 1981 saw major social unrest and full-blown rioting in London, Liverpool, Bristol and other major cities. The people at the cutting edge of the Thatcher experiment weren't becoming more industrious and virtuous – they were out of work, levelling their own streets and lobbing molotov cocktails at the police, all of which was doubly embarrassing to the government in the light of its incessant knee-jerk "law and order" posturing. The idealogues couldn't accept that their theories might be wrong, so they and their supporters cast around instead for alternative explanations. Sinister Trotskyite conspiracies, always a good bet, were duly trotted out, but the Tory press were soon stalking another scapegoat:... thus the "video nasty.

"Nasties" had originally been employed as a puerile designation for the spate of lurid horror novels that followed in the wake of James Herbert's success with THE RATS (1974). The first use of the term in connection with videos is lost in obscurity, but it's clear that "video nasties" were actually the latest (and greatest *) in a long series of cyclical establishment panics over advances in popular technology being mis-used by the lower classes. It's as well to remember here that back in the 1880s concern was raised in Parliament over the growth of Britain's railway network on the grounds that it would allow hordes of marauding proletarians to move around the country, murdering the well-to-do in their beds. But it has always been advances in popular entertainment technology that have been regarded as particular cause for alarm by the powers that be: "Penny Dreadfuls", the cinema, horror comics and TV have all, in their turn, been held responsible for juvenile delinquency, breakdowns in moral values, the decline of Western Civilization as we know it, etc, and each has been perceived as having new features, peculiar to themselves and progressively more effective in rousing the brute that lies just below the surface of working-class man.

The uniquely alarming feature of video was the facilities it provided to re-wind, play back in slow motion and freeze-frame choice moments of violence so that they could be – in the words of James Ferman, secretary of the British Board of Film Censors – "viewed over and over again by people teetering on the brink of using material in the wrong way". And of course, the material that was getting out on video did seem, to the untrained eye, to be a lot "harder" than anything that had gone before...

"Too many people believe that a video nasty is something like a hotted-up Hammer horror film. It's not. It's something entirely different."
Conservative MP Graham Bright, who lent his name to the Video Recordings Bill that would eventually become law and ban the"nasties".

"These video nasties are not spine-chillers in a tradition that stretches back to Conan Doyle and Edgar Allan Poe."
THE DAILY MAIL, 30th May, 1983.

"Nasties are far removed from traditional suspense and horror films. They dwell on gory scenes of murder, rape, sado-masochism, cannibalism and Nazi atrocities."
THE SUNDAY TIMES, 23rd May, 1982.

The picture being painted is of a startling new development in horror movies which almost comprises a movement, a kind of nasty "New Wave". In fact, perusal of the Director of Public Prosecutions' "nasties" list indicates precious little homogeneity, with well-crafted "message" movies (however contentious that message might be) like CANNIBAL HOLOCAUST juxtaposed cheek-to-jowl with home movie-like exploiters such as CANNIBAL TERROR. Further perusal explodes the myth of startling newness. LAST HOUSE ON THE LEFT and NIGHT OF THE BLOODY APES, for instance, had been made approximately ten years before "video nasty" hysteria broke out, and Herschell Gordon Lewis' BLOOD FEAST a full two decades!

It's easier to understand how it was possible for the authorities to group this diverse grab-bag of disparate films together under the tatty banner of "nasties" if one considers the cossetting for so long given to British cinema-goers by the BBFC, the effect of which has been to "protect" delicate British sensibilities from the realisation that yes, horror has indeed moved on from the days of Sir Arthur Conan Doyle. This is why the video explosion of the early '80s and brief period of non-regulation came as such a rude awakening.

The British Board of Film Censors was set up by the cinema trade and industry in November 1912 to navigate itself safely through the veritable maze of legislation that could be brought against its perceived improprieties, including even the Vagrancy Laws of 1824 and 1838 (making provision for the control of "disorderly houses"), which could be used when all else failed, and actually were by Mary Whitehouse in the late '60s and early '70s to try and stop screenings of Marco Ferreri's grotesquely satirical LA GRANDE BOUFFE / BLOW OUT, among others. Largely as a result of the consistent failure of such actions, the Criminal Law Act (1977) abolished much of Britain's piecemeal legislation in this regard and brought the cinema under the control of the Obscene Publications Acts of 1959 and 1964, whose famous – and famously vague – litmus of obscenity is drawn from the Hickling judgement of 1868(!), that an item is obscene if it exhibits "a tendency to deprave and corrupt". Members of the public lost their right to bring actions against cinemas, the Director of Public Prosecutions reserving that right for himself, and provision was made for the defence of films on the grounds of "the public good", which could include the defence that a film was "of outstanding artistic merit".

It has been the BBFC's task then, to avert prosecutions (under the OPA since 1977) for the industry that created it, which it does by censoring and specifying audience age-limits for the material that local licensing authorities pass for screening in the cinemas that fall under their jurisdiction. As the statutory bodies in law, these authorities can disregard the BBFC, passing material that it has banned, or, as is more often the case in these instances, the converse. In effect though, in the vast majority of cases, the BBFC's classification certificates are what count, and bring de facto immunity from OPA prosecutions (though private cinema clubs, which can by law operate without reference to certification, are subject to such prosecutions, as in notable cases involving ANDY WARHOL'S FLESH in 1970 and Pasolini's SALO – 120 DAYS OF SODOM in 1977).

The Board's deliberations in discharging this prime directive are informed by familiar British prejudices. Film critic Derek Malcolm, an opponent of the Video Recordings Act and defence witness in the NIGHTMARES IN A DAMAGED BRAIN show-trial, has said: "The whole thing has a class basis, the idea that contentious material goes out to 'ordinary' working people who are assumed to be incapable of controlling their own lives and making their own choices. A previous censor once actually said to me: 'It's all very well for sophisticated middle-class people going to the ICA to see ANDY WARHOL'S TRASH, but think of the effect on the working-class man in Manchester'."

But Malcolm, as a well-educated Englishman, has made some dubious class pronouncements of his own, as have other members of the intelligentsia professing an aversion to censorship. For instance Peter Nicholls, deploring the prosecution of VTC over their video release of Andrzej Zulawski's POSSESSION, wrote in The Sunday Times (23rd September, 1984): "Surely it is manifestly ridiculous to prosecute this middle-class Art-house movie as if it somehow belonged in the same category as the films of genuine sex and sadism – the so-called video nasties that appear on the police proscribed list" (a statement which completely ignores the fact that POSSESSION, despite its impeccable middle-class credentials, also appeared on that list!).

The babblings of confused liberals, however, seem almost palatable in comparison to the stark crassness with which the establishment pursues its class agenda. Home Office sociology adviser Dr Clifford Hill's infamous and totally discredited (**) VIDEO VIOLENCE AND CHILDREN document had the audacity to report that working class children were in particular peril from the "nasties", even though, as Brian Brown (whose Television Research Unit conducted Hill's research, only for the good Doctor to totally ignore it in favour of his own pre-conceptions) later revealed, the questionnaires used to obtain data contained no questions that could have revealed the socio-economic status of the correspondents. The Hill report concludes with laughably sophomoric political predictions about the state Britain will be reduced to should the "nasties" go unchecked: "When the level of breakdown of social order reaches a certain point, a situation is created where left-wing revolutions occur and right-wing dictators after the pattern of Hitler may arise and pose as social saviours. They may be eagerly supported by those who see no alternative to the chaos in society, and thus they achieve power."

But hang on — wasn't it precisely Hitler and co who burned books they disapproved of (presumably videos would have gone the same way, had they been around), before they progressed to burning people that they considered sub-standard? And if that seems too fanciful an analogy, consider the words of the Lord Chief Justice, Lord Lane, delivered in his November 8th, 1983, Darwin Lecture, "Do we get the criminals we deserve": "Human beings are imitative, and the less strong-minded, the more imitative they are. We get the results in the criminal courts crimes of sexual sadism so recondite and horrible that you wonder where the idea came from as you look at *the unimaginative and sub-standard human being* in the dock ... Sometimes the puzzled police-man says 'What on earth made you think of doing such a horrible thing to her?' The answer occasionally reveals the truth: Well, it's them books and films, innit?'." (My italics).

It's clear, despite the vocal protests of those such as Mrs Whitehouse (who just two days after Lord Lane's lecture, wrote, in a letter to The Times: "The whole problem of violent obscenity ... is destroying our culture") that the true architects of our culture's collapse into some kind of sinister new order can be found within their own ranks. By reducing the complexities of man as a moral agent to a simple-minded "monkey see, monkey do" equation; by refusing to acknowledge that man has an inherent dark side that he must learn to accommodate to the needs of civilized society (as postulated by both the Christian doctrine of Original Sin and the Freudian notion of anti-social instinctual drives); and by substituting for all that the paranoid scenario of an Evil outside of us and attempting to get in (through the medium of video or whatever), they are chipping away at the Judeo-Christian ethical bed-rock of the culture that they profess such concern for. Hence such absurdities as Lord Longford campaigning for the suppression of pornography and simultaneously for the release of child-torturer Myra Hindley, or The Daily Mirror taking the moral high-ground over that pathetic little film S.S. EXPERIMENT CAMP while calling for real-life Nazi criminal Rudolph Hess to be freed from Spandau Prison.

I won't attempt to fathom the affinity our self-proclaimed moral guardians, the Longfords, the Lane's, the Whitehouses, The Daily Mirrors, Mails, et al, seem to feel for the desperate deeds of these notorious individuals and movements: it's sufficient to point out that their muddled moral revolution / reaction is itself the unwitting force for a cultural disintegration that will take us down the shortest road to where the burning of books, videos and ultimately people can begin in earnest.

(*) "The impact that this sick, money-making corruption is having on illiterate minds is going to make previous anxieties about violence on TV look like worries about the impact of Enid Blyton" wrote Lynda-Lee Potter in THE DAILY MAIL on the 28th June, 1983.

(**) But not before the gutter press had enjoyed a field-day with its "findings".

THE VIDEO CHILLERS UNLEASHING MAD KILLERS

WHEN Robert Sartin went on his gun rampage through the streets of his quiet town, he claimed he was driven by a voice from a video. He told a court that he had become obsessed with Michael Myers—the chilling central character in the Halloween movies. There have been several macabre episodes in which people claim they have been driven to evil by the exploits of video madmen. SUE CARROLL and ALLAN HALL investigate the video chillers.

From yesterday's Sun

JAGGED EDGE

● STUDENT Mark Branch, 18, had video parties with his pals—eating popcorn while blood splashed in buckets across the TV screen. Then he tried it for real, stabbing an 18-year-old girl with a long-bladed hunting knife and mutilating her body.

He hanged himself four days after the 1987 murder in Greenfield, Connecticut. Police Captain David Crossland said the killing was similar to the opening scenes of the Jeff Bridges horror film Jagged Edge.

BRIDGES: Killing

I SPIT ON YOUR GRAVE

● *PENSIONER Dick Slater wept as his son Ian was detained for life for causing grievous bodily harm to a ten-year-old girl and attempting to rape her.*

Mr Slater and his wife Barbara let their son watch films of sex and violence like the notorious I Spit On Your Grave because they believed it was part of growing up.

In this particular video nasty three gang rapes are featured, and the woman victim takes revenge. Each man is killed in a unique manner. One is seduced and castrated in the bath.

Dick, from Blackburn, Lancs, said later: "I thought he just treated them as a laugh."

CRIMES of PASSION

● EIGHTEEN-year-old Robin Gecht was a ticking time-bomb of frustrated emotions who blew up after he watched the Ken Russell film Crimes Of Passion, about a priest who terrorises a prostitute.

Satan-worshipper Gecht left his Chicago home after seeing the movie, which stars Kathleen Turner. He stalked the streets of the Windy City with a long-bladed hunting knife until he found a 19-year-old prostitute.

He stabbed her 30 times.

TURNER: Passion

COMMANDO

● THE Arnold Schwarzenegger film Commando was cited as the deadly influence on crazed drifter Patrick Purdy, 26.

Purdy armed himself with an AK-47 assault rifle and opened fire on children in the playground of an elementary school in Stockton, California, killing four boys and a girl under six and wounding 34 more.

We shall never know how long it was between his last seeing those films and the killings because he took his own life.

FUZZ

● *FOUR teenage delinquents were jailed for life for pouring petrol over 70-year-old tramp John Cartina as he slept on waste ground in Boston, Massachusetts.*

They then danced around his body as he writhed in agony, trying to put out the flames.

The youngsters later said they were given the idea by watching a B-movie thriller called Fuzz . . . where a man dies in EXACTLY the same way.

British censors refused to grant the film an 18 certificate, but it is a cult shocker in the States.

THE THING

● CHRISTOPHER MEAH, a 30-year-old mini-cab driver, raped and nearly killed his neighbour in London's East End.

The woman was threatened with a carving knife when she refused to commit a sexual act with Meah, and she was slashed three times.

He was jailed for life after a court heard he was always watching videos—particularly The Thing and The Last House On The Left. He claimed in his defence that as he raped and stabbed the women he felt like he was watching a film of himself.

FLESH EATERS

● *KENNETH SMART, a 22-year-old fork-lift truck driver, had fantasises about tying up young men, fuelled by The Zombie Flesh Eaters, in which people were tied up, and The Wanderers—about the taking of hostages.*

After watching the videos Smart, from Chippenham, Wilts, took his best friend 18-year-old Terrance Preston to a wood, bound him up with shoelaces, gagged him with his own socks—and beat him to death.

Smart was jailed for life after a judge condemned him as "a dreadful danger to the public."

PHANTASM

● *MASS murderer Donald Harvey was called The Angel Of Death because he poisoned 25 people in a Cincinnati hospital. When he was taken in, he blamed his problems on watching video nasties like Phantasm—where a steel ball which sprouts razor blades is embedded in people's skulls.*

Harvey said the "reckless regard" for life portrayed on the TV gave him "a chilling thrill . . . something akin to a climax when you make love."

PHANTASM: Skull

FRIDAY THE 13th

FRIDAY: Torture

ROD MATTHEWS was a 14-year-old Boston schoolboy who enjoyed watching the horror film Friday The 13th with his pals.

He even collected machetes and an ice-hockey goalie mask as used by Jason, the gruesome character in the series of low-budget movies. In the films, Jason mentally tortures his victims before killing them. Matthews is in a mental institution, probably for life, after taking a baseball bat in 1987 and bludgeoning his classmate to death . . . "to see what it felt like."

RAMBO

● BRIAN BRITTON worshipped the Rambo films so deeply, he thought he WAS Rambo.

Britton, 16, saw the Sly Stallone character as a way out of his real-life quarrels with his family and on March 22, 1989, toting two pump-action shotguns, he executed his father Dennis, 44, mother Marlene, 42, and brother James, eight.

When police surrounded the New York house and asked his name he yelled back, "Rambo."

SLY: Influence

FATAL ATTRACTION

● *RONALD LEE, 29, brooded for a year about what to do to get back at his lover Mybrit Schaller, 26, who had dumped him for another boyfriend. He found his answer after seeing the film Fatal Attraction.*

Lee went to her home in New Jersey with his semi-automatic rifle, and blasted her to death as she hugged new boyfriend Gerald McCord in front of the TV.

Then he turned the rifle on himself.

FATAL: Blasted

The Sun
2nd May 1990

METAXA CORP. presenta · A PETER NEWTON Film

ABSURD

Producida por: JACK MACDONALD · RICHARD HALLER
RGE EASTMAN · EDMUND PURDOM · ANNIE BELLE · IAN DANBY
FF · KATIA BERGER · ANJA KOCHANSKY · CHARLES BORROMELL
KASIMIR BERGER · JOHN CART
N FRANKLIN   Montador: GEORGE MORLEY   Director de fotografía: RICHARD COHN
gida por: PETER NEWTON —   Música por: CARLO MARIA CORDIO
Decorador y ambientador: HELEN CROSBY · Color por: TELECOLOR

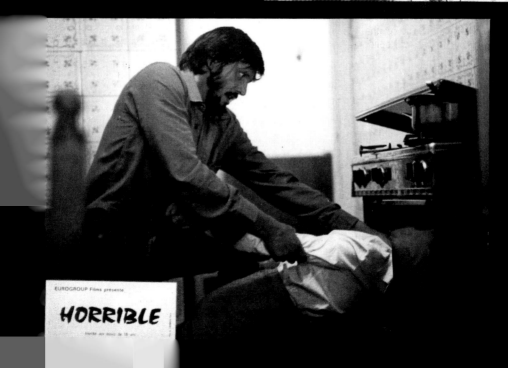

EUROGROUP Films présente

HORRIBLE

Interdit aux moins de 18 ans

THE SEDUCTION OF THE GULLIBLE

ABSURD aka ANTHROPOPHAGOUS 2/ ROSSO SANGUE / HORRIBLE. Italy, 1981. Video label: Medusa. Starring "George Eastman" (Luigi Montefiore), Annie Belle, Charles Borromel, Katya Berger, Kasimir Berger, Hanja Kochansky, Ian Danby, Edmund Purdom, Ted Rusoff. Camera: Richard Haller (Joe D'Amato). Written by "John Cart" (Joe D'Amato). Produced by "Peter Newton" and Donatella Donati. Directed by "Peter Newton" (Joe D'Amato).

The Beast is back, again played by "George Eastman" (this time sans crusty face make-up) in a quickie sequel-of-sorts cashing in on the inexplicable success of his original escapade. First seen jogging through a park, AB is attempting to climb over some rail-ings when a deranged Greek priest emerges from the bushes, tugs on his legs, and impales him ...yep, the old guts are already taking another bashing. Anthropophagous staggers into a nearby house, clutching his dangling intestines and upsetting its occupants (including the mandatory obnoxious kid and his bed-ridden sister, whose head is bolted to some kind of orthopedic torture device. Sensing he's not welcome, Mr Beast wanders off and is run over by the kids' drunk-driving dad. None of this puts the big guy off his food, and he's soon ambushing and dining on a hapless scooter-rider played by none other than Michele Soavi, who went on from bit-parts in D'Amato and Fulci movies to assisting Dario Argento, then directing STAGEFRIGHT, THE CHURCH, THE SECT and DELLAMORTE DELLAMORE. Winding up in a hospital, Anthropophagous drills daylight through a nurse's head with the kind of power tool that D'Amato believes is constantly at hand in the average American hospital, lobotomising a passing orderly with a bandsaw for good measure. Meanwhile the Greek priest is explaining to doctors and policemen that Beasty Boy is virtually idestructable because of the speed with which his blood clots. "Absurd!" observes one of the medics, and it's difficult to disagree. Explaining his own role in the affair, the priest reveals that he "serves God with bio-chemistry instead of ritual" and proceeds to the hard biochemical facts, such as Anthropophagous being possessed by Evil, and God's flame having gone out in him... and all because he spent some time adrift in an open boat! Back in the house the obnoxious kid is warning that "the Boogey Man" is back (does this remind you of any-thing?) but no-one will believe him. His screwed-in sister tells him not to pay any heed to the scare stories his empty-headed and malicious baby-sitter feeds him. She changes her mind when Anthropophagous parts said babysitter's hair with an axe and a friend of the family (played by horror/porno crossover "star" and D'Amato regular Annie Belle) has her head baked in an oven. Spurred to action, she packs her kid brother off across the street (again, just like HALLOWEEN), unscrews herself from the fiendish contraption and engages the Grim Reaper in hand-to-hand combat (why she was screwed to that thing in the first place will remain one of the great imponderables of our time), popping his eyes out with a compass. When mom and dad get home they are greeted by the spectacle of their daughter brandishing a bloody axe and the Beast's severed head.

This is one of D'Amato's better films, but as those whose masochism runs to Massaccesi-watching will know, that doesn't mean it's any good. It does hint at a grasp of pacing that is woefully absent from many of his other efforts, in which the all-important splatter scenes are separated by lengthy interludes in which nothing happens. There's always something happening in ABSURD... something pretty disgusting as a rule, which is about the best you can say for any D'Amato-directed horror film. "The Scum of the Earth" (as Bill Landis dubbed D'Amato), though, was later to surprise every-one by producing Soavi's stunning debut STAGEFRIGHT (written by Eastman/Montefiore as "Lew Cooper") and eventually proved that he could produce and direct half-way decent soft-core erotica with such films as the 11 DAYS, 11 NIGHTS series.

Current Status: Uncut version banned. Now deleted from Medusa catalogue

ABSURD

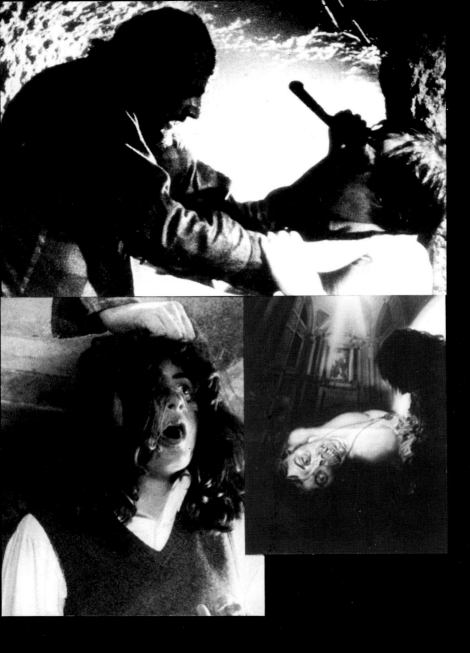

THE SEDUCTION OF THE GULLIBLE

THE ANTHROPOPHAGOUS BEAST aka ANTHROPOPHAGOUS / THE GRIM REAPER / MAN EATER. Italy, 1980. Video label: Video Film Promotions. Starring Tisa Farrow, Saverio Vallone, Margaret Donnelly, Vanessa Steiger, Mark Bodin, Bob Larsen, Simone Baker, Mark Logan, Rubina Rey, Zora Kerova and George Eastman. Camera: Enrico Biribicchi. Written by Luigi Montefiori and Aristide Massaccesi. Produced by Oscar Santaniello. Directed by Joe D'Amato.

Joe D'Amato, the indefatigable Sultan of Sleaze, has exhausted every avenue of exploitation in his notorious career, signing his prolific output with a bewildering array of aliases (including Michael Wotruba, David Hills, Kevin Mancuso, Peter Newton, Richard Franks, John Franklin and Steven Benson … even "Joe D'Amato" turns out to be a pseudonym, Aristide Massaccesi being his given name). His ANTHROPOPHAGOUS begins with a happy German couple on holiday in Greece, signalled by cheesy Zorba-style music on the soundtrack. She goes swimming and is dragged beneath the surface, he (his Walkman turned up loud), is oblivious to her fate until the old axe-in-the-face routine terminates his sun-bathing session. Meanwhile the ever-lovely Tisa Farrow (who built a career in Italian horror on the strength of big sister Mia's appearance in ROSEMARY'S BABY) meets a bunch of tourists in a cable car (including Zora Kerova, frequently martyred in these things) and everyone gets along so famously that they hook up for the rest of their vacation. Hereafter the film degenerates into tedious travelogue stuff which goes on for so long that you have to keep having to remind yourself you're watching a horror film. Have no fear, D'Amato is saving his energy for the boffo finalé.

The gang turn up at the coastal village where the Germans disappeared, and it seems they're not the only ones – the place is absolutely deserted, although someone has written "Go away" on a window. Investigating one of the houses, Tisa and co are confronted by a girl hanging herself from a great height, who spits blood all over them in her death throes. They find another girl, alive but terrified, blabbering about the friendly neighbourhood psycho-killer ("He's here," she insists, "I can smell him!"). They also discover a grungy old diary, cue flashbacks revealing regular D'Amato collaborator and all-purpose massive dude George Eastman (real name Luigi Montefiori) ship-wrecked, adrift in an open boat, and reduced to eating his wife and child to survive. As a result of this traumatic experience Big George has lost most of his hair, developed a heavy case of leprosy and taken to eating everyone he meets, pride of place going to the scene in which he induces labour in a pregnant woman by jumping up and down on her belly, then wolfs down the foetus (actually a skinned rabbit). The fact that this risible little scene was presented on British TV news as "a clip from a snuff movie" tells you all you need to know about the level of "debate" provoked by the "nasties" question.

Tisa and another girl hide out in the attic of a house but Anthropophagous punches through the roof to scalp Tisa's companion and pull out her thyroid gland. Tisa herself is about to end up on the menu when her only co-survivor appears out of nowhere and slams an axe into the belly of the Beast, resulting in a shower of offal. Game to the last, he pulls out several yards of his own intestines and starts chowing down on them before falling to the floor, apparently dead.

There's not a lot D'Amato could do to top that, but he gave it his best shot in ABSURD, aka ANTHROPOPHAGOUS II.

Current Status: Banned

HARRY NOVAK presents

AT LAST...
TOTAL
TERROR!

AXE

Starring JACK CANON
RAY GREEN • FREDERICK R. FRIEDEL
And Introducing LESLIE LEE as LISA • with DOUGLAS POWERS
FRANK JONES • CAROL MILLER • HART SMITH • GEORGE J. MONAGHAN • SCOTT SMITH
Music by GEORGE NEWMAN SHAW and JOHN WILLHELM
Produced by J.G. PATTERSON, JR. • Written and Directed by FREDERICK R. FRIEDEL
EASTMANCOLOR • a BOXOFFICE INTERNATIONAL PICTURES release

R RESTRICTED
Under 17 requires accompanying Parent or Adult Guardian

AXE aka THE CALIFORNIA AXE MASSACRE / LISA. U.S.A., 1977. Video label: Video Network. Starring Leslie Lee, Jack Canon, Ray Green, Frederick R. Friedel, Douglas Powers. Camera: Austin McKinney. Produced by J.G. Patterson Jr. Written and directed by Frederick R. Friedel

The skull-strewn pack promised "Total terror", but AXE turned out to be a mediocre flick I had already seen at the cinema as CALIFORNIA AXE MASSACRE with Robert Voskanian's ZOMBIE CHILDREN – a stultifying double bill put together under the auspices of L.A. drive-in specialist Harry H. Novak.The pre-titles sequence details the killing of two fags by three gangsters. One of the victims is forced to eat a lit cigar. In the aftermath of this rub-out the chief heavy decrees that he and his partners in crime had better keep a low profile till the heat dies down. Their idea of keeping a low profile turns out to be shooting up the local food mart. There's an impromptu food fight, then these desperate characters terrorise the checkout girl, checking out her charms and cracking jokes about her big melons – real Oscar Wilde stuff! The theatrical version leaves it there, but the video version (3 minutes longer at 68 minutes) has the hapless shop-girl stripped down to her underwear and subjected to a game of William Tell, frantically mugging in a feeble attempt to convey terror ... total or otherwise. After this false start our desperadoes do indeed lie low, billeting themselves on an isolated farm inhabited by a young girl, Lisa, and her paralysed senile father. When the boss bad guy tries it on she rebuffs his amorous advances with a straight razor, dumps his body in the bath and sections it with an axe. The same trusty axe is used to cool out the second bad guy when he gets wandering hands. Billy, the youngest and relatively sympathetic villain, discovers the body in the bath, and – to avoid becoming number three – he runs outside, straight into the cops who have turned up apropos of nothing, and who gun him down with similarly obscure motivation. Upstairs Lisa ladles out what looks like blood – but is hopefully tomato soup – to her feeble old man. Yep, she can look after dad, run a farm and see off hit men "Coz she's a woman, W-O-M-A-N..."

Current Status: Banned

ETERNA FILM

LA BESTIA IN CALORE

MACHA MAGAL · JOHN BRAUN · KIM GATTI

XIROS PAPAS · ALFREDO RIZZO

SAL BORIS

IVAN KATHANSKY

THE BEAST IN HEAT aka S.S. HELL CAMP. Italy, 1977. Video label: JVI Video. Starring Macha Magall, John Braun, Kim Gatti, Sal Boris, Alfredo Rizzi. Music by Giulian Sorgini. Camera: Ugo Brunelli. Written by Luigi Batzella. Produced by Xiro Papas. Directed by "Ivan Katansky".

"Ivan Kat(h)ansky" (aka Paolo Solvay, born Luigi Batzella)'s THE BEAST IN HEAT, clearly inspired by Don Edmonds' notorious ILSA series, concerns itself with "horrifing (sic) experiments of SS last days" in the words of its cumbersome subtitle. The prin-cipal experiment is the injection, by a slinky SS lady doctor (Magall), of some fiendish mega-aphrodisiacs into the troll-like Sal Boris (who also appeared in that immortal classic FRANKEN-STEIN'S CASTLE OF FREAKS, under the far more likely sound-ing name of "Boris Lugosi"). "My creature will give a display that will make the god Eros green in envy" boasts the Fraulein doctor, feeding a succession of local nubiles to the caged midget sex-machine, assuring her assistants that this constitutes research vital to the survival of the Fatherland, although her scientific detach-ment is rather called into

question by the way she jumps up and down, gleefully exhorting her protege to "go on … rape her … rape her!" Sal / Boris needs little encouragement, hamming it up in a Cosmo Smallpiece-like caricature of lust, mugging and smacking his lips into Batzella's on-rushing zoom lens.

There's also a "heroic partisans" sub-plot of dubious relevance (it seems to have been spliced in from another film). These scenes are so tedious as to make one yearn, improbable as it may seem, for a return to Mr Lugosi's cage (where he's to be found eating girls' pubic hair) and Magall's torture cellar, where one woman is being eaten by guinea-pigs and anothe rhas her fingernails extracted with pliers ("Stop it … you're hurt-ing me" she deadpans). Three male prisoners, hanging from the ceiling, are proving difficult to crack, so the doctor strips to the waist, and rubs her breasts all over one, who scornfully replies "You're nothing but a bitch on heat". Another is rather more enthusiastic, howling: "Don't waste your time with him … come here. I want you before I die". She castrates him for his presumption, justifying her action by posing the rhetorical question: "Which do you prefer? An asexual angel or an exciting devil?"Well, the partisans have very definite views on this - when their footage finally meets up with hers, the Fraulein doctor is forced into Bonking Boris's cage, but unfortunately they shoot her and her creation before the full measure of poetic justice can be meted out.

Current Status: Banned.

THE SEDUCTION OF THE GULLIBLE

THE BEYOND aka L'ALDILA / SEVEN DOORS OF DEATH. Italy, 1981. Video label: Vampix. Starring Catriona MacColl, David Warbeck, Sarah Keller, Antoine St. John, Veronica Lazar, Anthony Flees, Giovanni de Nava, Michele Mirabella, Al Cliver. Special effects and make-up: Giannetto de Rossi, Germano Natali. Camera: Sergio Salvati. Written by Lucio Fulci, Giorgio Mariuzzo and Dardano Sacchetti. Produced by Fabrizio de Angelis. Directed by Lucio Fulci.

Although Lucio Fulci had already directed 30-plus (and written approximately 130) movies, it was 1979's ZOMBIE FLESH EATERS (see review elsewhere in this volume) that brought him international recognition (not to mention notoriety), initiating a period of frenetic creativity. Foremost among the achievements of this period is that haunting masterpiece of quickie, low-budget Goth Cinema THE BEYOND, the most visionary and ambitious of his zombie series, in which, says Fulci: "I tackle Hell with an even more metaphysical elaboration than CITY OF THE LIVING DEAD … my idea was to make an absolute film … it's a plotless film, there's no logic to it, just a succession of images". No doubt the director intended this as his INFERNO, but what he has borrowed from that film, and from several others (you don't have to look too far into THE BEYOND to spot bits and pieces of THE SENTINEL, SUSPIRIA, THE SHINING, AMITYVILLE HORROR, DON'T LOOK NOW and many more) result in what is probably the best-plotted of his supernatural films, whatever stance Fulci the theoretician might care to take, and paradoxically, from such magpie borrowings, Fulci has here distilled something uniquely his own.

In the beautifully-tinted pre-titles sequence, set in 1927 New Orleans, a red-neck lynch-mob straight out of H.P. Lovecraft's "The Case of Charles Dexter Ward" converge on the Seven Doors Hotel to deal with a warlock named Schyke, whom we see composing a canvas of bodies heaped high in a frigid wasteland. Despite his protestations that the hotel has been built on one of the Seven Gates of Hell and that he's the only one who can keep it closed, Schyke is chain-whipped, crucified and showered with acid. There follows a breezy quotation from The Book of Eibon (a figment of Lovecraft acolyte Clark Ashton Smith's imagination): "You will face the Sea of Darkness and all therein that may be explored". The book bursts into flame as the titles appear and Fabio Frizzi's mumbling monks take up the atmospheric music. A spellbinding opening!

In the present day Lisa (Catriona MacColl) inherits the hotel and, along with it, the mandatory case of ancestral vengeance. During the renovation of the building various workmen are maimed and killed and as a result Lisa makes the acquaintance of Dr. John McCabe (David Warbeck). She also meets Emily, a blind girl who alarmingly steps out in front of her car on a coastal road to warn Lisa of the danger she's in. Lisa shrugs off her warnings, arguing that the hotel is her last chance to make something of her life. Nobody else is aware of the existence of this Emily and Lisa loses some of her composure when she discovers that the house the girl seems to occupy during the night is abandoned and ramshackle during the daylight hours. In fact, the pre-titles sequence has established that Emily lived in the house in 1927, and she would seem to have partially inherited the mantle of sentinel.

Down at the morgue, the cadavers are getting restless, and the widow of one of the dead workmen becomes the second acid-head in the picture. Her daughter attempts to rescue her but is driven back by an advancing pool of corrosive crimson, setting up one of the most nerve-wracking suspense sequences in any Fulci film. The girl runs from door to door, finding each one in turn to be locked, and when she manages to force her way into the deep-freeze, it's only to find the place crawling with zombies. The girl is

Jetzt kommt er . . . der neueste Zombie-Film!

Die Geisterstadt der Zombies

KATHERINE MAC COLL · DAVID WARBECK · SARAH KELLER · ANTOINE SAINT JOHN
Regie: LUCIO FULCI · Musik: FABIO FRIZZÍ · Kamera: SERGIO SALVATI
Produktion: FABRIZIO DE ANGELIS · FULVIA FILM S.R.L. ROM im *Alemannia* · *arabella* · F

next seen at her mother's funeral, her eyes clouded by the cataracts which signify that she has been claimed for The Beyond (Fulci: "Their sight has no raison d'etre anymore in this lifeless world").

As in CITY OF THE LIVING DEAD, corpses turn up all over the place then disappear just as abruptly, and one stormy night Lisa is confronted with the spectacle of Schyke nailed up in his old room. By the time the doc arrives, the warlock has gone, though the nails remain. Cue the mandatory "head pushed towards sharp object" sequence, which ends with the hotel's Mrs Mop hanging on the end of a nail which has pushed one of her eyeballs right out of its socket.

Lisa spots a copy of The Book of Eibon in an antiquarian book-seller's window, but when she goes in to buy it, it has vanished into thin air. Her surveyor looks up the hotel's plans in a local library, but just as he discovers the secret of Hell's gate a bolt from The Beyond knocks him to the floor. He lies paralysed in a pool of blood as infernal spiders emerge from every corner of the room to chew up his eyes, lips, tongue, etc … a charming little sequence! Meanwhile the architectural plans disappear from the pages of the book. Elsewhere a deputation of zombies, led by Schyke, turns up to escort Emily back to the underworld. Her guide-dog fights them off, but as she hugs it gratefully, it rips her throat out.

The memorable climax has MacColl and Warbeck chased around hospital corridors by hordes of shuffling zombies, Warbeck shooting deadsters' heads off in the time-honoured fashion, and to spectacular effect in the case of the little zombie girl previously seen in a deep-freeze full of ambulatory cadavers. By sheer weight of relentless rigor mortis the protagonists are forced into the hospital basement, which they are alarmed to find has become, simultaneously, the basement of the hotel several miles away, suggesting the all-encompassing nature of the Evil underlying and permeating our reality. As they explore further we realize that they are, in the words of the prologue, "exploring the Sea of Darkness", trapped in the wasteland depicted on the warlock's canvas, and revealed as blind in the shocking final shot.

This vision of Hell ("An immobile world where every horizon is the same") is typical Fulci alchemy, extracting visual poetry from the meanest of resources. It certainly impressed Paul Schrader as a cursory glance at his big budget CAT PEOPLE remake (also set in New Orleans) will testify. Fulci is fond of recounting how when he studied at The Experimental Film Centre in Rome under Antonioni and Visconti, the latter told him: "You know film and you have a lot of courage": His detractors would no doubt substitute "nerve" for "courage", but THE BEYOND is an admirable achievement, audacious in conception and execution, Fulci's most satisfying integration of Lovecraft's dime-store demonology with the gleeful cruelty of E.C. Comics, not to mention Italy's own sadistic comic strips.

Fulci is well served by the contributions of several regular collaborators – Gianetto de Rossi's FX work is painstaking (literally for the extra who allegedly had part of his shoulder blown off and was asked to do another take!), Fabio Frizzi's score is the best of the series, with themes intelligently developed and married to the action, Cinematographer Sergio Salvati renders a New Orleans that seems accessible only to Italians (see also Lamberto Bava's MACABRO) and Vincenzo Tomassi's editing effectively enhances the hallucinatory ambience.

Current Status: Re-released by Elephant Video, then VIPCO "Cult Classics" with additional cuts.

THE BEYOND

While His Nubile Young Girl
Victims Screamed Out Their
Life Blood, He Prepared the
Most Horrendous Of All Feasts.

Box Office Spectaculars, Inc.
Presents

An Admonition:
IF YOU ARE THE
PARENT OR THE
GUARDIAN OF AN
IMPRESSIONABLE
ADOLESCENT —
DO NOT BRING
HIM OR PERMIT
HIM TO SEE THIS
MOTION-PICTURE

BLOOD FEAST

MORE GRISLY THAN EVER IN BLOOD COLOR!
Introducing CONNIE MASON YOU READ ABOUT
HER IN PLAYBOY

PRODUCED BY DAVID F. FRIEDMAN   •   DIRECTED BY HERSCHELL G. LEWIS

BLOOD FEAST. U.S.A., 1963. Video label: Astra Video. Starring Thomas Wood, Mal Arnold, Connie Mason, Lyn Bolton, Scott H. Hall, Toni Calvert.. Written by A. Louise Downe. Original thematic music: Herschell Gordon Lewis. Producer: David F. Friedman. Photographed and directed by Herschell Gordon Lewis.

Frank Henenlotter, director of BASKET CASE, remembers his first youthful exposure to BLOOD FEAST: "We heard rumours that there was a film at this drive-in that showed breasts ... that's the only reason we went, watching this girl undress, hoping we'd see a flash of her breast, and all of a sudden this guy comes in and cuts off her leg! We all panicked and ran!" The sequence that proved so traumatic for Henenlotter is clearly a lowest common denominator reworking of the famous shower scene in PSYCHO, not only in its setting but in the fact that it involves the early demise of a sympathetic character ... at least we assume she would have been, but we never get the chance to find out, because BLOOD FEAST doesn't have any characters, just cyphers to be wheeled in and killed off in the finest traditions of Grand Guignol. The unfortunate bather's fate sets the tone for the rest of BLOOD FEAST and indeed, for the whole crimson career of that pioneer, that conquistadore of gore, Herschell Gordon Lewis.

Hailing originally from Pittsburgh (where George Romero would later pick up his gory trail), HGL lectured in English at the University of Mississippi but escaped from the Groves of Academe to form Box Office Spectaculars with producer Dave Friedman, churning out a succession of lucrative nudie pictures. But the lucre of the skin-flick waned when the majors began to muscle in on their territory, and as Lewis recalls: "In early 1963 I felt the nudie cycle was going in the wrong direction. There are only a certain number of ways you can show girls playing basketball!" (Lewis's BOIN-N-G! was probably the definitive statement on this aspect of the human condition). Trading in his nudie cycle, Lewis decided to grasp the thistle ... make that gristle! If Hollywood was going to annexe the skin-flic, he would stay one step ahead by moving on to material that they wouldn't dare touch (it would be another 17 years before the majors could bring themselves to dip their toes in the Lewisian bloodbath, signalled by Paramount's acquisition of FRIDAY THE 13TH, by which time Lewis was already retired in Florida).

The new age was heralded in by the back-to-back shooting of BLOOD FEAST on the set of BELL, BARE AND BEAUTIFUL – a showcase for the 44-inch charms of Virginia Bell – over a period of all of several days (the soft-core pedigree of BLOOD FEAST is evident in its gaudy lighting, static camera work, threadbare props, non-acting actors and vestigal plot). At the time it was even a bit daring to use the word "blood" in a title, and Lewis, who believed that the ad campaign was at least as important as the film, piled on the agony... "Nothing in the annals of horror quite like it... ghastly beyond belief ... You will shudder and recoil in horror at the sight of the slaughter and dismemberment of young girls for a weird and ancient ritual" etc, etc, ad nauseum.

Lurid ads were nothing new – BLOOD FEAST was a first in that it actually lived up to them! The film opens with the amputation (to the sound of "tragic kettle drums"!) that so disturbed Frank Henenlotter – one small step for Fuad Ramses but a giant leap for screen gore (not to mention a faltering hop for the girl in the bath). Fuad Ramses (Mal Arnold) is a crazed Egyptian exotic caterer whose determination to invoke the goddess Ishtar by building a perfect female body out of the constituent parts of his victims, provides the flimsy plot of BLOOD FEAST. "LEGS CUT OFF!" scream the headlines next day, and for an encore Ramses goes beach-combing and beats out the brains of a cat-suited cutie out spooning under the stars with her boyfriend. When questioned by the police, this guy really starts chewing the scenery, pulling faces and wailing "She wanted to go home! She wanted to go home!" over and over again as he meditates on

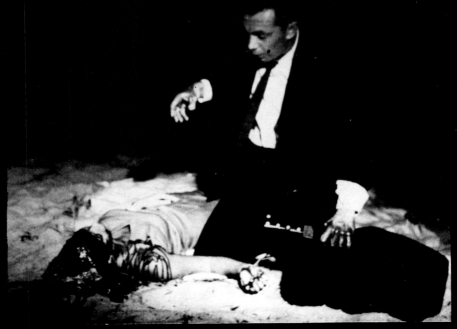

the wages of sin. Ramses' third victim has her tongue (actually that of a sheep) pulled right out of her head. Lewis says of Playmate Astrid Olsen: "She was quite adequate for the role – her mouth was big enough to hold this sheep's tongue and several others!" This tongue-in-cheek – or should that be tongue-out-of-cheek – attitude to actors is characteristic of Lewis, who once remarked that "an actor is like another commodity – you use it and you throw it away". He attached far more importance to the constitution of the stage-blood, which he mixed personally.

Connie Mason (another ex-Playmate, who was cast because of Friedman's infatuation with her toothy smile) is a member of the same book-club as the amputee in the bath and also attends lectures on Ancient Egyptian cults. "You know I've always been interested in Egyptology", this obviously empty-headed girl tells her boyfriend, who just happens to be a detective, in fact one of the extremely slow-witted cops on the case of the demolished girls. Another (un)fortuitous "plot"-twist has Connie's status-seeking mother hire Fuad Ramses to provide something really exotic for Connie's birthday party. Little does she know that this is to be the "Blood Feast" of the title. With a tongue, a brain and a leg, Fuad obviously has the makings of a serviceable goddess already (in one gratuitous scene he is shown roasting a pair of breasts in an oven), though just which bits of Connie's anatomy he plans to filch are left to our imagination. Although an ace Egyptology student, Connie just doesn't realise what peril she's in as the machete-wielding exotic caterer persuades her to lie on the kitchen table with her eyes closed. Just as he is about to deliver the coup-de-grace, the cops, for whom the penny has finally dropped, burst in and save Connie. Ramses is pursued across the city dump and expires in a garbage crusher. "He died a fitting death for the garbage he was" intones Connie's boyfriend, neglecting to add that his fate also provides a perfectly appropriate ending to cinematic garbage such as this.

Lewis himself readily concedes that BLOOD FEAST isn't very good, but insists on its historical importance as the first of its kind. Even that is a highly debatable claim, but BLOOD FEAST's massive influence over subsequent graphic horror product is indisputable – as a rough guide, just think of how many films have reprised the tongue-yanking gag. The much touted BLOOD FEAST 2 now looks like a non-starter, but Jackie Kong's BLOOD DINER is an enjoyably affectionate parody-cum-remake.

Current Status: Banned

Blessed are the meek
for they shall inherit...

BLOOD RITES

BLOOD RITES aka THE GHASTLY ONES. U.S.A., 1969. Video label: Scorpio Video. Starring Veronica Radburn, Anne Linden, Maggie Rogers, Hal Borske, Richard Romanos, Fib La Blaque, Carol Vogel, Hal Sherwood, Eileen Haves, Don Williams. Written by Hal Sherwood and Andy Milligan. Produced by Jerome Fredric. Photographed and directed by Andy Milligan.

BLOOD RITES turns out to be Andy Milligan's THE GHASTLY ONES. Anyone suckered into watching it gets to see two bad actors walking around in somebody's garden then being ripped to shreds by a retard rejoicing in the name of Colin. That's just the pre-titles sequence. Nothing else happens after this. Bugger all. Not a sausage. There's a vestigial plot about a family inheritance that provides the pretext for some boring, bloodless murders and lots of talking … oh, and Colin gets to eat a rabbit, fur 'n' all. Like all Milligan's films, BLOOD RITES boasts anachronistic "period" costumes and sets, to stop it dating and to ensure that as many people will want to see it with every passing year as wanted to see it when it was first released (i.e. not many). Incredibly, Milligan re-made this one (as LEGACY OF BLOOD) in 1972.

I don't know what else to say about BLOOD RITES except that I hope and pray I never again have to sit through anything quite so mind-numbingly *bad*.

Blessed are the meek
for they shall inherit…

BLOOD R[†]TES

Current Status: Banned

TECHNICOLOR. ECRAN LARGE

UN GRAND FILM DE **MARIO BAVA**

LA BAIE
SANGLANTE
(A BAY OF BLOOD)

BAY of BLOOD

MEDUSA

VHS

The Bay is a valuable piece of property that a lot of people would like to desalter. But when there are too many interested parties some of them must go. The first murder triggers a chain reaction of death from which there is no escape. The murderers become victims as the plot develops into wholesale slaughter.

Running time 90 mins. approx.

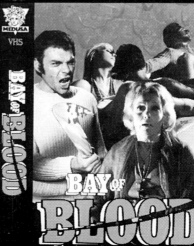

BAY of
BLOOD

Starring: Claudine Auger, Luigi Pistilli, Claudio Volonte

THE SEDUCTION OF THE GULLIBLE

BLOODBATH aka ANTEFATTO / BAY OF BLOOD / TWITCH OF THE DEATH NERVE / CARNAGE / THE ECOLOGY OF A CRIME / BEFORE THE FACT / LAST HOUSE ON THE LEFT PART 2 . Italy, 1971. Video label: Hokushin Video. Starring Claudine Auger, Luigi Pistilli, Claudio Volonte, Chris Avram, Anna Maria Rosati, Leopoldo Trieste. Camera: Mario Bava and Antonio Rinaldi. Written by Mario Bava, Joseph McLee (Giuseppe Zaccariello), Filippo Ottoni, Dardano Sacchetti, Franco Barberi. Produced by Giuseppe Zaccariello. Directed by Mario Bava.

Mario Bava was a true man for all horror seasons, as comfortable with eye violence as he was with subtle, atmospheric chills. Indeed, he pioneered graphic screen gore in his momentous monochrome debut, BLACK SUNDAY (1960). But for censorship and distribution hassles which dogged that film, Bava - not Herschell Gordon Lewis - would have been recognised as the guy who kicked off the whole gore ball-game. He also established the conventions of the giallo with THE EVIL EYE (1962) and 1964's BLOOD AND BLACK LACE (which made a profound impression on a young film critic named Dario Argento and whose villain sports a prototype Krueger kill-glove). When the American majorsfinally plucked up the nerve to jump on the gore bandwagon, Bava was already dead, but in typically Bavian fashion his ghost presides over 1979's ALIEN (which goes so far as to restage the scene from Bava's PLANET OF THE VAMPIRES in which the protagonists discover a huge, fossilized E.T.) and Sean Cunningham's FRIDAY THE 13TH (1980), an unacknowledged remake of ANTEFATTO. Ironically, the Bava film was marketed in America as a bogus sequel to Cunningham and Wes Craven's LAST HOUSE ON THE LEFT!

In a mansion overlooking a scenic bay, a wheelchair-bound Countess is hanged, only for the hangman to be stabbed repeatedly and dumped in that bay. So begins ANTEFATTO (released on video in Britain as BLOODBATH), an everyday story of genocidal folk rubbing each other out in their eagerness to secure inheritance of that bay and its surrounding real estate. Bava signals the unanimity of murderous intent with a totally unexpected shot following the Countess's death – after the old girl has taken the drop, his camera zooms in on her assailant's mandatory black leather gloves in the time -honoured giallo tradition, only to pan up, pull out and reveal his face ... no need to pussy-foot around concealing identities when *everybody* is guilty.

To delineate every step of the dance macabre would rob the viewer of the few addition-al surprises to be had from Bava's vestigial plot, which works like a charm on the screen but would read like a shopping list on the printed page. Suffice to say that after 11 graphic murders (encompassing machete maulings, stabbings, impalements, de-capitations and strangulations), the two surviving contestants step off the kill-go-round and are busy congratulating each other on how well they've done for themselves and their children when the cherubs in question pop up bearing shotguns to blow momand dadd away. "Gee but they're good at playing dead, aren't they?' enthuses little Nicoletta Elmi, before running down to the bay with her brother to enjoy their inheritance.

This final childish twist throws an ironic light on adults' acquisitive graspings, and suggests why BLOODBATH was singled out for prosecution when many of the inferior stalk 'n' slashers it spawned escaped scot-free. Sure, it features children killing adults (always dodgy territory, witness the NIGHTMARES IN A DAMAGED BRAIN saga) and remains the definitive "have sex and die" movie (four hot-to-trot teens who turn-up in a lime-green beach buggy are dragged into the kill spree, their death throes hideously choreographed to simulate orgasmic thrashing), but I suspect that the real reason for BLOODBATH's hostile reception in the Britain of the early '80s was its depiction of soul-less, crude characters driven by the banal desire for ever-increasing financial gain, no matter what the cost to their fellow man. The hysterical Thatcherite response to Bava's bloody parable was no more than the howl of Caliban recognising his own reflection.

Current Status: Mooted Medusa 1984 release, as BAY OF BLOOD, never emerged. Finally re-released under that title, with cuts, by Redemption ten years later.

THE SEDUCTION OF THE GULLIBLE

BLOODY MOON aka COLLEGIALAS VIOLADAS / PROFONDE TENEBRE / DIE SAEGE DES TODES. Spain / Germany, 1981. Video label: Interlight Video. Starring Olivia Pascal, Christoph Moosbrugger, Nadja Gerganoff, Alexander Waechter, Jasmin Losensky, Corinna Gillwald, Ann-Beate Engelke, Antonia Garcia. Written by Rayo Casablanca. Produced by Wolf C. Hartwig. Directed by Jesus Franco.

Spanish sleazemeister Franco is a low-rent counterpart to Luis Buñuel, obsessed with the conflict between a pleasure-denyingsociety and overwhelming sexual drives. His films resolve this conflict in a sado-masochistic compromise, occasionally to startling (if not exactly polished) effect, more usually with utmost banality. BLOODY MOON begins at a ludicrous al-fresco freak out, where hep-cats are getting down to insufferable disco pap. Couples slink off into the bushes and the air is thick with entreaties like "Just melt in my arms" and "caress me gently ... everywhere!" (those hot-blooded Latins, eh?) We see the shot of the moon that will preface all the killings and hear the words "Miguel, I'm your sister! Don't look at me that way! Go back to the dance!" Miguel contents himself with stealing a girl's undies then somebody's Mickey Mouse mask to surreptitiously seduce one floozy. At the height of her passion she rips the mask off to reveal Miguel's scabby face. When she screams her displeasure, he carves her up with a pair of scissors. All this is filmed in P.O.V. style, a-la HALLOWEEN, so it comes as no great surprise when the next thing we see is one of those "Five years later" captions. Miguel is discharged from a booby hatch into the care of his sister, who's admonished to "avoid references to that unfortunate night ... he might not be cured"

Thence unfolds a saga of intrigue over an inheritance at a mysterious language school populated by, among others, a sinister shears-brandishing gardener, Antonio the tennis ace/super stud, the suspiciously smooth proprietor and a bunch of tedious girls who lust after Antonio and spend their time in puerile sexual discussions. Meanwhile Miguel's dumpy sister is exciting him to the point where he loses control, grovelling and slobbering over her chubby legs. Can't you see they won't let us love each other?", she chides him: "Everyone around us is judging us ... if we could just get rid of everyone!" First to go is the old biddy whose money is up for grabs, then one of the girls is stabbed in the back and turns up dead in the closet of her best friend, who's improbably persuaded that this find was a product of her vivid imagination, over-stimulated by lurid paperbacks. One of the girls trails the principal to the coast, where he is involved in some shady transaction. A big polystyren boulder nearly falls on her. When another girl is menaced by Miguel's sister's pet python, Antonio decapitates it with the shears and we are subjected to a shot of the scaly head thrashing around in a pool of reptilian blood. Yet another girl is taken by an unseen stranger to an old mill, lashed to a slab, and starts prattling: "You shouldn't want to do that to me – that's the craziest thing that ever happened" (hyperbole surely) "...If that's the way you like it, ok. It's a bit perverse (sic) but I'll try anything – so long as I get back to the club on time. Don't tie me up so hard, my poor backside is aching" (Well stop talking through it, woman!) "... but as they say, pain is good for pleasure, huh? I always wanted to make it with a Spaniard, they're so hot blooded and imaginative, you never know what to expect – you don't have to do all this, you know I'm not planning on running away. I said I was game for anything, I have a weakness for strong men..." and so on). Understandably infuriated by this incessant brainless babbling, the unseen bondage fan starts up the buzzsaw that features so prominently on the BLOODY MOON pack, and stemms the flow of verbal diarrhoea by sawing a shop-window mannequin ... er, I mean the hapless victim's head off (cue much squirting of tomato ketchup). Back at the college the plot resolves itself with some indecipherable revelations about who inherits off whom. To nobody's great surprise the principal is revealed as the killer, Miguel's sister is revealed as his lover, and she announces her total contempt for Miguel and his incestuous attentions, following up with some catty observations about his complexion. Unfortunately for her, Miguel has been eavesdropping on all this. Dusting off his trusty chainsaw, he reduces his tormentors to grungey gouts of gushing gristle. The End, thank Christ!

Current Status: Uncut version banned. Re-released by VIPCO with cuts

BLOODY MOON

THE
BOGEY
MAN

●VIPCO●
presented

Suzanna Love · Ron James · John Carradine
also starring
Nicholas Love · Raymond Boyden · Felicie Morgan
Written, Directed and Produced by Ulli Lommel · Music by Tim Krog
Executive Producer Wolf Schmidt

SEE WARNING ON REVERSE   Running Time 84 Minutes

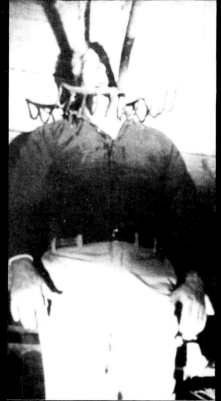

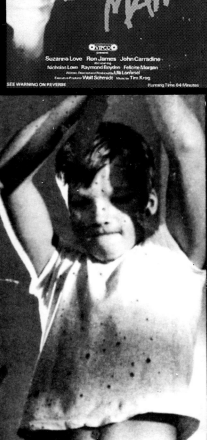

THE SEDUCTION OF THE GULLIBLE

THE BOGEY MAN. (U.S. THE BOOGEY MAN). U.S.A., 1980. Video label: VIPCO.
Starring Suzanna Love, Ron James, John Carradine, Nicholas Love, Llewelyn
Thomas, Felicite Morgan, Raymond Boyden, Jay Wright, Jane Prat, Bill Rayburn.
Special effects: Craig Harris. Camera: David Sperling and Jochen Breitenstein.
Written by Ulli Lommel, Suzanna Love and David Herschel. Produced and directed
by Ulli Lommel.

Fassbinder protege (TENDERNESS OF THE WOLVES, 1974) and former Factory associate (BLANK GENERATION, COCAINE COWBOYS) Ulli Lommel was by 1980 joining the rush to cash in on John Carpenter's HALLOWEEN. His film opens with familiar-sounding tinkly music as the peeping-tom camera prowls around a familiar -looking house. A woman spots her kids, Willy and Lacey, spying on her and her lover, so he chastises Willy, MOMMIE DEAREST-style, tying himto the bed. Freed by his sister, Willy stabs his tormentor to death. From here on the HALLOWEEN story is reversed – it's the victim who becomes the Bogey Man, a stocking-masked, super-natural-born killer surviving in a mirror (note the influence Lommel's film has exerted over the money-spinning NIGHTMARE ON ELM STREET series). 2 decades later, Lacey and Willy (now mute) are haunted by these events. Lacey's husband Jake takes her to see psychiatrist John Carradine. Under hypnosis, she spits, curses and threatens them in the voice of The Bogey Man (a combination of HALLOWEEN and THE EXORCIST – can't miss, right? Wrong!). Carradine prescribes a visit to the house where the killing took place. Jake drives Lacey over there, leaving Willy to muck out the barn, where, the town flirt chats him up, sensitively: "I think it's cute that you can't talk … it makes you different from all the other boys". Willy reacts by lifting her against the barn wall and half throttling her. Concluding that a mirror was influencing him during this violent out-burst, Willy goes around his house, painting all its mirrors black. The old house is inhabited by kids who don't mind at all when Jake and Lacey roll up and start "poking around". When Lacey enters the room where the dirty deed was done she sees the Bogey Man in the mirror and smashes it. Shame-faced, Jake collects the broken glass in a bag and takes Lacey home. The kids agree that breaking a mirror is bad luck, and "frees everything the mirror has ever seen". A shard starts glowing red and a heart-beat appears on the soundtrack as one of the girls retires to the bathroom to get ready for a hot date. Psychos, even incorporeal ones, are always enraged by teenage sex, so the kids are wiped out in three of the most ludicrous "designer deaths" ever – the boy is guillotined in a window frame, one of his sisters is attacked by a pair of scissors, and the other battered over the head by a cabinet door that snaps open through the power of the occult. Jake re-assembles the mirror back home, and characters are soon being dive-bombed by pitchforks. Lacey takes her obnoxious child fishing. As he dangles his feet off the prom we see some glass stuck to the sole of his boot, and reflected light plays on the other side of the bay where some frisky teens are having a barbeque as a prelude to heavy petting. What happens next is definite proof that a screwdriver rammed into the back of the head and exiting through the mouth is an invaluable aid to prolonged French kissing.

In the alleged climax Lacey has her blouse ripped off, then a splinter of glass pierces her eye as the mirror bathes the house in red and green light and dead characters fall out of every cupboard. The door falls in and a priest appears, wielding a huge cross. As he attempts to yank the glass from her eye (a biblical parable, right?), somebody off-camera pours strawberry jam over his bald patch (which memorable spectacle provides the pack shot). He plucks the glass out and staggers away, revealing the contents of the cutlery drawer embedded in his back. We didn't actually see this happening — maybe the SFX man was on his lunch break — but they're ripped off everything else, so why not CARRIE? Feeling enough is enough, the survivors throw the mirror down a well, from which a fireball rises into the sky. Willy regains the power of speech during this ordeal (ie he starts screaming his head off). The final scene involves Lacey and Willy looking forward to a bright future, but to no-one's great surprise the last thing we see is a glowing piece of mirror. THE REVENGE OF THE BOGEY MAN? You betcha.

Current Status: Re-released by: VIPCO "Cult Classics" in a cut version

THE BOGEYMAN

JEAN UBAUD, MICHAEL CO... ...CY BURGER
present a MIRAMAX...

THE BURNING

Starring
BRIAN MATTHEWS
LEAH AYERS
BRIAN BACKER
LARRY JOSHUA
and LOU DAVID
as Cropsy

The most frightening of all maniac films

"THE MOST TERRIFYING FILM OF THE YEAR."

18

A BRUTAL
HORRIFIC
ACT MADE
HIM KILL
AND KILL
AND KILL

THE BURNING

Cult Classic
FRIGHTENER

MUSIC BY RICK WAKEMAN

THE SEDUCTION OF THE GULLIBLE

> **THE BURNING. U.S.A., 1981. Video label: Thorn EMI. Starring Brian Matthews, Leah Ayres, Brian Backer, Larry Joshua, Jason Alexander, Ned Eisenberg, Carrick Glenn, Caroline Houlihan, Fisher Stevens, Lou David. Special effects: Tom Savini. Camera: Harvey Harrison. Written by Peter Lawrence, Brad Grey, Bob Weinstein, Harvey Weinstein and Tony Maylam. Produced by Harvey Weinstein. Directed by Tony Maylam.**

THORN-EMI must have been thinking: "Why us, Lord?": Though billed as "The most frightening of the maniac films", THE BURNING is an identikit example of the "teen campers in peril" sub-genre spawned by the success of FRIDAY THE 13TH (1980) and it seems rather arbitrary for the DPP to have singled it out for inclusion on the official "Video Nasties" list. Production values here are slightly lower than in Jason's slaughter-fests, but one thing that THE BURNING does share with FRIDAY THE 13TH is the make-up effects of Tom Savini, who took this job in preference to FRIDAY THE 13TH PART 2 because, he says, that film's out-of-wack storyline and continuity put him off – "Especially the idea that Jason was alive in some lake for all that time" (He was also offered better money to do THE BURNING, of course, and presumably it was a similar consideration that allowed him to overcome his philosophical objections and go to work on FRIDAY THE 13TH PART IV). In fact, with apologies to Mr. Savini, THE BURNING and FRIDAY THE 13TH PART 2 are virtually interchangeable, though the credits for this thing, which list an unbelieveably massive crew, insist that it took three people to write, then two to make a screenplay of what they see fit to describe as the "original story".

In the tiresome pre-titles sequence the waggish campers of Camp Blackfoot set out to scare obnoxious caretaker Cropsy with a worm-ridden skull containing a candle (readily available at all good stores). Unfortunately the gag results in Cropsy's bed catching fire and he becomes a human torch, leaping hot-foot into Lake Blackfoot (where presumably he met Jason and picked up some tips on coming back to life and jumping out of lakes when everyone thinks the picture is over). Cropsy winds up in hospital, described by a sensitive orderly as "a fucking Big Mac, overdone."

To no-one's great surprise, "five years later" Cropsy is discharged with some sound advice – "I know you resent those kids, but try not to blame anyone". After five years cooped up in intensive care a young Cropy monster's thoughts turn to what you'd expect them to turn to, so he nips off to the local red light area for a quickie. Even a prostitute gets a headache when she checks out Cropsy's charred visage, and when he presses his suit she succumbs to a fit of bad acting (she's not the only one – even by the standards of this sub-genre the general level of thespian attainment is appalling). Enraged, Cropsy stabs her and pushes her through the window. Realising his true vocation, he hightails it to the nearest Summer Camp, Camp Stonewater.

There's a veritable shoal of red herrings as we are introduced to the campers – the girls agonise over the state of their relationships while girlie-mags and condoms are delivered to the boy's hut; buttocks are peppered with buck-shot, and amid much masturbation wit the girls are referred to as "prime meat" (how true, how true); then there's the camp wimp Alfred, spying on girls in the shower, which is possibly intended as a Hitchcock hommage. Next up is the campfire sequence you'll know off by heart if you ever saw FRIDAY THE 13TH PART 2. Todd, the hunky camp counsellor, scares the new kids with the story of Cropsy, stalking the woods with a pair of shears (turns out to be a good guess!) "He's out there watching... waiting. So don't look – he'll see you. Don't breathe he'll hear you. Don't move ... YOU'RE DEAD!" at which point some eejit jumps out of the bushes in a feeble attempt to scare the living daylights out of everybody.

IMPORTANT NOTICE TO DEALERS.

RE-RELEASE OF "THE BURNING."

ON the 21st June, 1984, the Uxbridge Magistrates' Court dismissed a test case prosecution, brought by the Director of Public Prosecutions, against THORN EMI Video and Nicholas Charles Bingham pursuant to the Obscene Publication Act 1959.

On the 2nd July, 1984, the Director of Public Prosecutions confirmed that in the light of that decision and the fact that the film has a British Board of Film Censors Certificate, he has advised Chief Constables that any current prosecution of the "X" Certificate version of the film should be withdrawn.

Dealers may recall that in October, 1982 THORN EMI Video released this film only to discover three weeks later that they had inadvertently released a version which included the 15 seconds that the British Board of Film Censors had requested be cut to qualify the film for an "X" certificate.

THORN EMI Screen Entertainment is unreservedly opposed to the distribution of horror videos which have not received a British Board of Film Censors certificate advising of the suitability of a film for public viewing. Strenuous efforts were made to alert all dealers to this error and THORN EMI Video recommended that they return uncensored copies which would be replaced free of charge with copies of the edited version.

Although a large number of these cassettes have been returned, THORN EMI Screen Entertainment recognises that copies of the uncensored version are still in circulation and therefore wishes to repeat the offer previously made and inform dealers that until 31st September, 1984 they can exchange their video cassettes for the British Board of Film Censors approved version simply by following standard EMI return procedure.

In the event of a dealer having purchased a copy from a wholesaler, previous to opening an account with EMI, the cassette should be returned to the wholesaler concerned or sent to Colin Richards, THORN EMI Screen Entertainment, THORN EMI House, Upper Saint Martin's Lane, London, WC2H 9ED whereupon it will be exchanged.

Dealers who are unsure of what version of "The Burning" they possess, should check the label on the cassette itself. If it has a date stamp or is in a new style blue and white label, then dealers can be assured that it is a fully certified copy of the film.

However, it must be emphasised that should any dealer continue to distribute the uncensored version after the 31st September, 1984, THORN EMI Screen Entertainment will refuse to accept any responsibility or provide support for any action that may be taken by the Police in relation thereto.

THORN EMI
Screen Entertainment

THE SEDUCTION OF THE GULLIBLE

It's not till the kids go on a canoe trip that the stuff really starts hitting the fan. Cropsy interprets the "Have-sex-and-die" rule somewhat broadly, for the first victim backs out of sex in the creek before undergoing a DIY tracheotomy as she searches for her knickers, blood gurgling out over her breasts. The kids wake next morning to find that the canoes are missing, so they improvise a raft and set off back to camp. One of the missing canoes drifts into view, but when they paddle over to it, up jumps Cropsy, brandishing shears. With a dazzling display of dexterous hand-speed he stabs heads, slashes throats, pierces breasts and crops the fingers off a guy who raises his hands in a protective gesture. It was the latter amputation that prompted the police to bust the tape ("We caught 'em red-handed M'Lud!"), which in turn caused Thorn-EMI to recall THE BURNING and get out their own shears, re-issuing a version seven seconds shorter. But horror of horrors, they managed to return to the shops many copies with the offending seven seconds intact, so THE BURNING was withdrawn all over again. In the aftermath of this fiasco Thorn-EMI got the jitters and started censoring their product left, right and centre, including SUSPIRIA, a particularly brutal carve-up of HALLOWEEN 3: SEASON OF THE WITCH, and even EMMANUELLE 2!

Back at Camp Stonewater the discovery of the wrecked raft, not to mention a floating arm and fingerless corpses popping up in people's faces, leads to another outburst of hysterical over-acting. Subsequently, copulating teens are slaughtered in their sleeping-bags and pinned to trees with shears through their throats (c.f. FRIDAY THE 13TH). Surprising Cropsy in mid-slash, wimpy Alfred is pursued in P.O.V. Cropsy-vision to a handy-dandy disused mine, in which the socko-boffo climax unfolds. Todd charges to the rescue, and a flashback reveals that "Young Todd" was one of the pranksters who set off this whole unlikely chain of events in the first place (Well slap my face!). Who cares? Cropsy does, and with a fine sense of poetic justice he goes after Todd with an oxy-acetylene burner, leaving the viewer to ponder certain questions, e.g, while in hospital, how had Cropsy kept tabs on Todd's movements? Even more perplexing, how did Todd get a job as a camp counsellor when a mere five years earlier he had been responsible for broiling a camp caretaker?

Things are looking bad for Todd, but Alfred proves himself a man at the crucial moment, burying the shears in Cropsy's back. He falls so readily that you lose several credibility points if you don't guess that as Alfred and Todd leave arm-in-arm, Cropsy will gamely rise for another go. An axe in the face makes his comeback a short one, and the boys set fire to him again for good measure. The film closes with a reprise of the fireside scene (well clean my pants!) but any frisson of terror that this might have generated is stifled by the lamentable acting of those concerned.

One significant way in which the film does differ from FRIDAY THE 13TH is that it never spawned a BURNING 2, 3, 4, 5, etc ad nauseum (ain't that a shame?). Two BURNING alumini went on to bigger and (not difficult) better things, thesp Holly Hunter and editor Jack Sholder (who subsequently directed A NIGHTMARE ON ELM STREET PART 2: FREDDY'S REVENGE and THE HIDDEN).

Current Status: Uncut version banned. Re-released by VIPCO "Cult Classics", cut

KEINER
IST VOR IHNEN
SICHER –
AUCH DU
BIST ES NICHT!

Verleih :

ASPHALT-KANNIBALEN

THE SEDUCTION OF THE GULLIBLE

CANNIBAL APOCALYPSE aka APOCALISSE DOMANI ("APOCALYPSE TOMORROW")/THE CANNIBALS ARE IN THE STREETS / INVASION OF THE FLESH HUNTERS / SAVAGE APOCALYPSE / THE SLAUGHTERERS / CANNIBALS IN THE CITY. Italy/Spain, 1980. Video label: Replay. Starring John Saxon, Elizabeth Turner, John Morghen, Cindy Hamilton, Tony King, Wallace Wilkinson, Ray Williams. Special make-up effects: Giannetto de Rossi. Camera: Fernando Arribas. Written by "Anthony M. Dawson", José Luis Martinez Molla, Dardano Sacchetti, Maurizio and Sandro Amati. Produced by Maurizio and Sandro Amati. Directed by "Anthony M. Dawson" (Antonio Marghereti).

Francis Ford Coppola's APOCALYPSE NOW dealt with the dehumanising effects of the Vietnam War; Michael Cimino's THE DEER HUNTER portrayed post war social dislocation; but not until Antonio Marghareti's CANNIBAL APOCALYPSE did a film have enough guts to tackle the taboo subject of … cannibal G.I.s!! Italian splatter icon John Morghen (real name Giovanni Lombardo Radice) stars as Charlie Bukowski, whose commanding officer Hopper (John Saxon) discovers him in a pit somewhere in Indo-China, chowing down on fragrant crispy Vietcong with his buddy Tommy. APOCALYPSE deviates wildly from the cannibal code set down in CANNIBAL HOLOCAUST by dispensing with the jungle setting after this opening, the subsequent action unfolding back home in Atlanta, where Saxon is suffering the expected traumas and 'Nam flashbacks. His troubles begin in earnest when Morghen is released from "The Hospital for Nervous Disorders".Distracted at the cinema by a couple's heavy petting antics, Morghen forgets his popcorn and dives in on their ecstasy, biting lumps out of her throat. Audience reaction to this is understandably hostile, so he holes up in a shopping mall, shooting caretakers and Hell's Angels who wheelie in after him. Heavy social comment here, as Charlie sings: "Yankee Doodle went to Vietnam, just to shoot the Vietcong, Yankee Doodle got shot up... and called it maca-ro-neee!" "He'll be singing through his ass-hole by the time I've finished with him" hisses hard-boiled police captain McCoy, obviously a music lover. He calls in Hopper, who was just making some progress with the jailbait next door, i.e. biting her midriff (this girl gives the lie to any notion that all Italians are stylish, favouring traffic-light tights and lurid spangled hot pants).

Charlie is talked out and returned t hospital, where he and his equally anthropophagous army buddy Tommy waste no time spreading the cannibal plague. "What I don't understand", says one character: "is how a social phenomenon such as cannibalism can become a contagious disease" (and this indeed is the $64,000 question). "By some sort of biological mutation due to psychic alteration" is the answer (would you buy used Cronenberg from this man?) From here on things escalates rapidly – the police captain walks into his precinct house to find one of his men lunching on a police-woman's breast: "Oh my God son, put it down" he pleads. Back at the hospital, a French kiss terminates in tongue amputation. Saxon eventually "comes out" and springs his pals from the hospital, then they embark on a spree of cannibalism across Atlanta. A garage forecourt attendant is killed and his leg sawn off for a snack, the camera dwelling lovingly on the action as a "Baker Street"-style sax blows on the soundtrack. The vengeful Hell's Angels from the mall appear, wearing neatly-pressed denims. "I want that motherfucker in the back seat" demands their leader. Instead, he and his chapter are bitten, kung fu–d and eye-gouged into submission. There ensues a car chase, at the end of which most of the cannibals are shot or torched in a sewer. Inevitably Morghen's demise is the most spectacular, a drastic evisceration by shot-gun. Marghereti doesn't waste the chance to poke his camera around in the wreckage of Johnny's plumbing.

Saxon escapes and returns home, where he and his wife are reconciled in a suicide pact. "Call the coroner", says McCoy "and tell him this fucking nightmare is over." But no film of this calibre would be complete without a silly twist ending, and the final shot reveals that the luridly dressed Lolita next door has stocked the fridge with chunks of her dismembered momma.

Current Status: Banned

CANNIBAL APOCALYPSE

CANNIBAL FEROX

Unvorstellbares wird auf der Kino-leinwand zur grausamen Wirklichkeit!

Die Rache der KANNIBALEN

JOHN MORGHEN
BRIAN REDFORD
ZORA KEROWA
VENANTINO VENANTINI

Regie: UMBERTO LENZI
Kamera: GIOVANNI BERGAMINI
Eine DANIA-MEDUSA Filmproduktion. Rom. im Verleih der ⁄*arabella* Film

THE SEDUCTION OF THE GULLIBLE

> *CANNIBAL FEROX aka MAKE THEM DIE SLOWLY / WOMAN FROM DEEP RIVER. Italy, 1981. Video label: Replay. Starring John Morghen, Lorraine de Selle, Bryan Redford, Zora Kerova, Walter Lloyd, Meg Fleming, Robert Kerman. Special effects: Gino de Rossi. Camera: Giovanni Bergamini. Produced by Antonio Crescenzi. Written and directed by Umberto Lenzi.*

Umberto Lenzi's CANNIBAL FEROX cashes in on the definitive CANNIBAL HOLOCAUST, dispensing with that film's sophisticated dual narrative format but doubling up on the violence (reflected in its overkill ad campaign, promising/threatening "24 scenes of extreme and explicit violence … banned in 31 countries"). In Deodato's film the bad guys are despatched quickly, albeit gruesomely. In FEROX the natives' revenge takes the form of prolonged, ceremonial torture. As in Nick Roeg's WALKABOUT, the wilderness action is bookended by familiar urban scenes for dramatic contrast. Two heavies whose collective vocabulary seems to consist exclusively of the phrases "shit face" and "mother fucker" are searching New York for a drug-dealer named Mike (John Morghen), but he's hotfooted it to safer climes, a cannibal infested jungle! There he meets a lady professor (Lorraine de Selle) with a shaky grip of methodology – she plans to disprove three reported incidents of cannibalism in the belief this will establish that "cannibalism as an organised human practice does not exist and never has existed …the mythical lie of the cannibal ferox". Her colleague puts the argument more succinctlyl – "Man eats man is bullshit". Deep in the jungle though, natives are chewing on maggots ("How disgusting") and maggots chewing on natives (also pretty disgusting!) When our heroes reach a village Mike demonstrates white supremacy by frenziedly stabbing a pig to death. Censured for this act, he snaps: "D'you get off on ecology, huh, twat!" Morghen appears to have picked up the endearing habit of addressing everyone as "twat" from his HOUSE ON THE EDGE OF THE PARK co-star David Hess, but his character is not incapable of charm. Who could possibly forget the tender moment when he seduces Pat (Zora Kerova) by giving her cocaine and telling her: "I had you nailed the minute I saw you … a hot pussy little whore who came down here looking for freedom; a victim of puritanical breeding seeking release for strange new feelings"?

Mike progresses from killing pigs to raping natives, which seems to excite Pat, though she draws the line when he starts shooting the local:"Get off my case, motherfucker!" he chides her. Mike rationalises his brutish behaviour as a reaction to "a bad scene"that befell his friend: "They castrated him with a macheté…" he remembers: "then they ate his genitals!!!" (delivered with much rolling of eyes and gnashing of teeth, this line is invariably greeted with hysterical audience laughter). Flashbacks reveal that it was actually Mike himself who tortured, castrated and gouged the eyes out of various natives while wired on coke. When the natives catch up with them, the kid gloves are off. Pat has her breasts skewered on hooks, by which she is hauled into the air and left to dangle. Mike is tied to the village totem pole and poked with spears. He spits in the chief's eye, an act of bravado he instantly comes to regret. Wiping his eye, the chief pulls out Mike's honky schlong and whacks it off (all in unflinching close-up) with his macheté. While the cannibal chorus line wave their spears in the air and give it the old college cheer, he swallows the Morghen organ in one go (that's what I call deep-throating!) Now Mike really proves his mettle (or perhaps the invigorating properties of cocaine): escaping from the cannibals; having his hand chopped off as punishment when they recapture him; then escaping yet again only to be recaptured a third time. At this point, the cannibals decide enough is enough; besides, they're starting to feel a bit peckish, and reasoning that the best brain food is brain food, they wedge Mike under a table with a hole in its centre, through which the top of his head protrudes. They lop this exposed portion off with that trusty macheté and … hey presto! Brains in a bowl! Even Mike can't manage another escape after that. Lorraine de Selle has to share a sub-merged bamboo cage with fat bloodsucking leeches, but slips away before the full measure of cannibal retribution can be meted out to her. The film closes with her presenting her doctrinal dissertation on the non-existence of cannibalism. So go figure!

> *Current Status: Uncut version banned. Cut version deleted by Replay*

EUROGROUP Films presente
**CANNIBAL
HOLOCAUST**

The legendary "Piranha bait" scene: never included in any release print

CANNIBAL HOLOCAUST. Italy, 1979. Video label: Go Video. Starring Robert Kerman, Francesca Ciardi, Perry Pirkanen, Luca Giorgio Barbereschi, Salvatore Basile, Ricardo Fruentes, Gabriel Yorke, Paolo Paolini. Special effects: Aldo Gasparri. Camera: Sergio d'Offizi. Written by Gianfranco Clerici. Produced by Franco Palaggi. Directed by Ruggero Deodato.

Deodato's first foray into cannibal territory was the starkly-titled CANNIBAL (aka THE LAST CANNIBAL WORLD / THE LAST SURVIVOR) in 1976. Made in the Philippines, it details the harrowing ordeal of Massimo Foschi, who falls among primitives (including the ubiquitous, invitingly-named Me Me Lay), is caged and subjected to various indignities, only escaping after he has participated in a human bean feast. Foschi's disgust at this initiation is rendered by the non-too-subtle expedient of mugging into the camera from point-blank range, which was to become a staple shot at this point in the plot of subsequent sagas of ignoble savagery. CANNIBAL was widely denounced as "racist" for its depiction of under-developed humanity, and Deodato appeared to take this accusation to heart. His seminal CANNIBAL HOLOCAUST is a brilliantly mounted critique of the whole "mondo" school of film-making. Sure, it climaxes with natives pulling their white visitors limb from limb and scarfing down their remains, but Deodato establishes along the way that the imperialist bastards had it coming! By means of an audacious dual narrative technique he also poses uncomfortable questions about the ethical status of this whole area of "entertainment". Ludicrous but oft-repeated media claims that CANNIBAL HOLOCAUST is a for real "snuff movie" merely testify to the effectiveness of the whole enterprise.

The film opens with a know-it-all TV reporter commenting that: "Man is omnipotent, and will soon conquer space, yet only just a few hours flight from NYC, people are still living in the Stone Age". The report shows a crew of mondo film-makers jetting off to unspecified South American parts to shed some light on the situation. The next we hear of these guys, they're missing, presumed dead and a second mission, led by Professor John Monroe (Robert Kerman) is sent to discover their fate.

Monroe is disturbed at the macho behaviour of the hard-assed Spanish hunter who is assigned to show him the ropes (or should that be the vines?) in the jungle. This guy captures a native and forces him to lead them to the Tree People. Their reluctant guide is treated like an animal, rewarded for "good behaviour" with cocaine blown in his face. En route to the Tree People's place, they witness the local punishment for adultery, which involves violation with first a huge rock, then a mud-pack pitted with sharp stones. They find the Tree People, the general consensus among whom seems to be that the first expedition were bad news, specifically their filming activities (c:f. Dennis Hopper's THE LAST MOVIE). When Monroe gains their confidence by steeling himself to eat human flesh, they show him a shrine fashioned from the mortal remains of the first camera-crew and their photographic paraphernalia. The natives are all in favour of Monroe taking the footage back with him, as though this will somehow exorcise evil

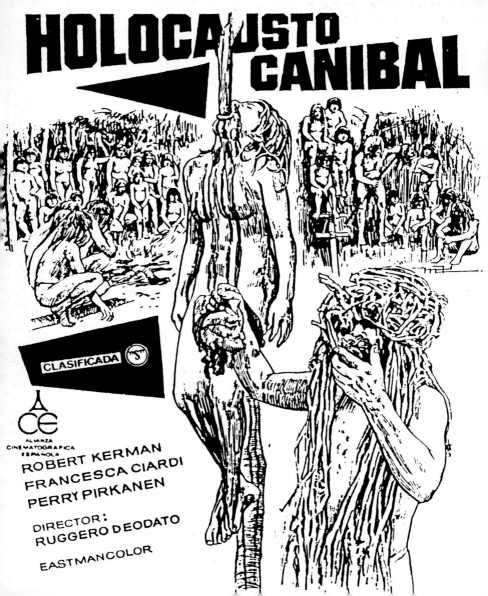

THE SEDUCTION OF THE GULLIBLE

spirits. Back in America, the salvaged film is prepared for transmission as "The Green Inferno", but Monroe begins to have doubts when he checks out the late team's previous effort, "Last Road to Hell", a crude collage of atrocities that got into legal difficulties when it was alleged that some of the killings in it were specially set up for the camera (a clear reference to the notorious real life case of Jacopetti and Prosperi's 1965 Mondo AFRICA ADDIO). The anecdotes of those who worked with them lend weight to this adverse impression.

The developed film initially reveals an obsessive cataloguing of the unpleasantness and discomforts of a jungle expedition, but when the makers tire of this they begin to kill and torture animals to spice things up a little. By the time they meet the Tree People they are ready for rape and murder, planning to pass it off as inter-tribal warfare. Alan, the leader, excitedly declaims sub-Nietzchian piffle about the weak giving way to the strong as he supervises the burning alive of a group of Tree Persons. One of the TV people viewing the film opines that it should be broadcast so that people can make up their own minds — it seems fair enough that if the whites brought their fate upon themselves the world should be told, rather than left to believe it was because of the "savagery" of the natives, but Monroe (and Deodato) argue that the film should be banned — a startling (but not unique) example of a "video nasty" which argues for the suppression of "video nasties"! Monroe believes that the audience can be desensitized and brutalized "The more you rape their senses, the more they seem to like it".

What they see next convinces the others of Monroe's argument: After a woman is seen impaled on a sharp pole, followed by a mob-enforced brutal abortion (both among scenes that were heavily trimmed for Go's British release), the natives strike back in the chillingly realistic climax. The expedition's flight is hampered by their obsessive filming of the chase (c.f. the well-documented demise of some real-life war reporters): "We've really put ourselves in the shit this time, staying to film the last bit" says Alan "... now I don't even know where we are". One by one they are caught, beaten, castrated, efficiently stripped down to skeletons and eaten. Alan becomes a victim of his own philosophy when his keenest disciple tells him that it's more important to get the film back to civilization than to stay and help him. It's the sorcerer's apprentice who falls last: The moment of death, recorded on his face, takes up the final few frames of film (PEEPING TOM in the jungle?). As he leaves the studio, Monroe wonders "Who are the real cannibals?" (Well Prof, they're the guys who eat people!)

"Nobody had heard of CANNIBAL HOLOCAUST..." boasted its British distributor "... till I wrote to Mary Whitehouse complaining about it. Once she got in on the act I couldn't run off enough copies to meet the demand". It soon became clear that this would-be wise-guy had actually shot himself and the trade in the foot, providing as big a push for the censorship bandwagon as S.S. EXPERIMENT CAMP's tasteless poster and the whole SNUFF fiasco. As with SNUFF, not everybody was convinced that the Special FX *were* Special FX. Lord Lane, Britain's Lord Chief Justice, appeared to think that people were really being eaten in it, and the director was embroiled in a long-running court-case back home in Italy over the alleged "obscenity" of his film. He was eventually acquitted, only for all negatives of the film to be destroyed in a mysterious fire. The spectre of a possible jail sentence hanging over his head appears to have chastened Deodato, who now likes to play down HOLOCAUST and HOUSE ON THE EDGE OF THE PARK, and has even cited the mawkish kids-dying-of-cancer effort LAST FEELINGS as his personal favourite among his own films. Once a director of infinite visionary promise, Deodato now churns out anaemic horror efforts that are unworthy of his talent.

Current Status: Banned

WHEN
THE BUTCHER
GOES BERSERK....

ATLAS INTERNATIONAL presents
ELOY DE LA IGLESIAS'S

THE
CANNIBAL MAN

starring VINCENTE PARRA as Marcos
with EMMA COHEN · EUSEBIO PONCELA · LOLA HERRERA
Produced by JOSE TRUCHADO   Directed by ELOY DE LA IGLESIA

CANNIBAL MAN aka THE APARTMENT ON THE 13TH FLOOR / LA SEMANA DEL ASESINO Spain, 1972. Video label: Intervision. Starring Vincente Parra, Emma Cohen, Eusebio Poncela, Vicky Lagos, Ismael Merlo, Charlie Bravo, Rafael Hernandez, Lola Herrera, Valentin Tornos. Camera: Raoul Artigot. Produced by Joe Truchado. Written and

Iglesia's film was lumped in with the FEROX's and HOLOCAUST's of this world by Intervision when such titles were in fashion. Shortly afterwards, when it became fashionable to seize and destroy those movies,it followed FEROX and co into the flames. Under its original monicker it might well have escaped, being not so much a gorefest as a darkly comic Iberian answer to Wim Wenders' THE GOALKEEPER'S FEAR OF THE PENALTY (though thankfully nowhere near as tedious), which proceeds with relentless nightmare logic towards an interesting, if not entirely effective, twist ending.

One Monday night, slaughterhouse worker Marcos (Vincente Parra) gets into a brawl with a taxi-driver who objects to him necking in the back seat with his fiancée Paula. The next day, they learn that the taxi-driver is dead and Paula urges Marcos to turn him-self in to the police. When he declines to do so she tells him that "a marriage can't be built on lies" and that she's leaving him. Enraged, Marcos throttles her, helping himself to a perverse, protracted kiss as she dies. On Wednesday, Marcos takes his brother into his confidence, and is again advised to throw himself on the mercy of the law. Instead he takes a spanner down from a curious display of tools that adorns one of his walls and beats Stephen's brains out with it, then sits and agonises over a photo of himself and his brother as boys in the arms of their mother. On Thursday Stephen's fiancée turns up, discovers his body and has her throat slit by Marcos, who is by now going through his murderous paces coldly and mechanically. Her father arrives on Friday, rants about his daughter's honour, and receives a meat-cleaver full in the face for his trouble. Marcos takes time out from his kill-spree on Saturday, and Rosa the randy bar-maid rolls up on Sunday to seduce him and suggest that redemption is a possibility. Unfortunately she won't be dissuaded from prying into the repository of his putrefying secrets, and Marcos is compelled to silence her by smashing her head repeatedly against the wall. Marco's last caller is a lonely homosexual, who's been making thinly-veiled passes at the protagonist throughout the picture, and reveals that he has witnessed the on-going slaughter-fest in Marcos' hovel from the window of that apartment, on the 13th floor of a towering luxury block. He offers to assist in the disposal of the bodies, and Marcos – unwilling to injure the only person who has offered him any support or understanding – finally gives himself up to the police.

TAOT13F embroiders a persistent thread in Spanish cinema, from Jesus Franco to Luis Buñuel (whose masterly LOS OLVIDADOS is recalled by shots of boys playing football on a wasteground), that of a repressive social order's doomed attempts to keep the lid on unruly human desiresl (just as the rank odour of Marcos' suppurating victims cannot be disguised, no matter how many air-fresheners he employs). Marcos is a frustrated man: his manipulative fiancée seems more concerned with his promotion prospects than with giving him the affection he needs; they have to keep their affair a secret from her family, which is why they end up snogging in a taxi; finally, the taxi -driver's disastrous intervention provokes Marcos into taking drastic action against a world which seems hell-bent on denying him happiness and fulfilment.Marcos' problems are compounded by rigid class barriers. In a suspenseful sequence where his work-mates throw around his hold-all, stuffed with human remains, they chide Marcos that he's "not one of us anymore … he'll soon be moving into one of those fag high-rise apartments". His admirer comments "I ought to be with my own class".He has it tougher than most, of course: "I can't be sure of my own future", he tells Marcos, and our last sight of him is as he contemplates a jagged shard of glass. Given that the repressive society de la Iglesia is portraying in CANNIBAL MAN is patterned, and not so loosely, on the actual society that he was living and working in, this is courageous stuff.

Current Status: Re-released by Redemption Video with 1 second cut

CANNIBAL MAN

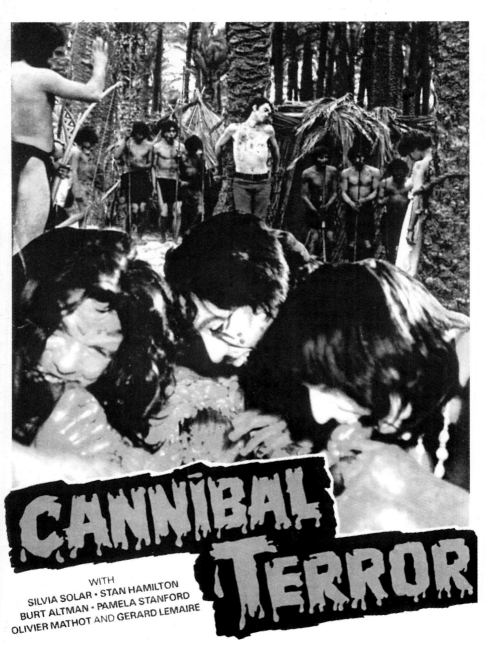

MODERN FILMS
VIDEO

CANNIBAL TERROR

WITH
SILVIA SOLAR · STAN HAMILTON
BURT ALTMAN · PAMELA STANFORD
OLIVIER MATHOT AND GERARD LEMAIRE

93 minutes Colour   **V.H.S.**

THE SEDUCTION OF THE GULLIBLE

CANNIBAL TERROR. France, 1981. Video label: Cinehollywood. Starring Sylvia Solar, Pamela Stanford, Burt Altman, Tony Fontaine, Michael Lavry, Gerard LeMaine, Olivier Mathot, Stan Hamilton, Anthony Mayant. Written by H.L. Rostaine and Ilona Kunesova. Produced by Marius Lasoeur. Directed by "Allan W. Steeve" (Julio Perez Tabernero).

"Allan W. Steeve"s CANNIBAL TERROR is a French man-eating effort that follows the Italian model closely but incompetently. The film's tone is encapsulated in its opening scene, involving two mean-looking dudes breaking into a yacht. What they're after is uncertain, but the extent of their vocabulary is clear enough: "Can't you open the fucking door?" "Shit... oh shit." "Shit... what are you doing?" "Shit... oh shit." "Fuck... oh fuck it! No fucking idiot could get that door open... made me look a fucking fool!" Striking out as cat burglars, they try their hand at kidnapping, abducting a little boy and making for a safe house in the depths of some jungle while the ransom is sorted out. Their jungle guide advises them that cannibals lurk behind every bush. "They'd love to put you in the soup" she warns "but if we don't stop, there's no sweat." But there's perspiration aplenty when their jeep breaks down. Disregarding her own warnings, the guide wanders off into the undergrowth and is promptly ambushed by the locals – a less than convincing spectacle. The "cannibals" – who seem more interested in playing tug-of-war with the unfurling animal intestines than eating them – overact shamelessly, grinning like loons as they brandish offal at the camera. Further inept editing ensures plenty of shots of people standing around waiting for cues.The kidnappers make it to their jungle safe-house, and no sooner has their host gone away on a business trip than they tie his wife to a tree and rape her (a feat accomplished without any unzipping his trousers). When hubby gets home he tfeeds them to the locals, while the kidnapped kid is led off to play in a cannibal kintergarten. By the time his parents arrive, acting on a hot tip-off, there's not much left of the 'nappers. "The gangsters got all the punishment they deserved", the tribal chief assures them, indicating what is supposed to be the severed head of the baddy-in-chief: "He got all the pain and suffering that was coming to him." So did anvone who sat through this piece of garbage!

Current Status: Removed from DPP list. No re-release scheduled

ASTARON
BRUT DES
SCHRECKENS

Het zaad van Mars
«CONTAMINATION»

Technicolor

CONCORDE FILM

regie Lewis Coates
Ian Mc Culloch
Louise Marleau
Gisela Hahn

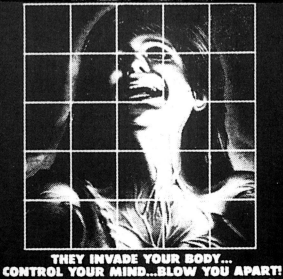

THEY INVADE YOUR BODY...
CONTROL YOUR MIND...BLOW YOU APART!

ALIEN
CONTAMINATION

...ET DEMAIN
CE SERA VOTRE TOUR!

CONTAMINATION
UN FILM DE LEWIS COATES

THE SEDUCTION OF THE GULLIBLE

CONTAMINATION aka ALIEN CONTAMINATION / ALIEN 2. Italy, 1980. Video label: Video Independent Productions. Starring Ian McCulloch, Louise Marleau, Marino Mase, Siegfried Rauch, Gisela Hahn, Carlo De Mejo, Carlo Monni. Alien Cyclops designed by Claudio Mazzoli, constructed by Giorgio Ferrari. Special effects by Giovanni Corridori. Camera: Giuseppe Pinori. Written by "Lewis Coates" and Erich Tomek. Produced by Claudio Mancini. Directed by "Lewis Coates" (Luigi Cozzi).

Cozzi's low-rent monster-mash was originally entitled ALIEN 2, but they didn't get away with that for long. It's opening plunges us into a "Marie Celeste" situation, in fact it's a virtual remake of the intro to Lucio Fulci's ZOMBIE FLESH EATERS as an abandoned boat, floats into New York harbour. "This looks like the officers' mess" observes a coast guard official, and "mess" is the operative word, because before you can say "shiver me timbers", mutilated sea-dogs are falling out of every cupboard. The culprits are nasty green pods from outer space, distant relatives of those in ALIEN and INVASION OF THE BODY SNATCHERS, but rather more immediate in their effect — when these pods ripen they burst open and so do any Earthlings reckless enough to be in the vicinity. The coast guards are soon exploding in a shower of offal, all filmed in such super-slow motion as to make a Sam Peckinpah offing look like fast-forward.

The human race responds swiftly — all the Italians in New York are soon on the case. Dr Stella Holmes (Louise Marleau) takes control. "I'm a colonel, directly responsible to the President, Special Division Five", she barks: "... put Emergency Plan Seven into effect". Stella enlists the aid of Police Lieutenant Arris (Marino Mase), the sole survivor of the initial incident, and also Hubbard, an astronaut who was laughed out of NASA when he returned from Mars claiming that his colleague was killed by pulsating pods. Holmes finds this guy residing in alcoholic squalor, but galvanizes him with some catty reflections on his virility ("In this state, you couldn't even get it up with a crane!") What a ball-breaker!

Hubbard repeats his story, the accompanying flash-back sequence — depicting his ordeal in a cave at the Martian pole — is gripping stuff, comparing very favourably to the corresponding scene in ALIEN when you consider the films' respective budgets. The atmospheric Goblins score (re-used in ZOMBIE CREEPING FLESH) does no harm either. Hubbard is played by Ian McCulloch, who's had to deal with threats to mankind that come floating into New York harbours before. OK, so he came off second best when he tangled with ZOMBIE FLESH EATERS ...will he do better against the galactic greenies?

Our heroes trace the pods to a waterfront warehouse, which is stormed by. SAS types. The warehousemen duck any awkward questions by the simple expedient of exploding in slow motion. Stella theorizes, straight off the top of her head, that the pods are to be placed in the Big Apple's sewer system, there to incubate and blow up a large section of the city. "National security is at stake" she warns: "... and possibly even more than that!" The film relocates to South America, signalled by the expected outbreak of stock footage. Villainous locals smuggle pods into Stella's bathroom while she's taking a shower, but the boys rescue her, setting the scene for the climactic confrontation on a coffee plantation that has been turned over to the cultivation of pods, an operation run by Hamilton, the supposedly dead astronaut, his will directed by the dreaded Alien Cyclops ("...It's slimy, slithering appearance more than made up for by the fact that it has all the mobility of a toaster oven": FANGORIA magazine.)

The Cyclops mesmerizes Arris with its throbbing yellow eye then sucks him into its gaping maw. Stella's next on the menu but Old Mother Hubbard, despite undergoing another Mars flash-back (makes a nice change from all those 'Nam flash-backs) shoots the cyclops in the eye, which for some reason causes Hamilton to burst into flames. The army turns up on cue to round up the Martian minions and close down the plantation, but that's not the end of the story — back in NYC, pods are ripening in sidewalk garbage piles. One of them bursts as the credits roll.

Current Status: Re-released by European Creative Video with cuts

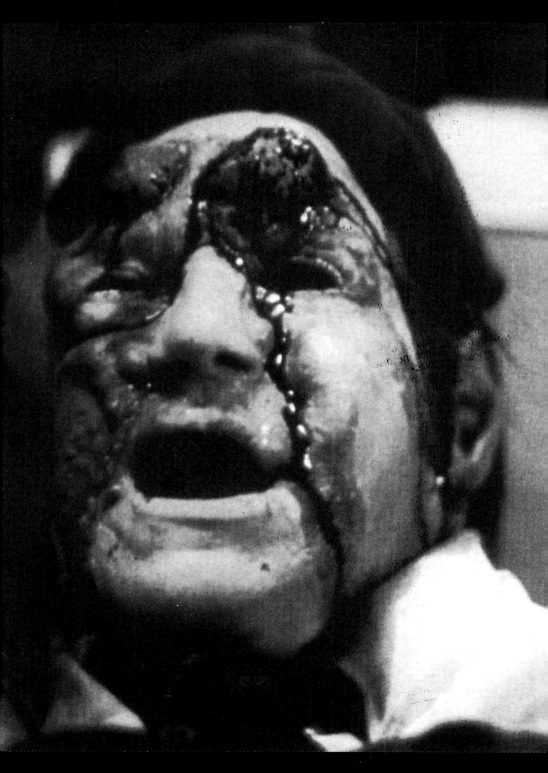

THE SEDUCTION OF THE GULLIBLE

DEAD AND BURIED. U.S.A., 1981. Video label: Thorn EMI. Starring James Farentino, Melody Anderson, Jack Albertson, Dennis Redfield, Nancy Locke Hauser, Lisa Blount, Robert Englund. Special effects: Stan Winston. Camera: Steve Poster. Written by Ronald Shusett, Dan O'Bannon, Jeff Millar and Alex Stern. Produced by Ronald Shusett and Robert Fentress. Directed by Gary A. Sherman.

DEAD AND BURIED was one of the bigger-budgeted films to end up a "nasty", probably because most of that big budget was spent on some genuinely nasty Stan Winston gore effects. The firstvictim is a camera buff mooching around on the beach (we see a sign bearing the ironic message: "Potter's Bluff – a new way of life") till he comes across a blonde piece of jail-bait willing to give her all in the cause of art. "Do you want me?" she pouts and before you can say "Is the Pope a Catholic?", up springs a gang of yobbo fishermen to beat him over the head with blunt instruments. He's photographed, then burned alive. This surreal introduction has the flavour of a gored-up AVENGERS episode, but you ain't seen nothing yet. The forces of law and order, led by Sheriff Dan Gillis (James Farentino) find this unfortunate planted in an upturned car. Then zany local mortician Dobbs (Jack Albertson) rolls up with big band jazz blaring out from the stereo in his meat wagon. As they peruse the crispy head it opens its mouth and screams! Bandaged up in intensive care like a Mummy, our photographer friend is understandably perturbed to see that the nurse whose tender loving care he has been consigned to is none other than the little tease on the beach, and she's brought along a nice big syringe to stick in his one remaining eye. He finally givues up the ghost. But not for long! He's soon back with a new identity, mingling happily with his killers (includingRobert "Freddy Krueger" Englund). The zombie secret is given away far too early, probably because the makers of this film figured they have one more boffo revelation up their sleeves... of which more later.

Desperate Dan's scratches his head a lot and utters inane lines like: "What kind of maniac is loose around here?" Then he discovers that his teacher wife includes the occult in her lesson plans. This black magic woman is played by Melody Anderson (whose illustrious CV also includes the Dino FLASH GORDON and POLICE WOMAN CENTREFOLD) As if "Janet and John go voodoo" wasn't enough, Gillis now unearths a porno flick starring his spouse. Neighbourhood goons are shown leering through the window as she entertains a mystery guest then stabs him to death. Just to round off his day, Gillis runs over and is then mugged by a jay-walking zombie. Elsewhere a family inexplicably take a descent of fog as their cue to wander around a derelict house until swashbuckling zombies swing through the windows to get them. Next, a doctor investigating some grisly scraps of evidence is waylaid by the Potter's Bluff Glee Club in his lab. As usual it's the jail bait who takes a leading part, inserting tubes up his nostrils and pumping in acid! Needless to say, he is soon back conferring with Gillis, assuring him that dead men don't come back, even though he is the living(?) proof that indeed they do. Several more unlikely occurrences lead the sheriff to confront Dobbs the mortician, who, it turns out, is honing his professional skills by snuffing people and bringing them back as zombies: "It's an art. I'm an artist. Call it black magic, call it medical breakthrough, but I'll take my secret to the grave!" Of course he has no intention of ever getting into one. When Gillis shoots him, Dobbs thanks the sheriff for the opportunity to "become one of my children", hooking himself up to a bottle of zombie juice. "There's one more thing you should know, Dan" comments Dobbs, running the unexpurgated version of Melody's stag film and revealing Gillis himself as the victim! That's right folks, in case you couldn't work it out from his performance ... James Farentino is a zombie!

Although it's unarguably daft, and for much of its length suffers from the surprisingly flat, TV movie-like direction of Gary DEATH LINE Sherman, DEAD AND BURIED does have a genuinely nightmarish quality about it, not only due to the graphic violence but also the metaphysical queasiness of the finalé, which recalls a classic episode of Boris Karloff's THRILLER television series, THE INCREDIBLE DR MARKESAN.

Current Status: Re-released by The Video Collection

"Texas Chainsaw Massacre" director Tobe Hooper gives you another orgy of blood and terror!!

STRONG UNCUT VERSION!!

DEATH TRAP

VIPCO

Starring
Neville Brand, Mel Ferrer, Marilyn Burns,
William Finley, Carolyn Jones & Stuart Whitman
Directed by: Tobe Hooper Produced by: Mardi Rustam

SEE WARNING ON REVERSE

RUNNING TIME 90 MINS. APPROX.

THE SEDUCTION OF THE GULLIBLE

DEATH TRAP aka EATEN ALIVE / STARLIGHT SLAUGHTER / SLAUGHTER MOTEL / HORROR HOTEL / AMOK U.S.A. 1976. Video label: VIPCO & VCL. Starring Neville Brand, Mel Ferrer, Carolyn Jones, Marilyn Burns, William Finley, Stuart Whitman, Roberta Collins, Kyle Richards, Robert Englund. Camera: Robert Garamico. Written by Tobe Hooper, Mardi Rustam, Alvin L. Fast and Kim Henkel. Produced by Mardi Rustam, Mohammed Rustam, Samir Rustam, Larry Huly, Robert Kantor and Alvin L. Fast. Directed by Tobe Hooper.

DEATH TRAP opens with a point-blank close-up of Robert Englund's bejeaned crotch, the zipper descending as he introduces himself … "My name's Buck, and I'm a-rarin' to fuck!" What a career pinnacle... even Englund's "Freddy" antics pale into insignificance beside this mouldy milestone, a spectacle so cheesy and sleazy that the only way to enhance audience appreciation of it would be to hand out scratch 'n' sniff cards with a patch marked "rancid smegma". "Why don't you turn over and get up on your knees for ol' Buck?" continues our loathsome cowboy, but the gal he's asking, though on the game, isn't game for any anal antics. Back-door man Buck complains to Madame Miss Hattie (Carolyn "Morticia" Jones), and as compensation he gets two bimbos for the price of one. What the anal virgin gets is slung out of Miss Hattie's establishment. She wanders around until she comes across the Starlight Motel, a garish neon vision floating in the bayou mist, within whose dilapidated walls sits Judd the proprietor (Neville Brand), ranting incoherently as he squints at girlie magazines through a looking glass. Deciding that his new guest is morally deficient, Judd stabs her repeatedly with a rake and feeds her to the crocodile (Judd is mortally offended if anyone mistakes it for a mere alligator) that inhabits the swamp overlooked by his motel.

The next folks who sign in are Hooper regular William Finley, black-wigged TEXAS CHAINSAW MASSACRE alumnus Marilyn Burns and their cute little daughter. Judd's crocodile wastes no time scarfing down her puppy, after which Finley has a barrel of laughs, tormenting the girl by barking like a dog. Weirder still, he grovels at Burns' feet, begging her to stub out a cigarette in his eye(!) Eventually he steps onto the back porch with his rifle, aiming to gun down that thar' scaly varmint, but Judd mows him down with a swing of his scythe and a further torrent of verbal diarrhoea. Just as he is about to deliver the coup-de-grace, Judd's patently rubber pet crashes through the railings and drags Finley head first into the swamp. Judd ties Burns up in her room but her daughter escapes and runs underneath the building, where she spends the rest of the movie oscillating between the Scylla of scythe-wielding Judd and the Charybdis of his hungry crocodile. Judd chases Burns and the kid around until predictably falling victim to his own croc. Hooper's final shot is a heavy-handed quotation from Peter Pan, as ol' Judd's wooden leg rises to the surface of the swamp... perhaps it was this that recommended Hooper to Steven Spielberg, who would produce POLTERGEIST for him.

Hooper's TCM follow-up was compromised by a veritable battalion of interfering producers and he has disowned the film, which emerges as a live-action E.C. comic, lit in such a way that individual frames suggest comic panels, six years before George Romero's rather too literally executed CREEPSHOW (1982). Its cast of oddball characters and crocodile ex-machina are straight out of the E.C. canon, in particular "Country Clubbing", a Jack Davis epic that appeared in HAUNT OF FEARS # 23 (1954). Hooper's evocation of rural idiocy in the shit-kicking south-side of the Moronic Inferno benefits no end from another of TEXAS CHAINSAW MASSACRE collaborator Wayne Bell's jarring "found" scores (so often and so badly imitated in scores of subsequent zero-budgeted schlock horrors), which perfectly compliments the rubbish spewing from Judd's relentless radio. If anything, all this places DEATH TRAP closer to Buñuel's documentary of in-bred, atrophied humanity ("Words cannot express the horror of their mirthless grins") LOS HURDOS / LAND WITHOUT BEAD, than to TEXAS CHAINSAW, though like Hooper's debut it is based on the notorious exploits of a real-life demented ghoul – one Joe Ball, who fed his victims to five pet alligators.

Current Status: Re-released by VIPCO "Cult Classics" with 25 secs cuts

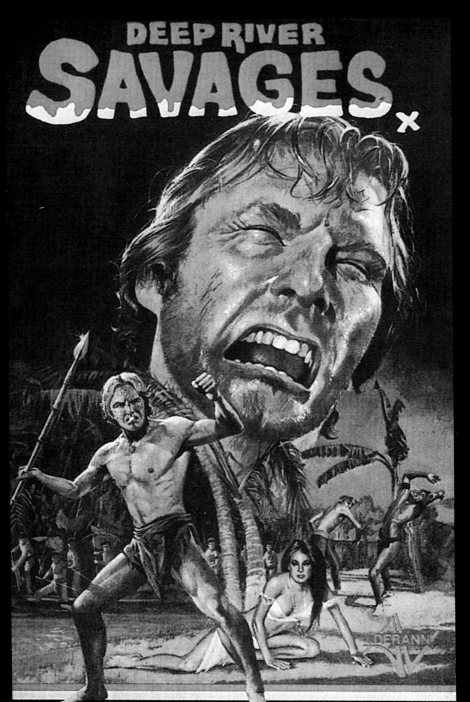

THE SEDUCTION OF THE GULLIBLE

DEEP RIVER SAVAGES aka THE MAN FROM DEEP RIVER / NEL PAESE DEL SESSO SELVAGGIO / SACRIFICE. Italy, 1972. Video label: Derann. Starring Ivan Rassimov, Me Me Lay, Pratitsak Singhara, Sulallewan Suwantat, Ong Ard, Prapas Chindang, Tuan Tevan. Camera: Riccardo Pallotini. Written by Francesco Barilli and Massimo d'Avack. Produced by M.G. Rossi. Directed by Umberto Lenzi.

"A story of raw savagery, tribal torture and one man's courageous fight for survival, respect and the delicate and fragile love of a beautiful native girl ... a compelling film in which character relationships are brilliantly developed and a richness of human emotions are played out against the bizarre and tortuous rituals of the primitive world." Don't worry, despite all this hearts and flowers stuff on the pack, you're in for some typical Umberto Lenzi sleaze.Ivan Rassimov, having killed a native at a Thai boxing match, heads for the steamy Thai interior and pronounces: "I'm sick to death of this trip ... I wish I was at home drinking a pint". Viewers will agree, as all their least favourite pieces of stock footage are trotted out yet again (if I see those bloody storks in that tree again!) When the cannibals roll up, Ivan tries the diplomatic approach ("Leave me alone, you bloody savages") but they drag him back to their village, where the first thing he witnesses is a guy getting his tongue cut out ... BLOOD FEAST has a lot to answer for, but it's MONDO CANE that serves as the real "inspiration" for DEEP RIVER SAVAGES, its subsequent violence mostly directed at our little furry and scaly friends. Hardly a minute goes by without a snake being flayed, a pig gutted, a mongoose forced into a life-or-death struggle with a cobra, etc, etc ad nauseum. Adding most to the nausea is the scene in which a monkey has the top of its head lopped off, boiled-egg style, so the tribe can snack on warm simian brains for supper. Lenzi was to try out this trick on a human (well, John Morghen's) cranium during CANNIBAL FEROX.

Rassimov, though, is treated to the life of Riley after he has saved the chief's son with an impromptu tracheotomy. Memorably, he is allowed to take part in a ritual where the village men file past a hut and put their hands through a hole. The aptly named Me Me Lay sits blindfolded on the other side while the men take turns squeezing her breasts and feeling between her legs. The budget wouldn't stretch to a MAN CALLED HORSE-type ritual for Rassimov's formal initiation into the tribe, so instead he is lashed to a vertical rotisserie which turns slowly as the villagers aim their blow-pipes at him through cubby-holes. Now Rassimov gets down to bringing up a family with Me Me, but neighbouring tribesmen are soon viewing her as lunch. She escapes, but one of her friends is not so fortunate, and when Rassimov catches the intruders in the act (to the accompaniment of jolly music!) he shows how thin the veneer of civilization is by hacking out their tongues. So it's nosurprise that even when Me Me dies of a tropical disease, he elects to turn his back oncivilization and stay with the tribe that adopted him.

Current Status: Removed from DPP list. No re-release scheduled

DEEP RIVER SAVAGES

Colour 85 minutes
VTC 1022

THE SEDUCTION OF THE GULLIBLE

DELIRIUM aka PSYCHO PUPPET. U.S.A, 1979. Video label: Video Tape Center. Starring Turk Cekovsky, Debi Chaney, Terry Ten Broek, Barron Winchester, Bob Winters, Garrett Bergfeld, Nick Panouzis. Special effects: Bob Shelly. Camera: John Huston and Bill Mensch. Written by James Lowe, Eddie Kreli, Richard Yalem. Produced by Sunny Vest and Peter Maris. Directed by Peter Maris.

DELIRIUM's derivative plot finds the cops investigating a series of dubious "suicides", all involving violent crims who have been acquitted on technicalities. "If this shit carries on", remarks a detective "...we can all go fishing", and the viewer will soon wish he had acted on this suggestion. These cops rival those in BLOOD FEAST for sheer inability to put together screamingly obvious clues, but it seems a sinister organisation of right-wing industrialists and military men, who operate a kangaroo court in a cellar, have decided to clear the scum off the streets. They've recruited disturbed Vietnam Vet Charlie, who moonlights from his vigilante day-job by killing nubile girls. The first ends up stabbed and impaled on a door, an effect Maris is so (inexplicably) pleased with that he treats us to flashbacks of it at several inappropriate points. Next, Charlie picks up a scantily-clad, hitch-hiking Bo Derek clone shortly before undergoing a particularly florid Nam flashback which culminates in him crashing the car. Girls … what would you do? Run, right? Well, this one coolly announces: "I'm going for a swim", strips off and jumps in a nearby pond. When Charlie refuses to join her, she taunts him about the size of his manhood. Charlie shuts her up by drowning her. He adjourns to a graveyard to continue his flashback in peace and the root of his problem is revealed – a Vietnam massacre and the murder of a hooker who mocked him when he failed to rise to the occasion. Charlie's boss Stern turns up to eliminate his wayward employee and the film "climaxes" in a three-way shoot-out with the law. Apropos of nothing, Stern now has a 'Nam flash-back of his own, running at the police and shouting orders to imaginary troops, until he's shot down (all inter-cut with endless stock footage of helicopters taking off). Perhaps Maris himself was suffering a flashback by this point!

Re-released on the Viz Movies label as PSYCHO PUPPET.

cinehollywood

THE DEVIL HUNTER

Al Cliver, Gisela Hahn, Robert Foster

THE SEDUCTION OF THE GULLIBLE

THE DEVIL HUNTER aka THE MAN HUNTER / MANDINGO MAN HUNTER / SEXO-CANIBALE. Italy/Spain/West Germany, 1980. Video label: Cinehollywood. Starring Al Cliver, Ursulla Fellner, Silvia Solar, Gisela Hahn, Werner Pochat, Burt Altman, Robert Foster. Camera: Juan Soler. Written by Julius Valery and "Clifford Brown". Produced by Franco Prosperi. Directed by "Clifford Brown" (Jesus Franco).

DEVIL HUNTER was originally to have been directed by Amando de Ossorio, but when he dropped out the property devolved into the careless hands of perennial Spanish sleazemeister Jesus Franco, whose prolific output ranges in quality from the fairly watchable (JACK THE RIPPER, FACELESS) to celluloid atrocities such as … well, such as THE DEVIL HUNTER. BLOODY MOON, another Franco entry on the "Video Nasties" list, is instantly recognisable as a Spanish giallo – albeit scraping the bottom of that genre's barrel – but DEVIL HUNTER represents Franco at his most amorphous, baffling and boring. Utilizing the sets, locations, general tone and certain cast members from his 1979 film CANNIBALS / WHITE CANNIBAL QUEEN (many of the same ingredients turn up in the contemporary CANNIBAL TERROR, a monstrosity described elsewhere in this volume), Franco turns in a stultifying, sexist, racist fantasy in which starlet Laura Crawford (Ursulla Fellner) is abducted and taken to some Third World locale. Here the natives live in fear of the eponymous Devil, offering him frenzied tribal dances and chained maidens in supplication. The Devil, when he turns up, is a major disappointment, being nothing more than a tall black guy with ping pong eyeballs. But boy, can he eat pussy … no, really, he actually eats it!! Meanwhile Fellner, in chains (a major Franco fetish), is being raped by one of the kidnappers, while CONTAMINATION's Gisela Hahn enjoys the spectacle from her hammock. Al Cliver (Pier Luigi Conti), in low-rent Indiana Jones threads, is charged with liberating this damsel in distress. He's flown out to that unspecified Third World jungle in a chopper, then, true to Franco form, he spends an eternity wandering around in the undergrowth not actually doing anything. Eventually he arranges with the nappers to swap the girl for a suitcase stuffed with money. They keep the girl and try to shoot Cliver, but anticipating this turn of events, he has stuffed the suitcase with worthless paper (unfilmed Franco scripts, perhaps, if such a thing exists). Now the bad guys start getting picked off by The Devil (Hahn's head is beaten in with a rock) and the natives prepare Fullner for consumption … none of this being as interesting as it might sound. Cliver scales the cliff on top of which the sacrifice is to take place and incredibly, his cliff-scaling exploits are rendered by that staple expedient of the old BATMAN TV series, i.e. Franco's camera is laid on its side and Cliver is filmed crawling across the floor! It's for the individual viewer to decide whether this is more or less ridiculous than the spectacle of Al with his arm – supposedly amputated by natives – conspicuously tied behind his back in Franco's CANNIBALS.

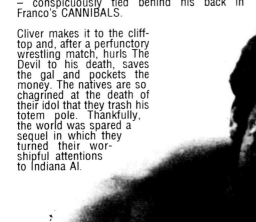

Cliver makes it to the clifftop and, after a perfunctory wrestling match, hurls The Devil to his death, saves the gal and pockets the money. The natives are so chagrined at the death of their idol that they trash his totem pole. Thankfully, the world was spared a sequel in which they turned their worshipful attentions to Indiana Al.

Current Status: Banned

Everyone has nightmares about the ugliest way to die.

DON'T GO IN THE WOODS
"...alone!"

R WARNING
CONTAINS SCENES OF GRAPHIC VIOLENCE

Starring NICK McCLELLAND

JAMES P. HAYDEN · KEN CARTER & TOM DRURY as "The Monster"

MANSON INTERNATIONAL
Copyright / 1981 Double 5 Productions (Astral) Ltd. all rights reserved

THE SEDUCTION OF THE GULLIBLE

DON'T GO IN THE WOODS aka DON'T GO IN THE WOODS ALONE. U.S.A., 1980. Video label: Video Network. Starring Mary Gail Artz, Ken Carter, Jack McClelland, James P. Hayden Tom Drury, David Barth. Camera: Hank Zinman. Written by Garth Eliassen. Produced by Roberto and Suzette Gomez. Directed by James Bryan.

It's identikit "stalking and slashing in the woods" time again, with nothing to distinguish D.G.I.T.W.(A.) from a score of identical home movies in this densest of sub-genres...come to think of it, Jim Bryan's film does have one feature that sets it apart from its peers, none of which can boast(?) a theme song based on "Teddy Bears' Picnic". I kid you not! Check this out ...

"Don't go into the woods tonight, you probably will be thrilled.
Don't go out in the woods tonight, you probably will be killed.
There's a friendly beast that lurks about,
And likes to feast, you won't get out,
Without being killed and chopped up in little pieces ..."
etc, etc, etc ...

Actually H. Kingsley Thurber's little ditty serves as a convenient summary of the "action". Things kick off with Craig, leader of a gang of townies out camping for the weekend, warning his charges that "the most dangerous animal in the woods is man" and that "the most important rule is this ... never, NEVER go into the woods alone". No prizes for guessing that the campers' unanimous response to this "most important rule" is to wander off into the woods alone at the earliest available opportunity, to be garotted, stabbed, hung up in sleeping bags, impaled on booby traps and have various limbs lopped off themselves, all to a bouncey electronic organ accompaniment of the kind you hear playing at ice-hockey matches.

"It's gonna be one of those summers!" complains one of the inept cops assigned to the case, dead ringers for those in THE LAST HOUSE ON THE LEFT. To nobody's great surprise there then ensues a lot of wandering around in those damn woods, punctuated by some more killings, the culprit eventually revealed as a retard in a fur coat who packs a mean homemade lance. Finally some campers gang up on this guy and beat him to death (a couple of Jason-like resurrections are of course thrown in along the way) with sticks and machetés.

"Everyone has nightmares about the ugliest way to die" screams the pack. Right, and mine involve being strapped to a chair while an endless succession of these things unspool before my eyes!

Current Status: Banned

Home VIDEO Productions
Don't Go Near the Park
Produced & Directed by
LAWRENCE D
ALDO
DISTRIBUTED BY
THE FIRST NAME IN VIDEO
THE LAST WORD IN ENTERTAINMENT
HORROR

THE SEDUCTION OF THE GULLIBLE

> *DON'T GO NEAR THE PARK aka NIGHTSTALKER. U.S.A., 1979. Video label: Intervision. Starring Aldo Ray, Meeno Peluce, Tamara Taylor, Barbara Monker, Crackers Phinn, Linnea Quigley. Camera: William De Diego. Screenplay by Linwood Chase and Lawrence D. Foldes. From the original story "Sanctuary for Evil" by Linwood Chase. Produced and directed by Lawrence D. Foldes.*

"12,000 years ago" – and this is all true, it says so in the credits – prehistoric teenagers Gar and Tra (Meeno Peluce and Barbara Monker) are being carpeted for blood-drinking, incest and cannibalism, activities intended to secure them eternal life. Given that this was their aim, the "punishment" meted out to them seems somewhat perverse – they will live for 12,000 years, then – "when the twin stars of the wolf realign" - they must sacrifice a virgin descended from the tribe. This will the eternal life they covet, but failure will lead to damnation "for eternity upon eternity". "We are your children!" wails Tra, but their accuser is unmoved by her protestations... "so bad it's good", you're thinking, but DGNTP is so bad it's awful", and that's the verdict of trash icon Linnea Quigley, who made her screen debut in this mind-numbing clinker. Anyway, time flies, and 11,984 years later ("16 years ago") we find a distinctly shit-faced looking Gar (who has wisely changed his name to Mark and assumed the guise of a businessman), disemboweling and scarfing down the innards of a young angler. Gar/Mark is refreshed and rejuvenated while the boy's corpse withers before our very eyes. Gar receives a message in an echoing telepathic voice, from sister Tra (now "Patty'), urging him to father a child so that they can sacrifice it when the wolf stars are realigned. "I want eternal life!" she rants. "So why can't she just get a man and beget her own child?" you may well be asking. Well, the years have taken their toll on Tra too, though she also resorts to periodic cannibalism as a restorative.

Gar strikes up a relationship with the young Quigley, who quickly bears him a daughter. Gar, possibly motivated by a desire not to have the silliest name in the film, insists on calling the brat Bondy, in honour of a former girlfriend ("She was a good dancer"). Bondy grows up to be Tamara Taylor, on whom Gar lavishes all his attention, neglecting Quigley now that she has served her purpose. It's the final straw when Bondy is given a golden amulet on her 16th birthday: "Gold?!!" whines Quigley. "... I only get copper!!!" "That's right, bitch!" responds Gar, sensitively: "... she just happens to be better than you!" Understandably, Quigley packs her bag, and Bondy also decides to hit the road. She is immediately picked up by a van-load of sleazoids (including demented writer/producer/director Lawrence D. Foldes) with rape on their minds. "You wanna take a walk on the wild side?" asks one. Another tells her: "We just wanna squeeze your nipples", which is apparently intended to be reassuring. Bondy calls on her father, at which point that prehistoric amulet glows red and the van explodes, torching the low-lifers but leaving Bondy unscathed. She finds her way to a ranch populated by delinquent children, presided over by none other than Tra/Patty, now sporting a ludicrous eye patch. Poor old Aldo Ray ("Taft") stumbles in to warn them that Patty is "Satan" and that they should stay away from the local park. To illustrate his point we see shots of girl campers having their guts pulled out and eaten in the park.

Bondy starts having nightmares about being dragged into a coffin, then Gar turns up and takes her for a stroll in that park which she wasn't supposed to go near. "The time has come," he reveals. "Remove your clothes and assume your natural state." "Cowboy" arrives to save Bondy from being sacrificed, but is blammed by laser beams that shoot from the eyes of Gar and Tra. Bondy briefly turns into the cave-granny who initiated all this, and announces that the balance of nature, which these prehistoric delinquents have destroyed, will now destroy them. Flames engulf the eccentrically named bad guys, whose victims then rise from the dead to turn the cannibal tables. Eeveryone piles into that park to play, and a fluffed freeze-frame ending suggests that Bondy is about to disembowel Nick the obnoxious and sexually precocious midget, the first time in the whole movie that the audience canreally get whole heartedly behind what is happening on screen. Don't bother seeing this crappy movie! A cheap shot, but sound advice anyway...

> *Current Status: Removed from DPP list. No re-release scheduled*

Don't Look in the Basement

R

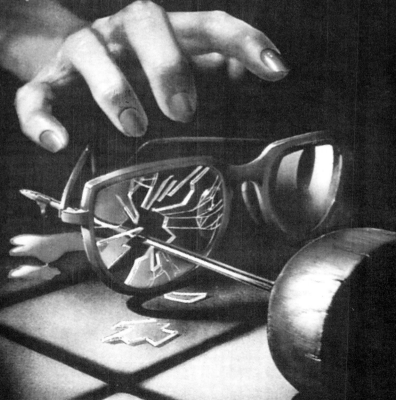

A FEELING OF UNEASE CREPT OVER HER ....

THE SEDUCTION OF THE GULLIBLE

DON'T LOOK IN THE BASEMENT. U.S.A., 1973. *Video label: Derann/Crystal. Starring Jessie Lee Fulton, William Bill McGhee, Robert Dracup, Harryette Warren, Michael Harvey, Jessie Kirby, Hugh Feagin, Betty Chandler, Camilla Carr, Gene Ross, Anne MacAdams. Camera: Robert Alcott. Written by Tim Pope. Produced and Directed by S.F. Brownrigg.*

The Stephens Sanatorium is run along liberal lines, its inmates encouraged to go ape-shit as a solution to their mental problems. Thus "Sarge" (Hugh Feagin) dresses in army fatigues and waits for an invasion that only he knows is coming, "the Judge" (Gene Ross) rages about the sins of the flesh, and an amiable lobotomized black guy named Sam (William Bill McGhee) sucks on a lolly-ice and generally acts like a goon. It was Sam's case that convinced Dr Stephens (Michael Harvey) of the need for an alternative to psycho-surgery. We see him encouraging the Judge to chop wood with an axe: "with every stroke he's reaching into the cellar of his unconscious brain" enthuses the doc, but the Judge soon starts chopping at him.

Psychotherapist Charlotte Beale (Jessie Lee Fulton) arrives to take up her new position, but gets a frosty reception from the sanatorium's new head, Dr Geraldine Masters (Anne MacAdams). The most ancient crone in the place, Mrs Callingham (Rhea MacAdams) warns Charlotte to get out of the sanatorium as soon as possible. Soon afterwards, the ol' girl turns up spitting blood and fragments of her tattered tongue, pretty well proving her point. There's a marvellous scene in which a telephone engineer arrives at the sanatorium to fix the phone and is challenged by Dr Masters as to why he didn't give her notice of his visit. "Well your phone's not working and your receptionist has no tongue" he repliesh. The engineer is pulled into a closet by a libidinous lady inmate, who's so upset by his rejection of her superannuated advances that she stabs him and keeps his body to cuddle up to.

Meanwhile, Charlotte is trying to continue Dr Stephens' progressive policy, but Dr Masters is taking a tougher line, e.g. burning Sarge's hand for disobedience. The patients respond by freaking out and killing each other. One unfortunate girl gets her eye impaled on a paper spike by the judge. Charlotte goes down into that basement and discovers Dr Stephens, still alive but in a bad way. Unfortunately she construes his plea for help as another attack by a demented patient, and beats him to death. Now Charlotte realises that "Dr Masters" is actually one of the patients, killing off anyone who threatens her new found position of authority (this will have dawned on the audience long ago, even those who haven't seen the previous year's Amicus effort ASYLUM, so obviously the inspiration here). Sam, flashing back to his traumatic lobotomy, rescues Charlotte from the lunatic who has taken over the asylum, who is then dispatched by the revolting (in every sense of the word) inmates, queueing at the door, AIRPLANE style, with knives, axes and other weapons. Finally Sam reappears and chops down the judge with his own axe.

In the '70s and early '80s the mysterious Mr S. F. Brownrigg (died, 1996) churned out 4 minimalist yarns in which ranting, retarded obsessive characters, closeted together on threadbare sets, vent their spleen on – and eventually kill – each other, namely this, SCUM OF THE EARTH aka POOR WHITE TRASH PART II (1975), DON'T OPEN THE DOOR (1979) and KEEP MY GRAVE OPEN (1980). The hospital setting here is a natural for Brownrigg's oppressive world view. Much graphic violence has been excised from the British release (notably when Sam chops up the judge), a fact that together with the video's understated ad campaign ("A feeling of unease crept over her") makes one wonder why D.L.I.T.B. ended up on the dreaded DPP list. Well, apart from an apparent tendency for the police to seize anything with the word DON'T in its title, it would seem that the film invoked an old British prohibition, discussed in former British Board of Film Censors secretary John Trevelyan's illuminating memoirs, "What the Censor Saw", against inaccurate representations of psychiatric treatment.

Current Status: Removed from DPP list. No re-release scheduled

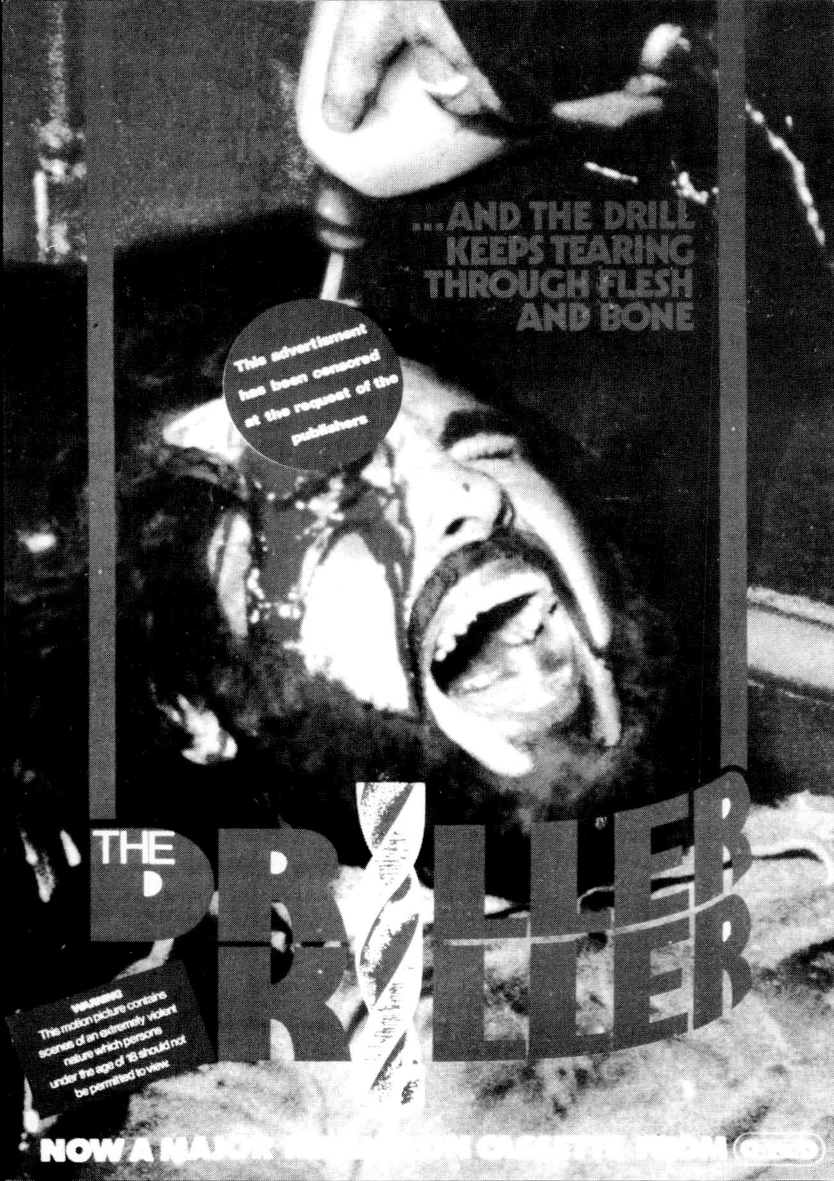

...AND THE DRILL KEEPS TEARING THROUGH FLESH AND BONE
This advertisement has been censored at the request of the publishers
THE DRILLER KILLER
WARNING
This motion picture contains scenes of an extremely violent nature which persons under the age of 18 should not be permitted to view.
NOW A MAJOR
ON CASSETTE FROM

THE SEDUCTION OF THE GULLIBLE

THE DRILLER KILLER U.S.A, 1979. Video label: VIPCO. Starring Jimmy Laine, Carolyn Marz, Baybi Day, Harry Schultz, Alan Wynroth, Rhodney Montreal. Camera: Ken Kelsch. Written by N.G. St John. Produced by Rochelle Weisberg. Directed by Abel Ferrara.

The infamous DRILLER KILLER, denounced and banned by those who never bothered to see it and often dismissed as boring by those who did, became an early and permanent fixture on the "video nasties" list due to its uncompromising sleeve. Too short on violence and long on arty pretensions to keep gorehounds happy, too sleazy for the Art-house crowd, THE DRILLER KILLER is seemingly loved by few.

Reno ("Jimmy Laine", alias director Abel Ferrara), an artist, lives in a PERFORMANCE-like open relationship with two girls, Carol and Pamela (Carolyn Marz and Baybi Day), who sit around stoned all day reading him "National Enquirer"-type newspaper stories (including the modern legend, the dog in the microwave) and restaging the shower sequence from AN AMERICAN WEREWOLF IN LONDON while he's out trying to sell paintings. The rent on their squalid appartment is long overdue, but Reno can't seem to finish the painting on which he is pinning his hopes for a big score. This meisterwerk turns out to be a unspectacular portrait of a bison, the eyes of which (and eyes in general) hold a strange fascination for him. Our misgivings over Reno's state of mind are hardly eased when we are made privy to his first (and for the moment, meaningless) flash-forward to himself being splattered with blood. Increasingly haunted by the spectre of destitution, Reno takes to hanging out with street people, sketching them, asking them how they ended up on the street, sometimes just staring at them, contemplating his probable future. Still he struggles to complete the painting. When Carol tries to assure him that it's perfect as it is, he rages: "You know how to bitch, how to eat, how to bitch, how to shit, how to bitch – but nothing about painting!" The girls get additional insight into just how flaky their paramour is becoming when he dives on a pizza they have ordered and starts guzzling it like an animal. Reno's painting grinds to a halt when a truly dreadful punk band named "Tony Coca-Cola and the Roosters" move into the building and commence 24-hour a day jam sessions. Tony Coca-Cola (the scarcely less oddly-named Rhodney Montreal) is a retarded would-be Lou Reed who calls everybody "man" and asks Reno: "Did you ever get into a rock 'n' roll trip, baby?" The final straw comes for Reno when he learns that these talentless idiots have got a lucrative recording contract (those who attribute some kind of "punk sensibility" to THE DRILLER KILLER have totally missed the point). Buying a portable power pack that he has seen advertised on TV, Reno takes to the streets with his trusty power drill and starts drilling daylight through the bums and winos that litter the New York landscape. He also skewers an art dealer who ridiculed his buffalo painting, and his girlfriend Carol's husband, who she has deserted Reno to go back to. The film ends in the dark with Carol trying to seduce her husband Stephen… or so she thinks. She's actually in bed with Reno (… and his drill?)

"The scenes depicted are explicit and very unpleasant" complained one critic: "Quite frankly they are disgusting". As if that weren't terrible enough, this pundit concluded with the observation that "the movie makes no contribution to the understanding of the human condition." In fact, DRILLER KILLER does provide a valid insight into the human condition, but one that is too subtle for its detractors to grasp. Those seeking illumination should check out Elliot Leyton's scholarly treatise "Hunting Humans" (Viking/Penguin). The impression of Ferrara as a director of some subversive intelligence was confirmed in his follow-up, the distaff DEATH WISH, ANGEL OF VENGEANCE / Ms. 45 (1980), in which he persuaded liberal critics, who had panned DRILLER KILLER as a "Video Nasty", to cheer on and make some kind of feminist icon out of Zoe Tamerlis, whose character is a mute, near catatonic moron, her victims often guilty of no crime more heinous than that of being male. Ferrara's subsequent career has netted him a fair bit of the folding stuff, but the artistic results have been mixed, to say the least.

Current Status: Banned

THE DRILLER KILLER

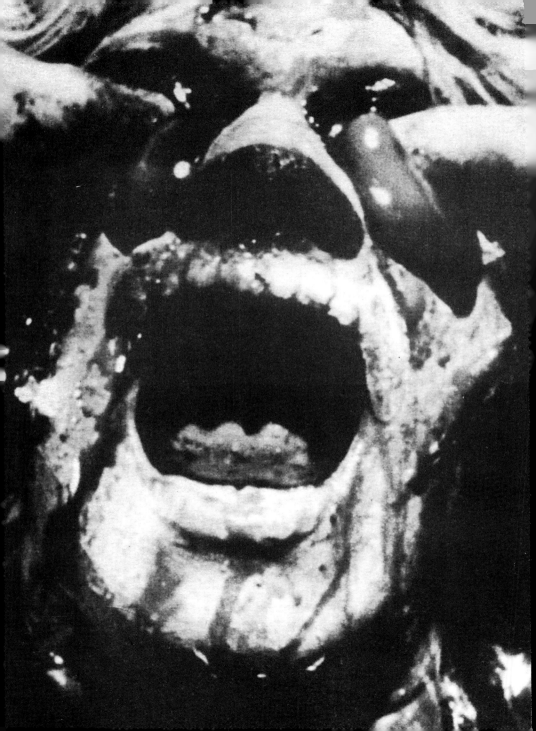

THE SEDUCTION OF THE GULLIBLE

THE EVIL DEAD aka BOOK OF THE DEAD. U.S.A., 1982. Video label: Palace Video. Starring Bruce Campbell, Ellen Sandweiss, Betsy Baker, Hal Delrich, Sarah York. Special effects: Tom Sullivan and Bart Pierce.Camera: Tim Philo. Produced by Robert G. Tapert. Written and directed by Sam Raimi.

SamRaimi's low-budget horror milestone marked time in America until its dynamite impact at the 1982 Cannes Film Festival, where it reportedly had Stephen King cowering behind his seat,, emerging to gibber that he had just seen "the most ferociously original horror film of the year". Raimi's real break came when Steve Woolley of fledgling British distribution company Palace Pictures, shopping at the American Film Market for Art-house fare to launch the company in prestigious style, wandered into the wrong screening room, was rivetted by the Raimi-patented "Shakey-cam" shot that opens THE EVIL DEAD, and stayed for the whole movie. On his say-so, Palace chairman Nik Powell picked the film up for UK distribution, and Palace's dynamic, over-the-top campaign ensured smash-hit status that would serve as a springboard for worldwide success, but ultimately backfired in spectacular style.

Despite its undeniably excessive gore quotient, THE EVIL DEAD received its '18' certificate in January 1983, sustaining only 37 seconds worth of trims at the hands of the BBFC ("Remove sight of Shelley chewing off her own hand" and "Reduce eye gouging and sight of resultant slime" were among their comments). The censors felt that this trimming would be quite sufficient, given the fantastical, non-imitative and unmistakably spoofy nature of the proceedings: King had been way off the mark to talk of "ferocious originality" - the film is a masterly melding and knowing piss-take of horror conventions, its H.P. (Lovecraft) sauce seasoned with a liberal sprinkling of Three Stooges-style buffoonery. Hip critics latched onto these parodic elements, and as Raimi pointed out: "You should try telling an actor to drink a cup of green bile then regurgitate it through her nose and mouth ... she can have a hard time taking it seriously! The movie is so far removed from what people experience in their daily lives that it's like a joke. And you can only be as offended by it as you could be by a bad joke." Palace's press notes dwelled on the film's "comic strip gusto" and its intention "to shock, jolt and amuse the experienced horror movie goer".

Those more concerned with prophecying the end of Western Civilisation than with going to experience horror movies didn't see the irony of Raimi's literally side-splitting comedy, taking at face value the film's hyperbolic claim to be "the ultimate in gruelling terror". As early as the first month of its release (February 1983), video copieswere seized by James Anderton's Manchester police. In the event all copies were returned, with apologies, to the shops from which they had been seized (the cops apparently BELIEVED that the video release was substantially "stronger" than the theatrical version). Dealers, fans and Palace personnel who thought that this was going to be the end of THE EVIL DEAD's problems were going to be shocked and jolted, if not exactly amused...

Mary Whitehouse and co now took it upon themselves to elevate THE EVIL DEAD to the position of "Number One Nasty" and proceeded with missionary zeal to agitate for the suppression of "that evil film". All they could offer to support this ludicrous billing was the apocryphal story of a child who had suffered a few nightmares after exposure to the film, but this was good enough though for the tabloid scum press, who stoked up anti-EVIL DEAD hysteria, resulting in an escalating series of seizures from high street video libraries. Proprietors invariably took legal advice to plead guilty to possession of an "obscene" item in the local Magistrates Courts, pay their fines and avoid the hefty legal costs involved in fighting a case. In this way Whitehouse and co. were able to maintain the fiction that THE EVIL DEAD was "obscene".

On 31st January 1984 Nik Powell wrote to the Association of Chief Police Officers to express concern and point out certain inconsistencies, e.g. that THE EVIL DEAD was BBFC approved, had played on more than 190 cinema screens to around two million people and had become the biggest rental hit of 1983 since its simultaneous theatrical

EVIL DEAD

CAN THEY BE STOPPED?

and video release on February 18th. His words fell on stony ground as the busts continued unabated. Palace solicitor Keith Cousins bemoaned the fate of dealers, many of them embarking for the first time, in the spirit of Thatcherite entrepreneurship, upon a business venture, who had no reason to suspect that what they were stocking – obtained from eminently respectable distribution companies – would come to be regarded as "obscene". Derek Mann of the Video Traders' Association argued for such dealers to be acquitted on a "statutory defence", and also for the rather more logical step of thedistributors being brought to court instead (a foreshadowing of what was actually to transpire in the EVIL DEAD case).

In an attempt to clarify the position in a test case, Palace subsidised the defence costs of the Leeds-based Barker Video Group, three branches of which had been raided in April 1983, with police seizing the inevitable EVIL DEAD among several other titles, four of which also had BBFC certificates and had already played theatrically in the Leeds area. The cloak-and-dagger police operation that had resulted in this bust adds several further bizarre twists to the story: a constable had joined the club, giving a bogus address, to gather evidence, although Barker already had 75 members of the West Yorkshire Police on their membership rolls, one of their shops was managed by the wife of a Detective Sergeant, and they had invited police to vet their stock when they opened! Palace backed Barker to the hilt, even flying Raimi over to testify at the trial, which took place in May 1984. THE EVIL DEAD was unanimously acquitted. "We put out more than 17,000 copies, which is a huge number in video terms," commented a happy Nik Powell. "We're glad that at last a jury has vindicated this very popular work." Emboldened by the outcome of the Leeds case, dealers began to contest the "obscenity" of THE EVIL DEAD in the Crown Courts. On 1st December 1984, at the end of a four day trial at Lewes Crown Court, Tony Bingharn, the proprietor of Peacehaven's 'That's Entertainment', was found guilty and fined £50 each for stocking BLOODY MOON, NIGHT OF THE DEMON and PRETTY PEACHES, but acquitted over THE EVIL DEAD (the jury failing to reach a clear-cut verdict on Lucio Fulci s ZOMBIE FLESH EATERS). "Out of all the films," the judge had commented in his summing up, "[THE EVIL DEAD] dealt with the realm of fantasy much more than any of the others, and perhaps the jury should think of it in a different light." Grimsby Crown Court (December 1984) became the third in a row to clear Raimi's movie, along with eight other titles, viewed over four days by a jury who were unanimous in their acquittal.

Just in case any of the film's supporters got too euphoric at this point, Peter Kruger, head of Scotland Yard's Obscene Publications squad, warned that "no matter how many dealer acquittals arise, I don't think it will be coming off the 'nasties' list before February." True to form, it took a lot longer than that – in September 1984 Nik Powell himself had been charged at Waltham Forest Magistrates Court, along with his companies, Palace Video and Palace Virgin Gold Distribution, of having obscene articles with intent to publish for gain, contrary to Section 2 of the 1959 Obscene Publications Act, the charges relating to 444 copies of THE EVIL DEAD seized from premises in East Leyton. The case was committed for trial at Snaresbrook Crown Court in July 1985 and on July 25th Powell and his companies were finally acquitted. Judge Owen Stableford took the unprecedented step of awarding the defendant's costs (in excess of £20,000) against the Director of Public Prosecutions, whom he castigated for "bringing the administration of justice into disrepute" by proceeding against THE EVIL DEAD despite the facts laid out in Powell's letter of the 31st of January 1984 and when obscenity convictions had resulted from only two cases out of the forty in which a full Crown Court defence had been mounted on its behalf.

Judge Stableford (the kind of guy who could restore your faith in British justice) was especially critical of the DPP's timing – "To launch these proceedings after the Video Recordings Bill received the Royal assent," (ie. 12th July 1984), "was, in my submission, quite wrong" – and the fact that, in the wake of the Leeds acquittal, Palace's solicitors had written to the DPP asking for all outstanding cases to be dropped ("the writer was concerned by the chaotic state of affairs from the point of view of his companies and those retailers to whom they supplied videos"), only to receive a

AT LAST.... IT'S BACK!!

SAM RAIMI'S

THE EVIL DEAD

"THE MOST FEROCIOUSLY ORIGINAL HORROR FILM"
STEPHEN KING

THE EVIL DEAD

PVC 2018A
COLOUR
APPROX 90 MINS

18

18

negative response, which the judge characterised as "inflexible and bureaucratic". "Unfortunately the DPP has not extended his right of superintendance over Chief Constables throughout the country" said Keith Cousins, who had also defended VTC in the POSSESSION case. Nik Powell expressed himself "extremely pleased for all concerned, especially my own family, to have won the case and I trust that the DPP will now do the honourable thing and drop any further prosecutions, allowing THE EVIL DEAD to be certified in line with the terms of the Video Recordings Act." In response to the outcome of the case, Chief Inspector Iain Donaldson, new head of the Yard's Obscene Publications Squad, announced that THE EVIL DEAD would at last be coming off the banned list in September (prompting the wishful-thinking headline "DPP Drops Dead" in one of the video trade magazines), the same month as the VRA came into effect, and added that he "would certainly be surprised if other cases involving the title went ahead."It must have come as a great surprise to him then when just a month later one Arvind Icahli of Firuji Hi-Fi & Video Shop in Kentish Town Road, London, was prosecuted for five films — FOREST OF FEAR, NIGHTMARE MAKER, UNHINGED, ZOMBIE CREEPING FLESH and ... THE EVIL DEAD! No directive had yet been given to remove the film from the list, a spokesman for the DPP's office revealed.

That was by no means the final twist in this sorry tale. Despite Powell's avowed optimism that THE EVIL DEAD would receive a certificate swiftly, things were not to be resolved so smoothly. The BBFC, whose very existence had been called into question over this matter, were understandably eager to cover themselves and procrastinated until May 1987, when a proposed re-release, theavily advertised in the trade press, was scrapped at the last minute due to Palace's inability to agree to the draconian cuts demanded. Bearing in mind the soft censorial rides that were subsequently given to the likes of SOCIETY and BAD TASTE, it's difficult to avoid the conclusion that THE EVIL DEAD had become a kind of boogey-film, the spectre of which could only be dissipated by complete dismemberment, much in the manner of its own Kandarian demons. Finally, in May 1990, the BBFC got their pound of flesh and a new version appeared in the shops, with a total of 65 seconds-worth of new cuts, including irritating ones during the (hardly imitable) melt-down climax, in addition to the inevitable emasculation of the famed tree-rape sequence.

In an interview conducted by Mark Kermode,Raimi complained: "What I don't like is the superiority and the smug attitude that they can see such things and they won't be affected by them... yet they're making a decision that others are too emotionally unstable to handle it." With characteristic modesty, he continued: "The real problem is not a movie like THE EVIL DEAD, because it's not really important whether that is seen. The real problem is, once the people allow the censors to determine what is right and wrong for them, once they've given them that power, who's to say that a politically disturbing picture, that differs from the view of the censors politically, shouldn't be censored? The people of Britain shouldn't allow them that power because soon they'll find out that other rights are being taken away from them one by one, till they don't have the right to speak at all."Indeed, it's not too fanciful to ascribe some right-wing method to the madness of pursuing Raimi's film so doggedly ... Nik Powell: "They may well have decided that win or lose, they would cause Palace such financial hardship that we would never handle a film like this again, or even put us out of business. It is extremely unusual, even under the Obscene Publications Act, to pursue a film after more than a couple of acquittals" (In April 1986 Powell admitted that: "If I had known in advance what I would have to go through for the film, I would have taken the easy way out"). Guy Collins,MD of VTC, had hit the nail squarely on the head after the POSSESSION acquittal: "I don't think it will change anything in that there'll still be charges against BBFC-certified material. It seems that there's some deliberate intention on the part of the DPP to bust a BBFC title, and once they've got that under their belt, they can go on to other things". An appealing game-plan, no doubt, to born-again reactionaries as they go into battle against the "communist-riddled" BBC, the "liberal establishment" and the whole legacy of those swinging, sinful '60s... anyone for a retrial of LADY CHATTERLEY'S LOVER?

Current Status: Re-released by Palace and PolyGram Video with cuts.

L'ORDINATEUR AU SERVICE DE SATAN

Messe
noire

Une Production LEISURE INVESTMENT
COMPANY CORONET FILM CORP
"MESSE NOIRE" (Evilspeak)
avec CLINT HOWARD R.G. ARMSTRONG
JOSEPH CORTESE
CLAUDE EARL JONES
HAYWOOD NELSON DON STARK
CHARLES TYNER Directeur de
la photographie IRV GOODNOFF
Producteurs associés
GERALD HOPMAN
et H. HAL HARRIS
Producteur exécutif
SYLVIO TABET
Scénario de
JOSEPH GAROFALO
et ERIC WESTON
d'après une histoire de
JOSEPH GAROFALO

Produit par SYLVIO TABET et ERIC WESTON   Réalisé par ERIC WESTON

THE SEDUCTION OF THE GULLIBLE

EVILSPEAK. U.S.A., 1982. Video label: VideoSpace. Starring Clint Howard, R.G. Armstrong, Joseph Cortez, Claude Earl Jones, Haywood Nelson, Don Stark, Charles Tyner, Lynn Hancock. Camera: Irv Goodnott. Written by Eric Weston and Joseph Garofalo. Produced by Eric Weston and Sylvio Tabet. Directed by Eric Weston.

The early '80s saw a cycle of grunt-bashing epics: AN OFFICER AND A GENTLEMAN, TAPS, THE LORDS OF DISCIPLINE... the wiggiest of the lot was Eric Weston's EVILSPEAK (dig that punning title), whose class punch-bag doesn't get mad but gets even, using contemporary technology to harness the powers of Black Magic. One would have thought that this marriage of high tech, individual initiative an military virtues would have appealed to Thatcherites everywhere, but one would have been wrong...

The film opens with wailing choirs and Kahlil Ghibran quotations, as a chapter of heretical monks are drummed out of their monastery and exiledto a desert. Their leader Esteban swears the vow of vengeance on generations yet to come that it's customary to swear on such occasions. Cut to the present day, where we meet Stanley Cooper-Smith (Clint Howard, Ron's brother. Stanley is a welfare student at the John Paul Jones Military Academy, despised by officers andclassmates alike as a charity case and referred to by one and all as Cooper-Dick (yuk, yuk, yuk). Even the platoon fat boy is higher in the pecking order than Stanley. The chaplain pursues a vendetta against him, and the coach tells his own team to beat him up during a football match (they throw him in a pile of shit). But the real bane of his life is a drunken sergeant who apparently sleeps in a crypt... I've heard of The Peace Dividend, but this is ridiculous! Cooper-Smith has only two friends on the whole post – the cook who gives him a runty puppy so he'll have someone to identify with, and the camp pig-keeper (!) who warns him about the hideous threat posed by man-eating pigs. "That could have been you" he gibbers, as his charges tuck into a defenceless turnip. In trouble again, Cooper-Smith is handed the chore of mucking out the Sarge's crypt,. Naturally, he unearths a Lovecraftian tome. No-one bats an eyelid at Stanley schlepping around camp carrying a book with a huge pentagram on its cover, and soon he's boning up on theology, Esteban-style. "Satan's magic is the strongest", Esteban insists, and it would seem he has a point, because man-eating pigs are soon stampeding into bathrooms and eating naked girls. What's more, the sergeant falls down the steps of his crypt and breaks his neck. All this provokes an outbreak of corny dialogue along the lines of "What the hell is going on around here?" When the bullies kill Stanley's dog, he decides enough is enough, though he isn't above using the mutt's blood in a Black Mass. He summons up a demon with his computer as the unsuspecting jocks are in the chapel getting a pep talk from the padre prior to a big game. As he tells them that they're "being watched by the Great Referee in the Sky" and that "there'll be Hell to pay" if they lose, the figure of Christ on the cross trembles at such blasphemies. The nail flies off its wrist and into the chaplain's skull, to the consternation of the jocks, who soon have to contend with those carnivorous pigs and Stanley, floating above them with a sword to dole out disem-bowelments, decapitations and open-heart surgery. The whole place burns down as the film ends, but there's a suggestion that Stan the boogey-man will be back. As yet there's been no sign of him and it's unlikely that horror fans will lose any sleep on account of his absence – EVILSPEAK takes an eternity working up to its splatter pay off, and you're even cheated of that In the emasculated "Horror Classics" reissue.

Current Status: Uncut version banned. Re-released by Horror Classics with cuts

Nothing, but nothing, is left to the imagination...

STARRING
LINDA HAYDEN   UDO KIER

AND INTRODUCING
Miss FIONA RICHMOND

Exposé

ANNIE LIBERT   and   SEX RALLY   x

NOTHING IS LEFT TO THE IMAGINATION!
IN HER FIRST SCREEN ROLE

FIONA RICHMOND
BRITAIN's No.1 SEX SYMBOL

Exposé

FIONA RICHMOND ● LINDA HAYDEN ● UDO KIER
Written and Directed by JAMES KENELM CLARKE
Produced by BRIAN SMEDLEY-ASTON

THE SEDUCTION OF THE GULLIBLE

EXPOSE aka THE HOUSE ON STRAW HILL / TRAUMA U.K., 1975. Video label: Intervision. Starring Udo Kier, Linda Hayden, Fiona Richmond, Patsy Smart, Vic Armstrong, Karl Howman, Sydney Knight. Camera: Denis Lewiston. Produced by Brian Smedley-Aston. Written and directed by James Kenelm Clarke.

The only British "nasty", EXPOSE features exploitation Hall-of-Famer Udo Kier as a novelist getting his head together in the country, penning the follow-up to his block-busting debut. Work isn't proceeding too smoothly, because that blockbusting debut was actually written by somebody else, who killed himself when Udo stole his magnum opus. Kier is also distracted by his sex-crazed wife, typecast Fiona Richmond (their coupling intercut with that hoariest of cliché shots, a door banging in the wind), and flashback sequences involving somebody (presumably the plagiarised author) slashing his wrists. Kier packs Richmond off to London and installs a secretary who proves hardly less distracting, played as she is by Linda Hayden (jail-bait adornment to a string of low-budget early '70s British horrors), who spends half of her screen-time abusing herself with great gusto (her orgasms, conveyed by frantic mugging, are the most memorably amusing aspect of EXPOSE). She even takes time out from dictation to go upstairs and take herself in hand (who can blame her … Udo's prose, excruciating soft-core pap, would send anyone in search of something better to do, and the suggestion that the finished novel will be nominated for a Pulitzer Prize is patently preposterous). Having satisfied herself, Hayden calmly returns to work.

Hayden goes into a cornfield for yet another wank, and while she's gone, Udo – who's convinced that he knows her from somewhere – roots through her effects. Predictably, he discovers a massive dildo. Meanwhile two louts in ridiculous loon pants have discovered Hayden playing with herself and are busy raping her. Hayden feigns acquiescence, only to lull her attackers into a false sense of security, then she grabs her shot-gun and blows them away (clearly writer/director Kenelm Clarke has THE STRAW DOGS very much in mind, a parallel underscored by the casting of Hayden, a poor-man's Susan George, and the aka HOUSE ON STRAW HILL). She resumes her duties as if nothing has happened. Udo gets drunk and starts ranting about the demands made on him by editors and publishers. After further weird flash-back sequences he makes a heavy pass at Hayden, but she seems content to let her fingers do the walking. Udo summons Richmond back, but she ends up in bed with Hayden. Taking a bath, Richmond discovers the body of Udo's housekeeper (Patsy Smart) in the airing cupboard and is then herself stabbed by a mystery assailant … except that there's no mystery about the identity of the killer. It is of course Hayden, who now trains her rifle on Udo and reveals that her husband was the guy whose work was ripped off (another non-surprise). She pursues him into the field and is just about to blow his brains out when one of the rapists she shot previously leaps out of the corn to stab her to death.

Udo Kier has appeared in some wild and sleazy movies (FLESH FOR FRANKENSTEIN, MARK OF THE DEVIL, SUSPIRIA), all of which pale into insignificance when compared with the details of his wild and sleazy life. More recently he has cropped up in Madonna's SEX tome and "Deeper and Deeper" video, ACE VENTURA, etc. Richmond is a sex industry veteran, modelling for and putting her name to ghost-written columns in Paul Raymond girlie mags and appearing in soft-core flicks like LET'S GET LAID. At one point she discovered God and announced that she'd mended her wicked ways, but her "straight" acting career never took off, and economic necessity has prompted frequent returns to the sleaze business. Director Kenelm Clarke made a BBC documentary about sexploitation movies. Karl Howman, the rapist who intervenes at the end of the film, seemed doomed bit parts in the likes of this, but struck lucky with the successful sit-com "Brush Strokes", and is probably now better-known, in Britain anyway, than any-one else who participated in EXPOSE. How Howman must wish that the film would simply disappear. Anyone who's ever sat through the wretched thing will surely feel the same way, though reportedly Kenelm Clarke is planning (get this!) a remake.

Current Status: Re-issued on Siren label, late 1997, with 51 secs & 9 frames cut, notably from the rape scene.

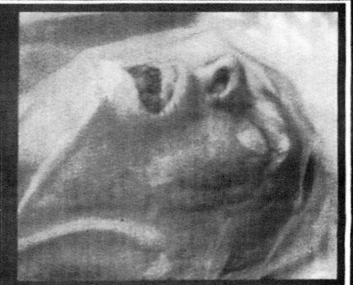

FACES
OF
DEATH

Explore man's greatest fear —
the fear of dying... the pain, the
joy, the sorrow. Terrifying, yet
fascinating, FACES OF DEATH is
an experience you'll never
forget...

COMPLETELY UNCENSORED

THE SEDUCTION OF THE GULLIBLE

> **FACES OF DEATH. U.S.A., 1981. Video label: Atlantis Video. Written by Alan Black. Produced by Rosilyn T. Scott. Directed by Conan Le Cilaire. Creative consultant and narrator: Dr Francis B. Gross.**

F.O.D.'s opening shot gets right to the heart of the matter, a heart pulsating away in its thoracic cavity, before a freeze-frame indicates coronary arrest. Cut to cheerful shots of cadavers in a morgue ... skin is being peeled off a skull, livers and lights are unpacked as bone-saws whirr away at various pieces of anatomy. Dr Francis B. Gross, earnest and bearded, bins his bloody gloves, washes his hands and commences his narrative: "Medical science cannot always have success" he solemnly intones: " ... and when death occurs, my expertise is called for." After urging the viewer to prepare himself for "a journey into a world where each new step might give you a better understanding of your own reality", he rails against those who refuse to recognise their "ultimate destiny". Haunted by recurring nightmares about funerals, Dr Gross (actually one Michael Carr) has travelled the world "compiling a library of the Faces of Death". The mondo footage kicks in here with Mexican mummies, Mexican bullfighting and even a spot of Mexican hat-dancing. Cut to the Amazon "where death becomes a mandate for survival". Insects eat each other (accompanied by tango music), piranhas strip anacondas to the bone, natives blow monkeys out of the trees with their blow-pipes and roast them on a spit ... "They eat all they kill" points out the doc, setting up a pointed contrast with some obnoxious yuppies we will later see pounding an unfortunate monkey's head in with hammers during "a most unusual dining adventure".

Representing Africa's "Faces of Death", Masai tribesmen are seen sucking blood out of their cattle. Leaving the Dark Continent, we take in the Western way of dealing with our farmyard friends — to the tune of "Old Macdonald" we learn that yes, it is indeed true that a chicken with its head cut off runs around and jumps up and down, flapping its wings. Ensuing scenes from a slaughterhouse cause Dr Gross some consternation, but he's the first to admit the hypocrisy of his reaction, and it should be borne in mind that most of those who were concerned to ban this thing are probably quite happy for animals to suffer so they can stuff their faces - they just don't want to see it happen!

Next we're off to a polar ice cap to witness thugs beating on seal pups with baseball bats. "I decided never to wear the skin of an animal on my back again" agonises the Doc. Good for him. During the subsequent piece on alligator poachers in the everglades, a palpably phoney "live news report" about a "nuisance alligator" shows the saurian in question surfacing to snack on some alligator hunters. "Oh my God ..." mouths a bored-looking bystander, " ... I can't believe it". Neither can we, but Dr Gross seems rather tickled by this ironic conclusion. A lot of the footage from here on in is of distinctly dubious authenticity, including "a political assassination" and further phony "news footage" of cases in which people have supposedly run amok and slaughtered their families. Our genial host muses that "perhaps there is a maniac killer in all of us, waiting to ignite". Who knows, but there's certainly a lousy poet igniting inside the doc...

> "In a world with no sound, their cries go unheard,
> The reality of life becomes totally absurd,
> The counting of time is considered a crime,
> And the money one earned, not worth a lone dime.

> "So here they will lie, for the rest of the night,
> Their bodies remain still, in darkness and light,
> But don't be afraid, for it will happen to you,
> When all will stop and your body turns blue."

FACES OF DEATH

Prepare yourself for the ultimate experience.
This video cassette will change your attitude
to life.

Executive Producer: William B. James
Producer: Rosilyn T. Scott
Director: Conan Le Cilaire

TRUE LIFE HORROR
Colour - AVP 601

THE SEDUCTION OF THE GULLIBLE

After an interview with Thomas Nyoguchi, the celebrity L.A. coroner on whom QUINCY is based ("Life on this planet is a transitory trip ..." he offers: " ... the spirit goes on after death"), Dr Frank begins to wonder if he's going to suffer a violent death. Keep up all that cod philosophy and terrible poetry and there's a fair chance, Doc!

Now he turns his gimlet eye onto capital punishment. "A graduate of the penal system is taking his final exam" states the Doc, caustically, as "Larry de Silva" is prepped for Ol' Sparky. The electrocution is an elaborately-staged pantomime (punctuated by such terse lines as "the room began to smell like burning flesh"). The doctor doesn't seem too impressed with capital punishment, concluding that if this is the best answer we can come up with, then we need to rethink our entire judicial system. Meanwhile, back in "the Middle East", candid camera captures a judicial decapitation. Sitars and "Om" chants on the soundtrack herald Frank's fearless exposé of a San Francisco death cult. "They believed the power of everlasting life was found within the organs of the dead", he informs us: " ... after their leader explained his reasons, I knew I was dealing with a maniac." "We are free, we are there, we are beautiful!" enthuses the maniac as his acolytes slice open corpses, tuck into their innards and get down to some frenzied sex (all faked). More interesting, but only fleetingly screened, are the real-life antics of Bible-bashing Kentucky red-necks who demonstrate their faith by speaking in tongues, drinking poison and dervish-dancing with snakes. Sly old Dr Gross can't resist telling us that one of the dancers died from a snake bite soon afterwards.

What else? Full moon suicides, dead guys in cryonic suspension, bloated floaters ("this young man was at the prime of his life ... maybe he took too much for granted"), "a savage bear attack" (the critter in question clearly wrestling playfully with its trainer), shots of litter accompanied by some wretched folky droning: "Jesus doesn't live here anymore" (your guess is as good as mine), anti-nuke protesters, concentration camps ("I personally don't know if this face of death could ever be repeated" ... tell 'em that in Cambodia and Bosnia, Doc!), disease, over-population, natural disasters, transport accidents, a parachute failing to open ("I wonder what thoughts went through the parachutist's mind"), a jet crashing ("The survivors are still, to this day, under psychiatric care.") Finally Gross tackles life after death, though he pronounces himself skeptable (sic) on this score. The testimony of "Joseph Binder, architect", a cock and bull story illustrated with preposterous "haunted house" special effects, convinces the good Doc, who's obviously not as "skeptable" as he thinks he is, that "death is not the end". F.O.D. concludes with an equally phoney birth (only the "mother"'s head and shoulders visible). "The end of the beginning ... or the beginning of the end?" asks Dr Frank: "I'll leave the decision to you."

While I can't really say that flipping through his "library of the Faces of Death" gave me "a greater understanding of my own reality", as promised, I did conceive a certain affection for the genial Dr Francis B. Gross ... what a rascal! He returned with director Conan Le Cilaire and the rest of the gang in FACES OF DEATH PARTS 2 and 3 (which concentrated almost exclusively on staged atrocities and recycled the original's "greatest hits" to ever-decreasing effect each time out), and PART 4 opens with his own cremation! File him in his own library ... under "Gross"!

Atlantis amputated 35 minutes, including the ersatz electrocution, the S.F. cannibal cult and various self-immolating religious fanatics from the first F.O.D. for its ill-fated British video release. Their mini-masterpiece of morbidity fared altogether better in the Japanese market – for which it had been specifically conceived – actually out-grossing STAR WARS for thirteen straight weeks, theatrically.

Current status: Banned

FACES OF DEATH

89 minutes of sheer terror

FIGHT FOR YOUR LIFE

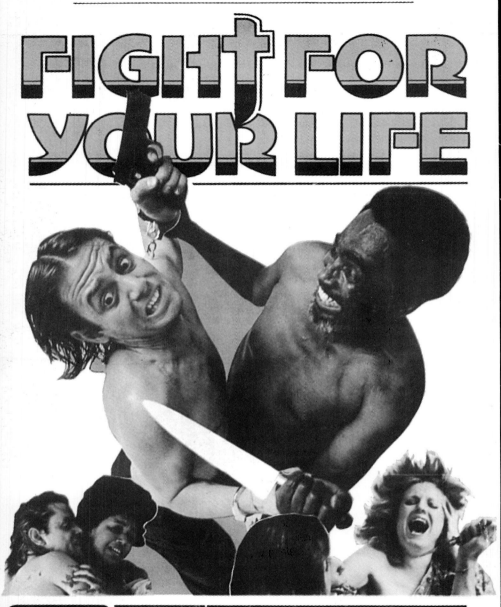

vision on video film company

THE SEDUCTION OF THE GULLIBLE

FIGHT FOR YOUR LIFE aka BLOODBATH AT 1313 FURY DRIVE / GETTING EVEN / HELD HOSTAGE / I HATE YOUR GUTS / STAYING ALIVE. Canada, 1977. Video label: Vision On Video.Starring Robert Judd, William J. Sanderson, Reginald Blythewood, Lela Small, Daniel Faraldo, Catherine Peppers, Yvonne Ross, Peter Yoshida. Camera: Lloyd Freidus. Written by Straw Weisman. Produced by William Mishkin and Robert A. Endelson. Director: Robert A. Endelson.

Robert A. Endelson's FIGHT FOR YOUR LIFE puts a race relations slant on the all-too-familiar "decent folk fight back" storyline pioneered by Wes Craven's LAST HOUSE ON THE LEFT, but torpedos its own anti-intolerance message with woeful ineptitude in the acting, scripting and directing departments.

Three convicts, a Chicano, a Chinaman and their redneck leader Jesse Lee Cain (William J Sanderson, best remembered as J.F. Sebastian in BLADE RUNNER) break out of jail and billet themselves on a God-fearing black family till the heat dies down. Jesse Lee spends most of the rest of the film humiliating and beating up on his reluctant hosts. The outside world only becomes aware of their ordeal when a little boy who calls at the house is killed by the convicts, cue the arrival of "Rule Book" Riley, a hilariously stereo-typical cop whose nickname derives from his rigid adherence to the letter of the law (the acting of the thesp who portrays him is also pretty stiff).

In what is obviously supposed to be a boffo twist, Riley holds his men back from storming the house when he learns that the black family have gained the drop on their oppressors. He's so disgusted by what's happened that he figures he'll leave the way clear for some Old Testament retribution. A nice idea, completely wrecked by more terrible acting from the cop and the fact that the black victims, given their chance to sock it to the bad guys, talk endlessly about how they're going to do it but actually do bugger-all! It's standard practice in these revenge dramas for the revenge to be anti-climactic (not, as critics allege, because the film-makers are more interested in the massacre of innocents than they are in "justice", but because taking their lead from Wes Craven and ultimately Ingmar Bergman's THE VIRGIN SPRING, they want to show that two wrongs don't make a right, that violence liberates nobody and corrupts everybody) but this is absolutely FEEBLE! So feeble that the racists gain the upper hand again, obliging the cops to storm the place and shoot 'em up. Before he dies, Jesse Lee considerately blurts out the motivation for his dirty deeds – his mom ran away with a black guy. Thank you Robert A. Endelson for conclusively proving that there would be no racism in the world if only black people would refrain from running off with white people's mothers – give that man a Nobel Peace prize! The saddest thing about Endelson's film is that the black characters are so one-dimensional and bathetic, one is tempted to laugh along with Cain's crude jokes at their expense.

Considered a "nasty" on video, F.F.Y.L. rated only an 'AA' certificate for its British theatrical release, which meant that the BBFC were then quite happy to let kids as young as 15 see it.

Current Status: Banned

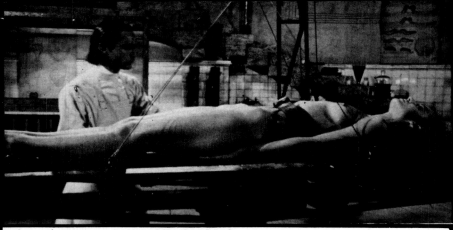

WE DARE YOU TO SEE... **ANDY WARHOL'S** 3 DIMENSION HORROR MOVIE!

ANDY WARHOLS
FLESH FOR FRANKENSTEIN x
starring JOE DALLESANDRO · UDO KIER · MONIQUE VAN VOOREN
introducing ARNO JUERGING · DALILA DI LAZZAR · SRDJAN ZELENOVIC

NAT COHEN presents an EMI Film Distributors Ltd

Music by CLAUDIO GIZZI

Written and Directed by PAUL MORRISSEY Produced by ANDREW BRAUNSBERG
EASTMANCOLOR Distributed by EMI Film Distributors Ltd

x 3 D
SPACEVISION
EFFECTS BY
THE HIRE OF SPECIAL 3D VIEWERS ARE
INCLUDED IN THE ADMISSION PRICE

EMI

THE SEDUCTION OF THE GULLIBLE

FLESH FOR FRANKENSTEIN aka ANDY WARHOL'S FRANKENSTEIN / IL MOSTRO E IN TAVOLA... BARONE FRANKENSTEIN / YOUNG FRANKENSTEIN. Italy/France, 1973. Video label: VIPCO & Video Gems. Starring Udo Kier, Monique Van Vooren, Joe Dallesandro, Carlo Mancini, Arno Juerging, Srdjan Zelenovic, Dalila di Lazzaro, Cristina Gaioni, Marco Liofredi, Nicoletta Elmi. Special effects by Carlo Rambaldi and Roberto Arcangeli. Camera: Luigi Kuveiller. Produced by Andrew Braunsberg. Written by Paul Morrissey. Directed by Paul Morrissey / Antonio Margheriti.

When one of Andy Warhol's freak acolytes shot and incapacitated him, he handed over his film set-up to Paul Morrissey, who expanded his concept of "The Cinema of Endurance" by alternating the usual boredom with grisly splatter FX in FLESH FOR FRANKENSTEIN (a title designed to cash in on the first film Morrissey directed for Warhol, 1960's FLESH) and BLOOD FOR DRACULA aka ANDY WARHOL'S DRACULA, shot back-to-back in Rome and financed by Carlo Ponti. As if to poke fun at those who detect proto-fascist elements in Mary Shelley's story, Morrissey relocates the action from its traditional German setting to Serbia. Baron Frankenstein, in the maniacal shape of Udo Kier, is building a perfect male from human remains, in the hope that it will mate with the ideal female which he has prepared, to produce an ethnically-clean Serbian master-race (prophetic or what?). The Baron grows impatient for the big event while waiting for the perfect male head to turn up and vents his frustration by ripping open the scars of his Venus so he can run his hands (and not only his hands!) around in her guts. With the aid of his goonish and equally disembowelment-fixated assistant Otto (Juerging), the Baron ambushes two shepherds on their way home from the local bordello and makes off with the head of one. The survivor (Joe Dallesandro) is employed at the Castle Frankenstein by the Baron's sexually voracious wife / sister (Monique Van Vooren). Understandably alarmed at seeing his friend's head on the monster's body, Dallesandro starts prying into the Baron's experiments. He is discovered and suspended from a chain above the lab, at which point the monster rebels, kills everyone except Dallesandro, and commits suicide. The film ends with the Baron's children advancing on Dallesandro, scalpels at the ready.

Its tempting to dismiss FFF as the self indulgent, tongue-in-cheek romp that it sets itself up as. Morrissey has expressed an admiration for CARRY ON films, and the teaming of Kier and Juerging is reminiscent of Pete 'n' Dud, only a lot funnier (Morrissey later directed Cook and Moore in an allegedly comic version of THE HOUND OF THE BASKERVILLES). Moreover, anyone who could leave so crude an actor as Dallesandro to improvise his own dialogue must have a keen sense of humour. However, there is much more than meets the eye to both FLESH FOR FRANKENSTEIN and BLOOD FOR DRACULA. Both films cock a snook at the aesthetic elite, the "beautiful people" who were Warhol's patrons. The aristocracy here are so jealous of their self-proclaimed superiority that they resort to incest to maintain it, and the Baron's excesses on the operating table can be read as a parody of the craze for plastic surgery among America's smart set. FLESH FOR FRANKENSTEIN pours scorn on such vanity with constant reminders that physical beauty is a highly perishable commodity. No wonder these films had to be made in Italy. BLOOD FOR DRACULA peddles a simplistic brand of Marxism, making a meal of the obvious parallels that can be drawn between vampirism and capitalism. This only serves to lend credence to claims that at least parts of these films were actually directed by Antonio Margheriti rather than the bellicose right-winger Morrissey. Margheriti took part in the explosion of graphically gory horror films in Italy during the late seventies and early 80's, so he would have been quite at home with the dangling intestines in FLESH FOR FRANKENSTEIN, rendered by Carlo Rambaldi and effectively showcased (as was Enrico Job's impressive laboratory set) by the 3-D process the film was shot in. Unfortunately, on the rare occasions that FLESH FOR FRANKENSTEIN is screened nowadays it is almost invariably shown flat. As a bizarre postscript to all this, Kier's oft-misquoted line: "To know Death, Otto, you have to fuck Life in the gall-bladder" was eventually given an ironic slant by Warhol's death from complications arising after a routine gall-bladder operation.

Current Status: Banned

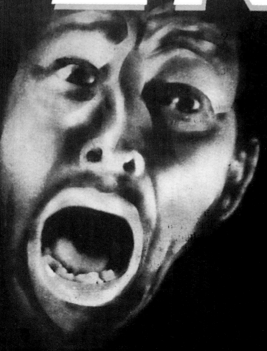

FOREST OF FEAR

THE SEDUCTION OF THE GULLIBLE

FOREST OF FEAR aka THE BLOOD EATERS / TOXIC ZOMBIES. U.S.A., 1979. Video label: Monte Video. Starring: Charles Austin, Beverly Shapiro, Dennis Helfend, Hariet Miller, John Amplas, Paul Haskin. Camera: David Sperling. Written, produced and directed by Chuck McCrann.

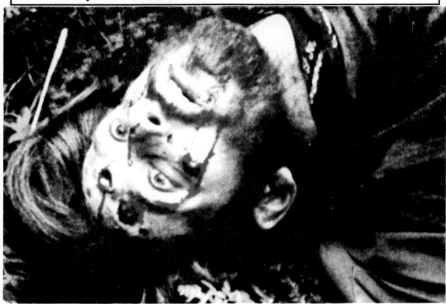

Just say "no-no!" Chuck McCrann's listless 16mm effort is a companion piece to David Durston's altogether more entertaining I DRINK YOUR BLOOD (1971. Drug-busting undercover cops infiltrate a dope plantation and are killed in a skirmish with the freaks who farm it. The government orders the ganja crop to be covertly dusted with Dromax, an ultra-powerful herbicide which is supposed to be banned due to its unpredictable side-effects (but who cares what happens to a bunch of no account drug-crazed long-hairs, right?) The dusted hippies go white, spit blood and fight over water ("You're acting like animals" says one of their non-dusted buddies, but he's wrong ... animals could act a lot better than this!) Meanwhile the drunken pilot who undertook the crop dusting and himself got dusted is killing his harridan wife. The affected hippies start eating raw meat and generally being gross, at which point their erstwhile buddies take a powder, but to no avail – the zombies apparently possess the ability to track them down by smell, like bloodhounds. They also sniff out a family camping in the woods, slaughtering pop. A good samaritan stops for mom but cancels out his good deed by stopping for the zombies too, resulting in both their deaths. Little Amy and her handicapped brother, left to wander the zombie-infested forest, are rescued by two couples on a camping holiday. Tom Cole, one of their rescuers, just happens to be working for the drug enforcement agency). His brother is eaten by toxic zombies but everyone else escapes to seek refuge in a moronic backwoodsman's shack. When zombies turn up with flaming brands he throws his guests out to avoid his shack getting torched. The zombies torch it anyway and eat him. Now the two guys who ordered the crop-dusting turn up "to do some house-cleaning". Various people and zombies are shot and eaten. Tom and the kids are still alive at the picture's rather arbitray end.

Undistinguished, thoroughly forgettable stuff. One of the crooked drug cops is played by John Amplas, who's rather more famous for playing MARTIN in the George Romero film.

Current Status: Banned

Frozen Scream

Directed by Frank Roach
Produced by Renee Harmon

DISTRIBUTED BY

THE FIRST NAME IN VIDEO.
THE LAST WORD IN ENTERTAINMENT.

HORROR-COLOUR
A-AE 0433

THE SEDUCTION OF THE GULLIBLE

FROZEN SCREAM. U.S.A., 1981. Video label: Intervision. Starring: Renee Harmon, Lynne Kocol, Thomas Gowen, Wolf Muser, Bob Rochelle, Lee James, Sunny Bartholemew, Wayne Lieberman. Written by Renee Harmon, Doug Ferrin, Michael Soney and Celeste Hammond. Camera: Roberto Quazada. Produced by Renee Harmon. Directed by Frank Roach.

"Death is just a transitory thing…often temporary, sometimes curable." In an attempt to prove this, Frank Roach has whipped together half-baked science, half-assed mysticism, zero production values, a script penned by an idiot or three, actors seemingly suffering from rigor mortis, and his own faltering grasp of basic cinematic grammar, to produce a clinker of the highest order. Roach begins as he means to go on, with enigmatic shots of a ghostly woman superimposed over a beach, while on the soundtrack a female Bela Lugosi sound-alike intones: "Ever since the creation of life man has dreamed of immortality. The pursuit of eternal life has always been devoured by death itself." For no apparent reason this is followed by a bunch of Cash Flagg clones butchering a couple making out by their pool. These intense young men in duffle coats are next seen harassing a certain Tom Gerrard (Wolf Muser) who apparently drops dead of a cardiac arrest.. Tom's wife Ann (Lynne Kocol) starts having ludicrous sub-Bergmanesque dreams involving herself, her dead husband and a beautiful blonde with flowing hair and big hooters. She confides in Kevin (Thomas Gowen), a cop who resolves to get to the bottom of Tom's mysterious demise, not least because he has his own amorous designs on Ann. She also consults Dr Lil Stanhope (Renee Harmon, whose Transylvanian tones featured in the opening sequence). Lil assigns Ann a nurse named Catherine (Sunny Bartholemew) who just happens to be a dead ringer for that dream blonde. Just in case anybody isn't totally confused, Roach now throws in mystifying flash-backs to a pagan hootenany presided over by Catholic priest, Father O'Brien (Wayne Liebman). Challenged as to the orthodoxy of all this, Fr O'Brien concedes that the participants are perhaps being a bit over-exhuberant, but basically it's all about young people having a good time. Aren't they just—"Oh Lord of Night" they chant, "List' to our runes, call out now beyond the Moon…love and immortality, love and immortality"... party animals, huh?

Ann has another ludicrous dream, in which she has an orgasm, then slashes her arms, all under the gaze of the mystery blonde. Elsewhere Kevin investigates Tom's experiments with rats, which have apparantly produced a pack of soulless rodents! Fr O'Brien is strangled in his confessional (how's that for over-exuberance?), then the Cash-clones turn their attentions to Ann, warning her to lay offs. We proceed to an out-door disco. Various pagan revellers in funky disco threads show out with their funky disco moves as duffle-coated deviants lurk in the shrubbery strangling alsations. Catherine the nurse tries to strangle her dancing partner too, then takes a fit and collapses ("She's freaked out" observes an astute onlooker). As if all this wasn't sufficiently off the wall, Roach intercuts it with shots of a bare-assed dude standing at his window contemplating the Moon. Ann starts poking around in Lil's laboratory and discovers her hubby in the deep freeze along with various other guys, one of whom comes alive and chases her around. Kevin the cop turns up for the worst choreographed fist-fight ever – even worse than the disco dancing! Kevin is run over by a car and then there's a lot more running around. Finally it's revealed that Lili and her equally heavy-accented colleague, Sven (Lee James), have been experimenting with cryonics, subjecting human guinea pigs to ultra-low temperatures, which brought about retardation of the ageing process. The down side was that it also transformed the subjects into murderous, dufflecoat clad zombies. Ah well, back to the drawing board. Ann throws a BRIDE OF FRANKENSTEIN style switch that blows up most of the lab, but she still ends up as a cryonic zombie. The final shot reveals Kevin waking up in his hospital bed, only for Lili to administer an injection directly into his eyeball.

I'm reliably informed that somebody thought it worth their while to make a sequel to this thing, entitled ESCAPE FROM THE INSANE ASYLUM, but I can't honestly say that I'm over-keen to sit through it..

Current Status: Removed from DPP list. No re-release scheduled

FROZEN SCREAM

THE SEDUCTION OF THE GULLIBLE

> *THE FUNHOUSE. U.S.A., 1981. Video label: C.I.C. Video. Starring: Elizabeth Berridge, Cooper Huckabee, Miles Chapin, Largo Woodruff, Shawn Carson, Jack McDermott, Sylvia Miles, Kevin Conway, Wayne Doba, William Finley. Camera: Andrew Laszlo. Written by Larry Block. Produced by Derek Power and Steven Bernhardt. Directed by Tobe Hooper.*

THE FUNHOUSE "enjoyed" a brief tenure on the "nasties" list. It had previously played theatrically on a double bill with MY BLOODY VALENTINE (in those days genre enthusiasts could spend half their life in darkened flea-pits watching an endless succession of teen-slaughter epics, and some of us did), without inspiring any discernible outbreaks of serial killing. The picture begins with a combined HALLOWEEN-style P.O.V. shot and a PSYCHO-inspired shower attack that turns out to be a practical joke played on young heroine Amy (Elizabeth Berridge) by her brattish kid brother. This scene sets the tone for the rest of the picture, in which apparently macabre developments are continually resolved as jokes ... and vice versa. Amy goes out on a double date after promising her parents that she won't visit a touring carnival whose visits to other towns have been marked by the mysterious disappearance of local girls. No prizes for guessing that Amy is dared into breaking her promise by her thrill-seeking friends, a not particularly likeable bunch in the tradition of flawed Hooper characters.

In a sleazy Grand Guignol side show "Marco the Magnificent" (William Finley again) plays a gruesome joke with the aid of an audience "plant" – again, the theme of some-thing amusing that lies behind the apparently macabre without dispelling the impression that something even more macabre lies behind it. Then the kids are lured by a barker's patter to a freak show tent displaying two-headed cattle and a cleft-headed foetus in a jar, among other monstrosities. Amy's brother (Shawn Carson), who has followed her to the fair, is disturbed by the barker's assistant (Wayne Doba), who walks around out-side drumming up trade in a "Frankenstein" rubber mask and boots. So as not to lose face, Amy agrees to stay behind when the carnival is closed and spend the night in the Funhouse. During the deception of phoning her folks with a phoney story about where she's spending the night, she is harangued by a tatty old bag lady who gives her the ominous warning that God is watching her. That night up in the rafters of the funhouse, the friends witness a sexual transaction between the whorish fortune teller and the guy in the Frankenstein mask, barely supressing their giggles as he tries for a refund after ejaculating prematurely. Their amusement turns to horror when he flies into a rage and murders her.

The barker (Kevin Conway) arrives and chides his son for murdering "one of the family" ("I've told you I don't mind what filthy things you do to the locals"). He takes an even dimmer view of things when he discovers that the carnival takings are missing – one of Amy's friends is the culprit. When blamed for this, the killer goes apeshit, punching himself in the head and finally pulling off his mask to reveal the snot-spraying cleft-headed mutant beneath (a dead ringer for Mr Integrity himself, Trevor Barley). When one of the boys accidentally drops his cigarette lighter from the rafters, it alerts those below and guarantees a hot time in the ol' funhouse tonight. The balance of the picture is a chase through the macabre, threatening furnishings of the Funhouse, which burst into life at the most alarming moments – the tangible manifestation of the "illusion into reality and back again" motif. One by one they are picked off – the light-fingered Richie (Miles Chapin) has a noose dropped over his head from above and is hauled aloft. Shortly after this the others spot a shadowy figure getting into a Funhouse car and heading their way. Sinking a handy-dandy axe into his head, they realise, too

Something
is alive in
the Funhouse!

THE FUNHOUSE

THE SEDUCTION OF THE GULLIBLE

late, that the shadowy figure is Richie. Now this doesn't necessarily make sense, but it certainly serves its purpose of making the audience jump, and recalls both the Lazarus-like rejuvenation of Grandpa and the apparently dead girl leaping out of the deep freeze in THE TEXAS CHAINSAW MASSACRE. Michele Soavi was obviously impressed, adapting this scene for John Morghen's demise in STAGEFRIGHT, and Soavi's mentor Dario Argento also quotes liberally from THE FUNHOUSE in PHENOMENA.

Amy's friend is trapped by the monster in a ventilation shaft and finds that the offer of sex is no good in the face of implacable murder. In the most poignant moment in the film, Amy is in a similar shaft when she sees her parents outside, come to collect her stop-out brother. They cannot hear her cries for help from the bowels of the Funhouse and drive off ... so near and yet so far. Finally Amy confronts the mutant in the Funhouse's clanking engine room. The splattery, sparky charnel-house finalé packs all the right punches, recalling briefly the intensity of THE TEXAS CHAINSAW MASSACRE, albeit in a somewhat stagey and contrived manner (emphasised by the strident PSYCHO-like music of John Beal). But it certainly works better than the climax of Russell Mulchay's RAZORBACK, which it clearly inspired. As Amy staggers out of the Funhouse, colliding with carney tramps in the early morning light, it seems as though the whole thing was a bad dream, but the bag woman's whispered, almost subliminal "God's watching you" indicates that she will carry a burden of guilt for the rest of her life.

THE FUNHOUSE was a natural for Hooper, whose penchant for scum-of-the-earth social-reject mutant outlaws was already well established. The carney code of looking after your own recalls the gabba-gabba fraternity of FREAKS (1932). and though Hooper is no Tod Browning, he manages to pose pertinent questions about the treatment of outsiders in society and achieves genuine pathos in the relationship between Cowman and his father. Despite its well documented production problems, THE FUNHOUSE stands head and shoulders above its many slice 'n' dice contemporaries and looks great thanks to the cinematography of Andrew Laszlo.

THE TEXAS CHAINSAW MASSACRE was a glorious debut for Tobe Hooper, but to quote Jim Siedow in the ill-fated sequel, "after the glory came the shame". Hooper's "nasties", DEATH TRAP and THE FUNHOUSE serve to remind us that the decline in the quality of his work was not quite so precipitous as it might sometimes seem in retrospect. Though each is flawed, they look a lot better if instead of comparing them to TEXAS CHAINSAW you line them up against the garbage Hooper subsequently came up with: POLTERGEIST (in which his cinematic identity was drastically diluted), LIFEFORCE (in which it was dissolved entirely), INVADERS FROM MARS (make up your own put-down line for that piece of shit), SPONTANEOUS COMBUSTION (... words fail me!) and so on...

Note: Mark Morris of Redemption Video suggests that Tobe Hooper's film appeared on the official "nasties" list due to confusion with VIctor Janos's LAST HOUSE ON DEAD END STREET, bootleg copies of which were apparently circulating in the UK at one point under the alternative title THE FUN HOUSE.

Current Status: Re-released by C.I.C. Video

THE GESTAPO'S LAST ORGY aka L'ULTIMA ORGIA DEL III REICH. Italy, 1977. Video label: Video Film Promotions. Starring Marc Loud, Daniela Levy, Maristella Greco, Fulvio Riccardi, Antineska Nemour, Caterina Barbero. Camera: Claudio Catozzo. Written by Antonio Lucarella. Produced by Ruggero Gorgoglione. Directed by Cesare Canevari.

This is the most blatant rip-off of THE NIGHT PORTER (1974) to emerge from a dubious Italian cycle of concentration camp movies (it also lifts a gymnasium orgy directly fromTinto Brass' SALON KITTY [1976]). Its higher-than usual production values, arty aspirations and sporadic insights into the nature of sadism and power politics lift it a couple of rungs above, e.g. Sergio Garrone's Nazi brace. A pre-titles caption announces the film's theme: "When the superman wishes to amuse himself he must do so even at the cost of the lives of others" (sounds more like some Nazi apologist's corruption of Nietzschian philosophy than the bona fide Nietzsche quote it's intended to be taken as) while on the soundtrack Myriam Del Mare's plaintive wailings are punctuated by the guttural injunctions of Ingeborg Jordy.

Canevari's film is chaotically structured, with much frenzied flashing back and forth. A camp Commandant is imprisoned for war crimes, then we see him being released and paying a nostalgic visit to the site of his camp with his Jewish mistress/former prisoner Lisa. Inspired by memories of the good old days, they get down to the kind of cute that young couples all over the world go in for – y'know, she sucks on his pistol, he inserts it between her legs … real romantic stuff like that. Now we flash back to Lisa's first day at the camp: an SS woman, seeing that Lisa is beyond fear and despair, tells the Commandant (while sodomising him with the butt of a whip) that they must make Lisa fear death and love life before they kill her. To this end she is dipped in quick-lime (which looks more like calomine lotion), then head-first into a cage full of hungry rats while the Commandant rants: "They'll eat your eyes first, then your nose and lips while you're still alive, then your brain and then you'll die" … any pity and terror that this scene might have evoked is soon dispelled by the fact that the "rats" are actually a cuddly bunch of squeaky gerbils! Naturally the upshot of all this is that Lisa falls in love with the Commandant, they start an affair and she conceives his baby. Everything is ducky until the moment of its birth, when the new daddy, instead of lighting up a big cigar, arranges to have his offspring taken away and incinerated. "It's the best way" he assures Lisa. She's not convinced and we flash forward to the present day just in time to catch her shooting him and then herself. Roll credits, reprise daft music. THE GESTAPO'S LAST ORGY attains at times a disturbing level of realism, but blows it with phoney touches like the camp doctor who lectures his colleagues on how "the true greatness of Germany" owes more to Goethe and Schiller than to Goebbels and Hitler.

Current Status: Banned

FULVIA FILM
PROUDLY ANNOUNCES

THE HOUSE OUTSIDE THE CEMETERY

DIRECTED BY
LUCIO FULCI

THE HOUSE BY THE CEMETERY aka QUELLA VILLA ACCANTO AL CIMITERO. Italy, 1981. Video label: Vampix. Starring Catriona MacColl, Paolo Malco, Giovanni de Nava, Dagmar Lassander, Ania Pieroni, Giovanni Frezza, Sylvia Collatina, Daniella Doria, Carlo de Mejo. Special effects: Giannetto de Rossi and Maurizio Trani. Camera: Sergio Salvati. Written by Dardano Sacchetti, Giorgio Mariuzzo and Lucio Fulci. Directed by Lucio Fulci.

The "out of the frying pan, into the inferno" device used by Lucio Fulci in THE BEYOND (see review elsewhere in this volume) and in MANHATTAN BABY (1982) is present in a modified form in THE HOUSE BY THE CEMETERY, adapted by Fulci and the ubiquitous Dardano Sacchetti from a story by ZOMBIE FLESH EATERS scribe Elsa Briganti. This one features only one zombie – a self made man at that - although Vampix's cover promises "demented marauding zombies".

H.B.T.C. has a throwaway sub-plot concerning a fin-de-siecle parallel universe, but the main thrust is secular rather than occult: Academic Norman Boyle (Paolo Malco) accepts from cameoing Fulci the brief of investigating what happened to a certain Dr Peterson, who took his research on suicide to heart, offing himself and his mistress in the titular house ("The times we have to live in!" mutters Fulci, darkly). Norman's wife Lucy (Catriona MacColl yet again) is told by their son Bob (Giovanni Frezza) that his not-so-imaginary friend May has been warning him of the peril that awaits them in the house, but of course this cuts no ice with his parents. Poor pudgy-faced Bob (played by Giovanni Frezza, who seems to pop up in every Italian horror movie of the early 80's) has been dubbed with a voice that grates on the ear like finger-nails being pulled across a blackboard, a fact that has most viewers rooting for the early demise of this supposedly sympathetic character.

May isn't bullshitting about the house – in the pre-titles sequence a teenage couple who snook in for a quickie have already been snuffed in graphic style, him scalped and stabbed in the heart with scissors, her having a knife rammed through her skull. Eagle-eyed Eagle Film (HOUSE's British cinema distributors) watchers will spot the girl as Daniela Doria, against whom Fulci seems to hold some kind of a grudge – she barfs up her intestines while necking with Michele Soavi in CITY OF THE LIVING DEAD, has her eyes eaten out by rats in THE BLACK CAT, and is mutilated with a razor-blade in THE NEW YORK RIPPER. Needless to say, the Boyles' stay in the house is not uneventful. People in the town recognise Norman, though he insists he's never been there before – another hint at dislocation of time and space. Enigmatic housekeeper Ania Pieroni comes with the property, much like Martha and Arthur in THE BEYOND. A cracked tombstone in the floor gushes crimson, and bats emerge from the cellar to attack the residents. Bob is plagued by premonitions of decapitation. Norman discovers that Peterson had become obsessed with a previous occupant of the house, a certain Dr Freudstein who was struck off at the turn of the century for "dabbling in bizarre surgical practices". He plays Peterson's last recorded message, a demented stream of consciousness. As we hear it Fulci's camera careers around what looks like a human abbatoir, and we hear children who are either sobbing or giggling.

This charnel house is down in the cellar, and so is Dr Freudstein, who has been keeping himself alive by grafting parts of unwilling donors onto himself. Curious Bob goes down and runs into the good doctor, who's got his killing head on. Norman, who's finally got the drift of what's going on, hacks at the cellar door with an axe, unaware that Freudstein is holding Bob's head against the other side. The suspense generated in this sequence rivals that of Christopher George rescuing MacColl from premature burial in

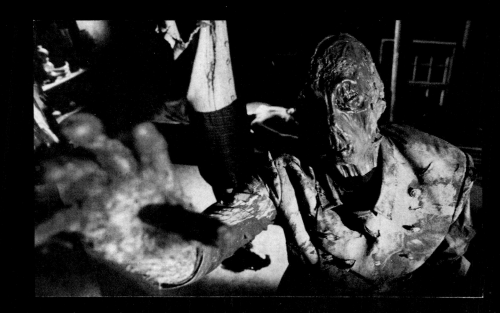

THE SEDUCTION OF THE GULLIBLE

CITY OF THE LIVING DEAD. Bob narrowly avoids the decapitation he's been forseeing throughout the picture, and before we have a chance to collect our breath, the Boyles are confronting Freudstein in his lair. Norman stabs the monster, maggots spilling from the wound, but Freudstein counters by tearing his throat out. Lucy carries Bob up a ladder that leads to the cracked tombstone, through which the terrified child tries to crawl as Freudstein drags his mother down to her death. He returns to Bob, but just as gnarled hands are tugging at the boy's legs, Bob is pulled up through the crack (a grotesque parody of birth, and a neat lift from NORTH BY NORTH-WEST), arriving in the aforementioned parallel universe just in time for tea with May and Mrs Freudstein.

Fulci ends with a quotation from Henry James, and though there are definite shades of TURN OF THE SCREW about HOUSE BY THE CEMETERY, the story is more firmly set in Lovecraft territory: Peterson's semi-lucid rantings could be coming from a Lovecraft character who has gazed too long and ventured too far into the Beyond; and Freudstein, when he finally appears, is a startling patchwork quilt of festering humanity, recalling the protagonist of HPL's "Cool Air". There's also more than a suggestion of CURSE OF THE CAT PEOPLE (1944) about Fulci's handling of scenes involving children.

Some critics have carped that for a film with a bogeyman named Freudstein, HOUSE BY THE CEMETERY was a bit thin on Freudian content,... not so! Bob's tombstone rebirth, his passage from the chaotic cellar (i.e. the unconscious) into a strictly regimented adult world, and the way HOUSE, like MANHATTAN BABY, uses the parallel world device to point up the differences between grown-up and childish thought processes, are all good Freudian stuff. Moreover, Freud's central thesis was the conflict between the sexual and the self-preservative drives, and though there's not much of the former in this film, there's plenty of the latter: Freudstein wants to preserve himself forever! Truly (to quote a gravestone seen in CITY OF THE LIVING DEAD) "the soul that pines for eternity". Developing the idea of an evil character who refuses to age and die, an old man using a rejuvenating agent was the culprit in THE BEAUTY KILLINGS, an early draft screenplay for Fulci's next and most notorious film, THE NEW YORK RIPPER (1982).

READ THE FINE PRINT.
YOU MAY HAVE
JUST MORTGAGED
YOUR LIFE.

DUE TO THE GRAPHIC NATURE OF THIS FILM, NO ONE UNDER 17 WILL BE ADMITTED

Current Status: Vampix version banned. Re-released by Elephant Video, then VIPCO

UN «THRILLING» PIENO DI SUSPENCE E DI PAURA CHE «MOZZA IL FIATO»!!!

la F·D CINEMATOGRAFICA
presenta

DAVID A HESS
ANNIE BELLE in

LA CASA SPERDUTA NEL PARCO

con **CHRISTIAN BORROMEO**
e con la partecipazione di **LORRAINE DE SELLE**
musica composta e diretta da **RIZ ORTOLANI**
regia di **RUGGERO DEODATO**

PER LE NUMEROSE SEQUENZE VERAMENTE SCABROSE IL FILM E' RIGOROSAMENTE VIETATO AI MINORI 18 ANNI

THE SEDUCTION OF THE GULLIBLE

HOUSE ON THE EDGE OF THE PARK. *Italy, 1979. Video label: Skyline Video. Starring David A. Hess, Annie Belle, Christian Borromeo, Lorraine de Selle, Giovanni Lombardo Radice, Marie Claude Joseph, Gabriele di Giulio, Brigitte Petronio, Karoline Mardeck. Camera: Sergio d'Offizi. Written by Gianfranco Clerici and Vincenzo Mannino. Produced by Giovanni Masini. Directed by Ruggero Deodato.*

Wes Craven opened a slimy can of worms when he pressed the plot of Bergman's THE VIRGIN SPIRING into service for his exploitation milestone THE LAST HOUSE ON THE LEFT. It didn't take long for other film-makers to start quoting, paying homage to, and plain old ripping off his movie. Aldo Lado's LATE NIGHT TRAINS (1975, also peddled in the States as – cringe – THE NEW HOUSE ON THE LEFT and attributed to "Evans Isle") adheres most closely to the original VIRGIN SPRING / LAST HOUSE scenario, differing only in that the action is set, yes, on board a late night train. Lado's movie is one very sick puppy indeed, which – surprisingly – never appeared on the DPP's "Nasties" list (though it was cited on previous hit-lists compiled by various regional police forces and seized from shops in areas under their jurisdiction). I SPIT ON YOUR GRAVE and the rather tame FIGHT FOR YOUR LIFE, are reviewed elsewhere in this volume.

HOUSE ON THE EDGE OF THE PARK borrows LHOTL's bogeyman-in-chief David Hess for the role of psychopathic car mechanic Alex, and teams him with Giovanni Lombardo Radice, aka John Morghen (who was lobotomised with a drill in Fulci's CITY OF THE LIVING DEAD, gutted with a shotgun in Marghereti's CANNIBAL APOCALYPSE and fell foul of tit-piercing, dick-chopping, brain-eating hottentots in Lenzi's CANNIBAL FEROX) as his retarded disco-dancing side-kick Ricky, unleashing this gruesome twosome in a swish pad full of smug yuppies, with the proverbial explosive results. After fixing the car of former Europorn starlet Annie Belle and wimpy Christian Borromeo, Hess talks himself and Morghen into a party where the jaded rich kids attempt to alleviate their boredom by humiliating these social misfits. Morghen is encouraged to take off John Travolta and most of his clothes, while Belle subjects Hess to the "now you get me, now you don't" routine. It's the final straw when they fleece Morghen in a rigged poker game. "They're taking you for a ride" snarls Hess, and when challenged by a bald elegant black lady he barks: "You heard me, twat!" The truce in the class war is well and truly over – now Hess robs, rapes and urinates on the beautiful people, while Morghen yammers encouragement from the sidelines, discouraging rebellion with a cut-throat razor.

A sweet young thing called Cindy comes a'knockin' at the door. Hess strips her, then sings a catchy little calypso number as he reprises his unique autograph technique from LAST HOUSE. At this point Morghen, who has been seduced and won over by one of the yuppies (his CANNIBAL FEROX co-star Lorraine de Selle) pleads with Hess to stop before things "go too far". Considering the gamut of atrocities which the yupps have already been put through, Morghen's definition of "going too far" beggars the imagination! It certainly irritates Hess, who seriously wounds Morghen with the razor and then breaks down when he realises what he has done, babbling invective at the woman who came between them, as the latent homosexuality that underscores their psychotic Laurel and Hardy act rises to the surface. The yuppies grab the opportunity to turn the tables, shooting Hess in the crotch. Emitting a curious high-pitched whine, Hess falls backwards into the swimming pool, all filmed in super-slow motion. Indeed, Deodato draws this moment out to such extraordinary length that the viewer could leave the room, fix himself a bite, eat it and come back to find Hess still screaming on his TV screen. Unfortunately Deodato felt the need to impose a contrived, pointless and frankly ludicrous twist ending on his film, detracting greatly from its impact. Nevertheless, HOTEOTP stands as one of the cinema's most viciously black essays in class warfare, and together with CANNIBAL HOLOCAUST seems to indicate that Deodato's filmography would be a formidable one indeed, had he not been worn out by censorship hassles and the commercial pressure to churn out such pap as the nauseating "kid-dying-of-cancer" weepie LAST FEELINGS.

Current Status: Banned

INTERCITY VIDEO

a bizarre love, a strange death.

I MISS YOU
HUGS & KISSES

STARRING: ELKE SOMMER AND DONALD PILON

With: Chuck Shamata, George Touliatos, Cec Linder. Introducing: Cindy Girling and George Chuvalo. Executive Producer – Steve Burns. Producer – Charles Markowitz, Murray Markowitz. Art Director – Carol Spier. Editor – Donald Ginsberg. Music – Howard Shore. Director of Photography – Don Wilder. Written and Directed by – Murray Markowitz. An Astral Films Release

DISTRIBUTION LIMITED

THE SEDUCTION OF THE GULLIBLE

I MISS YOU, HUGS AND KISSES. Canada, 1978. Video label: Intercity Video. Starring Elke Sommer, Donald Pilon, Chuck Shamata, Cindy Girling, George Touliatos, Cec Linder, George Chuvalo. Camera: Don Wilder. Produced by Charles Zakery Markowitz and Murray Markowitz. Written and directed by Murray Markowitz.

The ludicrous pack blurb promised something "for those who like their sex served up with some violence", which probably explains how this thing came to reside, briefly, on the "video nasties" list (where it was misspelt as "I MISS YOUR HUGS AND KISSES"). It turns out to be less of a horror movie than a thriller, and not a particularly thrilling one at that, but boy is the plot complicated! I'm convinced that any jury obliged to watch the film would be too busy trying to figure out what the hell was going on to reflect on its alleged obscenity – I.M.Y.H.A.K. is an absolute mess, flashing backwards, forwards and side-ways with scant regard for narrative cohesion or the sanity of hack writers attempting to compile synopses of "video nasties". It's as though the movie has been whipped up from the remnants of two or more earlier, unrealised projects.

Elke Sommer has her brains beaten out in the title sequence, then in quick succession we get her husband (Donald Pilon) being found guilty of her murder, escaping from the Eastern-bloc twenty years earlier and, as a child, being subjected to his dying father's rambling, home-spun philosophy about women. We flash forward to his meeting with Sommer, an elegant model, then to him telling a fellow Eastern-bloc escapee about their plans for marriage. His friend responds by ranting that Sommer is "… a money-grubbing little bitch from near Hamburg … she'll end up as a fat hausfrau … she doesn't even make a good whore … all she's got is that face, those tits… and that ever-open door of a cunt!" At various points in the past, present and future, we are introduced to Pilon's French mistress; yet another Hungarian refugee who was left for dead at the border by Pilon (a fact which he isn't too pleased about); and his heavy-weight boxer sidekick, whom Sommer offers $10,000 "to beat my husband to death." "But I only break arms and legs!" protests the scandalised pug.

Various characters with an axe to grind against Sommer are shown fantasizing about her dying in various grisly manners – she is run over, electrocuted in a swimming pool and has a paving slab dropped on her head, in scenes tinged a lurid blood red. Apropos of nothing, an escaped psycho turns up, stabbing and raping hitchhikers. Back at Pilon's trial, this guy is introduced as a defense witness, with the clear implication that it was him who murdered Sommer. "Do I look like the kind of person who'd hurt somebody?" he asks, and the answer is of course that yes, he does really. Nevertheless, Pilon is found guilty, which is, rather stupidly, played as a big shock – stupidly because the result of the trial was given away right at the start of the movie. Finally we see Pilon in jail, not looking very well at all. "The barbers put chemicals in my hair and it fell out", he complains, mugging into the camera: "The food is so bad that my face has broken out in boils." Then he starts agonising over the injustice of it all: "Was I prejudged because of my wealth? Was my mistake that I married a beautiful woman?" Frankly my dear, we don't give a damn.

I think that by the end of the film we're supposed to have arrived at some sort of conclusion about Pilon's guilt or innocence, but I lost the plot too early on in the proceedings to be able to hazard a guess. Murray Markowitz is not the only, and by no means the most notable Canadian genre film-maker, to have problems constructing his work in a coherent manner. David Cronenberg achieved international fame/notoriety years before he managed a truly "well-made" film with THE DEAD ZONE in 1983, leaning heavily on Stephen King's source material to come up with what many felt to be a distinctly un-Cronenbergian movie. Speaking of Cronenberg, his regular art director Carol Spier discharged the same duties on I MISS YOU, HUGS AND KISSES and George Chuvalo, who plays the boxer/hit-man (and was in reality a useful '70s heavyweight) turns up in Cronenberg's THE FLY, losing an arm-wrestling contest with Jeff Goldblum in spectacular, gory style.

Current Status: Removed from DPP list. No re-release planned

THIS WOMAN HAS JUST...

CUT, CHOPPED, BROKEN
AND BURNED FOUR
MEN BEYOND
RECOGNITION...
BUT NO JURY
IN AMERICA
WOULD EVER
CONVICT HER!

I SPIT on your GRAVE

AN ACT OF REVENGE!

Starring **CAMILLE KEATON** **ERON TABOR** **RICHARD PACE** **ANTHONY NICHOLS**
produced by **JOSEPH ZBEDA**
written and directed by **MEIR ZARCHI**
RUNNING TIME 98 MIN

THE SEDUCTION OF THE GULLIBLE

> *I SPIT ON YOUR GRAVE aka DAY OF THE WOMAN. U.S.A., 1978. Video label: Astra Video & Wizard Video. Starring Camille Keaton, Eron Tabor, Richard Pace, Anthony Nichols, Gunther Kleeman. Camera: Yuri Haviv. Produced by Meir Zarchi and Joseph Zbeda. Written and directed by Meir Zarchi.*

Schlock distributor Jerry Gross revived the title of an obscure French anti-racist movie, I SPIT ON YOUR GRAVE, for Meir Zarchi's rape-revenge flick,d originally entitled DAY OF THE WOMAN. By means of a barnstorming ad campaign ("This woman has just chopped, broken and burned four men beyond recognition ... but no jury in America would ever convict her. I SPIT ON YOUR GRAVE – an act of revenge") Gross achieved for this movie the notoriety he desired: "The most reprehensible film ever made. Anyone who defends it must be hopelessly perverted" (Ralph Darren) ... "A vile film for vicious sex criminals" (Roger Ebert) ... "Impossible to defend. The Vice Squad ought to watch every person who actually buys a copy of this tape. It even managed to offend me!" (John Waters). And of course I SPIT became one of the most vilified "video nasties" after its release on cassette in Britain.

Perversely, film's strongest critics don't appear to have actually seen it – either that, or they're thick as two short planks. What other explanation is there for writing up a pro-woman, anti-rape movie as though it were the reverse? ISOYG tells the story of Jennifer Hills (Camille Keaton), who rents a place in the backwoods to get away from it all and write The Great American Novel. Unfortunately the local rednecks turn up and subject her to a particularly gruelling multiple rape. As well as punishing her body, Jennifer's tormentors strike at her soul by ridiculing and destroying her manuscript.

Jennifer subsequently goes after her assailants one by one, acting seductively and making out that she wants more of the same. This is the point at which the film's critics either walked out or crashed out: Jennifer is merely pandering to the rapists' idiotic conception of "what women really want" to lull them into a false sense of security, so she can get on with the aforementioned chopping, breaking and burning, which she pursues without mercy or pity. For once the revenge sequences (including the castration of the lead thug in his bath-tub) are as protracted and detailed as those depicting the atrocities which inspired them, and the film ends with a freeze frame of Jennifer triumphantly brandishing the axe with which she has just vanquished the last of her foes. It's hard to square tis with Ebert's description of I SPIT as "... a very cruel film that expands upon the notion that women are nothing but sexual playthings: Jennifer wants a career and for this sin against domesticity she is rewarded with the most humiliating violence at the hands of three macho men". Ebert's reference to "three macho men" skirts around the fact that one of the rapists is a retarded geek – surely Zarchi isn't representing him as an admirable role model? And the "macho men" themselves are actually pot-bellied, stupid, gullible slobs.

Marco Starr cuts the crap in an impressive piece entitled "J. Hills is Alive" in Martin Barker's book "The Video Nasties" (Pluto Press). Mr Starr is not "hopelessly perverted" or a 'vicious sex criminal", he just took the trouble to watch the whole movie. "ISOYG is actually a very good movie" he argues: "... well made, interestingly written, beautifully photographed and intelligently directed ... not the least of its surprising accomplishments is the militant stance it takes in favour of the woman it is supposedly degrading ... it portrays violent aggression and hatred towards women while simultaneously condemning those very attitudes. And it does this long before the violated heroine has her day of vengeance." Disputing Ebert's claim that I SPIT is telling women to get back in line, Starr argues that the film honours women's aspirations: "The rapists in ISOYG. believe that abused women should be thrown away and forgotten; the film-maker quite definitely does not ... the rapists' continuing refusal to recognise Jennifer's rights as a human-being make them seem monstrously inhuman – their ultimate deaths can only be viewed as inevitable." Exactly. So does I SPIT ON YOUR GRAVE glorify rape? Only if you consider it glorious to go through life minus your penis!

> *Current Status: Banned*

una película de
DARIO ARGENTA

Infierno

THE SEDUCTION OF THE GULLIBLE

INFERNO, Italy, 1980. Video label: CBS/Fox Video. Starring Irene Miracle, Leigh McCloskey, Daria Nicolodi, Eleonora Giorgi, Alida Valli, Sacha Pitoeff, Feodor Chaliapin, Veronica Lazar, Gabriele Lavia. Special effects: Germano Natali, Pino Leoni, Mario Bava (uncredited). Camera: Romano Albani. Produced by Claudio Argento. Written and directed by Dario Argento.

INFERNO establishes that Elena Markos, the witch who presided over Argento's SUSPIRIA, was one member of an unholy trinity, Maters Suspiriorum, Lachrimarum and Tenebrarum (Sighs, Tears and Darkness), the latter two operating out of Rome and New York respectively. Rose Elliot (Irene Miracle) learns their secret when she acquires a forbidden book from the antique dealer Kazanian (Sacha Pitoeff), and is alarmed to find her apartment building cited as the lair of Mater Tenebrarum. She writes to her brother Mark (Leigh McCloskey), a music student in Rome, who is so troubled by herletter that he immediately flys home. Before he even leaves, though, his girlfriend Sara (Eleonara Giorgi), who sought out a copy of "The Three Mothers" tome after reading Rose's letter, is stabbed to death by a spectral figure. When he arrives in Rome Rose is also dead, guillotined in a window frame by another demonic assailant. Like Suzy Banyon in SUSPIRIA, Mark becomes ill and is confined to the building, nursed by its sinister tenants. Investigating a series of secret passage-ways, he confronts first Varelli, author of "The Three Mothers" and designer of their dwelling places, then Mater Tenebrarum herself as the apartment block goes up in flames.

Argento dislikes the term "Horror Film", preferring to talk about the "surrealist connotations" of his work. This dreamlike sequel to / remake of SUSPIRIA, in which a wrong turning at the library leads the hapless Sara into a Medieval alchemist's lab, certainly lives up to that billing. Conventional narrative techniques are jettisoned in favour of an episodic, fragmented exposition based on the "poetic" construction of Alain Resnais' 1961 film LAST YEAR IN MARIENBAD (the casting of Pitoeff was a nod in this direction) but thankfully any resemblance to the Resnais bore-fest ends there, and the fact that the "Three Mothers" concept was borrowed from De Quincey's "Confessions of an Opium Eater" may give a truer indication of the (dis)orientation that Argento brought to the making of INFERNO. Due to its rejectionl of linear narrative, any appreciation of the film inevitably becomes an appreciation of the beautiful set-pieces with which it is punctuated. The controversy over whether Mario Bava supervised the memorable sequence in which Rose tangles with a skinny-dipping cadaver while diving for the brooch she dropped in a submerged basement is in a sense irrelevant – INFERNO's delirious accumulation of ever more beguiling images, to the detriment of its narrative, testifies most eloquently to the primacy of the Bava influence.

The most overblown scene of the lot is the one in which the Mother of Tears (Ania Pieroni) materializes in the middle of one of Mark's lectures. The presence of a beautiful, scantily-clad teenager stroking a cat goes completely unnoticed by the other students, as does the indoor wind-storm which develops to the strains of "Va Pensiero" from Verdi's "Nabucco". Dealing as it does with the plight of the Israelites in Babylonian captivity, Verdi's piece, resurfacing on the soundtrack in a series of synthesized variations by Keith Emerson, serves to underscore Argento's vision of humanity as the plaything of cruel, elemental beings. ("To them we are no more than dust" gasps Varelli as he dies.) Argento takes the ironic giallo convention by which the protagonist's amateur sleuthing leads to a sharp increase in the kill rate and expands it so that Mark's delving into the mystery of his sister's disappearance opens up vistas of cosmic horror. The various characters are impelled by their isolation and incomprehension through a terrain polluted by evil towards an inevitable assignation with death. "You were looking for me, just like your sister", Mater Tenebrarum tells Mark: "This is what you wanted!", revealing her true identity as an exterminating angel.

The message of INFERNO appears to be that every man is an island. The problem is that Argento has fused medium and message to the point of beautiful incoherence.

Current Status: Re-released by CBS/FOX, with shots of cat eating mouse deleted.

INFERNO

THE SEDUCTION OF THE GULLIBLE

ISLAND OF DEATH aka A CRAVING FOR LUST / DEVILS IN MYKONOS/ ISLAND OF PERVERSION. U.S.A./Greece, 1972. Video label: A.V.I. Video. Starring Bob Belling, Jane Ryall, Jessica Dublin, Gerarlo Gonalons, Janice McConnel, Clay Huff, Mike Murtagh, Jeremy Rousseau, Niko Tsachiriois.Camera: Nick Gardellis. Written, produced and directed by Nico Mastorakis.

This one begins deceptively, coming on like a travelogue about Mykonos and prompting horrible memories of Joe D'Amato's ANTHROPOPHAGOUS BEAST. But it's a travelogue with a difference, apparently narrated by a guy dying in the desert, and the depravity kicks in a lot earlier than in the D'Amato film. Chris, the narrator (played by Bob Belling), is seen having sex with Celia (Jane Ryall) in a telephone box to the accompaniment of pumping disco music. He dials her mother in London to give her the benefit of their orgasmic groans. "You're disgusting Christopher, disgusting" protests Mom, but she, and the viewer, ain't seen nothing yet! Chris starts feeling horny again, but is rebuffed by Celia, so he goes out into the garden and apparently fornicates with a goat, then he stabs the unfortunate animal to death. Celia slips out for an assignation with Jean-Claude, a Frenchman they met in a restaurant. She helps him whitewash the walls of his house, they playfully splash each other with whitewash and then get down in the dirt for some torrid sex action. Chris spies on and photographs all of this, then he beats up and nails Jean-Claude to the floor ("in the name of God, who punishes perversions, you sinful man!") while Celia takes photos. Deciding that Jean-Claude is thirsty, they pour whitewash down his throat until he dies. Next they attend a gay couple's engagement party. Celia gets drunk, but Chris abstains, telling her that drunkenness would blur his enjoyment of their excesses. After the party has broken up they return and Chris attacks the gays with a sword while Celia – you guessed it – takes photos. "God punishes perversions", rants Chris: "… and I'm his angel with a fiery sword, sent to kill dirty worms." "I believe in God" cries one of the gays, pleading for his life, only to be told: "Too late, my friend, he no longer believes in you anymore." One of the victims is forced to fellate a gun barrel, then has his brains blown out.

Chris rationalizes his behaviour as an attempt to protect children from corruption. He has an idealized view of how "innocent and pure" life on the island is for the simple peasant folk and rants that he is battling against the forces of moral decline (how all this is supposed to square with his amorous inclinations towards goats is anybody's guess). His righteous indignation is next aimed at a junky bar-maid who's got the hots for Celia (cue gratuitous lesbian scene) but before she can be dealt with there's the little matter of a cop who's been trailing them around the world and now appears on Mykonos – he ends up flying through the air on the end of a noose attached to an airplane.

Chris is picked up by Patricia, a rich, bored, matronly American. With Celia surreptitiously taking photographs, as ever, Chris gets down to his idea of foreplay, i.e. pissing on Pat's face. Pat is initially indignant, then starts getting turned on, so Chris beats her to death and buries her body with the aid of a dump truck. Celia is raped by drug-crazed hippies while Chris is out fishing. He returns to catch them in flagrante delicto, harpoons one of them and drowns the other in the toilet. What's more, the gruesome twosome contrive to cover their tracks by blaming the recent spate of killings on the dead hippies. Celia is getting fed up with all the killings anyway, and puts it to Chris that this is a logical point for them to call it a day, but he is determined to visit divine retribution on that lesbian barmaid. Meanwhile a novelist turns up and sensitively announces that he is seeking inspiration from Celia's rape. Celia goes round to the barmaid's place and watches her shoot up, then lets in Chris, who administers a drink and drugs overdose to the prostrate girl and improvises an aerosol flame-thrower to torch her with ("I was sure the best way for the filthy lesbian to die was for her to

ISLAND OF DEATH

The lucky ones got their brains blown out!!

ISLAND OF
DEATH

Starring BOB BELLING, JANE RYALE and NICO TSACHIRIDI
Written and Directed by NICO MASTORAKIS

burn" intones Chris in his role as narrator). The barmaid's crispy corpse joins all the others in their photo album. The inspiration-seeking novelist works out what is happening and tips off the police, who catch up with Chris while he's a raping a girl in the shower. Frankly, I was hoping that they'd gun him down, because the film had really started to wear out it's welcome at this point, but Chris skewers his victim with a scythe, evades the police and collects Celia, with whom he escapes into the countryside. A moronic shepherd (Niko Tsachiriois) extends the hospitality of his hovel to them. Chris gets on his soap-box about the "innocent" peasants being the true owners of the island and how he is cleaning it up for them. The half wit responds by raping Celia. With no toilet to drown him in, Chris contents himself with photographing the proceedings, is beaten up and buggered for his trouble, tied up and thrown into a lime-pit. This brings us right up to date, for it is from this very pit that Chris has been narrating the whole sleazy saga. Now he calls for help, but Celia seems to have decided that being raped by an oversexed village idiot is her idea of an idyllic existence. Chris reassures himself that he won't burn as long as the lime stays dry... but what was that? A spot of rain? Incidentally, it is revealed towards the end of ISLAND OF DEATH that Chris and Celia are not only lovers, they're also brother and sister. And there I was, thinking that they were such a nice, clean-living couple!

Even if you can forgive Mastorakis for writing, producing and directing this outrage, the theme-song, which he co-wrote, will drive you right up a wall. Take it away, Nico (as far away as possible!):

> "Mother, I've seen the wonders of today,
> Millions of people living like clay,
> Millions of whispers saying 'I'm dying'.
>
> Get the sword! Kill them all!
> Truth was born in a thousand meanings
> Jesus said: 'Look, I'm flying!'
>
> (Chorus)
> Desperation, understanding,
> Destination, isn't ending,
> Desperation, understanding,
> Destination, isn't ending..."
>
> and so on ...

Current Status: Banned. A heavily edited version was submitted to the BBFC by another video company, under the title PSYCHIC KILLER 2, but refused a certificate.

THE SEDUCTION OF THE GULLIBLE

KILLER NUN aka SUOR OMICIDI. Italy, 1978. Video label: Techno-film. Starring Anita Ekberg, Alida Valli, Massimo Serato, Lou Castel, Joe Dallesandro, Laura Nucci, Paola Morra, Lee de Barriault. Camera: Tonino Maccoppi. Written by Giulio Berruti and Alberto Tarallo. Produced by Enzo Gallo. Directed by Giulio Berruti.

Sister Gertrude (Ekberg) presides over a hospice for clapped-out clerics and Catholic charity cases. She's a tetchy, tyrannical hypochondriac who complains, against all the 'evidence, that she's got cancer, which is a pretext for her heavy morphine intake. The medical staff discourage Gertrude's bad habit, and Mother Superior Alida Valli tells her that "it is a nun's vocation to suffer" but she takes no comfort from these words, throwing a fit (to the soaring strains of a musical sawk) and attempting to disconnect a patient's life-support system. Gertrude entertains the patients with an account of one saint's martyrdom ("Her teeth were pulled out and boiling oil was poured onto her bleeding gums ... incensed by her passive acceptance, her torturers put a hot poker on her tongue, jagged needles through her cheeks and pins in her holy lips. Her soul still didn't leave her body so they chopped off one of her breasts..." etc, etc.) During this heart-warming little anecdote an elderly patient named Josephine takes her teeth out and puts them in a glass of water, which so infuriates Sister Gertrude that she throws said dentures on the floor and jumps up and down on them until they are powder. The old girl suffers a heart-attack and goes into a coma. Gertrude dithers over the life-saving injection she is supposed to be preparing until Josephine dies, then coolly announces to the doctor that "Josephine is among the angels now".

Dirty Gertie now steals a ring from Josephine's effects, goes AWOL and hocks it to finance a boozy night out on the town where she has public sex, LAST TANGO-style (Ekberg a tad too old and tubby for comfort) and stocks up on dope. Back at the hospice, she shoots up to the sound of psychedelic sitars and prays for absolution. Each of her drug interludes (for which director Giulio Berruti pulls out every psychedelic cliché in the book) is accompanied by the murder of one of the patients (variously bashed over the head with a lamp and thrown out of a window, strangled, kicked to death, etc. One old lady has her face turned into a pin-cushion in the manner of the martyr whose fate was described above). Not surprisingly, Gertrude falls under suspicion, but comfort is on hand from pretty sister Mathieu, who spends most of her time slapping down the amorous advances of patients – she only has eyes for Gertrude, who gets her rocks off by humiliating Mathieu, forcing her to confess to being "the worst kind of prostitute" and telling her to "get your stockings ... put them on or I'll beat you. I prefer men but if I have to do it with a woman she has to wear silk stockings". Mathieu lets slip to Dr Patrick (Dallesandro), that Gertrude is the killer, then attempts to buy his silence with sex. When word gets out to Mother Superior Valli, she arranges to have Sister Gertrude poisoned. Too late, it is revealed that Mathieu has been killing off the patients as some kind of obscure revenge against her grandfather, who sexually abused her as a child.

Nuns' dirty habits have been a popular theme for exploitive "exposés" since the Reformation, but such material now carries little shock value outside of Catholic countries (this one was deemed "unacceptable" by Catholic censorship bodies in Italy, peeved by the way it was marketed as a real-life case "from the secret archives of the Vatican.") The film's facile politicising is typical of a strand of Italian exploitation with pretensions to artiness, as is the assemblage of a cast that has seen better days in more exalted company: LA DOLCE VITA was long over for Anita Ekberg by the time she appeared in this; Alida Valli's Hollywood career had been terminated by the disclosure of her own "bad habit"; and Joe Dallesandro, although he never could act, previously did his non-acting for the bare-assed Emperor himself, Andy Warhol. Unfortunately KILLER NUN is inferior in every way to Gianfranco Mingozzi's FLAVIA (1975) which is altogether artier and gorier, boasting besides a far more compelling central performance from Florinda Bolkan as the rebel nun / priestess of violence / heretic of its title.

Current Status: Re-released with mimimal cuts by Redemption Video

PAGE # 115

THE SEDUCTION OF THE GULLIBLE

THE LAST HOUSE ON THE LEFT aka KRUG & AND COMPANY / SEX CRIME OF THE CENTURY. U.S.A., 1972. Video label: Replay Video. Starring David Hess, Lucy Grantheim, Sandra Cassel, Marc Sheffier, Jeraime Rain, Fred Lincoln, Gaylord St James, Cynthia Carr, Ada Washington. Camera: Victor Hurwitz. Produced by Sean S. Cunningham. Written and directed by Wes Craven.

In 1970 Craven and Cunningham made TOGETHER, a porno film starring a certain Marilyn Briggs (later "Chambers"). It was so successful for Hallmark productions that they bank-rolled the partnership to make a "no-holds-barred, knock-down, drag-out horror picture". Craven and Cunningham rejected the body count approach (which would eventually serve as the raison d'etre for the latter's FRIDAY THE 13TH) and decided that they could achieve maximum impact by focussing on one unspeakable act and its aftermath in unflinching detail. The result was THE LAST HOUSE ON THE LEFT, "a quantum leap into an unknown area of screen violence" in the words of its star David Hess.

An ominous pre-titles announcement warns that "the names have been changed to protect those still alive", and claims documentary status for the film, a device later appropriated — with more justification — by THE TEXAS CHAINSAW MASSACRE (1974. Like Tobe Hooper's film, LAST HOUSE derives much of its almost unbearable intensity from this quasi-documentary tone (enhanced in the blow up from 16mm). In fact the film's plot is copped, not from real life but from THE VIRGIN SPRING (1960), Ingmar Bergman's saga of rape, murder and revenge in Medieval Sweden.

Craven's opening establishes the happy suburban domestic life of the Collingwoods, earnest liberals who buy their daughter Mari (Sandra Cassel) a ban-the-bomb pendant for her birthday but fret over her attending a gig by "Bloodlust" (who sound like they owe a lot to the grisly theatrics of Alice Cooper) with her friend Phyllis (Lucy Grantheim), a girl who is definitely from "the wrong side of the tracks". Stopping off to score some dope on their way to the gig, the girls are kidnapped by a bunch of prison escapees — Krug (rhymes with "Droog") Stillow (David Hess); Junior (Marc Sheffier) aka "Junkie" (Krug has apparently hooked his own son on smack, all the better to control him!); Krug's girlfriend Sadie (Jeramie Rain); and Fred "Weasel" Padowsky (Fred Lincoln). The escapees' collective CV, as recounted in an OTT radio report, includes "murder, dope-pushing and rape … the triple slaying of a priest and two nuns … child molestation, peeping Tom-ism and assault with a deadly weapon." The girls are taken into a wood, sexually humiliated and mutilated, their ordeal given an added poignancy by 1) Mari's realisation that she's just a few hundred yards away from her home 2) by intercutting with her parents' preparation for her birthday party, and 3) by the fact that in these very woods 24 hours earlier, the girls had discussed their romantic aspirations. Phyllis, whom Mari's parents had been so distrustful of, tries to protect her throughout, and bravely attempts to decoy her escape, resulting in her own disembowelment by the vindictive thugs. Mari has Krug's autograph carved on her chest with a razor, wades out into a pond in a state of shock and is finally put out of her misery by a shot in the head.

Krug and co seek shelter at — you guessed it that last house on the left (an irritating throwaway reference to A CLOCKWORK ORANGE), the Collingwood house, and against their better judgement Mari's parents put them up for the night. During an excruciatingly awkward dinner party, Mrs Collingwood, worried about her daughter's prolonged absence, notices that one of the guests is wearing her birthday pendant, and later eavesdrops on them laughing about the murder of the two girls. Hell hath no fury like a disillusioned liberal, and after a curious Freudian nightmare sequence in which Weasel's teeth are knocked out with a chisel (the first sign of Craven's penchant for such dream sequences, which by A NIGHTMARE ON ELM STREET had expanded to become the whole raison d'etre of the movie) Mrs Collingwood "seduces" Weasel, then emasculates him during fellatio (look it up in a dictionary!) For an encore, she cuts Sadie's throat. The unstable Junior shoots himself (with his father's active encouragement!) and Krug himself is apparently beheaded with a chainsaw.

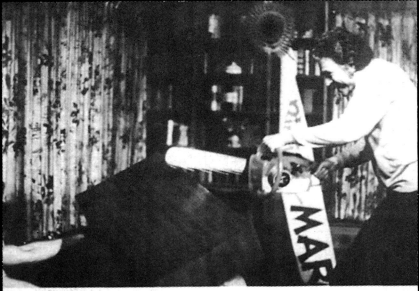

SEAN S. CUNNINGHAM FILMS LTD. Presents "THE LAST HOUSE ON THE LEFT"
Starring: DAVID HESS • LUCY GRANTHAM • SANDRA CASSEL • MARC SHEFFLER
and introducing ADA WASHINGTON • Produced by SEAN S. CUNNINGHAM
Written and Directed by WES CRAVEN • COLOR BY MOVIELAB [R] RESTRICTED

LAST HOUSE
ON THE **LEFT**

CAN A MOVIE GO TOO FAR?

MARI,
SEVENTEEN, IS
DYING. EVEN FOR
HER THE WORST
IS YET
TO
COME!

**TO AVOID
FAINTING**
KEEP REPEATING,
IT'S ONLY A MOVIE
..ONLY A MOVIE
..ONLY A MOVIE
..ONLY A MOVIE
..ONLY A MOVIE
..ONLY A MOVIE
..ONLY A MOVIE

...IT'S JUST

ACROSS THE

STREET FROM

"JOE"!

LAST HOUSE ON THE LEFT

WARNING! NOT RECOMMENDED FOR PERSONS OVER 30!

The film ends with the dazed Collingwoods surveying the carnage all around them. Although it's difficult to see how their revenge could, in the words of the notorious advertising campaign, "go too far", it certainly can't bring their daughter back, and they have lost their cherished self-image as civilised liberals, much like the protagonists of DELIVERANCE (1972). They don't even experience the elation that Dustin Hoffman feels at the end of STRAW DOGS (1971), in fact they have lost everything. No winners, no solutions, in the words of the theme song by David Hess ... "The road leads to nowhere."

LAST HOUSE was greeted with howls of protest, but distributors Hallmark cheekily recruited the critics to its promotional campaign, dressed up as an ongoing "debate" over that question of whether a film could "go too far". Nowdays producer Sean S. Cunningham seems loathe to discuss LHOTL, seemingly happier to acknowledge such junk as DEEP STAR SIX, but director Craven still defends the film staunchly (and even named his biggest hit's boogeyman "Krueger"): "Sometimes I think it was a terrible film to make ..." he admits: " ... other times I'm glad I was that angry. I have to be honest, even for me now it isn't a pleasant film to watch but I genuinely felt I portrayed what it felt like to kill somebody for real. The protracted violence was very human to me... nobody comes out of THE LAST HOUSE ON THE LEFT looking noble after they had killed somebody, even if they have killed for the right reasons."

Certain moments in the film make it impossible to deny Craven's serious intent, but although he was absolutely right to dehumanise the good guys and give the killers some positive features (they get all the best comic lines and are shown in the extraordinary aftermath of Mari's death to be capable of remorse), the director skates so recklessly over thin ice that it inevitably breaks – the crass antics of the local cops would be more at home in a Burt Reynolds "Good ol' boy" comedy than here, and the juxtaposition of the Krug gang's abominations with a wacky C&W song is nothing short of mind -bogglingly insensitive. Nevertheless, THE LAST HOUSE ON THE LEFT continues to exert a stranglehold over the imagination of all those who have seen it, so much so that apocryphal stories about "missing scenes" persist. Whether any such scenes actually exist is really beside the point – L.H.O.T.L.'s fly-on-the-wall intensity gives it enduring power matched by no other American horror film, bar TEXAS CHAINSAW MASSACRE.

Current Status: Banned

"DON'T OPEN THE WINDOW"

A NEWPORT RELEASE

THE SEDUCTION OF THE GULLIBLE

THE LIVING DEAD AT THE MANCHESTER MORGUE aka THE LIVING DEAD / BREAK-FAST AT THE MANCHESTER MORGUE / DON'T OPEN THE WINDOW / LET SLEEPING CORPSES LIE / NO PROFANAR EL SUENO DE LOS MEURTOS / FIN DE SEMANA PARA LOS MEURTOS/ NON SI DEVE PROFANARE IL SONNO DEI MORTI / WEEKEND PER I MORTI / LE MASSACRE DES MORTS-VIVANTS / INVASION DER ZOMBIES / DAS LEICHENHAUS DER LEBENDEN TOTEN, etc... Italy/Spain, 1974. Video label: Video Independent Productions. Starring Ray Lovelock, Cristina Galbo, Arthur Kennedy, Aldo Massasso, Giorgio Trestini, Roberto Posse, Jeanine Mestre, José Ruiz Lifante, Fernando Hilbeck, Isabel Mestre. Camera: Francisco Sempere. Special Effects: Giannetto de Rossi and Luciano Bird. Written by Sandro Continenza, Marcello Coscia, Miguel Rubio, Juan Cobos. Produced by Edmondo Amati. Directed by Jorge Grau.

Although DAWN OF THE DEAD set off an avalanche of (mostly Italian) imitations, George A. Romero's deadhead debut THE NIGHT OF THE LIVING DEAD spawned surprisingly few cinematic bastards. Jorge Grau's LIVING DEAD is the only memorable one, in fact I'm going to stick my neck out here and say that this multi-titled Italo-Spanish co-production is a better movie than Romero's historically important but rather overrated effort. Grau extracts maximum surreal and disturbing dislocation from the spectacle of cannibal cadavers shambling around the scenic beauties of England's Lake and Peak Districts, the sense of unease enhanced by a jarring stereo soundtrack (apparently a horror film first) which is guaranteed to put the viewer's nerves on edge.

The city of Manchester figures only briefly in the impressionistic opening (some sources have even mistakenly located it in London), with a hippy George (good name for an English hero, right?), played by Ray Lovelock, riding his trusty Norton out of town – which seems to be full of dying animals, Magrittesque businessmen in breathing masks and unexplained streaking females. A radio message warns against "hysteria when confronted with ecological problems, many of them exaggerated."

THE SEDUCTION OF THE GULLIBLE

MADHOUSE. U.S.A./Italy, 1981. Video label: Medusa. Starring Trish Everley, Dennis Robertson, Michael Macrae, Alison Bigger, Morgan Hart, Richard Baker. Camera: Roberto D'Ettore Piazzoli. Written by Ovidio G. Assonitis, Stephen Blakely, Peter Sheperd, Robert Gandus. Produced and directed by Ovidio G. Assonitis.

This is a real Ovideo Nasty from producer / director Ovidio G. Assonitis, the man who sacked James Cameron from PIRANHA 2, making him the film world's equivalent of the guy who turned down the Beatles. In homage to HALLOWEEN, MADHOUSE opens with a caption counting down the days to "Julia's birthday". Julia (Trish Everley) has a disfigured and hopelessly mad twin named Mary (Alison Bigger) who's a local booby hatch but seems to exert a strange telepathic influence over her sibling. This, we are told, has been going on since they were kids. On Julia's birthdays Mary would prick her with needles and burn her with matches. Their perceptive parents put these wounds down to psychosomatic manifestations of the nightmares Julia suffered about a big black dog. In the present day, various friends and associates of Julia are being attacked by a big black dog and stabbed by its maniacal owners. Julia's premonitions of doom are ignored by her psychiatrist. Meanwhile, the repetitive captions counting down the days to Julia's birthday are becoming increasingly irksome, as is the performance of an appalling little brat named Sacha who thankfully soon ends up as doggy dinner.

Father James (Michael Macrae), a priest who appears to be obsessed with the subject of family life, tells Julia that her premonitions of doom are tied up with guilt over the fate of her sister. He's organising a surprise birthday party for Julia – and what a surprise! All her friends will be there, decomposing around the birthday cake. Father James enlists the aid of Julia's landlady in lugging one such "guest" up the stairs in a hold-all. "It feels like a body", she quips. "It is", comes the deadpan reply. Julia arrives home and is surprised, but not pleasantly, by Father James' treat. Singing nursery rhymes, he wheels in her scab-encrusted sister. "I told you you'd never get away from me, Miss Perfect," says Mary. Julia argues, with good reason, that it's not her fault if Mary is deformed. "No, you can't make me well ..." is the chilling reply " ... but I can make you into a pretty close approximation of me." Father James appears to find this very droll and Julia breaks down, pleading to know why he's doing all this: "Tell her, Father," urges Mary, and a pregnant pause sets in, comparable to the moment in APOCALYPSE NOW when Marlon Brando, as Colonel Kurtz, is about to give the justification for his actions. Then, caressing scabby Mary, Fr James spills the beans on his descent into the heart of darkness, in the following words:

"There was a little girl" (he reveals) "and she had a little curl, right in the middle of her forehead. When she was good, she was very, very good, and when she was bad, she was horrid!"

Julia feels – not without some justification – that this just isn't good enough. "But you've killed them!" she complains. Jimbo is rather tetchy on this score: "Why is everyone so afraid of dying?" he barks banging his fist on the table. "It's not that bad. It s my business, basically. It's easy." "A piece of cake," pipes up Mary, waving around a piece of birthday cake. Fr James has a good old belly laugh at this jolly jape, then stabs Mary to death. By the time Julia's psychiatrist, Sam, rolls up to the rescue, Jimbo has progressed from nursery rhymes to grand opera, but before you can hum a snatch of the Va Pensiero chorus, that big black dog has launched itself at the shrink's throat. He slams the door on this hell-hound, its snarling head crashing through the wood, only for Sam to grab a handy dandy power drill and lobotomise it (or rather, a non-too-convincing glove puppet). Sam grabs an equally fortuitously placed axe and chops down Father James in mid-recital, which is the cue for Mary to pop up, Jason-style. She's soon knocked down again, this time for good though her voice echoes in Julia's mind, promising "You'll never escape me."

For his outro Ovidio quotes George Bernard Shaw... we can only speculate as to how Shaw the critic would have deployed his wit on this, er, truly unique effort.

Current Status: Banned. Deleted from Medusa catalogue

MADHOUSE

ROCK, ROCK, ROCK!

ALAN FREED · FRANKIE LYMON · CHUCK BERRY
CONNIE FRANCIS ...and many more!

ROCK, ROCK, ROCK.

Authentic Big Rock sound.
'Fabulous 50's', the era of
black leather jackets and
poodle skirts.

MARDI GRAS MASSACRE

Everyone is celebrating
nobody hears the screams
of the victims for the sacrifice.

DERANN VIDEO

THE SEDUCTION OF THE GULLIBLE

MARDI GRAS MASSACRE. U.S.A., 1981. Video label: Derann/Market Video. Starring Curt Dawson, Gwen Arment, Laura Misch, Cathryn Lacey, Nancy Dancer, Butch Benit, William Metzo, Ronald Tanet, Wayne Mack. Camera: Don Piel, Jack McGowan, Jack Weis. Written, produced and directed by Jack Weis.

The difference between "so bad it's good" and "so bad it's awful" could be characterised as the difference between the venerable BLOOD FEAST and Jack Weis's MARDI GRAS MASSACRE, a film with identical "plot" and production values, but considerably less appeal. This stupefying effort substitutes an unpronounceable Aztec goddess of evil for Ishtar, but that's about it as far as originality goes, because this deity also demands the bloody slaughter of young women. To this end an intense-looking guy (his portentious delivery of Weis's crummy lines ruined by an ill-fitting pair of false teeth) cruises New Orleans bars, picking up hookers, insisting to their pimps (one of them a brain-damaged hippy who speaks only in rhyming couplets) that he wants "the most evil woman" in the joint. Back in his basement dungeon these pick ups are tied up on an altar, treated to a soothing body rub, then rubbed out with a big ceremonial knife. First our intense friend slices through "the hand that accepted the money", then "the foot that brought you here" ("the foot"? Did they all hop there or something?) and finally "the part of you that you use for evil". This involves cutting into the girls' abdomens and pulling out their hearts, which seem for some reason to have migrated south from their thoracic cavities. The impromptu abdominal surgery is rendered by insert shots of a knife going into a pasty, rubbery-looking hide, and the effect is pretty convincing too, because the skins of the "actresses" concerned are also pasty, rubbery and unhealthy-looking.

The ritual occurs three times (the same gore effect each time) on consecutive Tuesdays leading up to Mardi Gras. Interpol informs the New Orleans PD that this pattern has been repeated over recent years, and if you're wonderingwhy Interpol is more clued in than the local cops, wait till you see the two dullards (perpetually squinting off camera at idiot boards) assigned the task of rounding up the culprit.. They visit one threadbare indoor set after another (including a nightclub apparently built inside somebody's garden shed) and one of them ("Frank… a good cop but a bad human being") starts an affair with a hooker named Sherri. It's a rocky road to romance for our star-crossed lovers – when she starts talking about marriage, he makes his feelings about her profession crystal clear. "At least I'm not a PIG!!!" she retorts. The Mardi Gras killer reunites them by chaining Sherri and two of her call-girl colleagues up in his dungeon, obliging Frank to burst in and rescue her. After a very unexciting car chase, the killer drives into New Orleans harbour.... but when his car is puller, there's no sign of him... only his mask.

Mardi Gras doesn't feature in the film until its final reel, when Mr Weis obviously sussed that he needed travelogue footage to pad things out to feature length. Then we get nothing but Mardi Gras, though as filmed by Weis it's so dull that you wonder why Peter Fonda and Dennis Hopper would cross the street, never mind the country, for it.

Current Status: Banned

NIGHT OF THE BLOODY APES

Warning–this film contains scenes of extreme and explicit violence

THE SEDUCTION OF THE GULLIBLE

NIGHT OF THE BLOODY APES aka LA HORROR PILANTE BESTIA HUMANA / THE HORRIBLE HUMAN BEAST / HORROR AND SEX / GOMAR THE HUMAN GORILLA. Mexico, 1970. Video label: Iver Film Services. Starring Armando Silvestre, José Elias Moreno, Augustin Martinez, A. M. Solares, Norma Lazareno, Carlos López Moctezuma. Special effects: Javier Torres Torija. Camera: Raúl Martinez Solares. Written by Rene Cordona and René Cordona Jr. Produced by Alfredo Salazar. Directed by Rene Cordona.

Ever since Fernando Mendez' seminal THE BODY SNATCHERS (1956) no self-respecting Mexican horror movie has been complete without its own wrestler / monster match-up. The busiest auteurs in this ludicrous sub-genre have been successive generations of the Cordona family (all bearing the christian name Rene, so don't ask me to start sorting out who made what). In 1962 the Cordona dynasty launched "Las Luchadoras" ("The Wrestling Women") upon an unsuspecting world with WRESTLING WOMEN Vs THE MURDEROUS DOCTOR, in which the eponymous heroines were called upon to enforce the Hippocratic oath with drop-kicks, head-locks and forearm-smashes. In 1963 the Cordonas knocked out a couple of entries in the Santo series (Santo being a fat man in a mask, any account of whose punch-ups with monstrous and mega--lomaniacal adversaries would fill a book on its own), namely SANTO VERSUS THE STRANGLER and SANTO VERSUS THE GHOST OF THE STRANGLER. But these were merely tune-ups for the Cordonas' masterpiece, which came the following year: WRESTLING WOMEN Vs THE AZTEC MUMMY in which, you won't be surprised to learn, the Wrestling Women took on an Aztec Mummy that was getting ideas above its station, also taking time out for a tag team confrontation with Mexico's answer to Fu Manchu and his Kung Fu-kickin' sisters. Not content to rest on their laurels, the Cordonas made THE INVISIBLE KILLER that same year.

In 1966 Las Luchadoras were clipping the wings of THE BAT WOMAN, and in 1967 Acapulco's local favourites, THE FISH MONSTERS, came unstuck against our in--defatigable heroines. Treasure hunting was in, big time, for 1968's Santo brace SANTO AND DRACULA'S TREASURE and TREASURE OF MONTEZUMA, and in the following year's WRESTLING WOMEN vs THE MURDEROUS ROBOT, those feisty wrasslin' gals kicked ass when one of their number was kidnapped by a mad scientist (mad scientists are ten-a-penny down Mexico way, incidentally). Also in 1969 the Cordonas pitted SANTO VERSUS THE HEADHUNTER, and still had time to make LOS JINETES DEL TERROR, in which leper gunslingers made Santo's day. This latter film is known in English language markets as either SANTO vs THE TERROR RIDERS or, rather more memorably, THE LEPERS AND THE SEX (!?!). 1971 saw SANTO IN THE MUMMY'S REVENGE, in which the Mummy fared no better against Santo than he had against Las Luchadoras. After 1972's INVASION OF THE DEAD, Cordona movies became more main-stream (well, as mainstream as you could reasonably expect, given their track record) as the Horror/Wrestling cycle began to peter out.

Most of the aforementioned will remain tantalising obscurities to English-speaking genre buffs (eat your heart out, gringo!) but the Cordonas NIGHT OF THE BLOODY APES received a British theatrical release (the only chunk of Mexican Horror/Wrestling to do so, on a double bill with NIGHT OF BLOODY HORROR, in October 1974) and attained a certain notoriety nearly a decade later, when designated one of the DPP's official "video nasties". Like just about every other Mexican horror offering, N.O.T.B.A. filches its basic plot from THE BODY SNATCHERS, but is untypical in that it omits the expected clash between wrestlers and monster (not "monsters": despite what we are promised in the title, there is, unfortunately, only one plasma-drenched Simian on parade here). Cat-suited cutie Norma Lazareno, who looks like a refugee from Skin 2 magazine, is relegated to a sub-plot concerning her lack of confidence after hurling one of her opponents out of the ring and into a coma, while her cop boyfriend (Armando Silvestre from WRESTLING WOMEN Vs THE AZTEC MUMMY) gets on with the sleuthing.

Lazarenzo's comatose opponent comes under the tender loving care of Dr Kraumann

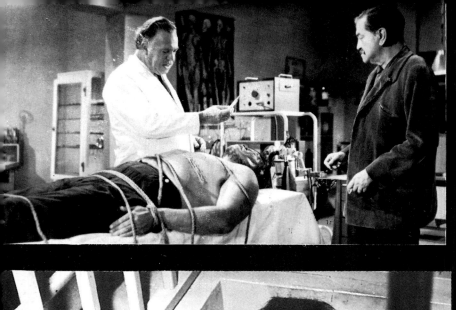

THE SEDUCTION OF THE GULLIBLE

(Jose Elias Moreno), who then learns that his son Julio is dying of Leukemia (pronounced "Loose-seam-ia"). He and his crippled assistant Goyo hot foot it to the local zoo (well, the crippled assistant does the best he can), to tranquilise and kidnap an Orang-utan which, by the miracle of not-so special effects, has become a man in a shabby gorilla suit by the time they get it back to their lab.

The good doctor announces that science has given up on Julio, but he'll be able to patch him up, just as he did for Goyo (not boding too well for Julio, I would have thought), and together they transplant the ape's heart into the body ("Come" deadpans Dr K: "…help me carry the cadaver of the gorilla to the incinerator.") For Julio's life-saving operation, Cordona cuts in documentary shots of actual heart surgery, and those who aren't so wimpish as to run screaming from the room at the sight of palpitating innards might stop to ponder where the phantom pair of hands came from – several mitts are seen paddling around in the chest cavity, while Dr Kraumann and Goyo seem only to have been equipped with the regulation two each.

Unfortunately the op's side-effects aren't exactly the kind you can gloss over – by means of inept lap dissolves Julio puts on about 100lbs and his once-handsome features begin to take on a distinctly neanderthal aspect. For good measure, his craggy visage appears to have been daubed with a thick coating of excrement. Heading out on a happy-go-lucky stroll, Julio spots a chubby senorita flaunting her towel-clad form in the window of her apartment. He climbs up the wall and ravishes her, though his ravishing style is cramped somewhat by an incongruous gallantry that compels him to stop and hitch up her towel every time it threatens to slip and compromise her modesty.

"I was prepared for everything but this" comments the doc, tranquilising Julio and taking him back to the lab. But Julio soon escapes and bushwacks a couple of young lovers out walking in the park, ripping his throat out and her dress off. There's a memorable shot (repeated several times) of the girl running towards the camera with her right breast hanging out and wobbling wildly, but when she dashes into a shop screaming for help her dress is all in one piece again. A chivalrous shopper who responds to her pleas for help is stabbed to death by Julio, who rounds off a very successful evening by subjecting an innocent bystander to the phoniest eye-gouging in movie history. A lady who stumbles upon this gory spectacle runs around in a traumatised state screaming "Oh! A dead man … a dead man … a dead man … a dead man!"

In an inspired fit of deductive reasoning, our man Armando tells his superior that, absurd as it may sound, these grisly crimes have been committed by a man who has mutated into an ape ("It could only happen in this century"). "I'll say it's absurd" scoffs the police chief, his lips flapping frantically in a vain attempt to keep up with the deranged dubbing: "…the proofs are insubstantial. It's more probable of late that more and more you've beenwatching on your television many of those pictures of terror!" Meanwhile, Dr Kraumann has been having his own moments of inspiration. He discards the ape heart and replaces it with that of the comatose lady wrestler (real op footage again). Does this second operation transform Julio into one of Las Luchadoras? No, that would be far too sensible! Instead, he goes ape again, pulling Goyo's head off (no great loss, really). The doc tries to stop Julio going on another kill spree and is injured in the process, so Julio tenderly tucks him up in bed, before embarking on his "last hurrah". He scalps a guy he meets walking down the street (pulling off his toupée to reveal a bald pate smothered in strawberry jam) then kidnaps a little girl and mooches around the rooftops of the city with her until the police close in on him. Julio's father arrives at the scene to remonstrate with him, but any poignancy that this scene might have had is scuppered by Julio's apish attempts to communicate, which closely resemble the yowlings of a cat on heat. Predictably, Julio releases his bored-looking hostage and is shot down by the police, bringing the curtain down on all this maniacal monkey business.

Current Status: Uncut version banned. Re-released by VIPCO with cuts

Warning–this film contains scenes of extreme and explicit violence

NIGHT
—OF THE—
DEMON

IFS

THE SEDUCTION OF THE GULLIBLE

NIGHT OF THE DEMON. U.S.A., 1980. Video label: Iver Film Services. Starring Michael J. Cutt, Joy Allen, Bob Collins, Jodi Lazarus, Richard Fields, Michael Lang, Melanie Graham. Special effects: Susan Brott. Written by Jim L. Ball and Mike Williams.Camera: John Quick. Produced by Jim L. Ball. Directed by James C. Wasson.

The IFS release of this one drew attention to itself with a sleeve warning: "this film contains scenes of extreme and disturbing violence" (not to mention lengthy scenes of people wandering around doing nothing in particular, plus some of the most ludicrous and inept gore FX in living memory). Opening with the bed-ridden and heavily-bandaged Professor Nugent telling his doctors "… about what's going on in that forest!", the chaotically-structured narrative proceeds to a series of flash-backs unfolding inside of flash-backs.Such plot as can be distilled from all of this runs as follows: Professor Nugent leads a team of anthropology students into some woods where Sasquatch sightings have been reported. As mentioned above, there's then lots of aimless wandering around, prompting one of the students, in an eerie anticipation of audience reaction, to comment: "I wish we could forget all this shit and go fishing." Thankfully all this tedium is punctuated by outbreaks of the graphic and ridiculous violence described above – a wood chopper is chopped up with his own axe; a silicone stuffed cutie and her beau are snotted while snogging in the back of his van; two girls are bear-hugged and simultaneously stabbed to death by the Sasquatch (the first good look we get at this alleged wild man of the woods, a tall high school kid with the remnants of a sliced-up fur coat gummed to his back, arms and legs); a camper is swung around and around in his sleeping bag, then flies off into the forest and ends up bloodily impaled on a branch; best of all, a biker relieves himself in a bush only for the Sasquatch to leap out, grab his manhood and swing him around by it!

Deep in the forest, the survivors discover "Crazy Wanda"s cabin. Wanda is a catatonic mute who, legend has it, gave birth to a monstrous baby, causing her fundamentalist father to burn himself to death at this "sign of Satan". Wanda throws a fit when shown a plaster cast of Bigfoot's big foot-print, so Professor Nugent calms her down with a spot of hypnotism. While under the influence, she speaks the truth about what happened between her, her Pa and the Sasquatch (cue yet another flashback) – she was raped by the Sasquatch ("as one last attempt to save its species from extinction," speculates the Prof), which then hung around outside the cabin awaiting the birth of its furry heir. Inside, her father whipped her ("I'm saving your soul, you ungrateful bitch") and attempted in vain to bring about an abortionl. When Wanda gave birth, her father killed the little critter, which so distressed her that she set fire to him. As a hysterical reaction to these terrible events, she lost the power of speech, and her father's followers went over to cannibalism and human sacrifice in honour of the Sasquatch, which they (for some reason best known to themselves) took to be the god Moloch. Immediately Moloch himself climbs in through the window and massacres everyone inside the cabin. Instead of making a run for it en masse, as though that would be somehow impolite, our heroes hold back in the manner of the bad guys in a martial arts movie, taking their chances one by one, each being trashed in their turn. Bigfoot disembowels one hapless dude and starts thrashing the others with his entrails, the first (and hopefully the last) intestine-whipping in screen history. Professor Nugent gets his face fried on a hot plate (thus the bandages), another guy's throat is cut on a jagged window-pane, a girl is bear-hugged to death, etc, etc, etc. All of this is rendered in slow motion (which hack directors always seem to believe capable of making silly things look scary) and to the accompaniment of irritating synthesizer belches andfarts.

Back in "the present", the Prof's doctors find his yarn a bit hard to swallow: "Unless his concept of reality changes, I'll have no alternative but to certify him as criminally insane." Rather harsh, considering that the Prof hasn't actually done anything criminal … which is more than can be said for the bozos who cobbled together this piece of junk!

Current Status: Uncut version banned. Re-released by VIPCO with cuts

ATLANTIS

She was lonely
He was all she had
No-one would take him from her —
and live.....

Named Best Horror Film
of 1982 by the Academy
of Science Fiction,
Fantasy, and Horror.

NIGHTMARE MAKER

THE SEDUCTION OF THE GULLIBLE

NIGHTMARE MAKER aka BUTCHER, BAKER, NIGHTMARE MAKER / THRILLED TO DEATH / MOMMA'S BOY / NIGHT WARNING. U.S.A., 1981. Video label: Atlantis. Starring Jimmy McNichol, Susan Tyrrell, Bo Svenson, Marcia Lewis, Julia Duffy, Britt Leach, Steve Eastin, Caskey Swaim, Cooper Neal, William Paxton. Special effects: Al Apone. Written by Stephen Breimer, Alan Jay Glueckman and Boon Collins. Produced by Stephen Breimer and Eugene Mazzola. Directed by William Asher.

"Madness and fanaticism add up to a vortex of blood that gives a new twist to the Oedipus story" screamed the pack. As the lousiest films tend to have the most lurid ad-lines, I wasn't exactly looking forward to NIGHTMARE MAKER, and I wasn't much reassuredby the fact that it had been named as "the best film of 1982" by the shadowy "Academy of SF, Fantasy and Horror". I was pleasantly surprised though, the picture being capably directed by William Asher (BEACH BLANKET BINGO, HOW TO STUFF A WILD BIKINI, 100 episodes of I LOVE LUCY...), even if its decidedly tame, TV movie content gives no clue as to why the DPP took such exception to it. Possibly the blood-stained lady on the cover was to blame (with more understated packaging I can't imagine that anyone would even have noticed NIGHTMARE MAKER). Perhaps it was tainted by association with that other Atlantis release, FACES OF DEATH?

The story tackles several - probably too many - social issues head on. "Little Billy"s parents leave him in the care of his Auntie (Susan Tyrell), who cares for him so much that she has drained the brake fluid from mom and dad's car, which crashes into the back of a lorry and decapitates them, leaving Auntie to adopt him. Fourteen years on, Billy (Jimmy McNichol) is a high-school kid who seems to spend all his time playing basketball. His over-protective Aunt is jealous of his relationship with pretty Julie (Marcia Lewis) but not above attempting to seduce a TV repair man. When he recoils from her superannuated advances she stabs him to death in a fit of pique. Billy arrives home to witness his death throes and is persuaded by his Aunt to tell the police that he discovered the TV repair man raping her and stabbed him to defend her. Homophobic redneck Lieutenant Carlson, played by big bad Swedish meatball Bo Svenson (I'd be more worried about the prospect of a clip round the ear from Bo Derek) hatches an alternative theory and pursues it, "Columbo"-style. Noting that high-school basketball coach Caskey Swaim and the dead man were lovers, and that Billy is the coach's star pupil, he decides that Billy killed the guy due to involvement in a gay eternal triangle. As the complicated plot thickens, macho Bo gets the wrong end of the stick at every turn, just like Arthur Kennedy in LIVING DEAD AT THE MANCHESTER MORGUE. Julie works out that Billy's Aunty is the real culprit when she discovers the skeletal remains of Aunty's ex-lover (for whom Billy has been serving as the substitute in her mind) down in the cellar (shades of PSYCHO here). Auntie chases Julie through the woods with a macheté (TEXAS CHAINSAW MASSACRE being the influence in this scene) but the young lovers manage to do away with her and also with Lt. Carlson, just as he is on the point of blowing Billy away. The "true story" epilogue casts doubt on its own veracity by revealing that "the jury unanimously acquitted Billy on the grounds of temporary insanity." I'm sceptical that a jury would deal so leniently with a cop-killer.

Performances are OK throughout, though Svenson's queer-bashing cop is played so meatily as to verge on ham. Joyce Bulifant's theme song "Little Boy Billy" could drive you right up the wall. NIGHTMARE MAKER is not a bad little film, if a little over- earnest. To see how its perverse themes could have been better developed, check out Lamberto Bava's superficially similar but altogether more accomplished MACABRE (1980).

Current Status: Removed from DPP list. Re-submitted to BBFC (as THE EVIL PROTECTOR) but refused a certificate

NIGHTMARE MAKER

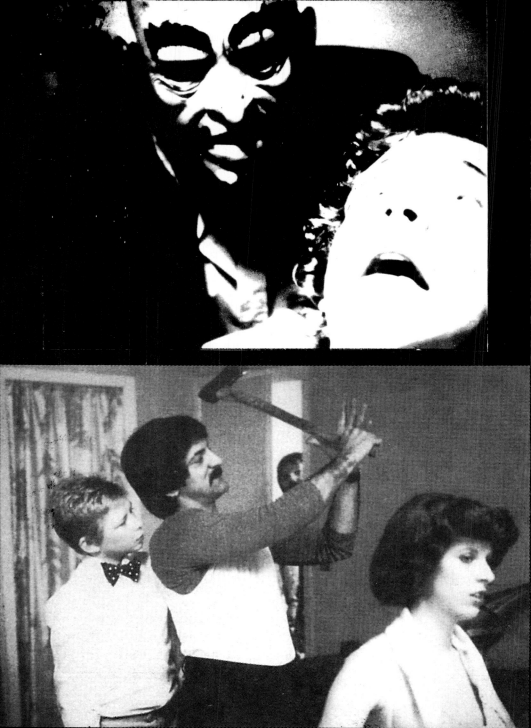

THE SEDUCTION OF THE GULLIBLE

NIGHTMARES IN A DAMAGED BRAIN aka NIGHTMARE / DARK GAMES. U.S.A., 1981. Video label: World of Video 2000. Starring Baird Stafford, Sharon Smith, C.J. Cooke, Mik Cribben, Danny Ronen, John Watkins, William Milling, Scott Praetorius, William S. Kirksey, Christina Keefe. Special effects: William Milling, Les Larrain, Ed. French. Camera: Gianni Fiore. Co-Produced by John L. Watkins and William Milling. Written and directed by Romano Scavolini.

NIADB is a film that has been dogged by more than its fair share of controversy, most notoriously when David Hamilton Grant was jailed for distributing it on video in the U.K. (although it had already played theatrically, with 60 seconds of cuts, on a double bill with Alfred Sole's COMMUNION). Previously, make-up FX ace Tom Savini had taken legal action to stop the film being hyped in America with what he represented as the spurious claim that he had been its FX technician (though Luca Palmerini's "Spaghetti Nightmares" tome reproduces a shot of Savini setting up an effect on the film's set). The World of Video 2000 release was promoted with a tacky, ill-received "Guess the weight of the real human brain in a jar" competition and the film's theatrical premiere was marked by the distribution of vomit bags, warnings in the foyer about its gruelling nature and ambulance-men conspicuously in attendance. It's difficult to avoid the conclusion that the unfortunate Mr Hamilton Grant eventually reaped what was sown by these wildly over-the-top promotional tactics.

As though in an attempt to distance itself from such buffoonery, the film bears the pretentious handle "SCAVOLINI'S NIGHTMARES IN A DAMAGED BRAIN" in its titles, establishing a subliminal and completely spurious link with such respectable Art-house fare as FELLINI SATYRICON. In fact, director Romano Scavolini's pedigree is more porno grind-house than Art-house, and it shows in every harshly-lit, statically-composed frame. Things kick off in slammo-bammo style, with brain-damaged George Tatum (Baird Stafford) dreaming that his bed is full of squirming female body parts. Trussed up in a strait-jacket, screaming his head off, George hardly comes across as a model of mental health, but his psychiatric custodians seem pleased enough with his progress under their loving care, to which he was consigned as "chief suspect in the sexual molestation and murder of a Brooklyn family."

Despite such trivial considerations as his amnesia, dream-fixations, seizures, schizophrenia and homicidal tendencies, George is let out on the streets. His first priority is to check out a few live sex shows, where the peep show dancers are intercut with flashbacks to his childhood discovery of pop trussed to the bed and being energetically ridden by a dominatrix, to which young George responded by grabbing a handy-dandy axe and dispensing a double dose of the Lizzie Borden treatment (predictably, most of the moral apoplexy generated by N.I.A.D.B. centred on this scene). George's next step on the sex-show circuit is to treat himself to a phone conversation with a dildo-wielding floozy who sits on the other side of a glass partition, driving our psychotic hero to such paroxysms of lust that he ends up writhing around on the floor, foaming at the mouth.

Having regained his composure, George slits a woman's throat, steals her car and makes for Daytona Beach, where he starts harassing his ex-wife Suzanne (Sharon Smith) by phoning her up a lot and generally hanging around the place looking menacing. His obnoxious, ever-smirking son "C.J." (C.J. Cooke) warns mom about the lurking loony, but is ignored due to his well-known penchant for tiresome practical jokes. When ticked off over one of these, the little rascal screams: "Nanny, nanny, boo boo, stick your head in doo doo" ... clearly this kid needs a good clip around the ear!

THE SEDUCTION OF THE GULLIBLE

George turns up at the window in a photo boyfriend Bob has taken of the house ("It's just like that Antonioni film, BLOW UP!" gibbers Bob, an obvious acid casualty). George rings one of his psychiatrists and complains that the dreams are taking over again, but the shrink reassures him that everything will be OK. Guess again, doc – George throws another fit, chews the carpet a bit, goes out and murders another girl, then drops in on Suzanne's place to give her a piece of his mind. Suzanne and hippy Bob have gone to a "business party" and the baby-sitter has invited her boyfriend over for a little party of their own. George registers his indignation at their promiscuous, dope-smokin' ways in the approved psychotic fashion (strangulation for him, ball-peen hammer battering for her). C.J. packs his kid sisters off to safety and breaks out the family rifle to blow holes in his dad. Predictably, it takes a lot of holes to put him down. All of this is intercut with George's youthful axe antics, reminding us that C.J. is just carrying on an honourable family tradition. Indeed, the final shot suggests that this smirking brat is now destined for a murderous career of his own. Thankfully we never got to find out, because after all the hassles associated with N.I.A.D.B, nobody was going to touch a sequel with a barge-pole.

Hamilton Grant's imprisonment for the heinous crime of distributing NIGHTMARES IN A DAMAGED BRAIN is particularly ironic in view of the Queen's Award to Industry that was handed out to Hammer Films in 1968. Hammer's THE GORGON (1964) and PLAGUE OF THE ZOMBIES (1966) had featured shocking decapitation sequences, and it is profoundly disturbing to consider that something which merited a Queen's Award in 1968 could result in confinement at Her Majesty's pleasure a decade-and-a-half later. Ah well, that's progress for you...

Current status: Banned

ISABELLE ADJANI   SAM NEILL

POSSESSION

un film de
ANDRZEJ ZULAWSKI

HEINZ BENNENT   effets spéciaux   CARLO RAMBALDI

images de BRUNO NUŸTTEN   musique de ANDRZEJ KORZYNSKI   directeur de production JEAN-JOSÉ RICHER

THE SEDUCTION OF THE GULLIBLE

POSSESSION. France/West Germany, 1981. Video label: Video Tape Center. Starring Isabelle Adjani, Sam Neill, Margit Carstensen, Heinz Bennent, Johanna Hofer, Michael Hogben. Special Effects: Carlo Rambaldi. Camera: Bruno Nuytten. Produced by Marie-Laure Reyre. Written and directed by Andrzej Zulawski.

Secret agent Marc (Sam Neill) and ballet tutor Anna (Isabelle Adjani) live with their son Bob (Michael Hogben) in pre-Glasnost Berlin, a city whose divisions and bleak ambience is reflected in their floundering marriage. Marc tells his paymasters that he's packing it all in to patch things up with his wife, but arrives home to find that she's taken things into her own hands and taken up with somebody (and I use the term advisedly) else. Marc goes calling on Heinrich (Heinz Bennent), with whom Anna has previously had an affair, but Heinz insists (after handing out a particularly bloody kung-fu lesson to Marc) that he hasn't seen Anna for weeks. Marc next enlists the aid of a private detective, who tracks Anna down to an apartment where he catches a glimpse of her secret lover, a slimy squid monster, before being killed by a broken bottle brandished by Anna.

What's sauce for the cheating goose is sauce for the gander, so Marc embarks on an affair with one of Bob's teachers, a dead ringer for Anna (played by Adjani in a wig and green contact lenses). A second private detective goes in search of the first one, who was his boyfriend, and discovers his body in Anna's apartment. He also discovers the monster. He shoots at Anna, who throws a fit and beats him over the head with a glass of milk, then shoots him dead. Heinrich is the next guy to beat a path to Anna's door. He tries to force his attentions on her, but his ardour cools when he spots the monster. Nor is he too keen on the private detective's head he finds in the fridge. Anna stabs him, then strips naked for her octopus, which is starting to look progressively more humanoid. Heinrich staggers to a phone-box to warn Marc about what's going on. Marc shows his gratitude by going round to Heinrich's place, torching it, drowning him in the toilet bowl (after telling him that his Yin-Yang balls are hanging from his Zen brain) and dancing a victory jig in the street. Marje, a family friend with her leg in a cast, turns up at Marc and Anna's apartment, apparently dying (another victim of the octopus). Marc slips a convenient body bag over her and then saunters over to Anna's new apartment, where he finds the saucy cephalopod giving her the benefit of its ninth tentacle.

Meanwhile Marc's absence from the world of international espionage is apparently hastening the onset of World War III. "Help us take care of a drowning world!" pleads his erstwhile spy boss,only to be told: "I met a man who loved everything and he ended up drowning in a flood of shit". "That's just details" insists the spy boss (well, maybe so, but presumably significant ones for the poor guy drowning in a torrent of turds). Now Marc goes into a monologue about the death of a dog he had when he was a boy. "So what?" interrupts the other man, not without some justification. Marc shoots some policemen, tears off on a motor-bike, crashes it, then confronts Anna and lover-boy, who has evolved into his doppelganger. Various police and/or secret agents turn up and mow down Marc and Anna, who are reconciled in a final, bloody, death-rattling kiss. Octoman survives to pay a visit on Marc's lover and his son, just as the Apocalypse breaks out. She seems quite pleased that the nukes are raining down, but little boy Bob takes self-preservative action ... he fills the bath with water and jumps in. So that's the plot of POSSESSION ... straight-forward really, isn't it?

Polish emigre Andrezej Zulawski's film represents a head-on collision between the European Art-house and Horror traditions (it might be helpful for the uninitiated to try and imagine how KRAMER VERSUS KRAMER might have turned out if directed by David Lynch from a screenplay by Arthur Janov), and the fall-out from this collision leaves

POSSESSION

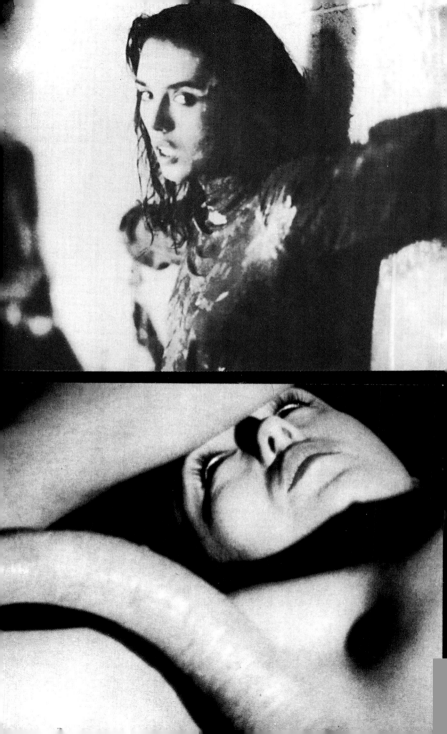

none of the participants unscathed. The principals (all bar the amorous octopus, who gives the most restrained performance in the picture) rant, rave and routinely throw fits, smashing up their surroundings and mutilating themselves, sometimes as the climax to one of their interminable debates about God, life, love and infidelity, sometimes for no apparent reason at all, and when Adjani starts ricocheting off the walls of a metro station and rolling around in the fluid that spews from her every orifice, she's apparently suffering a miscarriage. Reportedly, in the full-length version of POSSESSION (127 minutes as opposed to the British 122 – Americans had to settle for an 81-minute remnant), this astonishing scene is twice as protracted, with Adjani's body-slamming, bile-spraying antics running for a full ten minutes. "You come away from POSSESSION feeling destroyed" Adjani has said: "Zulawski's work is beyond movies. He's got no inhibitions. He doesn't obey any rules in terms of society, in terms of sin. He's got his own opinion of the devil, and it makes sense ... even if it's crazy."

Pretentious? Well, maybe, but Zulawski's film can't, in all fairness, be bracketed with those other blots on the copy-books of Neill and Adjani, OMEN 3 and the Hoffman/Beatty bomb ISHTAR. It's a lot harder to watch but at the same time a lot less cynical than either of those, testifying to some kind of crazed personal vision on the part of its creator, and we should perhaps applaud Zulawski's obstinacy while deploring his obscurantism. It's safe to say that POSSESSION is quite unlike anything you've ever seen anywhere else, though most wouldn't care to repeat this particular viewing experience again. Ironic, isn't it, that Zulawski should move from an Eastern-bloc country to the West in search of greater artistic freedom, only for his film to get bogged down in this kind of shit in the Mother of Western democracy, where – to compound that irony – POSSESSION had actually already been televised on Channel 4.

Sam ... star role

Sam film is branded a 'nasty'

A FILM starring TV heart-throb Sam Neil was branded a video nasty yesterday.

For the highlight of the movie Possession showed a woman making love to an octopus, a jury was told.

Police seized more than 600 cassettes of the film from CBS headquarters in West Kensington, London, Knightsbridge Crown Court heard.

Prosecuting counsel Thomas Richardson told the jury: "This is a film, set in Berlin, which you may find either highly artistic or deadly boring.

"There comes eventually a moment in the film when you will see a woman and some kind of octopus with long tentacles in simulated sexual intercourse."

The distributors of the video, Capital VTC, deny having an obscene article for gain.

The trial **continues.**

OCTOPUS CLEARED

A VIDEO of the award-winning film Possession was cleared of an obscenity charge by jurors at Knightsbridge Crown Court yesterday. The defence said a scene showing a woman and an octopus-like monster was not obscene because no one could possibly go out and imitate it.

Current Status: Removed from DPP list. Re-released by VTC after acquittal

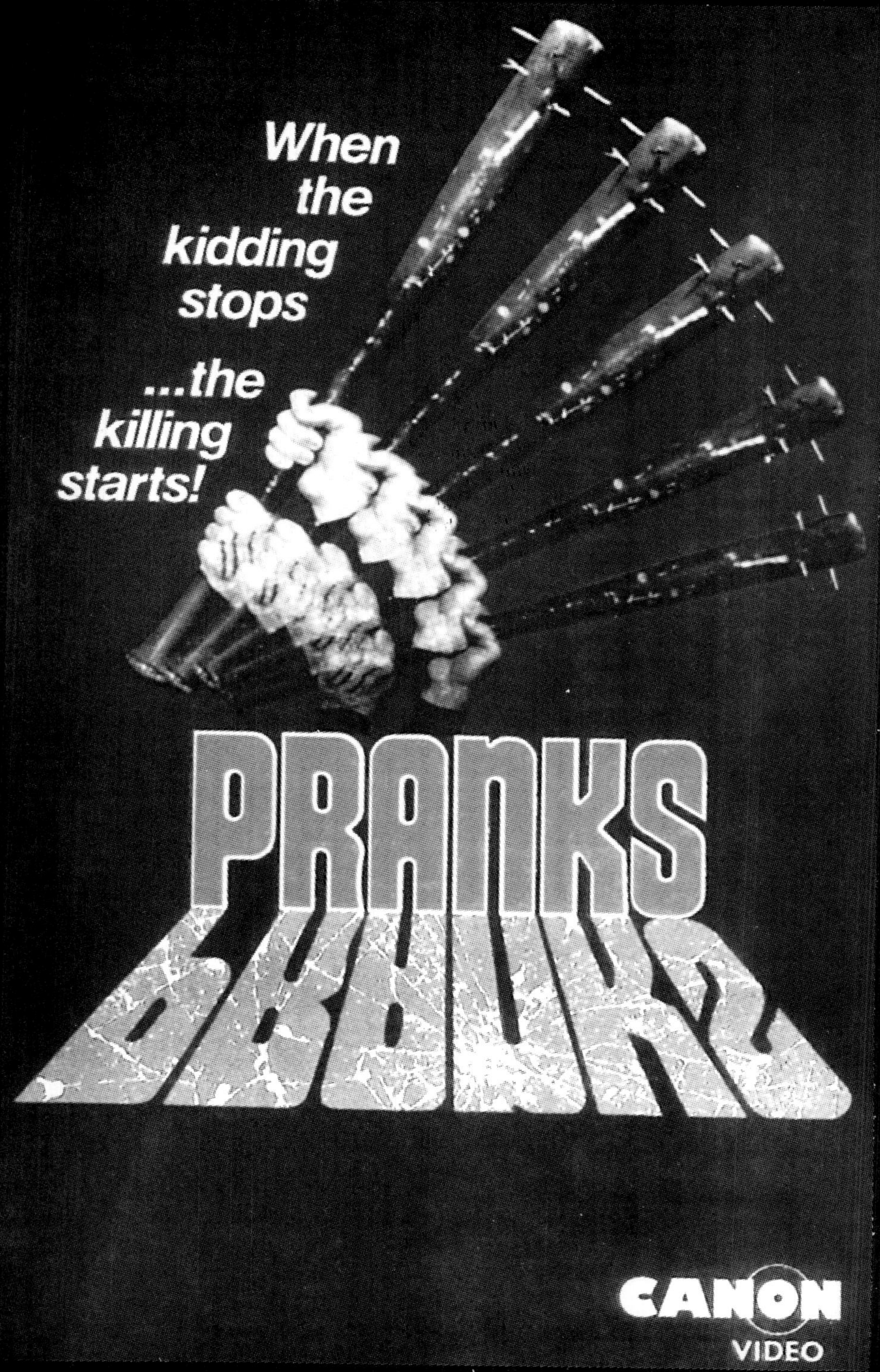

When
the
kidding
stops

...the
killing
starts!

PRANKS

CANON
VIDEO

PRANKS aka THE DORM THAT DRIPPED BLOOD. U.S.A., 1982. Video label: Canon Video. Starring Laurie Lapinksi, Stephen Sachs, David Snow, Daphne Zuniga. Make-up effects: Mathew Mungle. Camera: Stephen Carpenter. Written by Jeff Obrow and Stacey Giachino. Produced by Jeff Obrow. Directed by Jeff Obrow and Stephen Carpenter.

When five college kids stay behind at the end of term to close up their obsolete dorm, a zany time will be had by all, right? But like it says on the pack, "when the kidding stops, the killing starts", and kids as smart as this should have realised that such a set-up would act as a magnet to passing psycho-killers. The psycho-killer in question serves notice that he is not pussy-footing around by offing a whole family – dad gets a spiked club in the face and mom is garotted in their car, which is then used to run over their daughter (Decent Americans 0, Psycho-killer 3). Nicely tuned up, this nut case then heads off to clean up the dorm, power-drilling his way into the head of one student and boiling another in an indutrial-sized stew-pot.

So just who is responsible for all these desperate acts? Leading suspects are Emmett (the fat and greasy class-klutz) and a randy furniture removal man who's got the hots for Joanne (Laurie Lapinksi), our heroine. After discovering a bloody torso in the broom closet, Joanne stabs Emmett (who continues to stagger after her, begging to be heard) and finally kills him with the aid of Craig (Stephen Sachs), another of the surviving students. At this point Craig announces that the psycho-killer is none other than himself, a plot-point whose sole justification seems to be the fact that Craig has been such an anonymous character so far, no-one in the audience will have guessed that he's the culprit. His rationale for this kill-spree is equally flimsy—he's got a crush on Joanne and was jealous of everyone else (mitigating circumstances if ever I heard them, M'Lud).

His removal-man rival turns up for a climactic punch-up, during which the police arrive and order the good guy to turn around slowly and keep quiet or they'll kill him. The prostrate loony shows him a knife and informs him that as soon as he turns around he's "a dead man". It's a no win situation and when the removal man tries to extricate himself from it, the cops gun him down (this is easily the most well-wrought and suspenseful sequence in the picture). When the police leave – apparently not wishing to question Craig about the pile of bodies – he collects Joanne's unconscious body, carries it to the basement incinerator (mumbling endearments) and immolates it. The cops, on their way out, complain to each other about the terrible smell (of Joanne's burning body, as it happens!)

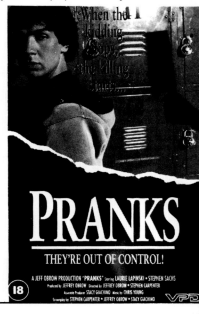

Obrow & Carpenter made the show-reel DEATH DORM in 1982 hawking it around investors and raising enough money to shoot PRANKS. THE EVIL DEAD was financed the same way. For all their drive though, Obrow & Carpenter taken together don't amount to one Sam Raimi.

Current status - re-issued by VPD, with cuts

PRISONER OF THE CANNIBAL GOD aka *SLAVE OF THE CANNIBAL GOD / LA MONTAGNA DEL DIO CANNIBALE. Italy, 1978. Video label: Hokushin. Starring Ursula Andress, Stacy Keach, Claudio Cassinelli, Antonio Marsina, Franco Fantasia, Lanfranco Spinola, Carlo Longhi, Dudley Wanagura. Camera: Giancarlo Ferrando. Written by Sergio Martino and Cesare Frugoni. Produced by Luciano Martino. Directed by Sergio Martino.*

PRISONER OF THE CANNIBAL GOD was made before CANNIBAL HOLOCAUST, and lacks the precise moral focus of that film and its imitators, throwaway lines about rapacious uranium prospectors exploiting the natives notwithstanding. "New Guinea is perhaps the last region on Earth which contains immense unexplored areas" according to the identikit prologue, but this is hard to believe, what with these Italian film crews all over the place. Sprinkled among the rampant stock footage we find Ursula Andress searching for her husband, who went missing while leading an expedition into the interior (this would appear to happen with monotonous regularity) and Stacy "Mike Hammer" Keach searching for the last of the Pooka tribe in an attempt to exorcise the memory of forced cannibalism — "You don't ... forget ... the taste ... of human flesh!" gasps Keach in a spectacular display of over-acting reminiscent of Richard Burton at his most maniacal. They set off for "The Mountain of the Cannibal God" (a god who eats gods? Surely some mistake here). En route they encounter a lot of cruelty to animals — a lizard is sliced open to the accompaniment of flaming bongos and farting synthesizers, but the organs that are supposedly pulled out of it are clearly those of a much larger animal, as if those nature equipped it with were simply not good enough for the exacting eye of director Martino. The ALF would be equally put out at the sight of a turtle involved in a life-or-death struggle with a crocodile, a situation so ludicrous that it was obviously contrived by chucking a turtle at the first passing crocodile.

Eventually they find the Pooka, but soon wish they hadn't. The eponymous cannibal god turns out to be Ursula's old man, putrefying noticeably. The Pooka thoughtfully daub his decomposing flesh all over Ursula's face, then she is washed in blood and decked out very fetchingly in feather head-dress and a leather outfit by Albanese, a designer-house that seems to have the Papuan cannibal concession sewn up. Ursula escapes and there is a predictable chase through treacherous jungle, with Pooka hiding behind every tree and jumping out of every river. She finally makes it home, a sadder and wiser woman (she'll never work for Martino again!) Joking aside, dependable genre-hopping journey-man Martino dislays his usual sure hand with sub-"Boy's Own" type yarns of stirring derring-do (see also his ISLAND OF THE FISHMEN, 1978 and THE GREAT ALLIGATOR, 1980) without ever really troubling the intellect, *a la* Deodato, or the stomach, *a la* Lenzi.

Current Status: Removed from DPP list. Deleted from Hokushin catalogue

PAGE # 149

PRISONER OF THE CANNIBAL GOD

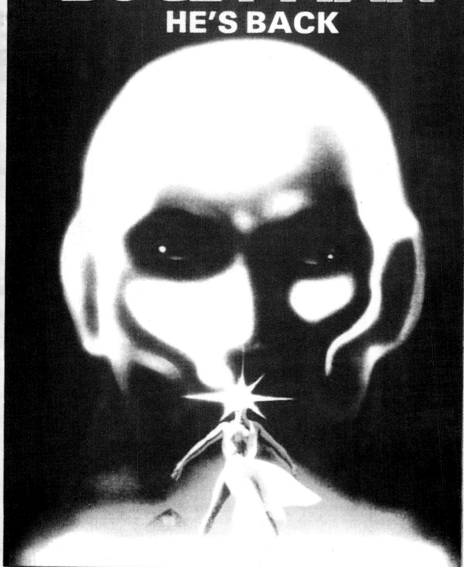

REVENGE OF THE BOGEY MAN
HE'S BACK

THE SEDUCTION OF THE GULLIBLE

REVENGE OF THE BOGEYMAN aka REVENGE OF THE BOOGEYMAN / BOOGEYMAN 2
U.S.A., 1982. Video label:Video Tape Center. Starring Suzanna Love, Shannah Hall,
Ulli Lommel, Shoto van Douglas, Bob Rosenfarb, Ahley Dubay, Rhonda Aldrich,
Sarah Jean Watkins, Rock Mackenzie. (In flashbacks): John Carradine, Ron James,
Nicholas Love, Felicite Morgan, Bill Rayburn, Llewelyn Thomas. Camera: Philippe
Carr-Foster, David Sperling, Special effects: CMI Ltd., Craig Foster. Written by Ulli
Lommel and Suzanna Love. Produced by Ulli Lommel and Bruce Starr. Directed by
Bruce Starr.

The original BOGEYMAN made big bucks for the ubiquitous Jerry Gross organisation. Lommel hesitated over making a sequel ("For fear of exploiting myself") but: "Then one day some financiers came to see me and said 'Here's half a million dollars. We don't care what you do, just make sure it's called BOGEY MAN 2'." Only it isn't, it's called REVENGE OF THE BOGEY MAN (1982). According to Lommel, it's autobiographical: A Hollywood producer is making a film about The Bogey Man and throws a party with pieces of that mirror as its centre-piece – "It is during thesefestivities that The Bogey Man makes his reappearance and kills everyone" (not beating about the bush eh?) "... I love the central idea of The Bogey Man not wanting to be exploited." Lommel is keen not to exploit himself, not to have his brainchild exploited, but doesn't seem so fussy about exploiting the public: THE REVENGE OF THE BOGEY MAN shamelessly re-uses footage from the first film (what on earth did they spend half a million on?), for which reason it too ended up on the "Nasties" list. Part 1 survivor Lacey (Suzanna Love, Ulli Lommel's real-life main squeeze) is lured out to Hollywood by her old schoolfriend Bonnie (Shannah Hall), who suggests that "a little therapy, some yoga and a few vitamins" will help her to overcome her ordeal. Once Lacey is out there, Bonnie starts pumping the gory details of that ordeal out of her for the benefit of her director husband Mickey Lombard (Lommel), who is planning to make a schlocky movie about the whole thing. Cue miles and miles of footage from the original movie – all your old favourites are trotted out, including those ludicrous designer deaths and a consultation with doctor of psychiatry John Carradine (consider that THE BOGEYMAN and BOGEYMAN 2 count as two different credits on Carradine's C.V., then take a look at some of his "appearances" in Jerry Warren movies and you begin to understand how the old boy's filmography came to be such an epic one).

Lacey has kept a piece of the original Boogey mirror, and insists that nobody but she must touch it, but Josef the butler gets his hands on the shard, causing Bruce Starr's camera to start bouncing around the walls of the house and Bonnie's daughter to start having nightmares about "the Boogeyman". He eventually shows up at a party thrown to help clinch the deal for the movie about him, and in his inimitable heavy-breathing P.O.V. style he bumps off the revellers with bottle openers, barbeque tongs, shaving foam, electric toothbrush and boring old garden shears. One girl has a car exhaust pipe rammed into her mouth and chokes on its emissions in a macabre parody of fellatio. With everybody else wiped out, Lombard and Bonnie take Lacey home to Maryland to visit her parents' grave. While she pays her respects they wait in the car. Bonnie tells Lombard it's a drag that the Boogie movie is now a non-starter. He insists that it's now more of a go-project than ever, at which point the Boogeyman's hand shoots out of the grave clutching a fragment of mirror and Lombard's car blows up. That's all, folks!!!

Lommel tries to use his previous collaborations with Fassbinder and Warhol to pass this junk off as an arty "film about film-making". It ain't ... it's a cynical rip-off, and the barbs which he aims at John Carpenter and Brian de Palma are particularly ungracious considering how heavily the first BOGEYMAN leans on Carpenter's HALLOWEEN and how obviously the "shock" ending of this thing has been, er, inspired by de Palma's CARRIE. Interestingly though, just as the original NIGHTMARE ON ELM STREET series owes an unacknowledged debt to the first BOGEYMAN film, so WES CRAVEN'S NEW NIGHTMARE (Craven's effort to prolong the shelf-life of that lucrative franchise) bears an uncanny resemblance to the, er, "high concept" of this cheap-jack exploiter.

Current Status: Removed from DPP list. No re-release scheduled

Is it a Nightmare?
or is it . . .

The Slayer

THE SEDUCTION OF THE GULLIBLE

THE SLAYER. U.S.A., 1981. Video label: VIPCO. Starring Sarah Kendall, Frederick Flynn, Carol Kottenbrook, Alan McRae, Michael Holmes. Camera: Karen Grossman. Written by J.S. Cardone and William R. Ewing. Produced by William R. Ewing. Directed by J.S. Cardone.

A painter suffers a recurrent nightmare about being throttled by a bogeyman named "the Slayer". This nightmare dates back to her childhood, when her pet cat turned up throttled in the fridge. She received psychiatric treatment after this incident, which she blamed on the aforementioned Slayer. She and her husband, together with her brother and sister-in-law, fly out to a remote island for a holiday ("It's the sort of place people dream about" the pilot tells them). On the island she recognises many buildings and landmarks from her dreams, sensing that something terrible is going to happen, but she can't convince the others. Needless to say, they're killed off in various gruesome ways. Her husband gets his head slammed in an attic trap door and swings around, gurgling blood in a protracted close-up. The brother has a fishing hook cast into his throat and is reeled off into the surf. The sister-in-law gets a pitchfork through her breast.

As a storm breaks out, our heroine locks herself upstairs. Having worked out that her dreams are intruding on real life (shades of ELM STREET, but four years earlier than the Wes Craven biggie), she drinks gallons of coffee, chain-smokes and even burns herself with cigarettes to stay awake. She seems to drop off and is woken by somebody forcing entry. She shoots this guy in the chest with a flare-gun, realising as the house goes up in flames that she's just killed the pilot, who had come to rescue her. Then the front door opens and in steps the Slayer, its rather mannequin-like appearance ruining this intended boffo moment. Finally, there's a surreal epilogue with the heroine, reborn as a little girl, receiving a black cat as a Christmas present (shades of the cyclical conclusion to 1945's DEAD OF NIGHT). Unfortunately imaginative little touches like this fail to lift THE SLAYER above the level of mundane adequacy.

THE SLAYER

Current Status: Re-released by VIPCO "Cult Classics" with cuts

THE SEDUCTION OF THE GULLIBLE

SNUFF aka THE SLAUGHTER. U.S.A./Argentina, 1974. Video label: Astra Video. Camera: Roberta Findlay. Written and produced by Michael Findlay. Directed by Michael and Roberta Findlay.

I'm sure that bona-fide "snuff movis" do exist, but t here's no way that anybody would be so stupid as to try and secure mass, mainstream distribution for them. That there are people stupid enough to pretend that this is what they are doing, and others stupid enough to take them at their word, is proven beyond argument by the notorious case of SNUFF. What actually happened was that U.S. exploiter Alan Shackleton of Monarch Films bought the rights to a quickie piece of crap called THE SLAUGHTER, which Michael and Roberta Findlay had shot in Argentina during 1971. To "liven things up at the end", Shackleton then put up a further $5,000, with which Michael Findlay (whose C.V. also included SHRIEK OF THE MUTILATED and various porno flics, and who later lost his life in a TWILIGHT ZONE-type helicopter decapitation atop the Pan-Am Building) filmed a palpably phoney epilogue in which somebody bearing the vaguest of resemblances to one of the actresses is supposedly killed by people purporting to be the SLAUGHTER crew. The new "livened up" version was released as SNUFF and promoted as a "snuff movie", Shackleton even going so far as to hire actors to pose as F.B.I. officers and harass people queueing outside of 42nd Street grind-houses to see the damn thing, grilling them for information on its production (how they were supposed to be wiser on this score than the F.B.I. was a minor technicality cheerfully glossed over by the merry men from Monarch). Perpetuating the sordid scam, Merlin's American video release of SNUFF was hyped with the line "Too real to be simulated, too shocking to be ignored", until public outrage forced a change in advertising policy. Britain's Astra Video never sank to quite those depths, and amended the U.S. advertising line: "The film that could only be made in South America, where life is CHEAP!" to: "The original, legendary atrocity, shot and banned in New York", though liner notes on both sides of the Atlantic agreed on the fundamentals: "The actors and actresses who dedicated their lives to making this film were never seen or heard from again" (Astra's decision to continue these dubious tactics in Britain was an own goal for the industry comparable to Go Video's enlisting of Mary Whitehouse in their CANNIBAL HOLOCAUST promotion).

"Legendary atrocity" is actually a fair summary of SLAUGHTER / SNUFF's "merits. I'm sure the actors and actresses who dedicated their lives to making it never were seen again, and equally certain that this had more to do with their primitive levels of thespian attainment than with any untimely demises. The film opens with hideous escapees from Herschell Gordon Lewis's SHE DEVILS ON WHEELS, tearing around on motorbikes to the accompaniment of a feeble "Born to be Wild" sound-alike riff. They secure a hippy girlin handy-dandy foot-stocks and treat her to a radical pedicure performed with pliers. These hags are under the hypnotic control of a complete dork calling himself "Sat-an", who plies his cycle-slut acolytes with drugs to subordinate their wills to his own. It must take a lot of drugs to achieve this because Sat-an is about as charismatic as a piece of plasticine. "Each one of you must obey my commands or you must die" he announces in the heavily reverbed way he has of announcing these things: "You do not live for yourselves, only for me and through me." No prizes for guessing that all this acid fascism is leading up to the stalking and assassination of Sharon T … er, I mean, a pregnant movie star (How tasteless can you get?!?). The narrative plods on in turgid zoom-happy style, punctuated by Sat-an's interminable rantings about the new world order that his murderous master-plan will inspire, until things just peter out at a totally arbitrary point and Findlay's famous "snuff" footage kicks in. God knows what they spent the 5 grand on! The "victim" is seen hanging around on a film set, supposedly that of SLAUGHTER, when one of the crew suggests that they "go over to the bed and turn each other on". "What, with all these people here?" she protests, only to be told: "They'll be gone in a minute." Instead of going, the crew start filming the heavy-petting session, and when she protests again, they lop off her hand and pull offal from under her T-shirt. "Let's get out of here", urges one of the cuprits. Good idea boys, and don't come back, ok?

Current status: Banned

SNUFF

violences...cruautés...

LE CAMP DES FILLES PERDUES

avec

MARCHA CARVEN   PAOLA CORAZZI

Un film de SERGIO GARRONE

THE SEDUCTION OF THE GULLIBLE

S.S. EXPERIMENT CAMP aka LAGER SSADIS KASTRAT KOMMANDANTUR. Italy, 1976. Video label: Go Video. Starring Mircha Carven, Paola Corazzi, Giorgio Cerioni, Giovanna Mainardi, Serafino Profumo, Attilio Dottesio, Patrizia Melega. Written by Vinicio Marinucci, Sergio Garrone and Sergio Chiusi. Produced by Mario Caporali. Directed by Sergio Garrone.

Walking into my local video emporium one day in the early '80s (so much has happened in the meantime that those days now seem like a life-time ago), I was mortified at the sight of the poster for S.S. EXPERIMENT CAMP, a truly nauseating piece of art-work that contributed in no small measure to the outbreak of censorship mania that culminated in the stifling Video Recordings Act. With a poster like that, the film just had to be a harrowing catalogue of torture and degradation, right? Wrong! In spite of reviews to the contrary, all written by people who never actually saw the film, S.S. EXPERIMENT CAMP is, in the words of Martin Barker: 'the most pathetic of all the Nasties". The most harrowing thing in it is the title sequence's use of authentic photographs of skeletal Nazi victims, a sharp contrast with the well-fed "inmates" depicted in the film. Director Sergio Garrone's vision of a concentration camp owes more to Butlins than Belsen, with guards passing among the prisoners, handing out cigarettes.

There's even a hospital ward for those who fall sick! The experiments which are mentioned in the title actually consist of people fucking in giant fish tanks while scientists in white coats stand around taking notes.

The occasional torture scenes are thrown in almost grudgingly, and all the victims have to do to end their torment is swear allegiance to Adolf Hitler. One girl who refuses to participate in an orgy is dumped into a barrel of ice – "she's frigid, so let's make her frozen!" quips one of the guards. That's about it for atrocities … apart from the commandant's testicle transplant! He's shown, in a flash-back, picking up a Russian prostitute on the Eastern front and enjoying some serious fellatio, until she gives him the ol' "I spit out your gonads" treatment. That's right, he fell for the oldest trick in the video nasty book! When the cream of Aryan soldiery (a suspiciously Latin-looking bunch) are brought to the camp to participate in sex experiments, the castrated commandant starts viewing the hunkiest of them as a potential goolie donor. The guy is a sensitive soul when one of his comrades asks him if he's looking forward to the experiments, he replies: "I think every time you open your mouth you talk shit!" The other soldier ponders his reply for about five minutes, then blurts out: "Hey, I don't like that last remark you made … about shit!"

The commandant blackmails the camp's Jewish (!) doctor into performing the necessary transplant operation (rendered by hilarious shots of some unfortunate animal's sweet-meats wobbling around in a kidney bowl) after which our soldier boy experiences problems making love to his Jewish girlfriend (who bears a faint resemblance to Meryl Streep but that's the closest Garrone gets to SOPHIE'S CHOICE). He breaks into the commandant's office and shoots him, but not before muttering the immortal line: "OK you bastard… what have you done to my balls?" Yep, the dreaded S.S. EXPERIMENT CAMP actually turns out to be a comedy classic.

Current Status: Banned

TENEBRE

UN FILM DE
DARIO
ARGENTO

COLOR

ANTHONY
FRANCIOSA
DARIA
NICOLODI
JOHN
SAXON
Y LA PARTICIPACION DE
GIULIANO
GEMMA

> **TENEBRAE aka UNSANE / SHADOWS. Italy, 1982. Video label: Videomedia. Starring Anthony Franciosa, John Saxon, Guiliano Gemma, Daria Nicolodi, Christian Borromeo, John Steiner, Veronica Lario, Lara Wendel, Ania Pieroni. Written by Dario Argento and George Kemp. Special effects: Giovanni Corridori. Camera: Luciano Tovoli. Produced by Claudio Argento. Directed by Dario Argento.**

TENEBRAE turned out to be a throwback to the giallo genre for Argento, rather than the expected conclusion to his "Three Mothers" trilogy. No doubt he was disheartened by the critical response to that INFERNO and the miserable distribution it received in the U.S. at the hands of 20th Century Fox. The opening of TENEBRAE reads like an inversion or crossing out of events in its unsuccessful predecessor – like INFERNO it opens with a quotation from a book (extolling the joys of murder) but this time it's a crime thriller, "Tenebrae", whose author Peter Neal (Tony Franciosa) flies from New York to Rome to promote it, reversing Mark Elliot's journey. When he arrives he is informed by the police that a passage in his book has inspired a copy-cat razor killing, indeed that pages of it were found stuffed down the victim's throat. This victim, a sluttish petty thief, is portrayed by Ania Pieroni, who played a supernatural siren in INFERNO. The killer bombards Neal with phone calls and photos detailing his ongoing kill-spree – a feminist journalist (Mirella D'Angelo) who slammed Neal's work as pernicious sexism is razored to death along with her lesbian lover (after an epic Louma crane shot in which Argento's camera effortlessly circumnavigates every nook and cranny of their house, in one fluid take with no cuts), then a maid from his hotel, pursued by a vicious doberman, blunders into the killer's house. Discovered gathering evidence, she is butchered with an axe. The author turns detective, aided by his secretary Anne (Daria Nicolodi) and gopher Gianni (Christian Borromeo), their investigations given increased urgency by the killer's announcement that he will soon be ready to deal with "the great corrupter himself". Prime suspect is Christiano Berti (John Steiner), an uptight journalist who seems to be obsessed with Neal's writings, but this line of inquiry terminates when Berti becomes the next axe victim. Neal is back to square one and sightings of his fiancée Jayne (Veronica Lario), supposedly back home in New York, add to the mystery. Neal's agent Bulmer (John Saxon) is the next victim, stabbed to death in a busy shopping mall in broad daylight. Gianni, who witnessed Berti's death, becomes convinced that it contains the key with which to unlock the whole mystery, and returns to the scene of the crime, only to be garotted by the killer. Anne discovers that Jayne is staying in a villa outside of town and arranges to meet her there, setting up the mind-boggling finalé, a brilliantly choreographed dance of death involving a succession of devilish twists and the demise of just about everybody who hasn't already been killed off....

TENEBRAE, though technically mesmeric, is ia disappointingly retrograde step thematically after the experimentation of SUSPIRIA and INFERNO. Such a tactical retreat was perhaps inevitable following the commercial failure of the latter, and the lucrative stalk-and-slash cycle generated by the success of John Carpenter's HALLOWEEN (1978) cannot have escaped Argento's attention. TENEBRAE expands the tired "slasher" format to operatic proportions, but was released simultaneously too late to ride the crest of the slasher wave and just in time for a wave of censorship in Britain that saw Argento consigned to the DPP's blacklist along with a host of hack directors not fit to lace his Gucci loafers."Inspired" by the mindless violence of LA (where he himself was the victim of prolonged harassment by a disturbed fan) Argento announced the theme of TENEBRAE as "to kill for nothing – that is the horror of today", but contradicts himself by packing the film with convoluted motivations, pulp psychology and confusing kinky flashbacks (featuring the beautiful trans-sexual "Eva Robbins" aka Roberto). His most enigmatic comments on TENEBRAE claim that it is set in a depopulated world of the near future – repeated viewings reveal nothing that would bear this out, and as Argento has declined all opportunities to elaborate, one can only conclude that he is dissembling, trying to claim for his straightforward murder mystery a profundity which simply isn't there. Similarly, talky scene   intended as a refutation of the "sexism" charge, are nothing of the sort, merely stringing together a few platitudes about "Women's Lib".

> **Current Status: Planned re-release by Redemption Video has not materialised**

THE SEDUCTION OF THE GULLIBLE

**TERROR EYES aka NIGHTSCHOOL. U.S.A., 1980. Video label: Guild Home Video.
Starring Leonard Mann, Rachel Ward, Drew Snyder, Joseph R. Sicari, Nicholas
Cairis, Karen MacDonald, Annette Miller, Bill McCann, Margo Skinner, Elizabeth
Barnitz. Camera: Mark Irwin. Written by Ruth Avergon. Produced by Ruth Avergon
and Larry Bab. Directed by Ken Hughes.**

"The advantage of doing exploitation movies," Rachel Ward once reflected, " ... is that they happen so quickly and are out and gone so fast that you can get away with murder in them and it doesn't really matter because nobody really sees them." Famous last words – inclusion on the DPP's "Video Nasties" list brought TERROR EYES, and Ward's inept (to put it mildly) performance therein, to the attention of a far wider audience than it would normally have reached. Perhaps it was the spectre of TERROR EYES that drove poor Rachel into her short-lived "retirement".

Just in case the ghastly sub-Forrest Ackerman punning of the title hasn't already tipped you off, the opening sequence of TERROR EYES leaves you in no doubt that you're in for a slice of premium-grade turkey: A macheté-wielding psycho in full biker leathers and crash helmet (black leather gloves are usually considered quite sufficient) menaces a woman on a slowly-revolving merry-go-round, but instead of just getting off and running away, the woman is content to sit there pulling faces until she gets her head lopped off.

Police Lieutenant Judd Anderson (Leonard Mann) and his insufferable wise-cracking Armenian partner – who single-handedly proves that Armenians are not exactly on a par with the jews when it comes to ethnic humour – discover the missing bonce in a bucket of water. This being the second time that such an unlikely fate has befallen local anthropology students, the cops gate-crash a lecture by anthropology lecturer Professor Millet (Drew Snyder, an astonishing Ron Atkinson-lookalike) and find him showing slides from his holiday in New Guinea among the headhunters. All this, plus the fact that he tends to rant and rave, to anyone who will listen, about the savage that lurks beneath the thin veneer of civilisation in every man ... and still the thick-headed cops don't have him pencilled in as prime suspect.

As it happens, he's only a red-herring, but one would have thought that the question of his possible guilt might have crossed their minds. Anyway, when asked for his advice, the best he can manage is: "You know, I think you're dealing with a psychotic killer here". Give that man a big cigar! The coroner is equally prone to pronouncements of the gratingly obvious, e.g. "It's a neat job of decapitation – the head is completely severed from the body" ... well, yes, that's often the way with decapitation, isn't it?

THE SEDUCTION OF THE GULLIBLE

The killings continue, with heads turning up in ditches, round the U-bend in toilets and even in a pan of Irish stew. The killing of an aquarium attendant (during which the killer demonstrates a total disregard for the laws of reality by jumping out of a closet that he/she couldn't have possibly gotten into in the first place) provokes the following memorable exchange between the cops :

"The old head in the tank routine... it's weird."

"To do that he had to climb three flights of stairs, carrying the head... just to throw it in a fish tank."

"See... like I said... it's bizarre."

"The question is... why?"

"So what's the answer?"

"Beats me."

"Maybe the killer was a sailor and he thought she was some kinda mermaid."

(After lines of dialogue like that, few would complain if writer Ruth Avergon, who also produced this farrago, had her head submerged in a bucket of water).

Despite the presence of another red-herring, a peeping tom who spends most of his time shinning up drainpipes to spy on lesbians, anyone with two brain cells to rub together (which lets out the cops) can easily work out that the killer is actually Millet's nubile student girlfriend Eleanour Adjai (Ward). At the "climax" of the picture she reveals to him that she's having his baby and she has to decapitate any girls he might take a fancy to and immerse their heads, because that's the way things are done in New Guinea (sounds reasonable enough).

With the police closing in, the Prof. decides to take the rap, wheelying off on his motorbike and performing tiresome Evel Kenevel-style stunts until someone does us all a favour and runs him over. "Holy shit! Looks like his neck is broken!" opines the Armenian cop as the Professor lies in the road with his eyes crossed and what looks like Ribena dribbling out of his nostril. At the funeral Lt. Anderson (for whom the penny has finally dropped) collars Adjai and extracts a promise from her that "the ritual is over". But is it? In a yawn-inducing epilogue, Anderson gets into his car and is seemingly attacked by a macheté-wielding biker. Guess what? It s Armenia's number one practical joker. "Who did ya expect?" asks this merry prankster, "the headhunter?" No, lame brain, we expected you and we were dead right.

Two things make TERROR EYES bearable – the rib-cracking dialogue (I can't resist quoting another bit...

"Isn't head-hunting illegal, even for an anthropologist?"

"What's that supposed to mean?"

"Nothing, except I suddenly find myself up to my neck in heads – heads in duck ponds, heads in fish tanks, heads in buckets, and then I come here and find more heads")

and the presence of Ms. Ward, who looks quite wonderful even if she does drawl her lines like John Wayne on mogadon. She looks particularly wonderful in her shower scene, during which the Prof turns up and does what any red-blooded male would like to do with Ward in a shower ... he smears red powder paint all over her(!??). Ah well, whatever turns you on ...

The stalk 'n' slash flick was so much in vogue during the early '80s that some unlikely figures contributed to the genre. TERROR EYES was directed by Ken Hughes, whose CV also includes CROMWELL and CHITTY CHITTY BANG BANG ... and there's another sub-Forry Ackerman pun in there somewhere!

Current Status: Removed from DPP list. Re-released by Guild & VIPCO

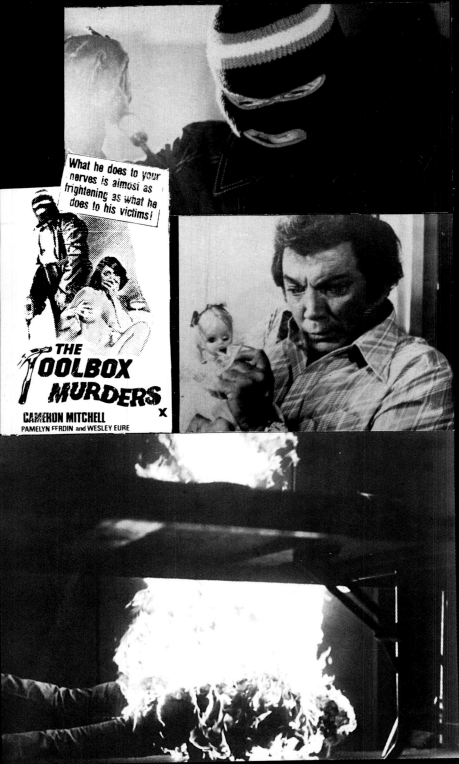

What he does to your nerves is almost as frightening as what he does to his victims!

THE TOOLBOX MURDERS

CAMERON MITCHELL
PAMELYN FERDIN and WESLEY EURE

X

THE SEDUCTION OF THE GULLIBLE

THE TOOLBOX MURDERS. U.S.A., 1978. Video label: Hokushin. Starring Cameron Mitchell, Pamelyn Ferdin, Wesley Eure, Nicholas Beauvy, Tim Donnelly, Aneta Corsaut, Faith McSwain, Marcie Drake. Camera: Gary Graver. Written by Neva Friedenn, Robert Easter, Ann Kindberg. Produced by Tony Didio. Directed by Dennis Donnelly.

In the summer of 1980 it occured to me that a new, mean spirit was abroad in the horror genre, characterized by a kind of film that routinely trotted out scenes of unconscionable violence with no pretence that it was doing so to make some spurious sociological point (as in DAWN OF THE DEAD) or to provide you with a hero that you couldroot for as he or she defied death to overcome insurmountable odds (as in ALIEN), but just for the sheer hell of it, just to see how much you could stand, just – in the words of Chas Balun- to "kick you in the balls and make you lick up your own vomit.". Chas has already drawn attention to the historical significance of the eye-skewering scene in Lucio Fulci s ZOMBIE FLESH EATERS, and it was, coincidentally, at a double bill of that movie and Dennis Donnelly's THE TOOLBOX MURDERS that the penny dropped for me concerning this new trend in Terror movies. It was no great surprise then, when both films later turned up on the "Video Nasties" list.

Donnelly's film (erroneously identified on the "Nasties" list as THE TALLBOX MURDERS) sets off at a cracking pace and for the first twenty minutes or so really lives up to its exploitive title). A ski-masked psycho spends his time spying on the self-abusive and promiscuous pastimes of the women who inhabit an apartment building, then takes his toolbox over there to hammer home some moral points. The most notorious scene in the film has a floozy masturbating in her bubble bath when the balaclavad bad guy bursts in, chases the soapy girl around the room (humming tunelessly all the while), and despatches her with nail-gun shots to the belly and head. The notion of "wayward" female sexuality being punished couldn't be any more explicitly represented. Hokushin's British release, identical to the BBFC-certified 'X' print, trimmed the under-water hitch-hiking but not the nail-gun attack, which says something about their sense of priorities.

This killing is punctuated by confusing, sepia-tinted flashbacks to a girl falling out of a car and dying. Turns out that she was Kathy, the daughter of Vance (played by – aaaargh! – Cameron Mitchell), apartment-block caretaker and Toolbox Murderer (as only the dim-witted cop, played by Tim Donnelly, seems to have any trouble figuring out). Devastated by the death of his "innocent" daughter, this bozo has decided to purge the world of immodest girls. He also kidnaps Laurie (Pamelyn Ferdin), whom he appears to believe is Kathy, ties her to Kathy's bed and surrounds her with Kathy's toys, then launches into an endless self-justifying rant that stops this hitherto pacey film dead in its tracks. "That woman ..." he slobbers "... she did terrible things to her own body ... it was unnatural ... unnatural!". Sensing that the film is going nowhere fast, Mitchell overacts maniacally in a vain attempt to hold audience attention, playing with dolls, sucking lollipops, spewing biblical quotations and singing hymns (not to mention the worst ever recorded rendition of "Sometimes I feel like a motherless child"). Meanwhile, Laurie's brother, Joe (Nicholas Beauvy), reveals to Vance's nephew Kent (Wesley Eure) his suspicions that Unc is the Toolbox Murderer. Kent's attitude is that the family which slays together stays together, so he douses Joe with petrol and torches him, revealing a musical gift the equal of his Uncle's as he croons: "Joey, Joey, burning bright." Kent goes to tell Uncle Vance but seems surprised to find him keeping company with a bound girl. An argument breaks out over Kathy's supposed "innocence", Kent revealing that he knew her in a biblical sense. Vance grunts a lot and calls Kent a heathen, then attacks him, only to be stabbed to death. As if the film's credibility wasn't already shot to ribbons, Donnelly now has Kent express the belief that Laurie is Kathy. "You can't remain a little girl for the rest of your life", he tells her, then rapes her. When he tells her that he's killed her brother, Laurie stabs him to death. A closing captioattempts to convince us that what we have just seen actually took place in real life. Sure it did, and so did the events depicted in PLAN 9 FROM OUTER SPACE!

Current Status: Removed from DPP list. Deleted from Hokushin catalogue

PAGE # 165

AVATAR
COMMUNICATIONS

VIOLENCE
BEYOND REASON.
VICTIMS
BEYOND HELP...

UNHINGED

AVATAR COMMUNICATIONS

UNHINGED. U.S.A., 1982. Video label: Avatar. Starring Laurel Munson, J.E. Penner, Sara Ansley, Virginia Settle, John Morrison, Barbara Lusch, Bill Simmonds. Camera: Richard Blakesee. Written by Don Gronquist and Reagan Ramsey. Produced and directed by Don Gronquist.

"The nightmare begins when you wake up" screamed the poster, and truer word was never spoken, as I discovered while dozing through lengthy passages of this in my local flea-pit. Considering some of the quality releases that are consigned straight to video these days, it's hard to believe that this Don Gronquist home-movie was granted a theatrical run back in the early '80s … maybe it *was* just a bad nightmare.

The action, what there is of it, concerns a bunch of tearaway girls whose car breaks down in the woods. They are taken in by a weird family, presided over by a crinkly matriarch. There's a dinner sequence that seems to go on for about four hours. Nothing happens, and to make matters worse, it happens from the same angle – no inserts, close-ups or reaction-shots whatsoever. Eventually we get to the supposedly boffo revelation that a gender-bending hillbilly has hung two girls up among the sausages and hickory-smoked hams in his garden shed. The supposedly dead girls appear to be supressing a mutual fit of the giggles. Those who've paid good money to see this garbage probably won't see the joke.

"Horror beyond belief – Victims beyond help" (and audiences beyond keeping their eyes open).

Unutterably bad. Deadheats with BLOOD RITES as the worst "video nasty" of them all. Avoid at all costs!!!

UNHINGED

Current Status: Removed from DPP list. No re-release scheduled

THE HOSPITAL WHERE YOUR NEXT VISIT... WILL BE YOUR LAST

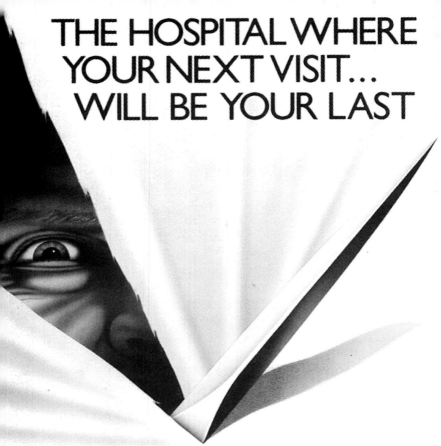

VISITING HOURS

CBS/FOX VIDEO

THE SEDUCTION OF THE GULLIBLE

VISITING HOURS. Canada, 1981. Video label: CBS/Fox. Starring Michael Ironside, Lee Grant, Linda Purl, William Shatner, Leonore Zann, Harvey Atkin, Helen Hughes, Michael J. Reynolds. Camera: Rene Verzier. Written by Brian Taggert. Produced by Claude Heroux. Directed by Jean-Claude Lord.

Michael Ironside, the renegade telepath in Cronenberg's SCANNERS, is typecast here as a hulking psycopath named Michael, whose bigoted father has instilled in him a hatred of independent, successful women (photos of those he has beaten and killed form a macabre, skull-shaped collage on his bedroom wall). He develops a fixation onTV journo Shelagh (Lee Grant), his resentment sharpened by the contrast in their social statndings — he polishes the floor of the her studio. Michael breaks into Shelagh's house, strips off and bedecks himself in body jewellery), kills the maid and, on Shelagh's return, pursues her around the place. Shelagh is injured while escaping and taken to hospital. Michael puts a florist's sign on his van, drives over and breezes in. There's an ironic scene in which he eaves-drops on Shelagh telling the police what a scum-bag he is, but being in no position to avenge the insult he consoles himself by turning off an old lady's life-support system, sticking around to rattle off a few polaroids of her death throes. A nurse who rushes in to the old girl's assistance is stabbed to death and another nurse, Deborah (Linda Purl), is photographed and noted as a future victim.

Unwinding in a bar, he attracts the amorous attentions of a waitress but ignores her and picks up Lisa, a biker girl, instead. Back at Michael's apartment, while he changes into his rubber bathing costume, she reads the framed letters that adorn his walls, reproductions of hate mail that he has sent to various newspapers, castigating a broad spectrum of minority groups. "You want the whole damn world to yourself?" asks the girl. "Yeah, I'd like that" deadpans Michael, before pouring beer over her and beating her up. Lisa seeks aid at a woman's clinic run by Nurse Deborah ("He chewed me up so bad because he couldn't make it", she confides: "Well, he won't get away with it"). Michael visits his father, now a drooling old loon in an institution. Flashbacks reveal him beatingup and raping Michael's mother, who responds by throwing hot chip-fat in his face. Michael bluffs his way into the hospital again, only to find that Shelagh is otherwise engaged in the operating theatre. He kills the new occupant of her bed and then dons surgical apparel (slaying anyone who challenges him) so as to participate in the operation, a truly horrifying, paranoia-inducing scenario, although the opportunity for him to make a fatal intervention thankfully does not arise. Michael is chased by security guards (several of whom he manages to maim) and arrives back at his apartment to find the walls smeared with excrement and the centre-piece of his collage, a photo of Shelagh, missing. Lisa the beaten biker has taken it to Deborah, who is phoning Shelagh to warn her when Michael appears from under her bed and stabs her. Now he really goes berserk, flushing down bottles of uppers with gallons of booze and smashing his arm into broken glass to get admitted into casualty for a final try at snuffing Shelagh. Hel rampages aroud,, disconnecting every life-support system he can find until he reaches his target, grabbing her and ranting that for once she is going to have to listen to him. Shelagh cuts all this masculine protest short by splashing a conveniently-placed corrosive fluid in his face, then stabs him several times.. She ends up soaked in Michael's blood, devastated... her pacifist principles hopelessly compromised.

VISITING HOURS is actually rather more analytical of machismo and misogyny than is usual in these things. Brian Taggert's script is in no way ambivalent about Michael's bathetic crusade and its genesis in a disturbed childhood that has left him an emotional cripple, exactly the kind of loser whose faltering identity can only be bolstered by preying on women. No way is he presented as a figure to be admired or emulated, the charge that has been thoughtlessly levelled at this most thoughtful film.The picture became one of the first "nasties" to play on "Sky Movies", the satellite channel owned by Rupert Murdoch, whose tabloids had done so much to foster "video nasty" paranoia. It was subsequently televised on the terrestrial ITV network, prompting a hatful of complaints to William Rees-Mogg's ludicrous Broadcasting Standards Council.

VISITING HOURS

You feel your Heart POUNDING,
You know It's out there,
You can't SCREAM,
NOW IT'S AT YOUR THROAT—

NIGHT of the HOWLING BEAST

starring PAUL NASCHY • GRACE MILLS • GIL VIDAL   SILVIA SOLAR • LOUIS INDUNI
in GEVACOLOR   a CONSTELLATION FILMS INC. release   [R]

THE WEREWOLF AND THE YETI

TWO BLOODTHIRSTY BEASTS
IN DEADLY COMBAT

CANON VIDEO

THE WEREWOLF AND THE YETI

PAUL NASCHY • GRACE MILLS • GIL VIDAL
DIRECTED BY
M.I.BONNS

LA MALDICION DE LA BESTIA

PAUL NASCHY   GRACE MILLS · SILVIA SOLAR   Director M.I. BONNS

THE SEDUCTION OF THE GULLIBLE

THE WEREWOLF AND THE YETI aka NIGHT OF THE HOWLING BEAST / MALDICION DE LA BESTIA. Spain, 1975. Video label: Canon Video. Starring "Paul Naschy", Grace Mills, Castillo Escalona, Silvia Solar, Gil Vidal, Luis Induni. Special effects: Alfredo Segoviano. Camera: Thomas Pladevall. Written by Jacinto Molina. Produced by Modesto Perez Redondo. Directed by Miguel Iglesias Bonns.

Writer, actor and occasional director "Paul Naschy" (Jacinto Molina Alvarez) is the amiable buffoon of Spanish Horror cinema. This ex-weightlifter's attempts to create an Iberianequivalent of the great Hammer and Universal cycles (on a budget of about two pesetas per movie) have to be seen to be believed, ranking amongst the most jaw-droppingly out-of-wack celluloid offerings on offer. It's impossible to come down too hard on this crud, because Naschy's heart is so obviously in the right place and he goes about his misguided task with such undeniable gusto, often suffering extreme physical discomfort to achieve the desired effect (in 1972's HUNCHBACK OF THE MORGUE, his finest hour, Naschy was bitten repeatedly by a pack of rats!), in the manner of a latter-day Lon Chaney. Actually, Naschy is more often compared to Lon Chaney Jr., due to an interminable series of movies (initiated in 1967's THE MARK OF THE WOLFMAN aka FRANKENSTEIN'S BLOODY TERROR / HELL'S CREATURES) in which he stars as tragic wolfman Count Waldemar Daninsky.

THE WEREWOLF AND THE YETI, Naschy's eighth outing as Daninsky, opens with Yeti-hunting anthropologist Silas Neumann discovering his moth-eaten quarry in Katmandu and falling prey to it. Cut to Britain (stock footage of Westminster bridge, accompanied on the soundtrack by bagpipes droning "Scotland the Brave"!), where another Yeti-buff, Professor Lacomb, is enlisting the aid of Count Waldemar in an expedition aimed at capturing the beast ("You're an anthropologist and a psychologist ... besides you know Tibet and you can speak Nepalese." He's also conducting a pretty hot affair with the Prof's daughter Silvia [Grace Mills]). Arriving in Tibet, the expedition is hampered by heavy weather, demon-fearing sherpas going AWOL, and outbreaks of ill-matched stock footage depicting native dervish dances. Naschy, looking even more like the Michelin Man than usual in his snow gear, wanders off to collapse in the wilderness and is rescued by two scantilly-clad cave-dwelling bimbos. "He is very strong," opines one of the girls: "He will be a good companion "...and a passionate lover," adds her partner.

True to form, as soon as he comes around Naschy whips off his balaclava and roll-neck pullover, baring that legendary barrel-chest to the world, and starts making serious woopy. Subsequently he discovers his new girlfriends eating an itinerant sherpa, and is obliged to reduce them to smoking skeletons with a handy-dandy wooden stake. At this point the full moon rises in the sky, and Naschy's love-bites convert him into a novelty shop werewolf (learning well from his Universal and Hammer mentors, Naschy has never given undue weight to internal logic in his films or continuity and consistency in this series – the Daninsky werewolf has a different set of origins every time out). This proves to be a blessing in disguise because the rest of the expedition has been captured by a horde of tartar roughnecks whose leader, the dreaded Saga Khan, has certain radical ideas on acne treatment – nubile girls are flayed and flaps of their dripping skin draped over his spotty features (It was this aspect of WEREWOLF AND THE YETI that brought it to the DPP's attention). To cut a very long story short, Naschy lopes into tartar H.Q., trashes the bad guys and liberates Sylvia, then the Yeti (remember him?) turns up for a perfunctory wrestling match. Finally Sylvia discovers – just like that – the herb which will transform Naschy from a nasty brutish wolfman back into a nasty, brutish John Belushi lookalike... and presumably they all lived happily ever after.

Current Status: Banned

VIDEOTAPECENTER

A young woman's
nightmare of incest
and castration.

THE WITCH
WHO CAME FROM
THE SEA

THE SEDUCTION OF THE GULLIBLE

THE WITCH WHO CAME FROM THE SEA. U.S.A., 1976. Video label: Video Tape Center. Starring Millie Perkins, Lonny Chapman, Vanessa Brown, Peggy Feury. Camera: Ken Gibb. Written by Robert Thorn. Produced and directed by Matt Cimber.

Molly (Millie Perkins) sits on the beach in Santa Monica with her nephew and niece, the unfortunately-named Tad and Tripoli, lecturing them on what a morally upright man her sea captain father was, and encouraging them to follow his stalwart example. As she compares Grandad to Christopher Columbus and Abraham Lincoln, Molly is surreptitiously ogling the crotches of beach boys going through their gymnastic work-outs. Later, watching TV, Molly opines that an actor in a razor-blade commercial "looks like Poppa". Her sister Kathy, Tad and Tripoli's mom, contradicts her. "He was a drunken bum" she insists: "an evil bastard … and more than anyone, you knew it." Flashbacks appear to indicate that Daddy dearest was a child molester who dropped dead of a heart attack while raping the young Molly.

Molly fantasizes about tying up, dominating and finally castrating with a razor blade two football players she has seen on TV. While working behind the bar at "the Boathouse", a joint owned by her sometime lover "Long John"(!), Molly sees a TV news bulletin indicating that this "weird sex scene" actually took place. A famous film star named Billy Batt – who just happens to be a regular at the bar – now takes a fancy to Molly ("For a sailor, she's got awfully sweet knockers") and invites her to a party full of famous film folk. Showing her a reproduction of Botticelli's "Venus", he explains the myth of how the goddess was born from the Mediterranean after the castrated testicles of a god were flung into it ("The sea was knocked up. Venus was the child"). But when he comes on to her, Molly bites and breaks one of his fingers. "You bit me, you cunt!" he observes.

Improbably, McPeak, the guy in the razor ad who's supposed to look like "Poppa", picks Molly up and takes her home. When he undresses her he discovers a mermaid tatooed on her belly (at "Jack Dracula's Tattoo Studios", no less), its tail rising from a curly black sea. "Television makes people so much kinder, doesn't it?" she asks McPeak, before attacking and killing him with a razor. As the police close in on her, Molly retires to the bosom of her family. With the obnoxious Tad and Tripoli in attendance, Long John and Sister Kate supervise an O.D. for her. By the time the cops roll up she's dying, hallucinating herself as a lone yachts-woman.

The constant repetition of sea-faring imagery, and the confusing (almost VIDEODROME-esque) blurring of reality and illusion, real-life and TV, ultimately don't add up to much, certainly not to the high tragedy that director Matt Cimber clearly intended. VTC marketed THE WITCH WHO CAME FROM THE SEA as a dick-pruning exploiter, with heavy emphasis on the razor in their pack design, together with the shout-line: "A young woman's nightmare of incest and castration … Molly has a way with razors! She uses them with devastating effect. She cuts men down to size in an effort to revenge herself of her father's sexual perversions." Gorehounds moved by this lurid line of prose to seek out THE WITCH WHO CAME FROM THE SEA will have been disappointed by the thoroughly bloodless nature of the proceedings, and confused by the episodic, impressionistic narrative.

The much-reviled I SPIT ON YOUR GRAVE does it all so much better.

Current Status: Removed from DPP list. No re-release scheduled

WOMEN
BEHIND BARS

THE SEDUCTION OF THE GULLIBLE

WOMEN BEHIND BARS. France/Belgium, 1977. Video label: Go Video. Starring Lina Romay, Martine Steed, Nathalie Chappell, Roger Darton, Ronald Weiss, Denis Torre. Written by R. Marceignac. Camera: Gerard Brissaud. Produced by Pierre Querut. Directed by "Rick Deconnink".

Although WBB is officially credited, if that's the right word, to "Rick Deconnink" (sure thing, you guys), one suspects the veiled hand of Jesus Franco at work. The plot, nicely encapsulated in that penny dreadful title, is "arse-deep in Franco territory" (to quote Ian Caunce). The presence of Franco s real-life paramour and frequent screen victim Lina Romay (and the fact that she is required to discharge her debt to society by submitting to torture and electrocution), not to mention such characteristic camera work as repetitive zooms into the actresses' pubic tresses, all serve to lend credence...

This torrid little saga begins with randomly culled travelogue footage, horrendous canned music and a poor man's Sam Spade voice-over courtesy of "Milton Warren, insurance man" (recalling Franco's LA CHICA DE LAS BRAGAS TRANSPARENTES, released in Britain as PICK UP GIRLS on Atlas Video). "Shirley Field" (Romay)'s slaughter of her lover at a dive called the Flamingo Club ("He betrayed me with a mulatto slut") plus some impenetrable stuff about pilfered diamonds serve as the pretext for whisking our heroine off to jail, where despite the liberal protestations of the warden (who bears too striking a resemblance to Sardu in BLOODSUCKING FREAKS for us to take these protestations seriously), the predictable outrages are trotted out. Things never get quite as extreme as in Franco's GRETA, THE MAD BUTCHER / ILSA, THE WICKED WARDEN but there's always the possibility that this British release is incomplete.

The inmates' time is spent lounging naked around their cells, sexual assignations with the warden easing the monotony and earning them minor privileges. No such avenue is open to sultry, Juno-esque Romay, the warden expressing a preference for "blondes with sexy asses". He does however detail one of his conquests to spy on her ("Life is shit and there's no shortage of stoolies in the shithouse"). Romay is discovered reading a note from Milton Warren, insurance man, who is planning to break her out of jail and get to the bottom of the diamonds affair. For this she is hung naked in chains (a trademark Franco fetish) and whipped, then subjected to the aforementioned electrocution. As her body convulses, the camera zooms in on her wobbling breasts (yep, this has to be a Jesus Franco movie). The ordea over, Romay is offeredr a conciliatory gift of cologne. She seems happy to accept this olive branch. "Why should I hold grudges against a little punishment?" she reasons: "You're the warden, you must enforce discipline." Then she adopts an ecstatic expression to drench herself with this present. "I find you as beautiful when you're laughing as when you're suffering," lusts the warden, who seems to be reconsidering his prejudice against brunettes.

Having lulled the old perv into a false sense of security, Lina pulls a gun (god knows where she's been hiding it) and marches him out of jail to a rendezvous with Milton Warren, insurance man, and a mystery dude played by (*I knew it!*) Jesus Franco, who lectures the warden on his moral failings (look who's talking) then shoots him dead. For Romay it's "out of the frying pan, into the fire" because back at their H.Q. her rescuers take turns beating up on her to elicit the whereabouts of those diamonds (remember them?), till she confesses that they're located in the basement of the Flamingo Club (did it really not occur to anyone to turn that place over?). Romay takes Franco there, reveals some incomprehensible (because uninteresting) sting, shoots him and absconds to Vera Cruz with Milton Warren, insurance man. "It's true, we've committed murder," muses Milt as the credits roll: "But who were the victims? People who deserved to die!" Careful, Jesus ... Feminists and film fans alike might care to hoist you on your own petard. Incidentally, a catty comment made by one of the prisoners about the warden could serve equally well as a critique of Franco, the man and director, namely: "He's such a pig, but when he gets his hands on a pair of tits he doesn't know what he's doing."

Current Status: Removed from DPP list. No re-release scheduled

ZOMBIE CREEPING FLESH aka NIGHT OF THE ZOMBIES/ VIRUS / INFERNO DEI MORTI VIVENTI / APOCALYPSIS CANIBAL / HELL OF THE LIVING DEAD. Italy/Spain, 1981. Video label: Merlin Video. Starring Margit Evelyn Newton, "Frank Garfield", Selan Karay, Robert O'Neal, Gaby Renom, Luis Fonoll, Piero Fumelli, Patrizia Costa, Bruno Boni, Cesare Di Vito. Camera: Julin Cabrera. Written by Claudio Fragasso and J.M. Cunilles. Produced by Sergio Cortona. Directed by "Vincent Dawn" (Bruno Mattei).

Throughout the video censorship controversy of the early '80s, the media regaled us with scare stories of impressionable children being exposed to "nasties", with supposedly dire consequences. Well, my pet theory about ZOMBIE CREEPING FLESH (credited to Bruno Mattei, here adopting the pseudonym "Vincent Dawn" in a trans-parently desperate attempt to establish some kind of subliminal link with George Romero's DEAD trilogy), is that it was actually directed by one of those kids — quite probably a five year old — who had just seen ZOMBIE FLESH EATERS and decided that anything Lucio Fulci could do, he could do better … guess again, Chucky!

This ludicrous effort opens in "the Hope Centre", a biochemical plant in New Guinea where two workers are attacked by the first zombie rat in screen history (seemingly something of a fixation with Mattei, who would later direct the equally inept "rampaging rodents after the Apocalypse" epic RATS – NIGHT OF TERROR). Inexplicably, this is the signal for green gas to billow out, and for various people with boot polish smeared on their faces to stagger around biting lumps out of their work-mates. "If we can't stop the leak, we'll all be dead" someone remarks, matter-of-factly. Crack investigative reporter Margit Evelyn Newton heads into the Papuan jungle to get the facts, and meets up with a SWAT team that just happened to be there for no better reason than there having been one in DAWN OF THE DEAD. A good job too, because Newton's young son has just turned zombie and eaten his father. The SWAT team blow the kid's brains out in the approved manner and also waste the mandatory zombie priest, plus the sundry crusty undead who come leaping out of every swimming pool and staggering from behind every clump of trees. "Maybe they're drunks" opines camera-man Max as the decomposing deadsters shamble in his direction (remind me never to drop into his local for a swift one!)

Now Mattei cuts to a TV broadcast which ham-fistedly splices together footage of tribal rituals from all over the world, while a stern voice over gamely attempts to convince us that we are watching people running away from zombies. "We're going to scoop the world on a major disaster" gushes one TV executive. "If there's anyone left to report it to!" admonishes his colleague. Our heroes' progress towards the Hope Centre is punctuated by several laughable zombie attacks, ineptly ripped off from other movies,

ZOMBIE CREEPING FLESH

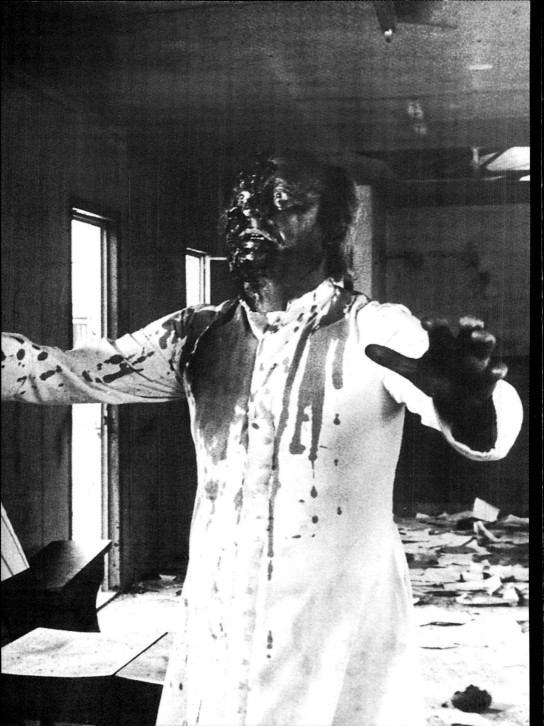

and padded out with miles of "National Geographic"-type stock-footage, much of which will be highly familiar to serious students of Spaghetti Splatter. The film's sound-track reinforces this sense of deja vu, cannibalising Goblin cuts from the scores of CONTAMINATION and Joe D'Amato's BLUE HOLOCAUST, among others.

Arrival at the Hope Centre reveals that its scientists were tackling the problem of Third World hunger, albeit from a slightly different angle to the one favoured by Bob Geldof ... they were developing a gas that would make the starving millions eat each other! No sooner does Newton learn the grim truth than she is torn apart and eaten by the now-zombified SWAT team. As if all this wasn't ludicrous enough, Mattei tacks on an epilogue in which bar-flies scoff at TV reports about a limbless cadaver chasing people around a morgue, only to be attacked by blue-faced deadsters.

It's a matter of personal taste as to this film's most rib-tickling moment, but nominees must include the scene where a SWAT man, besieged by zombies, dons a tutu and takes time out for a soft-shoe routine, and (my personal favourite) the United Nations sequence in which a badly-dubbed Third World representative rages: "YOU have murdered my people! YOU have treated them like a crowd of human lavae... like insects... savage beasts... prehistoric animals! They are running from their children, their parents, their brothers, transformed into vile creatures that feast on human flesh... monsters, killing without pity at all. Brother eats brother, mothers devour offspring in a chain of foul slaughter until nothing will remain but the bare earth, soaked in putrefying flesh!", only to be told: "Well, we'll continue tomorrow, Your Excellency ... good night" by the stiff upper-lipped Brit representative. Mattei's fondness for the climactic custard pie fight in DAWN OF THE DEAD results in several ludicrous sequences in which SWAT men single-handedly take on packs of zombies, baiting them with fire, avoiding their hungry jaws and addressing them as "stinking, putrid bastards, "you lousy bunch of turds" and "brainless monkeys", further advising them to "screw off!" and "get back to your graves!" The dialogue in general is laugh-a-minute stuff – a SWAT man who has just fought off a horde of the cannibal undead is asked: "What's eating you today?". Unwisely giving away the make-up secrets of FX man Guiseppe Ferranti, one SWAT man describes the zombies as "the guys with shit all over their faces". All performances are awful, particularly from the guy playing the supposedly hunky SWAT commander Mike London, but no matter – the ubiquitous stock footage is the real star of this one.

The British theatrical and Merlin video releases lost a sequence in which the SWAT team liberate political hostages, and also toned down much of the gore (most notably, Brits were denied the spectacle of Margit Evelyn Newton having her eyeballs pulled out through her mouth), which didn't prevent ZOMBIE CREEPING FLESH from creeping onto the DPP's hit-list. "Horror Classics", a short-lived label that specialised in emasculated re-releases of "nasties", later put out an even more watered-down version.

Current Status: Re-released by Horror Classics with cuts – Cert 18

THE SEDUCTION OF THE GULLIBLE

ZOMBIE FLESH EATERS aka ZOMBIE / ZOMBI 2 / ISLAND OF THE LIVING DEAD. Italy, 1979. Video label: VIPCO. Starring Tisa Farrow, Ian McCulloch, Richard Johnson, Auretta Gay, Olga Karlatos, Al Cliver, Stefania D'Amario, Ugo Bologna, Monica Zanchi. Special effects: Giannetto de Rossi. Camera: Sergio Salvati. Written by Elisa Briganti. Produced by Ugo Tucci and Fabrizio de Angelis. Directed by Lucio Fulci.

The last of the "video nasties", alphabetically, is the one that started it all, in terms of international recognition, for Lucio Fulci. Producer Fabrizio de Angelis (who sometimes moonlights as a director himself under the all-American monicker Larry Ludman) decided that Fulci was the man to helm his projected DAWN OF THE DEAD cash-in when he witnessed the head-crushing climax of Fulci's NON SI SEVIZIA UN PAPERINO ("DON'T TORTURE A DUCKLING", 1972). Benefiting from the efforts of a gifted team of collaborators (cameraman Sergio Salvati, composer Fabio Frizzi and, on make-up FX, the mighty Gianetto de Rossi) Fulci accomplished the difficult trick of making this quickie cash-in superior in every way to the film he was instructed to imitate. He managed to top DAWN OF THE DEAD (which scant months earlier had been regarded as some kind of "last word in splatter") for gore, serving the entrails up straight, without the misfiring social comment that becomes so tiresome in DAWN. These guys *are here to eat you* and it's going to take more than a custard pie fight with some Hell's Angels to spoil their appetite!

ZOMBIE FLESH EATERS takes the living dead out of the shopping mall and puts them back in the Caribbean, throwaway lines about voodoo supplanting throwaway lines about Venusian space-probes. A putrefying butter-ball sails into Hudson bay and bites lumps out of a harbour patrol cop before being shot by his colleague and falling overboard. "It's my opinion…' intones a solemn coroner as he inspects the cop's body: "…that the death of the poor bastard was caused by massive haemorrhage due to laceration of the jugular". Crack reporter Ian McCulloch is assigned to the story by his editor (a Fulci cameo) and, together with wide-eyed Tisa Farrow, follows a hot trail to the Island of Matul, hooking up en route with boatnicks Al ("I'm in everything") Cliver and gorgeous but wooden Auretta Gay. In a cheeky side-swipe at JAWS, Gay is menaced by a hungry shark, only to be rescued by a deep sea-diving zombie fish-eater (Tarantino once described this zombie / shark face-off to me as "the wildest scene in any movie, ever!")

On Matul they find Dr Menard (respected Shakespearian thesp Richard Johnson) struggling to put down an outbreak of zombie flesh-eating that his unorthodox medical experiments have brought about. In his colonial-style house, Mrs Menard (Olga Karlatos) is being stalked by a reanimated native, who punches through the window shutters and pulls her head out for a nibble, resulting in one of the most notorious scenes in any of the "video nasties", as her eye is impaled on a 14-inch jagged splinter (hereafter a sequence involving some sharp instrument or other being forced into somebody's cranium became mandatory in Fulci's horror offerings). There's an inept hommage

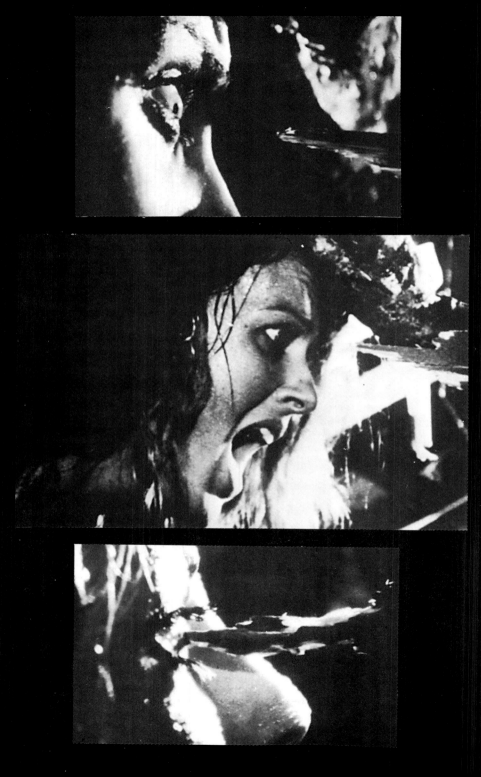

to/rip-off of this magical moment in Andrea Bianchi's laugh-a-minute zombie gut-cruncher NIGHTS OF TERROR aka ZOMBIE 3 / BURIAL GROUND. Anyway, back on Matul, Dr Menard sends our heroes over to check on his wife, whom they discover serving as the centre-piece of a zombie picnic. They have to bash the brains out of several zombies who want them to stay for dessert. When their land-rover breaks down, and in full knowledge that the dead are rising from their graves looking for people to eat, they lie down in an old Spanish cemetery and hold an impromptu necking session. To nobody's great surprise, and the delight of gorehounds everywhere, a zombie conquistadore appears and bites chunks out of Auretta Gay's throat. The others are chased back to Menard's hospital, which is soon besieged by the living dead.

The boffo climax has zombies popping up in windows and having their brains blown out like targets at a shooting gallery. Dead patients complicate matters by getting out of bed and biting the good guys, including Menard. When the zombies finally break the door down, our heroes hit them with improvised molotov cocktails. This gotterdammerung of the zombies (recalling both 1960's CITY OF THE DEAD and 1966's PLAGUE OF THE ZOMBIES) is tremendous crowd-pleasing stuff, and it's here that Frizzi's main theme, with it's thumping bass drum and hypnotic synthesizer doodlings, comes into its own.

The three survivors split, leaving the zombies to burn, but Cliver is confronted by a blue-faced Auretta Gay, who takes unfair advantage of their relationship to sink her teeth into him. McCulloch and Tisa sail back to New York with Al locked up in the bilge as substantiation for their unbelievable story. This turns out to be a case of carrying coals to Newcastle – as McCulloch turns the radio on to drown out the ominous moaning from below with "something more cheerful", he hears instead a maniacal news bulletin indicating that zombies have overrun and are taking bites out of The Big Apple. The final line of this broadcast always brings the house down: "We've just been informed that zombies have entered the building ... they're at the door ... they're coming in ... Waaaaahhhhh!!!"

VIPCO issued two versions of ZOMBIE FLESH EATERS, the "Strong uncut" one (93 minutes) and an 89 minute variant (identical to British cinema prints) that lost the eye-skewering, much of the intestinal barbecue and gallons of blood gushing from the respective throats of Auretta Gay and the harbour patrol cop who features in the opening scene. Nice try, VIPCO, but no cigar – both versions were consigned to the dreaded "video nasties" list.

Current status: "Strong, un-cut version banned. Vipco re-release is "un-cut cinema version", i.e. 89 minutes long.

"NASTY TIMES"
A CHRONOLOGY
OF VIDEO BASHING
1982-97

THE SEDUCTION OF THE GULLIBLE

1982

FEBRUARY's *Television and Video Retailer* reproduces letters of complaint over the poster for S.S. EXPERIMENT CAMP that appeared on the back cover of the January issue. Des Dolan of Go video argues that his company's advertising has got to be effective and can also serve the purpose of warning off the unwary. He reveals that the distributor's art-work feature da naked woman rather than one wearing panties: "To this extent (we) imposed our own moral censorship"."It is no use to me toning down my advertising" concludes Dolan "... if none of the other distributors follows suit. What the industry needs is some sort of guide-line that video advertisers can follow or at least refer to". The magazine concurs ("As the industry gets fatter and the publicity material spreads wider and wider, there must be a case for public moral acceptability"), but regrets that the industry is unlikely to come up with a voluntary code of practice.

MAY 7TH: *The Daily Star* reports that "the video boom is giving youngsters a chance to see some of the most horrific and violent films ever made". British Board of Film Censors Secretary James Ferman is described as being "furious" about this state of affairs, warning that: "they are watching shocking scenes that we would never allow in a cinema, even under an 'X'-certificate". He urges the government to tighten the law. A spokesman for the distributors organisation, the British Videogram Association (BVA) responds: "We hope to control this problem by asking retailers to follow a voluntary code of practice to be drawn up soon".

MAY 20TH: *Video Trade Weekly* reports World Of Video 2000's promotion of their forthcoming release NIGHTMARES IN A DAMAGED BRAIN – representative Pam Quinn poses for pictures outside a Surrey hospital with a bona-fide bottled human brain, offering £50 to whoever can guess its correct weight. Police are eventually moved to confiscate the offending chunk of grey matter.

MAY 23RD: *The Sunday Times* – "HOW HIGH STREET HORROR IS INVADING THE HOME". "Uncensored horror video cassettes, available to anyone of any age, have arrived in Britain's high streets. The videos – called 'nasties' in the trade – are freely available for sale or hire off the shelves of hundreds of shops catering for the video boom. They cost as little as £2 to hire for up to four nights. They exploit extremes of violence and are rapidly replacing sexual pornography as the video trade's biggest money-spinner. The 'nasties' are far removed from the suspense of the traditional horror film. They dwell on murder, multiple rape, sado-masochism, mutilation of women, cannibalism and Nazi atrocities". The piece cites DRILLER KILLER, S.S. EXPERIMENT CAMP, CANNIBAL TERROR, CANNIBAL HOLOCAUST, BLOOD FEAST and I SPIT ON YOUR GRAVE, and talks of highly realistic special effects (in BLOOD FEAST?!?) and the chance for renters to use slow-motion and freeze-frame facilities "to revel in the gory bits as often as they like", continuing: "...now the most notorious of the films, called simply SNUFF, billed as 'the original legendary atrocity, shot and banned in New York ... will be in the shops at the end of this week. The film shows gory scenes of extreme sadism, including rape, mass-murder and mutilation". While conceding that the film's claims to be a bona-fide "snuff movie" are highly dubious, *The Sunday Times* argues that whether the reports were true, or merely a sensationalist sales-ploy, "the product is horrifyingly convincing" (the writer has obviously never seen the movie) "and can now be viewed at home by anyone with a video recorder".

Mike Behr, MD of the film's British distributor Astra Video, redefining what the Ancient Greeks used to call 'hubris', is quoted as saying: "There's no censorship law on video at all. What can they do about it?" Home Office officials, though, confirm that the

THE SEDUCTION OF THE GULLIBLE

Obscene Publications Act (OPA) of 1959 does apply to video, but will make no further comment. A spokesman for video distributors VIPCO argues: "We are feeding a demand, not creating it. People want to see this sort of stuff, and we are giving them what they want. I agree that there's a lot of violence and that is probably bad, but who are we to decide? There really ought to be a line drawn somewhere, but there isn't".

The Sunday Times observes that the video boom is such a recent phenomenon that the Williams committee on obscenity and film censorship, which reported in 1979, didn't even mention it. Nor does the Cinematograph Bill, put forward by Conservative MP Peter Lloyd, which is currently before the House of Lords. "What worries me is not so much thepornography" says Lloyd "but the really harmful sadistic films with details of violence, especially against women". He argues that the OPA would be effective to cope with the perceived problem, if it was enforceable, " ... but the police do not have the man-power, and videos are difficult to deal with because you can't flip through them like a publication. Many people, including many MPs, do not seem to appreciate how violent, brutal and sadistic these sort of films are, and there has been insufficient research on their effects on audiences. My Bill deals with the problem of last year, but these video sales and rentals will be the problem of next year and the year after".

MAY 28TH: *The Daily Express* identifies "nasties" as "films which show castration, sadistic attacks on women and violence including the use of chainsaws or electric drills".

MAY 30TH: A *Sunday Times* article entitled "WATCHDOG IS UNLEASHED ON VIDEO HORROR" describes "nasties" as "films which specialise in extreme violence, sadism, mutilation and cannibalism" and reports that a high-powered BBFC/BVA working party has been set up with a brief to create a classification system for video, similar to that used in the cinema.The piece also reveals that Scotland Yard's solicitor is studying S.S. EXPERIMENT CAMP with a view to forwarding it to the Director of Public Prosecutions as a candidate for the first "nasty" to be prosecuted under the OPA. Peter Kruger, operational head of the Yard's Obscene Publications Squad: "The horror videos are a new concept and I think we are going to get involved with them more and more but we do not yet know whether we will be able to prosecute successfully. Even if we can, it may be some months before cases come to court". He invokes the "use in the home" argument, warning of the perils of video's slow-motion and freeze-frame facilities, and states that the police have received an increasing amount of complaints from people who have been shown offensive videos at parties or had them shown to their children.

The piece continues by reporting that trade and consumer magazines are attempting to "clean up" video advertising in the wake of the Advertising Standards Authority's upholding of three complaints against such ads. One for CANNIBAL HOLOCAUST was deemed to go "beyond the bounds of decency" and the DRILLER KILLER ad was described as "appalling". Strongest condemnation though, was reserved for the S.S. EXPERIMENT CAMP ads. The ASA stated: "We regret that some editors should be prepared to publish advertisements in which increasingly films of a violent or sexually perverted character were described in terms which, like the film themselves, were calculated to appeal to only the most degraded tastes". Chastened magazine editors have now agreed concerted action on this score. BVA director general Norman Abbott: "It is a competitive situation and everybody was trying to out-do each other and be more outrageous. But now the publishers have decided to put their own house in order and I think the problem of the advertisements has been partly solved". In the wake of last week's *Sunday Times* expose, ASTRA Video are now claiming that they have "severed all links with the tape SNUFF, which despite big orders", will not now be distributed (In fact, plenty of copies did get out – JM).

THE SEDUCTION OF THE GULLIBLE

MAY 31ST: The BBFC / BVA working party will present a system of video classification by the end of the year. Dealers will be asked not to stock un-classified tapes, but in the words of Norman Abbott: "It will be for the police to decide whether such material is likely to contravene legislation such as the OPA". Mary Whitehouse states that the working party is causing her "more rather than less anxiety". She objects to the presence on it of Lady Plowden (who recently sponsored defence funds for the ROMANS IN BRITAIN obscenity case, brought by Mrs Whitehouse against the National Theatre) and Lord Harlech, who as President of the BBFC had passed material "that would give cause for concern if shown on videograms". Mrs Whitehouse stresses that videos, intended for use in the home, can easily be seen by children, and urges the government to introduce "new and effective obscenity laws" to meet "the growing threat from videograms".

IT WILL SHATTER YOU!

DRILLER KILLER

This motion picture has been deemed TOO VIOLENT to be accorded a motion picture rating. There are no explicit sexual scenes. However, due to the violent nature of this film NO ONE UNDER 17 WILL BE ADMITTED WITHOUT BEING ACCOMPANIED BY A PARENT OR GUARDIAN

JUN 6TH: (*The Sunday Times*) "VIDEO 'NASTIES': YARD ASKS DPP FOR RULING". The Yard asks both the Attorney General, Sir Michael Havers, and Home Secretary Willie Whitelaw for statements about the "nasties" in view of "mounting public concern" over their effects on children. Superintendent Peter Kruger has sent three of the tapes in question – I SPIT ON YOUR GRAVE, DRILLER KILLER and S.S. EXPERIMENT CAMP ("All featuring extreme violence") – to the Director of Public Prosecutions, Sir Thomas Hetherington, seeking guidance: "We want to know where we should draw the line. This is a new problem for us, and we need to know where we stand". Professor Bernard Williams, whose committee on obscenity and film censorship reported in 1979, approves of this development: "This area of videos shown at home is rather poorly defined in relation to our recommendations. I think it is a good idea that we first test these films under the existing law". John Grant, Social Democrat MP for Islington Central, has tabled questions in the House of Commons, one asking the Attorney General for a statement on government policy towards prosecution of "those involved in making, distributing and showing horror and terror films which specialise in violence", and a second to Willie Whitelaw, asking him to meet the BBFC, the BVA and the Advertising Standards Authority to discuss courses of action and make a statement. *The Sunday Times* goes on to report that the BBFC/BVA working party "has been deeply disturbed by some of the material they have seen and it has been emphasised that any new system will be not be able to give a grade to the sort of material that would not pass a normal cinema certificate, which would exclude most of the nasties".

THE SEDUCTION OF THE GULLIBLE

JUN 13TH: (*The Sunday Times*) – "MORE VIDEO 'NASTIES' GO TO DPP". Scotland Yard's Obscene Publications Squad will this week view four more tapes that have been causing a fuss in the media, and the DPP is expected to decide within a month whether to go for the first OPA prosecutions of horror, rather than pornographic, tapes.

JUL 11TH: (*The Sunday Times*) Scotland Yard presses the DPP for a decision on whether the "nasties" they have submitted for his consideration can be prosecuted under the OPA. They state that until he has made a decision their hands are tied, with more and more "nasties" flooding into the shops. Their stated aim is to prosecute distributors rather than retailers at random.

AUG 7TH: (*Titbits*) "THE VILE SIDE OF VIDEO". "Butchery, cannibalism, rape are taking over from the sex movies ... a vast number of ordinary families feed happily on butchery, multiple rape, castration, cannibalism, mutilation of women and torture ... it is now felt that unless the Obscene Publications Act is invoked swiftly, the problem will escalate." Norman Abbott, director general of the BVA, is quoted as saying: "We are suggesting that the whole gamut of video films be classified, from the most innocuous to the most adult. But there are some films which are so violent that they may not be classified at all. We should not expect any of our members to handle such films but if they do, then we should have to amend our constitution and expel them". A spokesman for distributors VIPCO is allowed to point out that 20-40% of all videos hired out fall into the horror category, and that distributors are "catering for a demand for this kind of film, but we do not create that demand. It's the age-old story of giving the public what they want". But the piece's damning conclusion is that "video film makers are in a sick contest ... to make ever more horrifying 'nasties'." Throughout this diatribe, soft-core sex films are compared favourably with the "nasties"... well, this is *Titbits* !

AUG 8TH: (*The Sunday Times*) Prosecutions are to be made this week against at least three, and possibly as many as six "nasties". It is acknowledged that there are difficulties inherent in these being the first prosecutions of their kind and also that the vagaries of juries in different courts might lead to contradictory verdicts. It also remains to be seen whether prosecutions will be under Section 3 (which provides for seizure and forfeiture under a magistrate's warrant) or Section 2 (which allows for jail terms of up to three years) of the Obscene Publications Act. Successful Section 2 prosecutions would give "a clear ruling, which both the police and the more respectable members of the trade want so they know where they stand".

AUG 15TH: (*The Sunday Times*) The DPP is offering distributors a chance to avoid the risk of going to jail by agreeing to forfeiture and destruction of "nasties" under Section 3 of the OPA. Officers of the DPP consider that all seven of the tapes submitted to them by Scotland Yard contravene the Act, but it is felt that there is some justification for the view in the trade that no guidelines exist for how far a horror video can go.

AUG 17TH: (*The Times*) Several distributors are understood to have approached the DPP's office offering to destroy master tapes and cease sales. Although the DPP has decided in principle that Section 2 prosecutions could be taken against S.S. EXPERIMENT CAMP, I SPIT ON YOUR GRAVE, DRILLER KILLER, DEATH TRAP and CANNIBAL HOLOCAUST, there are at present no plans to start such proceedings.

AUG 31ST: Willesden magistrates order the forfeiture of 590 copies, plus masters, of DRILLER KILLER and DEATH TRAP which, the prosecution alleged "show scenes of extreme violence and multiple killings". The former is described as "an extravaganza of gory violence" and DEATH TRAP as "particularly disturbing", in that it features violence

THE SEDUCTION OF THE GULLIBLE

towards a woman in the presence of her child. Alex Cranbrook, representing VIPCO, describes the company as a reputable one which has handled the films in good faith, not knowing where the line is to be drawn. The company agrees not to distribute the titles any more and the DPP's office expresses satisfaction at being able to make its position clear at an early stage. Stephen Wooller, for the DPP, describes the Section 3 proceedings as "an exceptional course" and emphasises that in future, distributors will face Section 2 charges. Mary Whitehouse, instrumental in bringing these tapes to the attention of the police, slams the proceedings as "a farce" because of the absence of Section 2 prosecutions and insists that "the DPP should resign". A DPP spokesman describes her outburst as "unreasonable" and repeats that those who distribute the tapes in future will face fines and/or imprisonment under Section 2. Mrs Whitehouse's response to the "unreasonable" tag is to brand the films as "appalling and utter filth" and then admit that she hasn't actually seen them.

SEP 5TH: (*The Sunday Times*) – "NASTIES: THE BIG CLEAR-OUT". "The video trade is bracing itself for a series of police swoops to clear out the nasties". Dealers who continue to stock them are threatened with fines and/or imprisonment. The report continues: "All of the films exploit extremes of violence, particularly towards women, and show multiple murder, rape, mutilation and cannibalism". Derek Mann, chairman of retailers body, the Video Traders Association (VTA): "We now believe that a lot of police forces will be keen to take action, often spurred on by complaints from members of the public. We have had a lot of calls from traders who are very worried. Half are concerned that they might be doing something illegal, and the others are worried about a substantial loss of profit if they withdraw the nasties. We are advising them to take the titles which have already been through the courts off the shelves immediately, but we are also warning them that any film which exploits gratuitous violence may now be open to the same sort of prosecution as pornography. There are probably lots of other uncensored films around as bad as the ones which have been convicted and they may be liable under the Act".The police are warning that they will be pressing hard for Section 2 prosecutions if copies of the convicted tapes are found in any retail outlets.

SEP 24TH: Distributors Astra are ordered to forfeit 234 copies of I SPIT ON YOUR GRAVE, described by Croyden Magistrates as depicting "quite unnecessary violence". Again bemoaning the absence of Section 2 proceedings, Mary Whitehouse describes the proceedings as "a public scandal ... we have a situation today in which, given the choice between the distributors and the police, the DPP protects the interests of the distributors. What we need is a prosecution under Section 2 before a jury ... until we do we shall not know whether or not the Obscene Publications legislation is effective enough to control these video nasties". The DPP states that future prosecutions of these type of tapes will normally be under Section 2.

Presiding Magistrate George Mitchell says that he had been expecting the DPP to proceed under both Sections 2 and 3 of the OPA, after Section 2 papers were signed by Scotland Yard's Obscene Publications supremo Peter Kruger. Stephen Wooller for the DPP attributes this to a "breakdown in communications" between the Yard and the DPP's office and explains that the DPP was anxious to establish a ruling in these early cases due to the lack of precedents over video horror, and that Section 2 prosecutions would have taken months to establish the position. He points out that distributors with previously good records are now willing to surrender and cease distribution of "nasties".

OCT 20TH: A. written reply in the Commons indicates that the government is happy to let the BBFC and BVA work out a voluntary classification code for video. Meanwhile, the DPP warns that his "softly, softly" approach has come to an end

THE SEDUCTION OF THE GULLIBLE

Also this month, Thorn-EMI release THE BURNING on video, only to realise with horror, three weeks later, that the tapes have been struck from an un-cut master, including 15 seconds (notably the punch-line of the finger-snipping sequence) that the BBFC removed for the film to get its theatrical 'X' certificate. Copies are called in from dealers and replaced by the bowdlerised version, free of charge. In panic, Thorn-EMI also begin recalling and re-cutting the likes of SUSPIRIA and even EMMANUELLE 2.

DEC 16TH: Labour MP Gareth Wardell successfully applies to bring a Bill into the House of commons to outlaw the hiring of adult category videos to the young, "offering them protection where none exists at the moment". Wardell, the MP for Gower, argues that: "A young person or a child is today at perfect liberty to hire obscene videos from retail shops, to return to their home and clandestinely to view the material on a video machine. The information that I have collected ... has convinced me that the practice is both wide-spread and growing. It is appropriate today that the House should focus attention on the heavy responsibility carried by any parent that permits a video machine in the home. It is a potentially dangerous weapon that may be used to attack the emotions of our children and young people ... the obscenity law has clearly failed to keep abreast of developments in pornographic electronics". His Bill is given a first reading, but will ultimately run out of parliamentary time.

1983

edited by The Martin Barker
VIDEO NASTIES
Freedom and Censorship in the Media

JAN 2ND: In a *The Sunday Times* "Opinion" column, David Holbrook writes: "In some families, apparently, children are actually deliberately being shown films of buggery, rape and mutilation. Many see them because they are lying around the home. This, the NSPCC believes, is a new form of cruelty. The organisation consulted all its doctors and psychiatrists, who agreed that permanent damage could be done to children's minds by such pornographic and sadistic material, in which the detail is often powerfully real-istic, as in the depictions of castrations or scenes of someone boring through a human skull with an electric drill, bloodily" (how else?) Holbrook's piece is entitled "THE SEDUCTION OF THE INNOCENT", recalling Fredric Wertham's seminal horror comic-bashing essay of the '50s. (Martin Barker's books A HAUNT OF FEARS and THE VIDEO NASTIES [both 1984, Pluto Press], are recommended to anyone interested in the parallels between the anti-horror comics and anti-"nasties" campaigns – JM).

JAN 15TH: A group called "Angry Women", which was formed in the aftermath of the "Yorkshire Ripper" killings, claims responsibility for four window-breaking and fire-bomb attacks on video shops in West Yorkshire.

THE SEDUCTION OF THE GULLIBLE

JAN 29TH: *The Times* reports Norman Abbott's comments at a press conference during the Television '83 Conference. He stated that the voluntary system of regulation currently being worked out will remove the perils of capricious police action and the need for legal regulation: "The police cannot be expected to know much about these things and tend to respond haphazardly to Mrs Whitehouse and others who see themselves as guardians of public morality".

Also in this month: The BBFC and BVA issue a report leading to the amendment of British cinema classification categories to 'U' (Unrestricted), 'PG' (Under-15s accompanied by an adult), '15' (age 15 and over), '18' (age 18 and over) and '18R' (18 and over on a particular premises). THE EVIL DEAD is certified '18' after cuts.

Tougher times on the way for Nasty distributors

The recent seizure of two video cassettes described by the police as "unbelievably horrible" has raised the already loud outcry against the video 'nasties' to fever pitch.

Copies of **Faces of Death**, which includes amongst other scenes footage of a monkey being clubbed to death, have been seized from a video shop in London and handed over to the Director of Public Prosecutions.

Also under examination are copies of **Snuff**, a tape which purports to show genuine killings and was withdrawn by its distributors before release in this country. Some copies, however, have found their way into rental shops, and the DPP is now considering prosecuting

the distributors under Section 2 of the Obscene Publications Act which carries a maximum penalty of three years' imprisonment.

Until now, tapes have been prosecuted under Section 3 of the Act, which merely entails forfeiture under a magistrate's warrant. The relative lightness of this penalty has angered Mrs. Mary Whitehouse, who claims that fines and forfeiture orders together with the delay involved in bringing such cases to court is letting distributors off too easily. In reply, the DPP has promised that next time they consider a video obscene they will prosecute under Section 2 of the Act.

Further confusing the issue is the recent introduction of a classification scheme for video-tapes. The scheme is based on the new British Board of Film Censors' categories for cinema films which include a special 'Club' rating for those films which at present would be denied a certificate and restricted to screenings in private clubs. This movie is seen as an indication that the BBFC's role is changing from that of censorship to classification.

In the case of videotapes, however, the submission of tapes for rating will be at the discretion of the distributors concerned, although it is hoped that video shops will stock only those tapes which carry a rating.

The scheme is the brainchild

of the Video Working Party which, under the chairmanship of James Ferman, secretary of the BBFC, has been debating whether to treat video in the same way as publishing (i.e. something you look at in the privacy of your own home) or to legislate for it like the cinema.

The fact that the classification scheme for video is only a voluntary restriction seems to indicate that the debate is not yet settled. Certainly the distributors themselves seem confused and wary when it comes to the legality or otherwise of their tapes. Thorn-EMI recently requested dealers to return all copies of **The Burning**, after it

was discovered that the master tape from which the duplications were made was an uncensored version of the original cinema release. When the film first came before the BBFC, fifteen seconds were cut before an 'X' certificate was granted.

And in a recent raid by police on a Manchester video shop, several copies of **Endless Love** were confiscated even though the film was granted an 'AA' certificate when it was released in cinemas. The film is in fact a fairly innocuous teenage romance story but, according to the shop's owner, all the police were interested in was the slogan "She was 15" on the cassette's cover.

Video Viewer Feb 1983

FEB 3RD: In another written answer by one of it's spokesman in the Commons, the government indicates that it is still happy to let the BBFC and the BVA sort out self-regulation for the video trade.

FEB 18TH: Palace release THE EVIL DEAD simultaneously on video and theatrically, and almost immediately video copies are seized by Manchester Police, acting under the

THE SEDUCTION OF THE GULLIBLE

misapprehension that the cassette version is "harder" than the one seen at the cinema. All tapes are returned with apologies.

FEB 22ND: The Bishop of Edmonton writes to *The Times* about the BBFC/BVA working party: "More than grading and labelling is needed. There are some films for which 'not recommended' is the only appropriate classification. This would mean that they would not be legally available for sale, a ban to touch those who sell and hire as well as those who manufacture. We have to hold together rights in a free society. I believe the right to sell and make whatever you like is secondary to the rights of children to have protection around their emotional and spiritual growth, similar to that given to their physical growth. Without some sort of authorities with powers we should first of all be victims in the 'video jungle' and then, a little later, subjects of an oppressive censorship introduced by a society angered at excess".

MAR 2ND: A letter to *The Times* from Alan Gilmour, director of the NSPCC, states his desire for "an effective voluntary system with its own invigilating body set up by the suppliers" and adds: "It is disappointing not to have news of any development within the video trade, because there can be little doubt that legislation would be a clumsy alternative. Reputable dealers should be in no doubt of the degree of public concern nor of the will to support effective action".

MAR 10TH: Government spokesman Christopher Mayhew states that the BBFC / BVA report is ready and that their self-regulatory scheme for the trade can be implemented with the government monitoring how it works.

MAR 17TH: In a letter to Gareth Wardell, Home Secretary William Whitelaw says that: "...there is the very real point of principle that it would be wrong to involve the government so directly in matters of censorship ... If legislation is needed in this field we must clearly ensure that it is in the form best designed to achieve its objective without undesirable and unintended side-effects. As you know, the BVA are introducing their own scheme for voluntary classification and I think we both agreed that, if at all possible, it is preferable to rely on effective measures of self-regulation".

MAR 26TH: A conference representing 21,000 members of the Association of Cinematograph, Television and allied Technicians votes unanimously to campaign against "video nasties" depicting violence against women.

MAR 31ST: Minister Christopher Mayhew announces that he has received a copy of that BBFC / BVA report. A Videograms Standards Council is to be set up, and a prestigious chairman will soon be appointed to it.

APRIL. The police raid Barker Video in Leeds. A General Election is called for June.

APR 10TH: Mary Whitehouse presses for the Conservative Election manifesto to include tighter obscenity laws to control the "nasties". Mrs Whitehouse states: "The forthcoming election and the threat of video nasties has given a new impetus to our campaign. No party can afford to ignore the threat, and if the law is not changed, the spread of pornography via video and cable TV will do our children terrible damage". Home Secretary Willie Whitelaw assures her that the government will legislate if the Video Standards Council fails to secure effective self-regulation for the video trade.

APR 14TH: (*The Times*) "WAR DECLARED ON THE VIDEO 'NASTIES'." The voluntary classification code will be backed up by registration of video dealers. Dealers who fail to register by next September will be forced out of business by having supplies of tapes withheld. Any member of the BVA who continues to supply unregistered dealers will be expelled. Donald Maclean, BVA chairman, argues that legislation on the matter "would be fraught with undesirable side-effects". Vice-chairman Iain Muspratt says that there will be "no business, no future" for unregistered dealers and adds that although the scheme does represent a restrictive trade practice: "… we do not expect that to be a problem". Classification will start at once, using the same categories as are used for cinema releases. Cassettes will be clearly labelled with a certificate. The classifying body, the Videograms Standards Council, will be formed from representatives of videogram publishers, wholesalers and retailers, plus four people unconnected with the industry.

Norman Abbott of the BVA (which defines "video nasty" as "a phrase coined by the press that generally refers to material that can include disembowelling, castration, cannibalism and mutilation") sat in on the working party, and says: "I am trying to obliterate from my memory the terrible things we were subjected to. Some of the films stunned me". Iain Muspratt describes the "nasties" as "degrading muck" and adds that most dealers, as well as many parents, have been calling for a regulatory scheme such as the one that has just been worked out.

But when the Conservatives' Election manifesto is published, the following passage indicates a complete U-turn on video regulation and sends shock-waves through the industry: "We will also respond to the increasing public concern over obscenity and offences against public decency, which often have links with serious crime. We propose to introduce legislation to deal with the most serious of these problems, such as the spread of violent and obscene video cassettes".

APR 30TH: The media having prepared the ground for such preposterous claims, criminals start attributing their mis-deeds to the influence of video. At Cheltenham Juvenile Court, Gloucester, a 16 year old would-be rapist claims inspiration from CONFESSIONS OF A WINDOW CLEANER: "I watched the film and then went out because I wanted to have sex with a girl".

MAY. This month Raymond Johnston, a leading figure in Mary Whitehouse's "Festival of Light" pressure group, writes the paper CHILDREN AND VIDEO: A DANGER AND A PROPOSAL, a virtual manifesto for "nasty" bashers and highly influential on the upcoming Parliamentary Group Video Enquiry.

MAY 30TH: Mary Whitehouse asks the Independent Broadcasting Authority to preview the Channel 4 TV programme A GENTLEMAN'S AGREEMENT? (a feminist look at the video industry's attempts at self-regulation), due for broadcast on June 8th, to see that it does not "go too far" and contravene the Broadcasting Act in its use of illustrative clips from "nasties". The programme has already been moved back from its scheduled broadcast time of 8.30 p.m. to 10.15 p.m. An IBA spokesman says Mrs Whitehouse's request will be considered: "We do preview programmes anyway when we deem it necessary".

MAY 31ST: Senior IBA staff view A GENTLEMAN'S AGREEMENT? and a statement is issued that they had already intended to do so before receiving Mrs Whitehouse's request.

JUN 1ST: The IBA clear the Channel 4 documentary for broadcast. Meanwhile, the National Association of Head Teachers demands government action to protect children fro"nasties", claiming that they are playing a part in the increased incidence of sexual harassment of teachers by their charges.

JUN 3RD: Mary Whitehouse asks the DPP to stop the broadcast of A GENTLEMAN'S AGREEMENT? on the grounds that it contains excerpts from the convicted videos S.S. EXPERIMENT CAMP and I SIT ON YOUR GRAVE. Admitting that she has not viewed the documentary she is seeking to ban, Mrs Whitehouse continues: "It really would not have made the slightest difference, because I know very well what they are – we were responsible for bringing them before the courts" (She didn't bother to watch them then, either - JM). The police also express "surprise" that the programme will feature such clips, but Channel 4 responds that they have been chosen with care.

JUN 8TH: A GENTLEMAN'S AGREEMENT? is broadcast on Channel 4, the DPP advising Mrs Whitehouse that it would not be an offence to broadcast the clips in question on TV. The programme reveals that many parents deem "nasties" to be acceptable viewing for their children, and features an interview with Stephen Taylor, the first dealer to be prosecuted under Section 2 of the Obscene Publications Act. Though he believes his £600 fine was at least twice as big as it should have been, Taylor expresses himself "glad" that he was the first to be prosecuted: "If I had been the second, I might have got 6 months imprisonment". Clips screened include the patently phony immolation of women prisoners from S.S. EXPERIMENT CAMP.

JUN 9TH: On the day that the Conservative government wins a second term, *The Times* reviews A GENTLEMAN'S AGREEMENT?: "As one stockist of such films suggested, there is as much gruesome detail in a cassette on the Falklands War as in DRILLER KILLER or DEAD AND BURIED. Is there at work here an atrophied Puritanism that finds fiction more reprehensible than fact?" The review also argues that children are a lot more sophisticated in their reactions to what they watch than is generally supposed.

JUN 15TH: In *The Daily Express* one Graham Bright, Conservative MP for Luton South, defines "nasties" as "grossly offensive to all reasonable people", a line that would feature prominently in subsequent "clean-up" blitzes on various media.

JUN 27TH: A meeting of various concerned notables, first called by Viscount Ingleby in May, but postponed due to the Election, takes place in a room at the House of Lords. Lord Nugent of Guildford takes the chair, and after a discussion it is decided to seek out objective, factual evidence of the situation existing in the country, to guide Parliament "on a social situation that is giving concern and upon which there appears to be very little reliable evidence". Significantly, the meeting clashes with the Annual Assembly of the Methodist Church, so none of its leaders, who agreed to attend the earlier meeting, are available. The Reverend Brian Brown, a lecturer from Oxford Polytechnic, represents them, and volunteers to host the research in his Television Research Unit (TRU).

JUN 28TH: 18 year-old Mark Austin is sentenced to six years youth custody for rape, burglary and theft. "I got the ideas for the rapes from a video nasty", he claims. Robert Francis for the defence describes his client as a glue sniffing addict of low I.Q. who lived in a fantasy world dominated by violent videos. Judge Tudor Price agrees that the rapes were triggered when Austin's mind was "inflamed" after a viewing of I SPIT ON YOUR GRAVE. Despite the glue-sniffing and Austin's long track-record as a social misfit, Francis offered a more esoteric rationale for his client's behaviour: "His moral values were obliterated by seeing women degraded in video films. What he saw made him think that women were prepared to behave in a fashion that bore no relation to reality…" (See my review of I SPIT ON YOUR GRAVE for a rebuttal of this charge, which is so often, and so thoughtlessly, levelled – JM) "… he lived out his fantasies". *The Sun*, reporting this case, claims that: "The nasties usually include violent rape scenes which end with the victims enjoying the assault" … talk about bearing "no relation to reality"!

Daily Mail Campaign BAN THE SADIST VIDEOS

Lynda Lee-Potter in *The Daily Mail* : "The impact that this sick, beastly, money-making corruption is having on illiterate minds is going to make previous anxieties about violence on television look like worries about the impact of Enid Blyton!"

JUN 30TH: Prime Minister Margaret Thatcher's first clear Parliamentary comment on a "need for legislation": "I recognise the great concern caused by this matter. That is why we referred to it in our party manifesto during the Election campaign. It is not enough to have voluntary legislation. We must bring in a law to regulate the matter. My Right Honourable and learned friend the Home Secretary is now considering precisely what form the law should take.

The same day, a *Daily Mail* editorial launches that paper's "Ban the sadist videos" campaign "into top gear", as the video trade press publishes the following list of 52 "nasties", obtained from the Director of Public Prosecutions... ABSURD, ANTHROPOPHAGOUS BEAST, THE BEAST IN HEAT, THE BEYOND, BLOODBATH, BLOODY MOON, THE BOGEY MAN, THE BURNING, CANNIBAL APOCALYPSE, CANNIBAL FEROX, CANNIBAL HOLOCAUST, CANNIBAL MAN, CANNIBAL TERROR, CONTAMINATION, DEAD AND BURIED, DEATH TRAP, DEEP RIVER SAVAGES, DELIRIUM, DON'T GO IN THE WOODS, DON'T GO NEAR THE PARK, DRILLER KILLER, THE EVIL DEAD, EVILSPEAK, EXPOSE, FACES OF DEATH, FOREST OF FEAR, FRANKENSTEIN (Andy Warhol version), THE GESTAPO'S LAST ORGY, THE HOUSE BY THE CEMETERY, HOUSE ON THE EDGE OF THE PARK, I SPIT ON YOUR GRAVE, THE LAST HOUSE ON THE LEFT, THE LIVING DEAD, MAD HOUSE, MARDI GRAS MASSACRE, NIGHTMARE MAKER, NIGHTMARES IN A DAMAGED BRAIN, NIGHT OF THE BLOODY APES, NIGHT OF THE DEMON, POSSESSION, PRANKS, PRISONER OF THE CANNIBAL GOD, THE SLAYER, SNUFF, S.S. EXPERIMENT CAMP, TENEBRAE, TERROR EYES, THE TOOLBOX MURDERS (mis-identified as "THE TALLBOX MURDERS" on early listings – JM), UNHINGED, THE WITCH WHO CAME FROM THE SEA, ZOMBIE CREEPING FLESH and ZOMBIE FLESH EATERS.

JUL 1ST: *The Daily Mail* : "Within hours of *The Daily Mail* campaign moving into top gear, the Prime Minister admitted that voluntary standards of control would not work". Graham Bright, Tory MP for Luton South, who came top of the recent ballot for private member's Bills, announces his intention to resign his minor governmental post as Parliamentary private secretary to the two Home Office Ministers and introduce a Bill on the control of "video nasties" (such Bills often fail due to the limited amount of parliamentary time allotted to them, but this one was coming right from the top – JM).

JUL 2ND: *The Times* reports new Home Secretary Leon Brittan's "pleasure" at Graham Bright's topping of the private member's Bill ballot, also that Bright "had no comment to make on the details of the Bill, which will undoubtedly be drafted by the Home Office because he is going into hospital for a minor operation on Monday". Immediately following his topping of the ballot, Bright had also been offered a draft bill by Mary Whitehouse's National Viewers and Listeners' Association. "Mr Bright will have to resign as parliamentary private secretary, but that is no sacrifice compared with the gratitude he will earn from Mr Brittan and other ministers who were becoming embarrassed by the growing clamour for action inside and outside the Commons", continues *The Times*, leaving little doubt as to who is the real force behind "the Bright Bill". The purely figure-head role played by Mr Bright in the Bill that came to bear his name is entirely consistent with his subsequent, not exactly glittering, political career. He has emerged only rarely since the days of "video nasties", to agitate for the restoration of capital punishment (so much for non-violence) and the curtailment of prostitution and warehouse parties (so much for right-wing libertarianism).

JUL 6TH: A poll published by *Video Week* indicates a swing of opinion in the video trade − nearly half of the 100 dealers polled now support proposals for legislation, as opposed to voluntary self-regulation, against "video nasties".

JUL 7TH: A solicitor acting for distributors VTC writes to the police enquiring about that company's release POSSESSION appearing on a list of "video nasties". The police choose not to reply.

JUL 8TH: In a *Daily Mail* interview, Leon Brittan lets the cat even further out of the bag as to the real authorship of "the Bright Bill": "There is a widespread feeling of outrage. I was determined to get something through as soon as possible so we formulated a policy and Graham Bright has kindly taken it up. We could not get it through any faster if it was a government Bill".

JUL 13TH: Kenneth Smart, a 23-year old fork-lift truck driver, is jailed for life at Bristol Crown Court for tying up one Terrance Preston in a wood and killing him. In court he is described as "a sexual psychopath" obsessed with gay bondage fantasies, but the media chooses, inexplicably, to attribute his actions to viewings of Lucio Fulci's ZOMBIE FLESH EATERS.

JUL 15TH: (*The Times*) "A tough Bill designed to stamp out video nasties, with fines of up to £10,000 and imprisonment, will have its second reading in November". Graham Bright says: "We are after the cowboy backstreet dealers".

JUL 18TH: (*The Times*) "Mary Whitehouse will oppose any attempt to control 'video nasties' by a classification or licensing system without supporting legislation". In a submission to the Home Secretary, the NVLA President argues that the government's first priority should be legislation to control such material, setting out prohibited elements of violence and obscenity.

JUL 25TH: The DPP replies to a letter from VTC's solicitor, confirming that two OPA prosecutions of dealers involving POSSESSION are going ahead.

JUL 26TH: The second meeting of concerned worthies under the chairmanship of Lord Nugent considers research proposals and decides to implement them by setting up an academic working party, the "Parliamentary Group Video Enquiry", which isl supposed tocome up with unweighted conclusions. Despite its title, the working party is not a parliamentary body at all, rather a private one funded by individuals and churches (he who pays the piper ...). Sociology lecturer and Home Office adviser Dr Clifford Hill emerges as the most powerful figure in the team that will handle the upcoming enquiry.

JUL 29TH: VTC get an urgent call from the London offices of CBS, who have been distributing their video release of POSSESSION, informing them that police are on the premises, seizing 687 copies, plus the masters, of the tape. Sales are ceased, with 2,918 copies already having been sold.

AUG 4TH: In a *Daily Mail* piece entitled "'TAKEN OVER' BY SOMETHING EVIL FROM THE TV SET", one Dr Mathai tells of a boy "possessed" by a "nasty".

AUG 5TH: (*The Times*) "RAPIST WAS ADDICTED TO 'VIDEO NASTIES'". The wife of rapist Christopher Meah, who was yesterday sentenced to two life terms at the Central Criminal Court, blames "nasties" for turning him into "a sex monster". Obviously rationalising her decision to take this man as her soul-mate, Christine Meah contends: "When my husband first began watching these videos, we treated them as a sick joke. Now I am convinced that they changed his personality and that they should be banned".

Pin-pointing the real tragedy, Judge Gibbens, QC, described it as "a misfortune" that magistrates had allowed Meah bail, despite strong police objections, after two earlier attacks on women. Shortly afterwards he tied up, stabbed and raped a third. Robin Grey, QC, for the defence, claimed that his client was "sexually aroused" by an addiction to videos "of the most vile kind" (Meah allegedly "felt that he was looking at himself playing a video nasty film role" while carrying out his attacks), but also isolated another, more plausible reason for Meah's behaviour – brain-damage he had sustained after a car crash in 1978. Yet another factor which surely played no small part in what happened was revealed by Meah himself when he stated "I have been taking drugs and drinking, and the videos, on top of all that, drove me completely out of my head".

AUG 13TH: In the freedom and democracy-loving *Daily Mail*, Richard Neighbour makes the lofty proclamation that "The public has shown its preference, but in this case the public is wrong". (Watch out, the neighbours are keeping an eye on you!)

SEPTEMBER. A Gallup opinion poll, commissioned by the BVA to act as "a political dip-stick" for Graham Bright and lend weight to their claim that his Video Recordings Bill is in danger of going too far, indicates the depth of public confusion. "The Videogram Study, 21-27 September 1983" reveals that a majority of people surveyed were in favour of video censorship, but also that a large percentage believed video, and also TV, theatre, radio, books, newspapers and magazines were already censored.

SEP 23RD: The Parliamentary Group Video Enquiry rush out an "interim report" to coincide with the "Bright Bill"'s first day in the committee stage in the House of Commons. It claims that 40.4% of school children aged six and over have seen at least one "nasty". This finding is based on only the very small number of questionnaires that have been processed at this point, and the dubious figure has been further expanded by the group having ignored their own definition of "nasties", i.e. "films that contain scenes of such violence and sadism, involving either human beings or animals, that they would not be granted a certificate for public exhibition in Britain".

SEP 25TH: *The Daily Mirror* : "Violent, sadistic and perverted video films are as great a danger to a child's mind as any infectious disease is to the body. Yet children are being exposed to them every day. High street retailers, so obsessed with profit that they have

THE SEDUCTION OF THE GULLIBLE

these films on their shelves, plumb the depths of greed ... these obscenities can be bought or hired in any town".

SEP 30TH: Paul Mundy and Robert Peacock are jailed for four years and 21 months respectively for chaining and stabbing a kung-fu student. Despite the fact that their assault followed a drink and drugs binge, the media are keener to blame it on viewings of THE WARRIORS on video.

NOV 1ST: Police screen a 20-minute compilation tape drawn from six of the convicted "nasties" for MPs.

NOV 3RD: As the "Bright Bill" is published, outlining how the "nasties" would be banned by withholding certificates from them, and making provision for fines of up to £10,000 for those who deal in un-certified videos, Graham Bright reveals that any legislation might not take full effect until the end of 1985, as it will take 12-18 months to classify a back-log of 6,000 titles after his Bill becomes law next Summer. He is trying to ensure the backing of 99 colleagues that his Bill will require for its second reading on the 11th.

Recognising the accelerating climate of unreason, *The Guardian* argues: "anyone getting in the way too quickly risks being lumped together with child-molesters and sadists".

NOV 5TH: (*Times* lead article) "Video has come to Britain in a rush, faster than attitudes and laws can well adjust to... because prosecutions under the Obscene Publications Act are slow and fines very small, there has also been a rush of filthy and violent material profitably circulated with little regard to the law. Even those parents who are careful about what is shown in their own homes may find their small children coming home with the horrors after seeing JAWS or something much worse".

The piece acknowledges the double jeopardy faced by dealers, who will be liable under both the OPA and any proposed video legislation. On Bright's suggestion that the British Board of Film Censors grade videos, *The Times* comments: "To give (the BBFC) statutory powers over video, but not over film, would make it a most anomalous hybrid. Perhaps it is time to follow the recommendation of the Williams Committee and create a statutory film board, ending the role of the local authorities in this area".

NOV 8TH: Lord Lane, the Lord Chief Justice, calls for rigid and rigorous censorship of pornographic magazines and "video nasties", backed up by heavy penalties, in a Darwin Lecture entitled "Do we get the criminals we deserve?", at Cambridge University.

NOV 10TH: Mary Whitehouse as President of the National Viewers and Listeners Association, writes to *The Times*: "The whole problem of violent obscenity, which is destroying our culture, has its roots within our hopelessly ineffective obscenity legislation. That is the basic challenge, and unless the government faces up to this and takes action to deal with the problem on that level, then all other initiatives, however well intended will be purely superficial and cosmetic". She continues: "It would appear too that you have few qualms about the appointment of the BBFC as the classifying body. Are you not aware the films classified by that body have come before the courts? The inevitable corruption of judgement which has increasingly characterised the activities of that body should make it the last, not the first, alternative". She states her preference for a body independent of the film industry (consisting of child experts, teachers and women's groups) and commends the suggestion of John Smyth QC, who has studied the Bright Bill, to add "in the home" to clause 4(1), which states that the statutory authority will be responsible for determining "whether or not video works are suitable for showing".

On the same date, *New Society* carries a rare dissenting piece, "HOW NASTY ARE THE VIDEO NASTIES?" by Martin Barker.

NOV 11TH: MPs debate the second reading of Graham Bright's Video Recordings Bill.

NOV 12TH: Commenting upon the 20 minute compilation tape screened for MPs by the police, *The Daily Mail* says: "If it made MPs (and even hardened policemen) physically ill, then there cannot be much doubt that these evil artefacts should be kept out of reach of the young".

NOV 13TH: (*The Sunday Times*) In a piece entitled "WHY I DON'T ACCEPT THE NIGHT-MARE VIEW OF BRITAIN", John Mortimer QC, writes: "Lord Lane said that apprehended criminals seek to explain themselves by saying 'It's because of all them books and films, innit?' I wouldn't have thought that Lord Lane was accustomed to believe every word that captured criminals might put up by way of defence. To blame books and films for your crimes is a frequently heard mitigation in court. It may be that the roots of criminality lie far deeper and the possibility exists that neither Jack The Ripper nor Heinrich Himmler had ever seen a video nasty".

NOV 16TH: In a letter to The Times, Ivor H. Mills, Professor of Medicine at the University of Cambridge Clinical School, talks of physical addiction to brain chemicals produced by the viewing of "nasties".

NOV 17TH: (*The Times*) "VIDEO NASTY SICKENS EURO MPs". Graham Bright seeks European co-operation in Strasbourg, with the aid of "a Scotland Yard special video stitching together some of the more nauseating sections of the films available in local family video shops throughout Britain". The report recalls that a similar screening to British MPs earlier this month resulted in "half of them walking out, feeling ill". Members of the European Parliament, parliamentary staff and British journalists are now "treated to their first public viewing from the Yard's chamber of celluloid horrors". The article continues "Nasty is too weak a word to describe it. One girl had to rush from the viewing room to be sick and more than one journalist will be unable to give a full account of what happened. Several left, or turned their faces to the wall". The piece cites the "monkey scene" from FACES OF DEATH as the main cause of all this distress.

NOV 24TH: *The Daily Star* on Dr Clifford Hill's VIDEO VIOLENCE AND CHILDREN report: "Appalled researchers discovered that video nasties have replaced party games and conjurors at children's birthday parties".

NOV 30TH: At the Video Recordings Bill standing committee, responding to concern over the acquittal of two "Nasties" at Snaresbrook Crown Court on NOVEMBER 7TH, David Mellor of the Home Office replies that "the jury in the Snaresbrook Crown Court acquitted what in my view was one of the worst video nasties that I and several colleagues saw" (He's talking about THE EVIL DEAD! - JM) "That was an astonishing decision, but the jury acquitted it not because of an inadequacy in the law but because they used their judgement and arrived at a conclusion that may have seemed regrettable. The classic simplicity of the Bill is its proposal that the only matter of concern to the courts will be whether a video has a certificate."

By the end of this month, despite the belief of many MPs that it would not survive the parliamentary session, the "Bright Bill" has gone through its second reading in the

THE SEDUCTION OF THE GULLIBLE

Commons, without a single M.P. voting against it. At one point during the second reading, David Mellor opined that "no-one has the right to be upset by a brutal sex crime or a sadistic attack on a child or mindless thuggery on a pensioner if he is not prepared to drive sadistic videos out of our high streets".

DEC 3RD & 10TH: Two articles by Nigel Andrews, highly critical of the current video-bashing climate ("VIDEO NASTIES – OR VIDEO NAZIS?" and "THE VIDEO NASTY DEBATE SENSE AND CENSORSHIP"), appear in *The Financial Times*.

DEC 13TH: *The Times* – Roger Scruton comments, after a TV screening of THE DAY AFTER, that the post-nuclear holocaust drama "is...a particularly disgusting video nasty...That it should have been banned goes without saying. There is no more excuse for displaying a realistic depiction of nuclear catastrophe than for displaying a realistic picture of a woman being cut up with a chainsaw, or a live child being slowly disembowelled by hungry cannibals".

Restoring the balance of sanity somewhat, on the same date, a *Guardian* article by Maureen O'Connor demonstrates that Dr Clifford Hill's Parliamentary Group Video Enquiry derived parts of its findings on children's "Nasty" viewing habits from the questionnaire responses of as few as three children!

DEC 17TH: In a *Times* piece entitled "SHOULD WE THEN BAN 'NEWS AT TEN'?", David Hewson argues that TV news, videos of the Falklands War and even Shakespeare would fall foul of the prohibitive criteria being applied for the treatment of "video nasties" and goes on to report the following from the third sitting of standing Committee C on the Video Recordings Bill as indicative of the level of parliamentary debate:
Graham Bright (Conservative, Luton South): "There would be considerable scope for argument as to how far that" (an amendment which would replace the word "animal" with "sentient being") "would extend down the animal kingdom". I am advised, for example, that an amoeba might be considered to be sentient on the grounds that it would move away from noxious chemicals. Similarly ... I am told that a plant will respond to the force of gravity – if it is turned upside down, the stem and roots will start to grow in the opposite direction". Robert Maclennan (Social Democrat, Caithness and Sunderland): "Will the honourable gentleman explain why he thinks that exposure to the force of gravity could possibly be described as 'mutilation, torture, or other acts of gross violence'?" Graham Bright: "There is an element of force which is unnatural if one turns a plant upside down".

DEC 23RD: In a letter to *The Times*, Neville March Hunnings, editor of Common Market Law Report, warns about the prospect of "control by state organs in a manner not seen in this country since the Tudor licensing of the printing presses".

1984
"War is peace, freedom is slavery..."
("...censorship is classification"?)

JAN 3RD: "PONY MANIAC STRIKES AGAIN". A policeman investigating the sexual assault of ponies is quoted in *The Daily Mirror* as attributing the dirty deed to a "maniac (who) could be affected by video 'nasties' or a new moon".

JAN 15TH: In "Torturing the evidence", a Radio 4 programme presented by Michael Tracey, head of the Broadcasting Research Unit, it is revealed that laboratory research by Guy Cumerbatch of the University of Aston found the predominate reaction of his

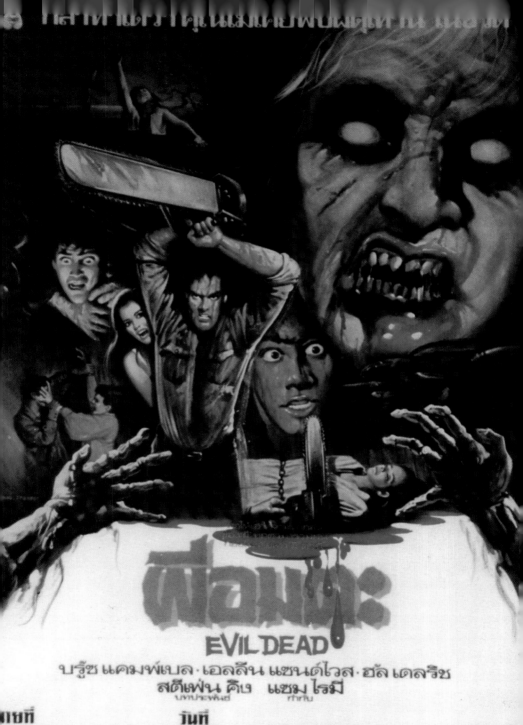

IT GOES
BEYOND
SURVIVAL!

IT GOES
BEYOND
CANNIBALISM!

IT GOES
BEYOND
YOUR WILDEST
IMAGINATION!

JOSEPH BRENNER presents

SACRIFICE!

WARNING:
FOR YOUR OWN HEALTH
AND SAFETY DO *NOT* EN-
TER THE THEATRE TILL
YOU ARE EMOTIONALLY
AND PHYSICALLY PRE-
PARED TO WITNESS THE
MOST FORBIDDEN ACTS
OF TORTURE.

SACRIFICE! A LENZI/ROSSI/ASSONITIS FILM
FOR ROAS PRODUCTIONS/MEDUSA/TECHNICOLOR/TECHNISCOPE
A JOSEPH BRENNER ASSOCIATES, INC. Release Ⓑ Ⓡ RESTRICTED

EXCELSIOR
URSULA ANDRESS
STACY KEACH
DE BLANKE
GODIN VAN DE
KANNIBALEN
LA MONTAGNE
DU DIEU
CANNIBALE
Regie SERGIO MARTINO
"THE MOUNTAIN OF THE

CONTAMINACION:
ALIEN
INVADE LA TIERRA

IAN Mc CULLOCH · LOUISE MARLEAU · MARINO MASE
Director: LEWIS COATES   eastmancolor

A NEW NIGHTMARE
FROM TOBE HOOPER DIRECTOR OF THE
TEXAS CHAINSAW MASSACRE

DEATH
TRAP

X

Starring NEVILLE BRAND · MEL FERRER · CAROLYN JONES · STUART WHITMAN

SE NON VOLETE SVENIRE CONTINUATE A RIPETERVI
E' SOLO UN FILM, E' SOLO UN FILM, E' SOLO UN FILM!

L'ULTIMA CASA A SINISTRA

CON DAVID HESS · LUCY GRANTHAN · SANDRA CASSEL · MARC SHEFFLER

REGIA DI WES CRAVEN

UNA PRODUZIONE THE NIGHT COMPANY NEW YORK
EASTMANCOLOR

David Hess **DER SCHLITZER** Annie Belle
Lorraine de Sele
Anca Lahres

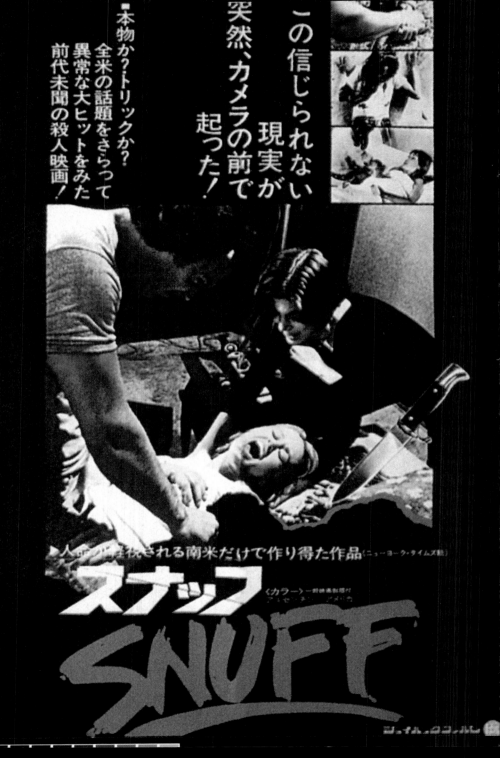

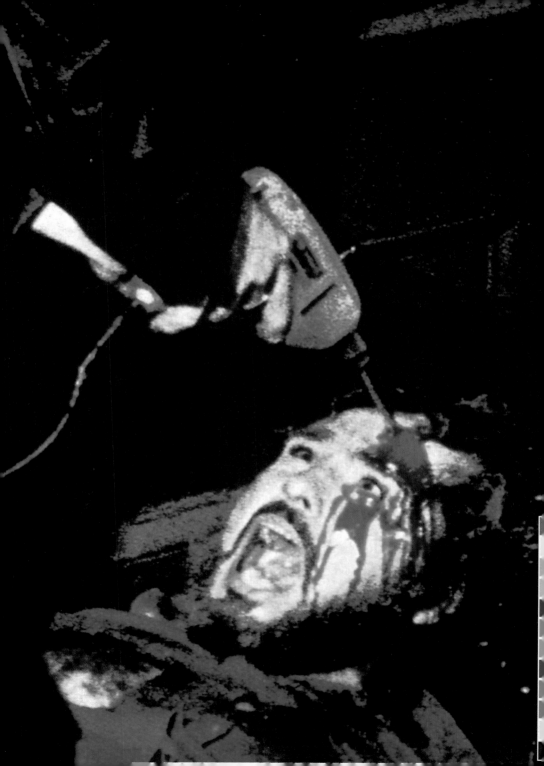

THE SEDUCTION OF THE GULLIBLE

subjects to DRILLER KILLER to be boredom rather than heightened aggression.

FEB 1ST: Judge John Evans QC, sentencing Stourbridge dealers Alan Perrins and Robert Hardwick to three month sentences, suspended for a year, at Dudley Crown Court, describes his viewing of the "nasties" for which they were prosecuted as "one of the most unpleasant experiences of my life" and talks of "unspeakable violence and sadism".

FEB 3RD: At the end of a 3 day test-case trial, David Hamilton Grant, secretary of the company that distributed NIGHTMARES IN A DAMAGED BRAIN, is sentenced to 18 months in jail, with a further 12 suspended, for possession of over 200 copies of an obscene article for publication for gain. Marketing director Malcolm Fancey receives a nine months suspended sentence and is fined £250. Works director Roger Morley is also fined £250. Summing up, Judge Christopher Beaumont declares: "People who make money out of this sort of obscenity, which can do much harm, have got to be punished". He ordered all the seized tapes to be destroyed. Grant's company, which distributed the title for WORLD OF VIDEO 2000, is in liquidation.

During the trial, the defence tried to show that the version of NIGHTMARES being prosecuted was similar to the one passed by the BBFC (which was actually 48 seconds shorter – JM) but Kenneth Richardson, prosecuting, argued that it "glorified and encouraged violence" and, on video, could easily be seen by children. Film critic Derek Malcolm, speaking as a defence witness, argued: "One remembers Dracula drinking the blood of young virgins sixty years ago, which was very shocking at the time". Describing NIGHTMARES as "among the better" horror films from a technical point of view, he continued: "You don't find a lot of profundity in this kind of film, but there is usually a moral of some sort. The moral in this case is that children are likely to be perverted by the excesses of the adult world". Richardson suggested that the film was itself one of those excesses, to which Malcolm replied: "That may be a view. It is not my view. Apart from a four minute sequence, there is very little that might disturb people".

Marjorie Bilbow of *Screen International* praised the "skill" with which NIGHTMARES had been made, opining that the mass under-25 audience would find it "not all that horrific". She described the film as "more intelligent, more thought-provoking" than FRIDAY THE 13TH, HALLOWEEN, THE EXORCIST or POLTERGEIST, with its director trying to say something about the parental guidance of children, the results of child neglect, and society's treatment of the insane. "I wouldn't wish a child to see it", she continued: "but that is surely the responsibility of parents and guardians of children". Doubting that the film's effects would be particularly harmful on a young mind anyway, she remarked in conclusion that "children have always enjoyed being frightened – that is part of growing up". Presumably arguing for an acquittal on the grounds of "artistic merit", she speculated that "in thirty years the film may be regarded in the same way as

THE SEDUCTION OF THE GULLIBLE

an early Hitchcock".

Derek Malcolm, more realistically, described it as "not a classic, but well-executed", provoking the testy retort "So was the German invasion of Poland" from Judge Beaumont (a remark that in its turn provoked Martin Barker to comment "Lord save us from such stupidity"). Malcolm also argued that PRIZE OF PERIL and Clint Eastwood's SUDDEN IMPACT, both released theatrically in the week of the trial, were infinitely more reprehensible, but that video was a soft target. He would later describe NIGHTMARES in *The Guardian* as "a more or less unexceptional horror epic with the usual bucket of blood in the last reel", adding the warning that if the "nasties" campaign continues: "we will quickly get the reputation of the most absurdly repressive nation in Europe". Recalling the experience of this trial, he commented: "There's no answer to this kind of ignorance, and no way of conducting a logical argument in courts of law dominated by judges and magistrates who have scarcely heard of Hitchcock", also quoting John Mortimer, QC, to the effect that: "to try and get the criminal law to impose standards of taste and morality is absolutely absurd".

FEB 8TH: David Mellor, Under-secretary of state at the Home Office, clashes with MPs over the role of the BBFC in classifying videos. Sir Bernard Braine, says that the Board has presided over a gradual decline in standards and he wants clearer guide-lines for it.

FEB 16TH: *Video Retailer* reports the comments of Austin Mitchell, Labour MP for Great Grimsby, as the Video Recordings Bill continues its passage through Parliament. He stated in the Commons that it has been "passed in a fit of inattention by the House. It has been cobbled together, especially at the latter stages of its consideration ... we are taking a sledge-hammer to crack a nut". Mitchell told the trade magazines: "This Bill has gone further than it ought to have done. I'm worried that with the BBFC coming closer under the Home Office's control, censorship could become much stricter".

The magazine also reports conflict in the trade between dealers and distributors over the cost of labelling cassettes and replacing old copies with the legally sanctioned new ones. Meanwhile, eight more dealers have been summoned to court in a continuing police blitz on video libraries in the Lancaster and Morecambe area. MANIAC, THE HILLS HAVE EYES, EMMANUELLE 2 and entries in the soft-core ELECTRIC BLUE series are among the tapes seized. Police officers tell dealers that they should be guided by what they are prepared to show their children (What are the implications of this for adult viewing? And what if the dealers were quite happy to show their children the "nasties"? – JM). The dealers are charged £4.31 each for the hire of video equipment so that the magistrates could view the films and £6 each for court costs.

Elsewhere, the Hill report is described as "totally discredited" after the resignation of the Catholic and Methodist members of its commissioning group, who have also removed their financial support. The row is over how fast the report has been drawn up. A Catholic spokesman talks of "dubious correlations and leading questions which ... distract from hard facts". The research was based on a survey of 6,000 children undertaken by Oxford Polytechnics Television Research Unit, who complained when it came out that they hadn't even processed their data, and that Dr Clifford Hill had misused that data. The group then removed both the data and the contract from their hands. The Reverend Brian Brown, head of the TRU, is planning a new survey along similar lines but with a wider brief to cover the whole range of children's viewing habits.

FEB 20TH: *Video Week* reports how video wholesaler Barrie Gold of S. Gold and Sons, High Road, Leytonstone, claimed in Snaresbrook Crown Court that distributor April

THE SEDUCTION OF THE GULLIBLE

Electronics "played a dirty trick" on him by supplying uncut versions of NIGHTMARES IN A DAMAGED BRAIN in 1982. In April of that year the BBFC had passed a cut version of the film and Gold claims that's the version he thought he had. His premises were raided in November of that year, with copies of DEATH TRAP, LAST HOUSE ON THE LEFT and CANNIBAL APOCALYPSE also being seized, resulting in a further three charges under the Obscene Publications Act. The jury were shown DEATH TRAP and CANNIBAL APOCALYPSE, but not the other two, which the defence did not dispute the obscenity of. Richard Du Cann, QC, defending, revealed that Gold got a letter from VPD in that year (1982), notifying him that they had had copies of LAST HOUSE ON THE LEFT seized, and he was going to send his four copies back to them – the four copies of that found on his premises had just been returned by customers and were due to be sent back. Gold also knew that DEATH TRAP had been withdrawn because it might be considered obscene under the OPA, and had received credits for its return. He had had no intention of supplying it for gain. Gold is acquitted, but will appear again in this chronology...

FEB 25TH: In *The Times*, Michael Tracey exposes the shortcomings of the Parliamentary Group Video Enquiry's VIDEO VIOLENCE AND CHILDREN report: "The problem is that almost every statement contained in the group's report and uttered at the press conference is denied by the other members of the research team who compiled the data, the members of Oxford Polytechnic's Television Research Unit". He reveals that when Graham Bright came top of the ballot for private member's Bills and announced his intention to introduce the Video Recordings Bill "what had been conceived as a study possibly lasting two years was suddenly under pressure to produce early results". The information from questionnaires was derived from teachers' comments rather than pupils' responses: "It is very difficult to see what can be claimed for such information, which of its nature can have no real social scientific significance". The TRU are quoted as stating: "Our main worry was that we knew the report contained assertions and exaggerated claims allegedly supported by factual evidence. We knew no grounds to support this statement. The report too was skewed and distorted and appeared to have been completed without any reference to the research data which we were still assembling. We know as a matter of fact that we did not collect much of the evidence cited". Furthermore, although there were no questions on TV ownership or socio-economic status in the questionnaire, the report contained comments on both, politically-loaded ones in the latter respect. Mysteriously, the report also contained comments from two nine year-olds in Coventry, Warren ("I like all the blood coming out") and Steve ("I like the bit in DRILLER KILLER where he puts a man up on sticks and then he gets a drill and puts it through his stomach and he screams for ages"), although no primary schools in Coventry were actually involved in the survey! Tracey reveals too how the TRU's print-out of data arrived on November 8th, and on November 14th they got a note telling them that their comments had to be with Dr Hill on 5pm that day so that the report could keep pace with the passage of the Bright Bill, i.e. "The body of the report was written before any statistical evidence was available". As if all this was not bizarre enough, Tracy finally reports how on November 25th, Hill actually launched a raid on the offices of the TRU, in which all data and correspondence was seized!

The maximum fine for offenders has by now been doubled to £20,000 (Graham Bright: "This will go a long way towards making sure that the Bill has teeth"), with prison a possibility for "more serious offences". David Mellor announces that the back-log of uncertified films, (under)estimated at 6,000, will get speedy certification, with summary treatment for "such obviously inoffensive material as MARY POPPINS, but with rigorous further analysis in relation to the Obscene Publications Act for '18' and 'R18' films".

MAR 4TH: *The Sunday Times* reports that a number of "nasties" (titles unspecified)

THE SEDUCTION OF THE GULLIBLE

have been seized by Suffolk Police from the new £1000,000 public library at Bury St Edmunds. A report has gone to the DPP, who will decide if there is a case to be answered. On the same day, in the same paper, in a piece entitled "CENSORS: THE REAL VIDEO NASTIES", John Mortimer writes: "It might be thought that a Tory government with an avowed belief in family responsibility would think that what we see and read in our own homes, and what we allow our own children to watch, is better decided by individual parents than by persons designated by the Secretary of State. It might be hoped that any government would resist the temptation to undermine constitutional liberties for the sake of apopulist, unthought out and unnecessary act of Parliament".

MAR 6TH: *The Times*. A letter from the Attorney General to BVA Chairman D. H. MacLean, referring to the Bill, currently in its closing stages in Parliament, says: "The BBFC are actively reviewing their criteria for the classification of video works to ensure that they do take into account the uniquely powerful influence of video and the fact that it is essentially home entertainment. My confidence that the VRA will resolve the difficulties the trade has encountered is enhanced by the amendment made at the Committee stage to clause 4 which now authorises the designated body to determine whether or not video works are suitable for viewing in the home".

MAR 7TH: The Parliamentary Group Video Enquiry publish their main research report, to coincide with the House of Lords debate, now with all the questionnaires processed. The percentage of children who have been exposed to "Nasties" has now gone up to 45.5%. The trash press headlines are predictable... "HALF OF CHILDREN SEE FILM NASTIES" (*Daily Mail*), "1 IN 2 CHILDREN SEE 'NASTIES'." (*Daily Express*), etc.

MAR 8TH: Hill claims that his figures are "totally reliable", but even Graham Bright pronounces himself sceptical: "I do question the validity of the research. It points at the problem but I do not think one can take that as conclusive evidence". His scepticism is, of course, well-founded. For instance, the highly-publicised "Children's Top Ten Nasties" mentioned in the report comprises THE EVIL DEAD, ZOMBIE FLESH EATERS, THE LIVING DEAD, THE BOGEY MAN, THE BURNING, I SPIT ON YOUR GRAVE, DEATH TRAP, ZOMBIE CREEPING FLESH, DRILLER KILLER and something called ZOMBIE TERROR, although there is no record of anything bearing that title ever having been released in Britain. Just one of the criticisms aimed at the Parliamentary Group Video Enquiry is that it did not introduce counterfeit titles to test the validity of children's claims about seeing "nasties", as though this basic verification measure was somehow "deceitful". Of course there was no deceit involved in the enquiry (no way!), though its compilers do appear to have included a spurious title through sheer incompetence.

Undeterred by such niceties, the Reverend Peter Liddelow, a working party member and headmaster, claims that the report's figures actually underestimate how many children have been exposed to "nasties". He tells the harrowing story of how children at his school "have had nightmares and then wake up and cannot get back to sleep. I find these figures quite appalling. These films are so dramatic and so realistic that children enter into the spirit of these films. It is poisoning and polluting their minds. It is going to have a degrading and devastating effect on the generation". Lord Coggan, the former Archbishop of Canterbury, says the statistics "portray a very serious picture. I think severe courses of action are called for in regard to these video nasties. The moral welfare of children is quite clearly at stake. It seems impossible even for parents who are concerned to guarantee their children don't see them".

MAR 16TH: As the Bill's third stage in the House of Commons is concluded, Sir Bernard Braine talks of "a grave and growing social evil which no civilised or caring society

THE SEDUCTION OF THE GULLIBLE

would tolerate" and "a filthy and pernicious trade". He criticises the BBFC ("its track-record does not inspire confidence") and warns that it must heed public opinion". At least recognising the contradictions inherent in his party (with all its rhetoric of freedom and de-regulation) presiding over a drastic extension of censorship, Sir Bernard blusters that what is happening is: "Nothing of the kind! What was being said was that no child should be exposed to the risk of an assault upon its mind by the horrific, filthy and damaging video material in circulation which ten year-old and even younger children were seeing". Harry Greenaway, Conservative MP for Ealing North, talks of welfare recipients who buy a VCR before food or furniture and neglect their children. He believes that the Bill is not going far enough. Mathew Parris, Conservative MP for West Derbyshire and the BVA's representative on the Video Recordings Bill standing committee, warns MPs about "a somewhat unsavoury note of self-congratulation that is beginning to creep in".

MAR 17TH: *Screen International* reports that Palace are considering legal action over the Hill report (which listed THE EVIL DEAD as a "video nasty") and against several papers for the way they reported it. "In the case of this particular film" states MD Nik Powell, "...there has yet to be a successful prosecution when defence has been made. The BBFC have made their judgement in granting it an '18'certificate, and we are now waiting for a jury to decide. The Hill report reference makes it virtually impossible now for the film to have a fair trial". The BVA is supporting Palace's criticisms of the report, and disagrees with its inclusion of a number of other titles in its "nasty" listings. Norman Abbott: "The report is significant in that it may influence some members of the House of Commons and House of Lords to swallow their scruples and vote in favour of the Video Recordings Bill". He adds that if the Bill is passed in its present form, it will make Britain the only European country to have state censorship of video.

MAR 18TH: (*The Sunday Times*) "VIDEO LAW CHAOS". The BVA, which originally supported the Bill, is now "totally opposed" to it. Norman Abbott: "We can't wait to get rid of the 'nasties' but the powers in the Bill are excessive. The censor is able to declare any films unsuitable for viewing in the home on any grounds political, industrial, religious...who knows what some future Home Secretary will decide to do?"Mary Whitehouse says that certificates will not deter her NVLA organisation from continuing to try to take video dealers to court under the OPA.

Also this month, a MORI opinion poll indicates that 65% of the public are opposed to Graham Bright's Bill.

APR 2ND: The Video Recordings Bill is read for the second time in the House of Lords. Labour peer Lord Mishcon says that it is aimed at "the filthy end of a quite reputable trade". He declares that he has "no hesitation in joining a war of extermination against those who traded in true video nasties". But Lord Houghton, one of the Bill's sternest critics, argues that if the evil is much smaller than alleged, then a voluntary effort to deal with it might be more successful and more easily mounted... are we to put all the video recordings through the censorship machine for a small minority of the films? It would be mounting an enormous apparatus of censorship in order to deal with a problem which could be got under control by voluntary means".

The Times reports that the BBFC has received DPP advice on video classification, with special reference to the "viewing in the home" factor and the consideration that children might watch them. This advice is not revealed to anyone else, prompting the BVA's Norman Abbott to remark: "It's like telling people not to drive too fast but refusing to say how fast is too fast". Graham Bright claims his Bill is already having a salutary effect on the "nasties": "The trade is backing off like mad, the supply is already drying up".

THE SEDUCTION OF THE GULLIBLE

APR 25TH: Casting further doubt on the Parliamentary Group Video Enquiry's findings, *The Guardian* reports researchers Bates and Cumerbatch's findings that 68% of 11 year-olds claim to have seen non-existent films.

APR 29TH: *The Sunday Times* predicts that the BBFC will reap great benefit from its classification duties under the Video Recordings Act, charging £2 per minute (working out at £180-£200 for the average feature) to view films, even those innocuous items whose certification will merely be a matter of rubber-stamping. The piece also mentions a growing tendency among distributors towards panic cutting, exemplified by Thorn-EMI's video release of HALLOWEEN 3 in a shorter version than was passed by the BBFC for its theatrical release. Norman Abbott: "It's regrettable that companies are doing this because they will have to get a BBFC certificate and under the procedure laid down for the censors the BBFC still collect their fees, even if they only have to nod approval.

MAY 4TH: In a letter to *The Times*, Mary Whitehouse and John J. Smyth, QC, deplore attempts in the Lords to block the Video Recordings Bill, and applaud Lord Mishcon's amendment to ban the export of "video nasties", which expedient, they claim, would avert "a flood of filth into Europe".

MAY 11TH: The Press Council raps *The Sun* (not exactly an infrequent occurrence) for misquoting Bristol Polytechnic Sociology lecturer Martin Barker as saying that he would "happily" show "video nasties" to his 9 year old daughter. Following his *New Society* piece "HOW NASTY ARE THE VIDEO NASTIES", (10th November, 1983), Barker was phoned by John King of *The Sun*, who eventually filed a report head-lined "LET KIDS SEE NASTY TV VIDEOS" and continuing "...a college lecturer switched on a furious row yesterday when he urged parents 'Let your children watch video nasties'." What Barker had actually said was that if his daughter had asked him if she could watch a "nasty" he would not refuse, but would want to talk to her about it.

MAY 12TH: The Scala cinema in London, in association with *Time Out* magazine, highlight what's going on with "REVENGE OF THE BRIGHT BILL", a 24-hr horror-fest comprising screenings of BLOODY BIRTHDAY, HELL NIGHT, THE BOGEY MAN, BASKET CASE, THE EVIL DEAD, DEATH TRAP, XTRO, HUMAN EXPERIMENTS, THE BLOOD-SPATTERED BRIDE, and SHOCK. The Scala has invited the entire Video Recordings Bill select committee to attend.

MAY 13TH: (*The Sunday Times*) Alluding to the up-coming trial of Leeds' Barker's Video on account of THE EVIL DEAD, THE BURNING and others, Irvine Rappaport of Palace Video comments: "At the moment the legal situation is very confused. I've asked the police how we are supposed to know if a video is obscene even if it has a certificate and they said that I should ask our solicitors. But when I asked if they had any more chance of knowing than I did, they said probably not".

At the end of May, Barker's Video of Leeds are acquitted of all Section 2 obscenity charges, with all the films, including THE EVIL DEAD and THE BURNING being found "not obscene".

JUN 9TH: Government ministers in the Lords are to attempt to crush efforts by Labour peer Lord Houghton of Sowerby to block the Video Recordings Bill. Lord Houghton, who opposes the Bill on civil liberties grounds, upset government hopes to get it through its report stage in one sitting on the 6th. He fillibustered into the early hours, then forced a division when there was not a quorum of thirty peers in the House.

THE SEDUCTION OF THE GULLIBLE

JUN 21ST: The British Film Institute is to bestow, in its annual awards, an award for commercial innovation to Palace, which is intended to indicate its support for the company as it goes through its legal travails. On the same date, Uxbridge magistrates dismiss a test-case prosecution brought by the DPP against Thorn-EMI and former executive Nicholas Charles Bingham over THE BURNING.

JUN 23RD: In a letter to *The Times*, Lord Houghton expresses mis-givings about the additional search-and-seize powers granted to police under the VRA and points out that dealers will face the double-jeopardy of prosecution under both that and the Obscene Publications Act. He also argues that "the real censor will be the Director of Public Prosecutions".

JUN 27TH: The Video Recordings Bill completes its passage through the Lords.

JUL 2ND: In the light of the Uxbridge case, the DPP is advising Chief Constables to withdraw any pending prosecutions of THE BURNING in its 'X'-rated version.

JUL 6TH-12TH: The Video Recordings Bill finishes in commons and gains the Royal Assent. Offences under the Act:
1) Supplying, or offering to supply, an uncertified videogram (tape or disc).
2) Possessing an uncertified videogram for supply.
3) Supplying, or offering to supply, a videogram to a person below the age specified in the certificate.
4) Supplying, or offering to supply, an 'R18' (restricted) videogram on premises other than a licensed sex shop.
5) Supplying, or offering to supply, a videogram in such a way that the labelling requirements are infringed, i.e. in an un-marked transit box or where the symbols and statements are of the wrong colour or have become defaced and obscured.
6) Supplying, or offering to supply, a falsely-labelled videogram .
Penalties:
The first two offences can result in a fine of up to £20,000 on conviction. The others carry a maximum of £2,000 fines. There is no provision for prison sentences. The Act empowers the police to search, seize and arrest. Videograms for which people are convicted under the Act are subject to forfeiture.
Exemptions from the Act:
Material designed to be informative, educational or instructive, or which is concerned with sport, religion or music, video games and videos produced for use in schools.
Exemption is lost if material deals "to any significant extent with:
1) Human sexual activity or acts of force or restraint associated with such activity.
2) Mutilation or torture or other acts of gross violence towards humans or animals.
3) Human genital organs, human urinary or excretory functions, or if the product is designed to any significant extent to stimulate or encourage acts listed in the above two categories.
Exempt supplies include:
a) If the supply is neither for reward nor in the course of business (e.g. a gift).
b) Where an original supplier supplies a videogram to another supplier, as long as it is not intended to reach the public.
c) Exports.
d) Supplying videos made to record events like weddings for those who took part in them, providing they don't depict or are designed to stimulate sex or violence.
e) Supplies to bona-fide cinemas and broadcasters, and the censoring authority are exempt, along with medical training films (though at one point Graham Bright had reportedly wanted the latter category to be included in the classification process).

THE SEDUCTION OF THE GULLIBLE

JUL 23RD: The Attorney General Sir Michael Havers announces in a written reply on the "nasties problem" in the House of Commons, that dealers will soon be able to get monthly up-dated lists of video titles which have been prosecuted under the Obscene Publications Act and those on which proceedings are pending, from local police forces, in a joint measure between the DPP and the Metropolitan Police. The Attorney General also gives the BBFC an outline of what the DPP takes into account when considering horror videos ("a source of particular difficulty"). A prime consideration is the likelihood that a significant number of those watching will be children or young people. Other relevant considerations might include:
a) Who is the perpetrator of the violence and what is his reaction to it?
b) Who is the victim, and what is his reaction?
c) How is the violence inflicted, and in what circumstances?
d) How explicit is the depiction of wounds, mutilation or death?
e) Is the violence justifiable in narrative terms?
"A work is likely to be regarded as obscene", Sir Michael states "… if it portrays violence to such an extent, or so explicitly, that its appeal can only be to those who are disposed to derive positive enjoyment from seeing such violence". Other relevant factors may include: violence perpetrated by children; self-mutilation, violent abuse of women or children; cannibalism; use of vicious weapons (e.g. a broken bottle); use of everyday implements (e.g. screwdriver, shears, electric drill); Violence in a sexual context. These factors are not exhaustive: Style can also be important – the more convincing, the more harmful. The Director of Public Prosecutions also has to have regard for the standards set by the courts – hence an arrangement for the results of concluded cases to be passed on to the Board by his office on a monthly basis.

JUL 27TH: The trade press reports that Avatar executive Robert Patterson has been told by the BBFC that THE LOST EMPIRE (a RAIDERS OF THE LOST ARK spoof) is to be viewed by an all-female viewing team due to concern about its "sexist" nature.

AUG 6TH: In a move intended to ease dealer difficulties in the interim period before implementation of the VRA, 62 films are identified as "Nasties" by the DPP and The Metropolitan Police, and dealers warned that to stock them incurs the risk of prosecution under the OPA. All the films listed have either been successfully prosecuted under Section 2 of the Act or are subject to pending proceedings, though no distinction is made between these on the list, which comprises: ABSURD, THE ANTHROPOPHAGOUS BEAST, AXE, THE BEAST IN HEAT, THE BEYOND, BLOOD BATH, BLOOD FEAST, BLOOD RITES, BLOODY MOON, THE BOGEY MAN, THE BURNING, CANNIBAL APOCALYPSE, CANNIBAL FEROX, CANNIBAL HOLOCAUST, CANNIBAL MAN, CANNIBAL TERROR, CONTAMINATION, DEAD AND BURIED, DEATH TRAP, DEEP RIVER SAVAGES, DELIRIUM, DEVIL HUNTER, DON'T GO IN THE WOODS, DON'T GO NEAR THE PARK, DON'T LOOK IN THE BASEMENT, DRILLER KILLER, THE EVIL DEAD, EVILSPEAK, EXPOSE, FACES OF DEATH, FIGHT FOR YOUR LIFE, FOREST OF FEAR, FRANKENSTEIN (Andy Warhol version), FUNHOUSE – CARNIVAL OF TERROR (sic), THE GESTAPO'S LAST ORGY, HOUSE BY THE CEMETERY, HOUSE ON THE EDGE OF THE PARK, INFERNO, I SPIT ON YOUR GRAVE, KILLER NUN, THE LAST HOUSE ON THE LEFT, THE LIVING DEAD, MADHOUSE, MARDI GRAS MASSACRE, NIGHTMARE MAKER, NIGHTMARES IN A DAMAGED BRAIN, NIGHT OF THE BLOODY APES, NIGHT OF THE DEMON, PRANKS, PRISONER OF THE CANNIBAL GOD, REVENGE OF THE BOGEY MAN, THE SLAYER, SNUFF, S.S. EXPERIMENT CAMP, TENEBRAE, TERROR EYES, TOOLBOX MURDERS, UNHINGED, THE WEREWOLF AND THE YETI, THE WITCH WHO CAME FROM THE SEA, ZOMBIE CREEPING FLESH and ZOMBIE FLESH EATERS.

The list will be updated every month and future lists will also include films prosecuted

THE SEDUCTION OF THE GULLIBLE

under Section 3 of the Act, which are not notifiable by police forces to the DPP. Chief Superintendent Peter Kruger of Scotland Yard's Obscene Publications Squad, who has compiled the list on behalf of the Association of Chief Police Officers, says: "Chief Constables will always be able to use the Act, but it has been indicated to all police forces that no video should be prosecuted unless a complaint has been made by a member of the public".

Derek Mann, chairman of the VTA, wants a more comprehensive list, though his main criticism is that the list doesn't specify which films are awaiting prosecution, nor which ones have been prosecuted unsuccessfully, e.g. THE EVIL DEAD. He bemoans the fact that if such a list had been available two years previously, it would have saved many dealers from criminal records, big fines and even prison. "Philosophically", he continues " ... we can also question this list as a form of pre-censorship by the police". He complains of the "devious" system used by Scotland Yard and the DPP to compile the list, which he characterises as "the thin end of the wedge": "After fighting for the publication of an official list for two years, it must seem a bit churlish to criticise the first issue, but the system being used by the police and the DPP in the compilation of the list is devious to say the least ... we have asked the DPP for a list of films which will be prosecuted under Section 2, but what they intend to publish is a list which contains films which probably have not been subject to any prosecution at all. It is for the courts to decide if a film is obscene, and until they have done so, the films in question should have no place on the so-called banned list".

The VTA wants a standard list operating across the country, with titles separated into three categories films successfully prosecuted under Section 2 at Magistrates' Courts, films successfully prosecuted under Section 2 at Crown Court level, and films where proceedings under Section 2 are pending: "Forget Section 3 – if the police believe a film is obscene, then let them prosecute under Section 2, where the case can be heard in Crown Court. In the past police have used Section 3 to gain convictions which would never have succeeded in front of a jury". He adds that dealers are keen to co-operate with the police but are suspicious of them.

The day after the issue of first list, a jury in Beverley, Yorkshire, acquits dealer Eddie Frankel over S.S. EXPERIMENT CAMP, CANNIBAL FEROX, CANNIBAL APOCALYPSE and NIGHT OF THE DEMON, on the grounds that the films are "not obscene", with the prosecution dropping charges against THE BOGEY MAN and ZOMBIE FLESH EATERS. Derek Mann, who was called as a defence witness, later states: "Increasingly, the decisions of the Crown Courts are exposing the wide gulf that exists between public standards of morality and the view held by the DPP. We would hope that decisions like this won't be overlooked by the DPP when issuing future lists".

AUG 12TH: Judge William Jalland says that Manchester has been "polluted in recent years" with "video nasties" and warns: "Those who peddle this type of perversion will be severely dealt with".

SEPTEMBER. Early this month, FROZEN SCREAM and VISITING HOURS are added to the official "nasties" list, disappointing those who believed that the furore was dying down. Peter Kruger, head of Scotland Yard's Obscene Publications Squad, states: "I had hoped that the list could remain static, but under present circumstances, I can only see it getting longer and longer". Countering charges that small, independent distributors are being made the fall guys, he continues: "It doesn't matter who distributes the film we are not interested in that. It's up to the DPP to decide ifr a title is obscene, and then we will enforce the law, no matter how influential or well-established a distributor is".

THE SEDUCTION OF THE GULLIBLE

SEP 2ND: *The Sunday Times* reports the revelation, at a debate on TV sex and violence, that the BBC is already re-cutting its TV programmes for video release, including the comedy programme THREE OF A KIND, starring Tracy Ullman. Paul Jackson, the show's producer, wonders: "How long will it be before people start telling us to think about the Bright Act before we make our programmes?"

SEP 10TH: The trial of VTC over POSSESSION begins at Knightsbridge Crown Court, with the company denying that they had an obscene article for gain. Although it was previously believed that the police took particular exception to a scene in which Isabelle Adjani throws a fit and apparently mis-carries in a metro station, plus an "imitable" scene in which Sam Neill drowns his rival for Adjani's affections in a toilet bowl, prosecutor Kenneth Richardson stresses certain gore FX and, especially, the scene in which Adjani apparently has sex with an octopus-like monster − "Its lingering treatment of explicit violence could be taken as an implicit approval or encouragement of it, and there is a bizarre portrayal of sex. If seen often enough, a film like this may tend to extend the limits of what a viewer finds acceptable, and in that way, the abnormal becomes normal".

Not surprisingly, after hearing the prosecution's opening submission, Mr Justice Phelan tells the jury: "Sometimes, in cases of this kind, when the prosecution has finished its evidence, a jury feels that they do not need to hear the case for the defence, and that they would never convict. I should like you to retire and consider if you feel that this is such a case". After retiring, the jury decide that this isn't such a case, and that they would like to hear the defence submissions, which, as conducted by Richard Du Cann, QC, alternate between ridiculing the notion that anyone could be depraved and corrupted by POSSESSION ("No-one watching this movie could possibly have relations with an octopus!") and extolling its artistic merits ("This film, set in Berlin, is a political metaphor for the division of Germany, parts of which you may find revolting, but that is not the test. Some may find the film highly artistic, or others deadly boring and deeply depressing. People of this standing in world cinema would make a film of this kind with the same integrity they would bring to any performance of artistic work"). He reveals that it has "won an Oscar in France" (actually an award at the Cannes Film Festival... it was also "Best Film" at the Trieste International Festival of Science Fiction Films and "Film of the year" at the London Film Festival − JM) and continues: "The story has a real purpose. It was made in Berlin, not in Hemel Hempstead, you know!"

SEP 12TH: After 2 hours, 14 minutes deliberation, 11 out of 12 jurors find POSSESSION "not obscene" (the dissenting party quite possibly being the lady who, when the film was screened, shrieked in alarm at the point where Isabelle Adjani cuts into her own neck with an electric carving knife). VTC are cleared of all charges, and awarded £50,000 defence costs from central funds. Guy Collins, the managing director of the company: "I was amazed that the DPP went ahead with the case. Sam Neill and Isabelle Adjani wrote detailed letters to me, telling me of their shock and amazement at the charge". But Collins identifies the method in this madness: "The DPP wanted to prove that a known Art film with awards and critical acclaim was something different when shown at home ... it seems there's a deliberate intention on the part of the DPP to bust a BBFC title, and once they've got that under their belts, they can progress on to other things".

Dealers are warned that the verdict gives no immunity from future prosecutions of this film, but Norman Abbott says he's asking the DPP to drop all charges against BBFC-certified material: "... which almost invariably result in acquittals. There is a system of certification for films in the cinema, and a similar process will soon be formulated for video. As a result of this decision, and many other recent cases, including one involving THE BURNING, it is evident that not only are certified films acceptable to the great majority of the public, but courts are also holding them to be not obscene. The BVA is suggesting that all cases pending under Section 2 of the OPA againstl BBFC-certified materia be dropped. It really is a waste of public money".

SEP 13TH: *The Daily Mail* reports on the POSSESSION acquittal at Knightsbridge Crown Court with typical subtlety...

'Octopus sex' film gets OK

A LAWYER claimed yesterday that a video showing a woman simulating sex with an octopus was not obscene — because viewers couldn't imitate the performance.

And a jury backed him up, acquitting the distribution company of a charge under obscenity laws.

Earlier, Mr. Richard Du Cann QC told them : "No one watching this video can possibly go out and have relations with an octopus.

"We're not going to pop into Harrods and get an octopus on our account."

Du Cann was defending the company Capital VTC who denied possessing an obscene article which might tend to deprave and corrupt viewers.

He told London's Knightsbridge Crown Court—which is next door to Harrods—that

SEP 14TH: In an interview with *Video Trade Weekly*, Scotland Yard Superintendent Peter Kruger denies that police are "on a witch-hunt", but concedes that random decisions by local forces have led to bad feelings from dealers: "When you consider all the terrible crimes we have to deal with – murder, rapes and real organised rackets – it's ridiculous to suggest that we are out on some witch-hunt against video". Head of the Obscene Publications Squad for four years, Kruger professes pragmatism: "I would hope that there will be more co-ordination between provincial police forces in the future. Each constabulary is completely autonomous and we at Scotland Yard have no say over what video titles are taken from shops in other parts of the country". "We don't want to deal with the legitimate companies like Thorn-EMI" he continues, "… or in fact any companies that are distributing titles with BBFC certificates. We are after those people who are clearly on the fringes – people who make no attempt to get their films certified. I do feel a great sympathy for some distributors and dealers – it's not always easy to judge whether a tape will be considered offensive. I always emphasise that our job is not to define what is obscene. That's the DPP's job. All we do is enforce the OPA once they've found a title to be obscene". He expresses the hope that more distributors than dealers will be prosecuted in future, but acknowledges that there might be a problem in that some of the earliest companies, e.g. Astra, have now gone out of business.

Kruger reveals that the "nasties" compilation tape that the police screened in Parliament was supplied by the Yard's Obscene Publications Department, but was not compiled for that reason, being a training tape for young officers: "Incidentally, just to put the record straight, a lot of national newspapers reported that Mary Whitehouse screened the same tape at the Conservative party conference. In fact what she showed" ("THE VIDEO NASTY", also later shown in Australia – JM) "… was actually a compilation of material which the DPP had ruled was not obscene. It included films like DEMENTED, I DRINK YOUR BLOOD, and MACABRE, none of which are on the official DPP list. That was just one of manyinaccuracies which appeared in the national press. *The Daily Mail* and others, who spearheaded the 'ban the nasties' campaign … have tarnished the video industry's image." He believes that police emphasis will shift away from "nasties" towards soft-porn.: "As far as we are concerned, the video nasty issue is just about dealt with. The list will continue to grow but we feel that the situation is now under control".

THE SEDUCTION OF THE GULLIBLE

SEP 17TH: *Video Retailer* reports that the VTA has added ten more title to the list of "nasties" which must not be stocked by dealers in their legal insurance protection policy – ANTHROPOPHAGOUS BEAST, BLOOD BATH, DON'T LOOK IN THE BASEMENT, FROZEN SCREAM, HOUSE ON THE EDGE OF THE PARK, MARDI GRAS MASSACRE, PRISONER OF THE CANNIBAL GOD, THE TOOLBOX MURDERS, UNHINGED and ZOMBIE FLESH EATERS. This brings their list to 33, considerably fewer than the DPP's list, with Derek Mann insisting that the VTA list is the definitive one because it includes only titles which have been successfully prosecuted under the Obscene Publications Act.

SEP 23RD: *The Sunday Times*, partly responsible for kicking off all this hysteria in the first place, is now having second thoughts, commenting on the fact that THE EVIL DEAD, acquitted in Leeds and Bournemouth, is to be prosecuted again: "Why is it that what is good enough for the film censor is not good enough for the police?". Peter Nicholls writes: "It is to be hoped that the censors will leave the long, if slightly tatty tradition of Grand Guignol alone" but he fears that the likes of THE EVIL DEAD "will be so heavily censored for video as to make them worthless".

The trade press reports that NIGHTMARES IN A DAMAGED BRAIN distributor David Hamilton-Grant has had his 18-month prison sentence reduced to a year with six months suspended by the Court of Appeal. However, in summing up, Lord Justice O'Connor warned that "those in senior company positions caught organising and making money out of a trade recognised as being a disturbing feature of society" could expect the courts to deal harshly with them.

SEP 29TH: *Video Business* reveals that wholesalers Wyndup, operating in the notoriously tough Manchester area, are refusing to stock CHILDREN OF THE CORN for fear of prosecution. Shortly afterwards, Hampshire's Chief Constable authorises the seizure of copies of that film from Isle of Wight dealer Tony Rees.

Also in September, Nik Powell, together with his companies Palace Video and Palace Virgin Gold Distribution, are charged at Waltham Forest Magistrates' Court with having obscene articles with intent to publish for gain, contrary to Section 2 of the OPA, the charges relating to 444 copies of THE EVIL DEAD seized from premises in East Leyton. The case is committed for trial in Snaresbrook Crown Court in July 1985.

OCT 1ST: In *Video Viewer*, Elkan Allan writes of the POSSESSION case: "Is this what we have a police force for? Is this what the courts are set up to deal with? Should a hundred or so grown men and women be wasting so much of their time over such trivia? Should a civilised society be persecuting works of art (good, bad, or indifferent)? Is this sort of charade to go on and on and on?"

OCT 15TH: The trade press reports that after its recent Crown Court acquittal, POSSESSION is to be re-released by VTC, after 18 months in limbo, re-packaged to emphasise its Art-house credentials. Guy Collins comments: "It's a shame that the DPP has not taken a broader view. There's no way films such as POSSESSION should ever have been prosecuted under the Obscene Publications Act. But common-sense does seem gradually to be coming to the fore". BVA chairman, Iain Muspratt maintains that: "If the lists are to have any validity as guide-lines for dealers, titles thrown out by the courts for not infringing the Obscene Publications Act must be removed without delay. We also note that no BBFC-certified film has been successfully prosecuted before a judge and jury, and would expect that the continuation of this endorsement of BBFC decisions by the courts will justify the DPP accepting that these titles should not be prosecuted".

THE SEDUCTION OF THE GULLIBLE

Shortly afterwards, it is announced that the DPP's "nasties" blacklist is to be divided into two sections, "successfully prosecuted" and "prosecutions pending". The new list places 43 titles in the former section: ABSURD, THE ANTHROPOPHAGOUS BEAST, THE BEAST IN HEAT, BLOOD FEAST, BLOODY MOON, THE BOGEY MAN, THE BURNING, CANNIBAL APOCALYPSE, CANNIBAL FEROX, CANNIBAL HOLOCAUST, CANNIBAL TERROR, CONTAMINATION, DEAD AND BURIED DEATH TRAP, DELIRIUM, DON'T GO IN THE WOODS, DON'T GO NEAR THE PARK, DRILLER KILLER, THE EVIL DEAD, EVILSPEAK, EXPOSE, FACES OF DEATH, THE HOUSE BY THE CEMETERY, HOUSE ON THE EDGE OF THE PARK, INFERNO, I SPIT ON YOUR GRAVE, THE LAST HOUSE ON THE LEFT, THE LIVING DEAD, MADHOUSE, MARDI GRAS MASSACRE, NIGHTMARES IN A DAMAGED BRAIN, NIGHT OF THE BLOODY APES, NIGHT OF THE DEMON, PRANKS, THE SLAYER, SNUFF, S.S. EXPERIMENT CAMP, TENEBRAE, TERROR EYES, TOOLBOX MURDERS, UNHINGED, ZOMBIE CREEPING FLESH and ZOMBIE FLESH EATERS.

Listed in the "prosecutions pending" category are: AXE, THE BEYOND, BLOODBATH, BLOOD RITES, CANNIBAL MAN, DEEP RIVER SAVAGES, THE DEVIL HUNTER, DON'T LOOK IN THE BASEMENT, FIGHT FOR YOUR LIFE, FOREST OF FEAR, FRANKENSTEIN (Andy Warhol version), FUNHOUSE – CARNIVAL OF TERROR (sic), THE GESTAPO'S LAST ORGY, KILLER NUN, NIGHTMARE MAKER, PRISONER OF THE CANNIBAL GOD, REVENGE OF THE BOGEY MAN, VISITING HOURS, THE WEREWOLF AND THE YETI, and THE WITCH WHO CAME FROM THE SEA.

FROZEN SCREAM, I MISS YOUR HUGS AND KISSES and WOMEN BEHIND BARS have been removed, their very brief stay on the list terminated by what a DPP spokesman describes as "a misunderstanding as to whether they had been successfully prosecuted or not". Peter Kruger suggests that THE FUNHOUSE, which has not been successfully prosecuted and according to Laurie Hall, CIC Video Managing Director, isthe same version as got a BBFC 'X' for theatrical release, will be dropped from the list next month.

BVA chairman Iain Muspratt: "We are very unhappy that there are titles on the list that have been deemed to infringe the OPA merely because a dealer has decided to plead guilty. This is very different to a judge and jury deciding that the films are obscene". Chief executive Norman Abbott agrees that there is still some way to go: "Titles which have not yet been prosecuted should certainly not be on the list. It kills a film stone dead, commercially – it's a bit like convicting a driver of drunken driving before he's been breathalysed". VTA Chairman Derek Mann calls the new-look, two-tier list "a great victory. The DPP has been forced into doing this by tremendous pressure... it's now obvious that the original list was an attempt to intimidate dealers into taking more than 60 titles off their shelves. Now as we dig deeper we find that only 43 films are definitely on the list and there are a further twenty with a very strong question mark hanging over them. Even if it takes 20 test cases we will continue this campaign, which we have been fighting for the past year. We see the DPP's latest move as a definite back-down and we are not giving up now".

October's *Monthly Film Bulletin* carries a "video nasties" feature entitled "MORE CONTROVERSY THAN DEBATE", comprising a highly critical essay by Julian Petley and an accompanying "nasties" check-list, which proves the essay's point about the level of confusion over "nasties" by being riddled with errors.

NOVEMBER. Early this month, inconsistencies are highlighted when of five titles seized from a Bethnal Green video shop, all listed in the "successfully prosecuted" section of the DPP list, only one (I SPIT ON YOUR GRAVE) is found to be obscene by a Snaresbrook jury.

THE SEDUCTION OF THE GULLIBLE

Also, VISITING HOURS comes off the "pending" section, the fifth removal in the last two months, reducing the list to 62. CIC have suspended sales and distribution while it has been on the list. Managing director Steve Mandy wrote to the DPP requesting details of any prosecution and was interviewed by the police. The title was dropped following the police report and further DPP consideration. Mandy says sales will resume immediately. The DPP denies any change of policy – each case will be tested on its merits, and this decision does not imply that any other films will be removed. But the list is getting smaller all the time, despite Superintendent Kruger's prediction that it would continue to grow.

NOV 19TH: The trade press reports that the DPP has instructed Hampshire's Chief Constable to return all copies of CHILDREN OF THE CORN seized from Isle of Wight dealer Tony Rees, recognising that the video is even more cut than the BBFC-passed theatrical version.

Towards the end of the month, in Cardiff Crown Court, Leslie Cartwright is found not guilty on a Section 2 charge relating to I SPIT ON YOUR GRAVE, with the prosecution offering no evidence. The case has taken two years to get to court since Cartwright's shop, on Clifton Street, Roath, was raided in October 1982 by police, who seized four copies of the film. John Williams for the prosecution conceded that a mistake which had been made in a police statement ruled the case out. The cassettes had been taken from a secured cabinet at the back of the shop though the police statement described them as being located "under the counter". "It cannot be proved" admitted Williams "that these films were in his possession for publication for gain", adding that charges involving NIGHTMARES IN A DAMAGED BRAIN had not been brought because publicity surrounding a case involving that film in September might prejudice a jury. Roger Everest, defending, said that a jury in Bradford earlier this year had ruled that I SPIT was not obscene, prompting Judge Watkin Powell, his feelings about Meir Zarchi's little revenge opus pretty clear, to remark: "I do not know the standards of people in Bradford, but I will say that in the past we have had some unusual decisions by juries. It may well be in the future that juries will accept that anything is not obscene, but as yet in this part of the world we have been spared that". Judge Powell also admonished that "People who run video clubs must be careful. If it is doubtful, it is dirty".

At Beverley Crown Court in Yorkshire, George Foster of Regency Video, Hull, is cleared of 4 Section 2 charges against CANNIBAL HOLOCAUST, LAST HOUSE ON THE LEFT, THE BEAST IN HEAT and CONTAMINATION: LAST HOUSE and CONTAMINATION were found to be "not obscene" by the jury, who accepted a statutory defence for the others.

After a humiliating series of defeats, the Attorney General is under mounting pressure to reconsider the natter of "statutory defence", the argument that in 1982 or '83 the dealers were not in a position to know that the films in question could be construed as obscenities, and that he should therefore "wipe the slate clean". The VTA's Derek Mann says: "We also believe that the results show that juries are of the opinion that many of the films are not obscene anyway." He adds that some VTA members had had OPA prosecutions hanging over their heads for 18 months, and that most "reputable" dealers had not stocked the titles on the DPP list for some time. His organisation is pressing this case to the Association of Chief Police Officers while it awaits results of research carried out by the Trading Research Unit into the whole question of prosecution of video retailers under the OPA.

DECEMBER. The list remains unchanged, but following recent court cases, THE BURNING will in future be identified as "un-cut version" when appearing on it.

THE SEDUCTION OF THE GULLIBLE

DEC 1ST: At the end of a four day trial at Lewes Crown Court, Tony Bingham of Peacehaven's That's Entertainment is found guilty and fined £500 each for stocking BLOODY MOON, NIGHT OF THE DEMON and PRETTY PEACHES, but acquitted over THE EVIL DEAD, the jury failing to reach a decision on ZOMBIE FLESH EATERS. The judge, in his summing up, stressed the fantastical, non-imitative nature of Sam Raimi's film.

Later in the month, Grimsby Crown Court becomes the third in a row to clear THE EVIL DEAD, along with eight other titles viewed over four days by a jury who were unanimous in their acquittal. However, Peter Kruger of Scotland Yard maintains: "No matter how many dealer acquittals arise, I don't think THE EVIL DEAD will be coming off the list before February". Nik Powell, who, together with his Palace companies, will be tried over the title next year, states: "I think it's ridiculous that every jury which has dealt with the film has cleared it and the DPP will still not drop it from the list. These verdicts will not have any binding effects on our court case because the DPP is so unpredictable". But Derek Mann repeats calls for the dropping of Section 2 charges where the alleged offence took place before the end of 1983: "We are asking the Attorney General to review the situation in the light of recent decisions made by the courts. We think there is now sufficient evidence to show that video retailers were not in a position to know that these films were likely to be obscene in 1982 or 1983".

DEC 11TH: Hampshire dealer Joe Case, prosecuted under Section 2 for eight titles (BLOODY MOON, CANNIBAL HOLOCAUST, CANNIBAL TERROR, DEAD AND BURIED, THE EVIL DEAD, THE HOUSE BY THE CEMETERY, MARDI GRAS MASSACRE and NIGHTMARE MAKER, five of which bear BBFC certificates) seized in a raid by Portsmouth Vice Squad in 1983, is acquitted in Portsmouth Crown Court. The Judge stops the case and directs the jury that it could decide to throw out the prosecution's case after just one witness, Joe Case himself, had been heard. The jury takes 20 minutes to decide to do exactly that and costs of between £18,000 and £22,000 are awarded to the defendant.

DEC 12TH: Joe Case is summoned back to court under Section 3 of the OPA with the summons citing more than 50 titles seized in the original raid, one or two of which are actually the same titles as those mentioned under the first prosecution.

DEC 24TH: At Plymouth Crown Court video dealer Bob Gordon of Southern Video is acquitted on four Section 2 charges over LAST HOUSE ON THE LEFT, NIGHTMARES IN A DAMAGED BRAIN, DRILLER KILLER and I SPIT ON YOUR GRAVE, after the jury fail to reach a verdict at the end of a week-long case. The tapes were seized by the Devon and Cornwall Constabulary on 8th December 1982. Charges relating to seized copies of CANNIBAL APOCALYPSE, CANNIBAL HOLOCAUST and S.S. EXPERIMENT CAMP were left on file by the police, which meant that if convicted the first four, Gordon might also have faced charges on the other three.

A virtually identical case takes place in Luton, again with the prosecution declining to go for a re-trial, reinforcing the VTA's appeal to the Attorney General to "wipe the slate clean" in cases where alleged offences took place before the end of 1983. Derek Mann describes these cases as "a triumph for common sense, very good news because I believe it shows the courts are at last beginning to understand that the situation dealers were in during 1982 and in early 1983 is very different to the situation today".

1985

JAN 14TH: At Peterborough Crown Court, dealer Harry Pearce of Cambridge Video Club in Huntingdon, is found guilty on the BBFC-passed THE BURNING (with the jury split 10/2) and S.S. EXPERIMENT CAMP, Judge Christopher Young fining him £500 on each offence. "I intend to do as much as I can to deter operators from inflicting on the public filth like this": states the judge: "You, as a schoolmaster, mindful of the problems of adolescent youth, were the brains behind a business which supplied these two films". His Honour also talks of a link between such material and "mindless violence". Pearce is ordered to pay £650 towards the costs of the prosecution, on top of his own defence costs, within 28 days, or face 28 days in jail. The DPP, who recently withdrew the 'X'-rated THE BURNING from the "nasties" list, will make no comment. Thorn-EMI, who, along with Palace Video and the VTA's Derek Mann, assisted Pearce in fighting the case, say they will assist in an appeal, a spokesman for their legal and business affairs department stating: "We feel most concerned by the decision ... because the film in question does not appear on any video nasties list".

Pearce, is to meet his thrusting young Tory MP (one John Major), who has expressed "concern" at certain "disturbing" aspects of the police's handling of the case, which has a peculiar history: Originally slated for last year, it was postponed when, at the last minute, police withdrew charges against four films and added a fresh six. "There should be an enquiry into why the charges were brought" complains the convicted dealer, who has been suspended from his job at Hinchliffe High, Huntingdon, where he has taught for ten years: "It's an issue of public confidence and freedom". He points out that he had written to police asking for advice several weeks before he was raided in October 1983, by which time the Go Video copy of S.S. EXPERIMENT CAMP for which he was called to account had been removed from his shelves, and reveals that he will be sending a circular around the trade to enlist support: "If the entire situation can't be sorted out, it's worth speculating whether it's worth being involved as a video dealer at all. If

the trade doesn't take a stand together now, there'll be little point in going on". Pearce was cleared on CONTAMINATION, which is withdrawn from the DPP list this month, plus three other certified movies:THE EVIL DEAD, CANNIBAL and ZOMBIE HOLOCAUST (illusttrated, left)

THE SEDUCTION OF THE GULLIBLE

JAN 21ST: In the trade press: "MIXED COURT-ROOM FATE FOR DEALERS". Neil Whatton, of Priory Video, Wigan, pleaded guilty to four Section 2 charges (relating to CANNIBAL TERROR, DON'T GO NEAR THE PARK, ZOMBIE FLESH EATERS and HOUSE BY THE CEMETERY) at Bolton Crown Court, and was fined a total of £500 and ordered to pay £100 costs by the judge. In another case at the same court, John Oakes of Electric Shop (also Wigan), was acquitted and awarded costs after pleading not guilty to Section 2 charges on ANTHROPOPHAGOUS BEAST, BLOODY MOON and PRETTY PEACHES. He used a statutory defence, testifying that before the raid in September 1983 he had destroyed 3,000 worth of tapes because of doubts about their legality.

JAN 24TH: The BBFC returns SUFFER LITTLE CHILDREN to independent wholesaler and distributor Films Galore, requesting several cuts before it can begranted an '18' certificate. The film was made at the Meg Shanks School, New Malden, whose pupils acted in it.

JAN 25TH: Police raid the London offices of Films Galore, seizing the masters and many copies of SUFFER LITTLE CHILDREN. On the same day, David Cronenberg's VIDEODROME is released on video by CIC, to high initial sales figures.

JAN 28TH: *Video Business* reports that Home Office information concerning prosecutions of videos under Section 2 may not be very up to date or complete, according to the VTA and Oxford Polytechnic. There exists "massive inconsistency" between the DPP hit-list and a list of titles actually prosecuted according to Brian Brown, the head of the Television Research Unit. Derek Mann is concerned that the DPP is basing his consideration of which films to prosecute on the nature of the likely audience for a film. A Home Office letter states that "the director considers in many cases a significant number of viewers will be children or young people". Mann is anxious to have the DPP explain the information on which this supposition is based.

On the same day, an open letter from Harry Pearce appears in the trade press, pointing out that the copy of S.S. EXPERIMENT CAMP he was convicted forwas seized from dead stock — "The whole trade should know that the police managed this by back-dating the indictment to include the one and only hiring this film had in '83. It means that any film any club has ever had in its possession can be charged, regardless of whether it has been withdrawn" and that CANNIBAL and ZOMBIE HOLOCAUST had never appeared on a DPP list — "The police are willing to have a go at anything", also that four of the films he was charged over had a certificate — "So much for the idea that the new

THE SEDUCTION OF THE GULLIBLE

'video' certificate will give the trade the security it needs". He re-iterates that he wrote to police, asking for help, 5 weeks before the raid. He urges united action, reveals that he has organised a petition, and appeals for defence fundcontributions: "The judge apportioned prosecution costs though they lost four and only won two, but would not apportion defence costs … another superb example of confusion and injustice".

The trade press also reports that TV viewers in the London area last week witnessed the destruction of £10,000 worth of adult videos belonging to Chelsea's Video Shuttle, arranged by the library's owner, Alex Neel. "It's time the industry grew up and recognised that its main business will always be in the renting of family-oriented product" states Neel, rather pompously. Warner Home Video was in on his publicity scam, vacated shelf-space being filled with 100 copies of POLICE ACADEMY (porn star Georgina Spelvin's blow-job sequence = "family-oriented product"?) As a further twist to all this tiresome self-publicising, Neel had a California cop overseeing the operation.

Also this month, BBFC President Lord Harlech is killed in a road accident, his untimely demise adding considerably to delays in implementing the VRA.

FEBRUARY. Early this month, Mike McNamara of Forum Video, Vauxhall, is acquitted on five Section 2 charges after pleading not guilty using a statutory defence. The jury finds FOREST OF FEAR, THE LIVING DEAD and THE SLAYER "not obscene", deciding that DON'T GO IN THE WOODS and NIGHTMARES IN A DAMAGED BRAIN are obscene, but accepting McNamara's statutory plea on them. The raid in which the films were seized took place in November 1983, before the publication of any official "video nasty" lists by the police. VTA-member McNamara, who was awarded costs from central funds at the conclusion of the six-day trial, later revealed that he would probably not have fought the case without the backing of the VTA's legal defence policy.

Also, Greater Manchester police add the following to their list of titles that have been forfeited in the Greater Manchester area – DAWN OF THE MUMMY, MASSACRE MAN-SION, MOTHER'S DAY, NIGHT OF THE SEAGULLS, ROSEMARY'S KILLER, SUPERSTITION and WEREWOLF WOMAN.

FEB 4TH: Films Galore threaten to sue the Obscene Publications Squad for £3,000 a day following the seizure of SUFFER LITTLE CHILDREN. Stewart Telfer, sales and marketing director, says: "It's video history. How can you seize a film off a distributor before cuts have been made by the BBFC and the film has been released? Under the Act a publication has to be released for gain for a crime to be committed".

VIDEODROME comes in straight at # 21 on *Video Week*'s top 50 rental chart but Video Business reports: "POLICE THREATS PROMPT 'VIDEODROME' WITHDRAWAL". Members of the mainly Nottinghamshire and Leicestershire-based Video Retailers Association have been advised to withdraw the controversial CIC release from their shelves, in the latest scare concerning that film. The Association has asked members not to stock the title pending a decision from the DPP on whether to prosecute it under Section 3 of the OPA. The Association took the action following normal liaison with local police, who warned of possible Section 3 charges.

CIC MD Laurie Hall protests: "We are very surprised at this development. VIDEODROME has been granted a BBFC '18' certificate. The film had to be edited to obtain this certificate and it is the edited version that CIC has released. CIC has gone to great lengths to ensure that dealers can stock and display VIDEODROME with confidence. The film was a legitimate theatrical release in this country, made by world-renowned director David Cronenberg, and I cannot understand why the video version should cause any problems". Dick Warren of the Association describes the decision to withdraw the film until a DPP ruling has been made as "a matter of policy" and urges the DPP to make such a ruling swiftly. He regrets any possible embarrassment to CIC, but says his priorities lie with the Association's members, upon whose best interests the body was acting: "I think CIC has been very badly advised to bring out VIDEODROME at this time, even if it is not to be prosecuted. I am very surprised that a responsible company like CIC should consider this release at this difficult period in time" (plans to release VIDEO-DROME last year were shelved by CIC due to the prevailing climate). As the BBFC's James Ferman explains to Video Retailer: "They made cuts on their own then decided to shelve the release until the political climate changed. They then submitted it to us for a video certificate and we passed it without any further cuts. I think the decision to release it now was made after the acquittal of comparably serious films like POSSESSION".

FEB 14TH: As reported in the trade press, a letter from James Ferman to Films Galore chief George Goodey encapsulates the problems being caused by the delayed implementation of the Video Recordings Act: "(The Act)... has not yet been brought into force so our certificate and the advice we give concerning it remains unofficial". Ferman points out that the un-cut SUFFER LITTLE CHILDREN, which contains acts of violence by children (c.f. the NIGHTMARES IN A DAMAGED BRAIN furore – JM) might fall foul of both the OPA and the Protection of Children Act (1978): "We have therefore asked for the reduction of explicit visual horror ... and we look forward to receiving a re-edited copy of the video in which time we will consider whether it has been made suitable for an '18' certificate to be granted". Goodey repeats claims that the police have taken a liberty and set a precedent by seizing the master prior to cutting or distribution, but neither Scotland Yard nor the DPP will make any further comment.

FEB 15TH: *Video Trade Weekly* reports that at Preston Crown Court, RPO wholesalers have been found not guilty on 3 Section 2 charges for THE BURNING (un-cut), PRANKS and CANNIBAL FEROX. Statutory defence was a main plank of their submissions.

FEB 18TH: The trade press reports how two Bradford dealers were cleared on obscenity charges after they agreed in a crown Court case not to stock any films that appear on the DPP's "video nasties" list. Derek Mann finds this worrying: "It's a subtle form of coercion. Having to accept that he will not stock any films that the police or the DPP care to place on the list, including those films which have appeared on the 'prosecutions pending' section, and are not yet found to be obscene, puts him at a considerable trading disadvantage to other dealers". VTA members Philip Smith and Michael Hardacre of Idle Video were cleared on the judge's directions at Leeds Crown Court after the prosecution offered no evidence on Section 2 charges against CANNIBAL APOCALYPSE, DEAD AND BURIED, THE GESTAPO'S LAST ORGY, THE HOUSE ON THE EDGE OF THE PARK and PRETTY PEACHES, because they made that promise and agreed to the destruction of the tapes. Costs were awarded to them from central funds.

Greater Manchester Video Retailers Association members have been recommended by the Association's viewing panel not to stock CIC's VIDEODROME, currently shooting up the rental charts, until any judgement has been made by the DPP. President Alf Morton tells *Video Week* that for the first time the panel has been unable to reach a majority verdict, with its six viewers split down the middle. "In the past we have been dealing with violence and horror. This is different. Taking it as a 90 minute film, there are only four scenes that are disturbing and they are all hallucinatory. Personally I don't consider it to be any more violent than some medical documentaries which show the insides of a man's stomach".

THE SEDUCTION OF THE GULLIBLE

MAR 4TH: (*Video Week*) Leicestershire video dealers are still waiting to hear if they can stock VIDEODROME. The whole saga began when local dealers screened it for police, seeking advice on its possible liability under the OPA, and the police passed it on to the DPP. He eventually gave local police "certain advice" but dealers were not let in on what this might be! The Video Retailers Association initially advised members not to stock the film but gave it the green light last week after a spokesman for the DPP told Video Week that the film had been ruled not obscene. The spokesman later retracted this statement and said that no decision had been made, only that "certain advice" had been given to Leicestershire police. Ken Blair, the Association's chairman, complains: "I find this totally unacceptable. Having told my members they were safe to stock the film, based on what the DPP initially said, I am not going to tell them to take it off the shelves again. It is about time we were told what advice the DPP has given to the police".

Video Week reveals "NO RESPITE FOR THE NASTIES": The Attorney General has turned down the VTA's request to drop all charges on the "prosecutions pending" section of the DPP list where the alleged offence was committed before the end of 1983. A letter to Derek Mann from the Attorney General's chambers points out that it was as early as the Summer of 1982 that films like DRILLER KILLER and I SPIT ON YOUR GRAVE came to the attention of the DPP and made the subject of forfeiture orders under Section 3 of the Obscene Publications Act: "It was clearly stated that subsequent publications of the same or similar material would be considered with a view to prosecutions rather than merely forfeiture. It would be inappropriate for the DPP to take an arbitrary date such as December 1983 and abandon proceedings in respect of offences before then. It would also be unfair on those who have already pleaded guilty or been convicted".

The letter adds that "all cases are considered by the DPP on their individual merits and account is taken of any evidence tending to show that a dealer was unaware, and had no reason to be aware, of the nature of the video in his possession. If the defence thought not enough weight had been given to that consideration, it is open to those representing the defendant to invite the prosecuting authority to reconsider the position". In answer to the VTA's request that the Attorney General should reconsider the whole question of the prosecution of dealers under the Video Recordings Act, because of recent Crown Court acquittals, the letter states: "Even if an acquittal is clearly based on the grounds of 'not obscene', it will not automatically follow that the DPP will not proceed with parallel prosecutions in other courts. There obviously might come a time when several similar verdicts persuade the DPP that he can no longer satisfy his first criterion for prosecution, that there is a reasonable prospect of conviction".

MAR 11TH: The trade press reports the acquittal of mobile video operator Errol Almond at Snaresbrook Crown Court. He had CANNIBAL HOLOCAUST, SNUFF, S.S. EXPERIMENT CAMP and DEBBIE DOES DALLAS, but they were not for hire on the day that the police swooped on his van.

MAR 18TH: On the same date, a "breakthrough" in relations between Manchester dealers and police is reported after a meeting between Inspector David Jones, new head of the Force's Obscene Publications Departmentr, and Alf Morton of the Greater Manchester Video Retailers Association. But Jones says his Department won't be reducing its vigilance: "I would love to have a better relationship with all the trade, but only so long as I feel dealers are genuinely trying". He reveals that the police's main concern is Section 2 material: "I would be surprised if you found much Section 2 material in shops in the Greater Manchester Police area now". "We are not arbiters, we act on what we believe anticipated public opinion will be and test it before the courts. It is for the courts to say and the verdict is different from time to time, although they are reasonably consistent. The police have no say, that's the purity of the system". Fielding complaints from dealers that they have been crying out for police guidance, with none forthcoming, he says: "We've certainly ironed out the problems now and Greater Manchester Police do issue a list", continuing: "There always was guidance given. It seems unfortunate that the responsibility for good citizenship has transferred to the shoulders of the police. I expect people not to put business acumen above principles of good citizenship". He maintains that responsible dealers do have the time to monitor the very small number of contentious titles on their shelves.

MAR 29TH: David Mellor MP is pressed for a new BBFC President to be appointed and the VRA to be implemented in the wake of concern over rapist Malcolm Fairley, known as "the Fox", and said to have been "influenced" by porn videos.

At the end of the month, the DPP officially tells CIC that their edited release of VIDEODROME is "not obscene". The decision was relayed in a letter from the Attorney General to the company's solicitors. Leicester police, having been informed of the decision, have also written to CIC, stating: "Having now received advice from the DPP … it would not be our intention to take police action with regard to any complaints its presence may provoke".

APRIL. Early this month, three titles are removed from the DPP's list – THE LIVING DEAD and THE SLAYER, after a series of acquittals, from the "successfully prosecuted" section, and THE BEYOND from the "proceedings pending" category. The DPP's office states that this action is being taken "in the light of recent court decisions". A spokesman for Scotland Yard's Obscene Publications Squad warns that they are still liable for seizure under Section 3.

APR 1ST: (*Video Business*) "DPP ACTION MAY SINK DISTRIBUTOR". Films Galore, the independent wholesaler and distributor which bought the video rights to SUFFER LITTLE CHILDREN, is faced with liquidation. Stewart Telfer says the DPP has acknowledged that the video was not available for distribution at the time it was seized by police. He also points out that the BBFC had agreed to grant it an '18' certificate subject to seven cuts totalling 2 minutes: "We received advance orders of 8,500 for SUFFER LITTLE CHILDREN as a result of our ad campaign" explains Telfer "… but because the DPP is still holding on to the masters we haven't been able to fulfil them". Castle Litho, which prints *Video Trade Weekly* (a magazine which has carried a lengthy series of ads for the film) has put in a winding up order and the company's bank account has been frozen. Company director George Goodey protests that unless the tapes are returned within the next few days, and compensation paid, Films Galore will be forced into "imminent liquidation", with the DPP replying that SUFFER LITTLE CHILDREN is "still under consideration" but refusing to say on what grounds.

Films Galore received £300,000 worth of advance orders for the tape, and if it could be released, that would off-set the £78,000 promotional budget. The Meg Shanks Film School, whose pupils acted in and made it has reportedly had to close down due to bad publicity. Before the seizure, Films Galore had agreed to back another five productions.

APR 8TH: *Video Trade Weekly* reports that Films Galore has overcome its liquidity problems and is going ahead with the release of SUFFER LITTLE CHILDREN on April 19th, following an all-clear from the DPP, whose principal assistant has sent a letter to Films Galore stating that "although parts of the film are indecent within the meaning of the Protection of Children Act, 1978, the public interest does not require the instigation ofcriminal proceedings under that Act". Managing director George Goodey says that the case has cost his company £225,000, and that a claim for compensation from the DPP is under consideration by the firm's solicitors. Joint MD Stuart Telfer complains: "It is a travesty of justice that decent, law-abiding, honest companies can be brought into disrepute by the actions of an authority arbitrarily seizing films". As a result of the DPP's decision, the Meg Shanks school will be re-opening on new premises.

APR 15TH: The trade press reports how Eric Hoddis was fined £2,000 at Manchester Crown Court for publishing two obscene titles for gain (one each for EVILSPEAK and BLOODBATH). Hoddis owns three shops in the Greater Manchester area, trading as Cheshire Home Entertainments Centres. The Manchester shop was opened in July 1983 and raided for the first time in September of that year. Hoddis told the court that before the police visited the shop, during the raid and before a subsequent raid, he had consistently sought police guidance on what was unsuitable stock, but that advice had not proved forthcoming. The films in question had been left on the shelf during the first raid, so he'd assumed that they were safe to stock. They had been supplied by reputable companies and there had been no complaints from customers. Hoddis disputed the obscenity of the tapes and they were screened for an 8 woman/4 man jury. It did his case no good at all when one of the women jurors fainted during the first few minutes of BLOODBATH. The judge recognised that he was running three legitimate shops but argued that even in the absence of police guidance, as a family man with two children, he should have asked himself what kind of effect these films might have had on them (ignoring the issue of what adults can watch and pre-supposing, that a dealer would be able to find the time to view every single one of the films he stocked). Maniacally mixing his metaphors, the judge said that Hoddis "had burnt his fingers dealing in nauseating filth".

It is also reported that Cyril Owen of Jubilee Video in Ashton-Under-Lyne, one of the biggest stores in the Manchester area, has been acquitted of obscenity charges at Manchester Crown Court. He pleaded not guilty on EVILSPEAK, THE FUNHOUSE and DON'T GO IN THE WOODS.

APR 26TH: A jury takes one hour to return not guilty verdicts on all four charges against Leonard Mathews of Archway Video in Archway Road, Highgate at Wood Green Crown Court (sitting at Snaresbrook). Mathews, who denied all four charges, has waited two years for the trial, following a police raid on January 25th 1983, during which a number of films were seized. Four were shown to the jury during the week-long hearing: I SPIT ON YOUR GRAVE, CANNIBAL APOCALYPSE, LAST HOUSE ON THE LEFT and S.S. EXPERIMENT CAMP. Police agreed that he had been co-operative and that most of his films had been "perfectly proper". The three-part defence conducted on his behalf by barrister Jacqueline Perry argued that three of the films had been taken out of his stock prior to the raid because of the bad publicity over them in the media, and were not for hire; CANNIBAL APOCALYPSE was for hire but Hoddis had had no reason to believe there was anything wrong with it (he did not watch every film in the shop); and anyway, the films were not obscene in law ("having a tendency to deprave and corrupt").

Towards the end of the month, Steve Bernard, RCA/Columbia chief, hits out at delays in the implementation of the VRA. The BBFC has refused to grant a certificate to BODY DOUBLE, which was scheduled for release by his company on May 10TH, but has now had to be pulled. Delays in VRA implementation have followed the death and non-replacement of Lord Harlech as President of the Board, and the non-publication of Home Office guidelines, all of which is causing grave concern in the industry.

MAY. In the first week of this month, legal inconsistencies are again highlighted – In Stockport, Dennis Bintcliffe is convicted on DRILLER KILLER, HOUSE ON THE EDGE OF THE PARK, NIGHTMARES IN A DAMAGED BRAIN and SNUFF, with charges against BLOOD BATH, BLOODY MOON and DON'T GO NEAR THE PARK withdrawn, while dealer Ashworth Handforth, with whom Bintcliffe traded as Diamond Mobile Video, is found guilty on CANNIBAL FEROX, CANNIBAL HOLOCAUST, HOUSE ON THE EDGE OF THE PARK, LAST HOUSE ON THE LEFT and NIGHTMARES IN A DAMAGED RAIN with charges withdrawn against CANNIBAL APOCALYPSE, DON'T GO NEAR THE PARK, and ZOMBIE FLESH EATERS. Bintcliffe is fined £250 on each guilty charge plus costs on each film, Handforth fined 100 for each "obscene" film plus £50 costs. Magistrates watched edited highlights of the films for an hour. Anthony Darnell, defending, said the offences had taken place in May 1983 before any publicity had alerted the trade to the notoriety of these titles, that both men had been easy prey to video salesmen and that the films were "appalling, with equally poor dialogue and acting". Police had watched the dealers' homes before making the raids.

MAY 6TH: The trade press reports the BVA's criticisms of Home Office proposals for bringing the VRA into force as "clumsy', with approximately 12,000 films needing video classification over the tight schedule laid down before parliament. From September 1st, 1985, all eligible new releases will have to be certified and properly labelled before release. The schedule for dealing with older material is as follows:
FIRST PHASE: By September 1st 1986, all English language material released theatrically before 1940, or which is not registered with the Department of Trade and Industry, must go through the process.
SECOND PHASE: English language titles registered with the DTI and distributed theatrically since January 1st, 1980, must be processed by March 1st 1987.
THIRD PHASE: English language titles registered with the DTI and theatrically distributed between January 1st 1975 and December 31st 1979 must be processed by September 1st, 1987.
FOURTH PHASE: English language titles registered with the DTI and theatrically distributed between January 1st 1970 and December 31st 1974 must be processed by March 1st, 1988.
FIFTH PHASE: By September 1st 1988, all other eligible material, including foreign language films, must be processed.

Titles become illegal merchandise on the arrival of the relevant deadline, unless they have been officially certified by the BBFC under the Act. Dealers will be provided with lists of films and their due dates by trade and industry bodies. As for packaging, videograms passed suitable for viewing in the home by the BBFC will have to carry their classification symbols on both the cassette and its case. The classification symbol alone must appear on one of the largest faces of the tape or disc. Cases will carry the classification symbol next to the title on the front cover, on the spine beneath the title and on the back, along with an explanatory note about the certificate. Where libraries use "transit boxes", those too will have to be labelled with the correct symbols. Where cassettes contain more than one work, e.g. feature film plus trailers, the entire cassette will have to be labelled with the most restrictive classification. The labelling regulations come into effect in accordance with the above time-table. BVA Director General Norman Abbott calls the regulations "both unwieldy and impractical... a great deal of unnecessary confusion... will arise purely because of the complexities of the system". The dealers' associations are also seeking last ditch concessions from the Home office. They complain that hundreds of their members will go bust and hundreds more remain in breach of an unworkable law. Concessions on complicated labelling regulations, which apply even to transit cases, are requested. Because so many titles will have to be removed from the shelf, the dealers representatives have also requested that the full three-year implementation period be used as a period of grace with no prosecutions.

Round about this time, the Greater Manchester Video Retailers Association Annual General Meeting warns that dealers could be fined £20,000 for stocking innocuous videos that have not been submitted for certification. "My members are astounded at the ease with which the government is going to devastate the industry" states GMVRA main-man Alf Morton: "To say they are concerned is an understatement". Meanwhile, the BBC and Independent Television Authority are objecting to their TV product being lumped into the same priority band as the "nasties".

MAY 8TH: The trade press cites the acquittal of a Grimsby dealer as evidence that convictions are less likely when dealers choose to fight cases. At the end of a two weeks trial at Grimsby Crown Court, John Allsop of Viewpoint Video was acquitted on Section 2 charges against seven titles, most of them bearing BBFC certificates: AXE, EVILSPEAK (un-cut version), THE SLAYER, TENEBRAE, TERROR EYES and UNHINGED, also on FLESH FOR FRANKENSTEIN, though that one is still subject to Section 3 charges and was passed over to a magistrate. Allsop will be contesting that too, along with twenty other Section 3 charges. "I credit the jury with having a great deal of common sense" he commented after his trial "... but not a great sense of humour". He had wanted to find the U.K. distributors of AXE to confirm that the film had a BBFC certificate but they couldn't be found so producer Harry Novak, president of Valiant Pictures Inc, over in L.A., confirmed its certification for him (NOTE: The version of AXE granted a theatrical certificate by the BBFC – as CALIFORNIA AXE MASSACRE – is actually slightly shorter than the version released on video in Britain by Video Network – JM).

MAY 13TH: The BBFC is reported in the trade press as being "not worried" about Warner and RCA/Columbia titles. Only one six second cut is demanded of any Warner film (MOTEL HELL) and only three titles are "temporarily" held back pending certification: FRIDAY THE 13TH, THE LAST TANGO IN PARIS and THE EXORCIST (the first two have, at the time of writing, been re-released but there seems no prospect of THE EXORCIST coming out of mothballs for the forseeable future – JM)

Also reported on this date: A Press conference has been held to introduce new BBFC President Lord Harewood, whose appointment had already been criticised by Mary Whitehouse due to his record of opposing theatre censorship in the '60s. "Give him a chance", storms Vice-President Lord Birkett: "... don't believe everything you read in the papers" (not a bad piece of advice for the Board-members to follow themselves). Monica Sims, the Board's other Vice President, said that responsibility for regulating children's viewing habits should lie with parents, and in another statement that would seem toindicate an admission of the whole exercise's pointlessness, Lord Birkett opined: "I would not dream of letting a six-year old watching an '18' film. But he may equally

THE SEDUCTION OF THE GULLIBLE

well pick up a razor blade or a carving knife". The new President, a movie buff who gave short shrift to a hack who asked if it was a comedown to move from directing The English National Opera to "the dingy world of video", stated that the Board's job "means a balancing of freedom and responsibility that most people believe in".

The BBFC has been, as expected, confirmed as the statutory body responsible for award-ing video certificates in line with the VRA. Appeals will be to a totally independent board, subject to the law, following the decisions of the courts. Ferman talks again of the need to prohibit videos that "can be viewed over and over again by people teetering on the edge of using material in the wrong way ... we are particularly cautious about rape scenes and also about scenes that depict criminal acts like the making of a bomb".

MAY 20TH: VTA vice-chairman Sid Thompson: "The Act is hitting the very people it was supposed to protect". it becomes apparent that a large number of children's videos, especially cartoons, are set to disappear, their distributors finding it too expensive, at £2 per minute, to submit them merely in order to have their certificates rubber-stamped.

Towards the end of this month, a couple are finally cleared of Section 2 charges that have been hanging over them for more than a year, during which time they have grown disillusioned and quit the business. Len and Lesley Gillard of Leisure Video, Droylesden, were finally cleared of three charges relating to ABSURD, DON'T GO NEAR THE PARK and NIGHT OF THE BLOODY APES, seized in a raid on their premises in September 1983. The Gillards were later told they would be prosecuted for seven titles – the above, plus THE EVIL DEAD, HOUSE BY THE CEMETERY, POSSESSION and CONTAMINATION. Three of those were dropped before the case came to court, CONTAMINATION later, on being struck from the list in January. Again acquittal occurred in a case where the VTA undertook a dealer's defence.
Note: The raid on the Gillards was the celebrated occasion on which the Oscar-winning APOCALYPSE NOW was seized, police mistaking it for CANNIBAL APOCALYPSE. No doubt Antonio Margheriti found this highly gratifying. Other mind-boggling seizures that occurred during the initial outbreak of "nasties" hysteria include: Sam Fuller's war epic THE BIG RED ONE (mistaken for a porno movie!); LASSIE COME HOME and THE BEST LITTLE WHOREHOUSE IN TEXAS (mistaken for their hard-core namesakes); Disney's THE DEVIL AND MAX DEVLIN (after hoax complaints by anti-censorship journalist Liam T. Sanford); even AN UNMARRIED WOMAN, seized in oneexample of extraordinary zeal in the pursuit of a return to "Victorian values"!

By now far fewer cases are hitting the courts, only 23 this year, with only three of those resulting in jury convictions. Droyelsden defence witness Derek Mann said he would be bringing these developments to the attention of the Attorney General, who has stated in the Commons that the DPP should have regard for the decisions of the courts. Mann is asking that a substantial number of titles be struck from the list. Three more are in this month DELIRIUM and THE TOOLBOX MURDERS from the "successfully prosecuted" section, and PRISONER OF THE CANNIBAL GOD from the "proceedings pending" category, TOOLBOX and PRISONER on being deleted from the catalogue of their distributor, Hokushin.

JUNE. The British Board of Film Censors becomes the British Board of Film Classification, with James Ferman, formally its "secretary", becoming its "director" (giving a whole new meaning to the term "director's cut"!)

JUN 3RD: As reported in the trade press, the judiciary is beginning to acknowledge certain legal inconsistencies. In "an astonishing" move at Liverpool Crown Court, two

THE SEDUCTION OF THE GULLIBLE

judges call a halt to separate "video nasty" trials, involving the same titles, for fear of the juries reaching conflicting decisions. In the words of Judge Edward Jones: "I would have found that intolerable".

Also in the news at this time, BVA representatives and Lord Harewood meet to discuss, among other things, a BBFC certification fee increase of 15%. The cost per minute of new English language film is now £4.60, a rise of 60p per minute. With its added VRA responsibilities, the Board is warning distributors that another "review" of charges can be expected in the new year. Norman Abbott expresses frustration that films like MARY POPPINS will need to be seen again at half-price, £2.30 per minute (in his words, "£2.30 too much!"). The BVA continues to insist that the VRA will have a negligible effect, while the dealers maintain that the loss of thousands of 'shelf-filler' titles will be damaging to the trade, forcing many of them out of business".

JUN 19TH: In what is seen as a "controversial" move, former "video nasty" CONTAMINATION is re-released on video by European Creative Films after being submitted to the BBFC with two minutes of cuts and granted an '18' certificate subject to one small additional cut being made. ECF head Ron Gale states: "The company does not intend to establish an image around re-releasing controversial horror product". ECF are offering dealers a trade-in on old, banned copies of the tape, with a reduced dealer price of £15 for the new one.

JUN 22ND: The trade press reports that the BBFC has withdrawn the theatrical 'X' (now '18') awarded to I FEEL IT RISING in 1980, after the discovery of an un-cut video version of the film carrying the Board's certificate. The video contains nearly 21 mins of material not approved for cinema exhibition (with 19 cut minutes restored, and the addition of a further two never submitted to the Board in the first place). Although distribution of the un-cut video does not itself necessarily constitute an offence, James Ferman says: "In our judgement this use of the Board's certificate cannot be permitted. Legal action will be brought against any company continuing to trade in this work while the Board's certificate remains on the recording". A BBFC spokesman described the Board's own action as "a grave step", taken against "an improper attempt to give legitimacy to a work which might have overstepped the limits of the criminal law".

For the third successive month, three titles are removed from the DPP's "Nasties" list: DEAD AND BURIED, TERROR EYES and THE WITCH WHO CAME FROM THE SEA. The list is now down to 53, i.e. 9 fewer than in March. Only one title has been added over the last 9 months, contradicting Superintendent Kruger's dire predictions. As has been the case with the majority of films dropped, DEAD AND BURIED and THE WITCH WHO CAME have been deleted from the catalogues of their distributors (respectively Thorn-EMI and VTC). TERROR EYES is still in distribution following a recent court acquittal, after which distributors Guild wrote to the DPP requesting that it be struck from the prohibited list, the DPP agreeing to this request.

JULY. Early this month, Lord Houghton calls for a Parliamentary debate on the VRA regulations, putting a motion for debate before the House Of Lords to annul them. While he concedes that there is no real chance of getting the regulations thrown out, Houghton says it will at least give critics of the new regulations the chance to get answers from the government.

In the second week of July, the Video Consultative Council which, under Lord Harewood, is to oversee implementation of the VRA, is formally launched by the BBFC. It comprises 24 members – 8 from local authorities, 8 from what the Board describes as

THE SEDUCTION OF THE GULLIBLE

"Individuals of personal distinction" (such as Lady Plowden, former chairperson of the Independent Broadcasting Authority; the Bishop of Peterborough; Professor Donald West, Medical Director of Cambridge Institute of Criminology; representatives of the National Society for the Prevention of Cruelty to Children, and other child experts plus, for some reason, "agony aunt" Claire Rayner).

JUL 22ND: Baroness Cox, responding for the government to questions put by Lord Houghton in the House of Lords, reveals that prosecution of dealers and distributors under the Obscene Publications Act could become a thing of the past once classification of videos under the Video Recordings Act gets underway in September. She says that the government shares Lord Houghton's concern over differences in police prosecution policy under the OPA relating to video. Houghton has said: "I believe the Obscene Publications Acts are being mis-used by the police authorities because in many cases prosecutions are taking place on the same work in different places even though acquittals have been secured". The Baroness states that OPA prosecutions of videos certified by the BBFC under the provisions of the VRA should be undertaken "only after the most careful consideration". She adds that the Home Secretary, Leon Brittan, is to advise Chief Constables that a specimen recording should be submitted to the DPP for advice before any OPA prosecutions in respect to videos classified by the Board. This system will stay in force until it is superseded next year by the introduction of the Crown Prosecutions Service, which will be the decision-making body for OPA prosecutions.

JUL 25TH: In what is seen as a test case, representatives of Palace Video appear in court facing OPA charges for distributing THE EVIL DEAD on video, only to be acquitted. (See full account in EVIL DEAD review elsewhere in this volume).

AUG 5TH: The trade press reports mixed results for John Smith of Alternative Video, Hampshire, in defending Section 3 charges at magistrate level. 90 titles were seized after a raid in October, mostly sex films, but also 16 which had BBFC certificates and which he defended with the aid of distributors, including Thorn-EMI, CIC, Warner Home Video, Polygram and VideoSpace. Magistrates viewed clips from 30 tapes, clearing eight of the certified ones (including XTRO, DEAD AND BURIED and THE FUNHOUSE, which has now been removed from the DPP's "nasties" list) but ordered John Carpenter's THE THING (which has been televised several times) to be destroyed! Other titles seized in the original raid included FRIDAY THE 13TH PARTS 1 & 2, BASKET CASE and MADMAN.

AUG 12TH: Director Michael Winner, who regards the VRA as "a disgrace", relates in the trade press how Lord Harewood told him: "The BBFC no longer has a free hand regarding video certifications". Winner, not a great admirer of James Ferman, continues: "It is now clear to me that the new law is to be implemented by a man who fervently believes in censorship". "British homes are full of perfectly normal people" argues the DEATH WISH director, "… not fiends", and complains that "scenes are cut from my films these days which would have been left in back in 1971 – the authorities in this country are becoming more and more censorious and the situation is becoming ridiculous. We used to have local authorities such as the Greater London Council to fall back on, now the country's viewing choice seems to be controlled by a sort of women's committee – the left wing isn't liberal enough and Mrs Whitehouse and the like are too much like social workers on the other wing".

SEP 1ST: The Video Recordings Act classification schedule rolls into effect.

The trade press reports how Thomas Radcliffe of Roker Video, Sunderland, was forced out of business following a Vice Squad raid on his premises before being found not

THE SEDUCTION OF THE GULLIBLE

guilty on three Section 3 charges (BLOODY MOON, CANNIBAL APOCALYPSE and CANNIBAL FEROX). A Durham jury heard that police seized various titles in a raid in October 1983, after which Radcliffe sought their advice on which titles he was safe to stock, receiving the response that police were unable to supply such information. His business dwindled because he played safe with stock and lost custom to dealers who didn't (so much for customer complaints instigating police action). Radcliffe entered the business in mid-'82 and his club had approximately 250 members. He told the jury that although he ordered films, he did not have time to view them all: "I could not continue the business because membership dwindled away. I was frightened to buy horror films that might result in me being taken to court. Members left because they could go to other clubs and get films that I was not stocking". The prosecution suggested that Radcliffe had "taken a chance" with some of the titles, to which he replied: "I borrowed between £16,000 and £18,000 from the bank to get this business going. I could not afford to take a chance. I simply wanted a business I could make a living from".

Also this month, six films have been removed from the DPP list – THE EVIL DEAD, as expected, plus BLOODBATH, CANNIBAL TERROR, DEEP RIVER SAVAGES, INFERNO and PRANKS, reducing the list to 41, and CANNIBAL FEROX will in future have " (un-cut)" behind its title on the list.

OCT 16TH: Shortly after the publication of a teachers' survey which reveals that "unsuitable" video and TV programmes are not, in the view of teachers, to blame for a perceived deterioration in school-kids behaviour, 86% of teachers citing instead "lack of clear standards and expectations at home" and "lack of parental example", thus casting even further doubt on the VIDEO VIOLENCE AND CHILDREN report, the third part of that infamous document comes out, concentrating this time on the dubious findings of psychiatrists concerning the effects of "nasties" on children's minds.

The report calls for state censorship of video, correctly identified as a call to lock the stable door after the horse has bolted by Norman Abbott: " 'Video Nasties' are illegal. End of story. You can't make something which is illegal more illegal … in view of the drastic action already taken by the authorities and the video industry, one can only speculate on the motives of the publishers of this report in releasing such an emotive document at this time. It is surely not possible to conceive of controls on home video more severe than those already imposed". Featuring prominently in Dr Clifford Hill's press conference to accompany the publication of part three is the apocryphal case of a little girl who told her head teacher that had learned all about sex from "a nasty film" (fortuitous turn of phrase, or what?) that her mother let her watch. The anonymous tiny tot concluded from her viewing that "sex is when a big man knocks you down on the floor and gets on top of you and you scream and scream because it hurts". The equally anonymous mother of this unfortunate waif, when called to account for her actions, apparently repled: "Well, she's got to learn about life sometime, hasn't she?".

Britain's gutter press have a field day with this gem, and generally with Dr Hill's latest ludicrous and apocryphal findings, also his dark forebodings of video-spawned anarchy in the UK, which only serve to highlight the hidden political agenda behind the whole "nasties" scam.

OCT 17TH: (*The Daily Mail*) "According to experts, rioters and child batterers are typical of a generation fed on a diet of pornographic and violent videos". (It's surely asking a bit much of young children corrupted by videos in 1981 to be battering their own children in 1985! – JM) *The Daily Express*, under the headline "THE VIDEO EVIL", concurs: "Recent shocking increases in child abuse, brutal sexual attacks, violent assaults and street rioting are at least partially explained by the wave of video filth that has swept through Britain's homes in the last three years", and reports Dr Hill's pulp-psychology diagnosis of the three-stage effect "nasties" have on the sensitive psyches of the young: "Initially they were shocked but continued exposure to scenes of violence ultimately led to desensitivisation (sic), a form of numbness. Then, finally, there was enjoyment. In the final stage youngsters' appetites were stimulated, they enjoyed the violence and craved more and more satisfaction ... and even more explicit scenes as they became addicted just as if they were hooked on drugs". Hill added that school violence has risen sharply over the last decade (but again, on any realistic time-scale, how could the blame for this be laid at the door of home video? – JM), following up with more anecdotal evidence concerning a boy suspended from school after attacking another pupil, who admitted to having seen 29 of the "nasties" (thoughtful of him to keep a tally) and the 5 year-old whose viewing led to "a sadistic attack on his pet cat".

As for those who argue against his "findings", Dr Hill is quoted by *The Express* as saying: "Believe me, the video film game is a multi-million industry, simply out to discredit research such as ours" (as if he and his cronies weren't doing a perfectly good job of that already). "Video pornography is a relatively new social phenomenon" (Hill is allowed to continue, inadvertently conceding that his own depiction of a generation of riotous anarchists weaned on the stuff is total garbage): "To those who say there is no sufficient hard evidence of the long term effect of such films, my answer is that it would be far too late to stop the damage if we were to wait until this generation had grown up to judge the seriousness of the situation". This is one sociology adviser to the Home Office who wants to have his cake and eat it.

The Express works itself into an indignant lather over such palpably phony Hill findings as a 10 year-old boy relishing "The bit in THE S.S. EXPERIMENT CAMP (sic) where a man has his eyes burnt out" (there is no such scene in the film), his girl classmate commenting on the scene where "something came out of a river and bit a lady's arm off" in ZOMBIE TERROR (there is no such film!) and yet another child enthusing about "the man who pushed his hands into someone's stomach and when he pulled his arms out his hands weren't there" (Obviously a description of THE THING, which is not a "nasty", and has played on British TV!) *The Sun* regurgitates all this under the characteristic headline "HORROR OF VIDEO NASTY KIDDIES".

OCT 18TH: *The Express* again ... "THE NASTY WAR" " ... bungling exposed our children to a year of video violence ... the censor acts but now the evil trade goes underground". "Behind the shock report that our young children's minds are being warped by video nasties, comes a tale of bungling bureaucracy". James Ferman is quoted, deploring the delay between the VRA's Royal Assent and its implementation in September '85, while Whitehall got its regulation proposals together, as "a very unfortunate bureaucratic delay". (*The Express* wrings its hands over this period when children were "without the protection of the law", but surely the paper's no-doubt responsible readership should themselves have been regulating their children's viewing, whatever "bungling" was going on in Whitehall). "Amazingly", the report continues, the Board was never sent a copy, nor even made aware of, the VIDEO VIOLENCE AND CHILDREN report (Probably just as well). *The Express* flaunts its chauvinistic prejudices on its sleeve with a lurid portrayal of a video dealer of "unspecified Mediterranean background" who leers about the killing he will make on the "nasties" black market, but Graham Bright expresses himself satisfied with the VRA: "It got the nasties off the shelves even before it became law. There has been a dramatic effect on what is available. By next year I think the nasties will have been put to bed", but the paper opines that "the irresponsible trade is still bound to go about its business, from suitcases if necessary. The police will have to monitor things very closely".

In a masterpiece of woolly editorialising and shaky grammar, *The Daily Mirror* thunders "BAN THEM ALL": "That's sense, not censorship. It's no use classifying some of them as unfit to show to children. Most of them are unfit to show to adults, either. To make them illegal is not to interfere with individual liberty, but to prevent pollution. There is no artistic or other merit in these films. They exploit perverted sex with children and animals" [WHAT?!?] "As Mr Gerald Kaufman said yesterday, crimes of violence have risen by 31% since Mrs Thatcher came to power. The blame for some of those crimes can be pinned on these videos. If the government means what it says about law and order it should ban them straight away". How bizarre that a Labour politician should blow the opportunity to castigate the Conservatives for their lamentable track-record on law and order, shifting the blame to home video, and that an alleged Labour organ like *The Daily Mirror* should give him the platform to do so.

OCT 20TH: Polly Toynbee remarks in *The Times* that defence pleas based on the warping influence of "video nasties": "... draw many a homily but rarely a lighter sentence from the bench".

OCT 28TH: The trade press reports how a former video dealer was given a conditional discharge for his second conviction under Section 2. Frederick Mortimer was found guilty at Snaresbrook Crown Court of possessing ANTHROPOPHAGOUS BEAST for gain and fined £150, but the jury found him not guilty on two other charges relating to UNHINGED and NIGHTMARE MAKER. Mortimer's West Ham library was raided in February '84. This was the second raid on his premises. In September 1984 Newham magistrates fined him £750 on two charges which resulted from a seizure 12 months earlier. 61 year old Mortimer sold his library in May this year so sentencing him, Justice Paiba said "You have now given up your shop and taken up something completely different with a view to retirement so I shall taken an exceptional course".

Video Trade Weekly reports: "OBSCENITY BATTLE LINES DRAWN. WHITEHOUSE TOUTS AMENDMENT BILL TO OUTLAW ALL MEDIA SEX AND VIOLENCE". Mary Whitehouse, President of the National Viewers and Listeners' Association, wrote to the Prime Minister last week and, largely ignoring the new VRA (except to point out that despite it, Obscene Publications Act prosecutions can still be brought against BBFC-certified material), pressed for major changes to the OPA. Stressing a need to protect both children and adults from obscene and violent videos, she argued that the current laws on obscenity are ineffective; "...incapable of controlling even the most extreme of video nasties..." i.e THE EVIL DEAD ("The number one Nasty"), which in her submission was only withdrawn from the DPP's list because of "the weakness of the law". The letter and its contents were clearly timed to coincide with the allocation of private members' Bills for the new Parliament on November 14th. National Viewers And Listeners' Association suggestions for a revised obscenity Bill include that an article can be judged obscene merely if it offends "a reasonable adult" on first viewing. Further amendments then seek to remove certain basic judicial safeguards, such as the right to call expert evidence in defence and the right to challenge the appointment of jurors, except in special circumstances. The current exemption of radio and TV would be ended.

The BVA respond immediately: "It must be remembered that as a result of a government statement in the House of Lords on July 22nd, obscenity actions against titles certified under the VRA would require the specific approval of the DPP, the inference being that he is most unlikely to agree to such prosecutions". An emergency meeting of the BVA is convened, involving lengthy discussions over a full counter-attack.

THE SEDUCTION OF THE GULLIBLE

A decision is to be revealed after the next full BVA council meeting.

Also in the trade papers on this date, it is revealed that the BBFC are certificating a hundred films a week, 80 of them videos. James Ferman: "We will have classified some 4,000 video features by September and that's remarkable. We are churning them out at the rate of around 100 a week" i.e. faster than he estimated to the Home Office.

NOVEMBER. Early this month, Keith Simpkins, who runs a shop in Collier Row Lane, Romford, Essex, is cleared at Snaresbrook Crown Court when a judge hears that the films in question "are no longer that obscene", following a string of recent acquittals. 75 tapes were seized from his premises in January 1984, including CONTAMINATION, DON'T GO NEAR THE PARK and THE EVIL DEAD. PRETTY PEACHES was still considered obscene "but not worth the time and trouble of going to trial". Judge George Coombe unsuccessfully urged the prosecution to go for it anyway. Simpkins argued that at the time of his arrest there was no list of "obscene" titles, but Coombe, who stated that if Simpkins continued to stock horror and adult tapes (which he categorised as "pornography") he would be leaving himself open to more police raids, refused to award him costs because the distributors of some of the films had been raided in the past and prosecuted for having obscene articles for gain. "The defendant quite knowingly took a risk" declared the judge, causing Simpkins to respond afterwards: "I haven't got a clue how I could have brought that upon myself. Every video shop in the area stocked those films, they are freely available today, and I am the only one to suffer. The judgement was totally out of order. It was frightening to hear the judge refer to all adult and horror material as disgusting, appalling, and the like, and it was clear to me that he regretted the decision of the prosecution not to bring any evidence".

NOV 18TH: Mary Whitehouse meets Home Secretary Douglas Hurd, who does not rule out a change in the obscenity laws, and is prepared to have further discussions with her on an area that is of "genuine government concern". But he stresses that before introducing any new obscenity law the government would have to be satisfied that it was acceptable to Parliament and that it would improve the situation if did become law. The same criteria would have to be applied to any private member's Bills. Mrs Whitehouse gets him to agree to look at research into links between "pornography" and sex crimes. She also gives him a report claiming that a quarter of TV shows contain some violence, based on a week-long monitoring of TV programmes by the NVLA. Hurd agrees to look at a tape of some of the programmes concerned. BVA director-general Norman Abbott says that with the VRA now in force he doubts whether the government would accept any legislation to further restrict the supply of home video, but warns that the NVLA's proposals to bring TV under the OPA is of major concern. Tory party chairman Norman Tebbitt said last week that the government will crack down on TV sex and violence.

NOV 21ST: The pernicious influence of TV, horror films and video is probably reflected in school-children's essays "full of gratuitous violence, unemotional killings, scenes of blood and gore and a lack of common humanity", writes teacher Christine Preston in the issue of *New Society* published today. She asked 240 thirteen year-old pupils to write what they might find in an elderly neighbour's garden shed, and swords, bayonets, stun guns, machetes and nuclear bombs were among the most popular items listed by her students. Apparently much mutilation and killing of people and animals was also taking place in neighbouring sheds too.

Towards the end of the month, the Methodist church joins the growing chorus of criticism for the VIDEO VIOLENCE AND CHILDREN report, stating that "the research was undertaken to prove a point of view acceptable to the group".

THE SEDUCTION OF THE GULLIBLE

BLOOD BATH, removed from the DPP's list in September, goes back on it, with the cut version of EVILSPEAK coming off.

DEC 1ST: DEATH TRAP, DON'T LOOK IN THE BASEMENT, NIGHTMARE MAKER and UNHINGED are taken off the list, the DPP taking note of mounting acquittals of these titles, particularly UNHINGED and NIGHTMARE MAKER, both recently cleared at Snaresbrook Crown court. Derek Mann, a frequent defence witness for dealers, says he has no record of any of these three films ever having been successfully prosecuted at Crown Court level and he wanted this principle to be extended to all similar cases: "They've had 18 months to justify the inclusion of titles like EXPOSE by coming up with guilty verdicts. If they've been unable to do so, it's time these films were removed".

In fact the remaining rump of 39 titles becomes the final version of the "nasties list" comprising: ABSURD (Un-cut), ANTHROPOPHAGOUS BEAST, AXE, THE BEAST IN HEAT, BLOOD BATH, BLOOD FEAST, BLOOD RITES, BLOODY MOON, THE BURNING (Un-cut), CANNIBAL APOCALYPSE, CANNIBAL FEROX (Un-cut), CANNIBAL HOLOCAUST, CANNIBAL MAN, DEVIL HUNTER, DON'T GO IN THE WOODS, DRILLER KILLER, EVILSPEAK (Un-cut), EXPOSE, FACES OF DEATH, FIGHT FOR YOUR LIFE, FOREST OF FEAR, FLESH FOR FRANKENSTEIN, THE GESTAPO'S LAST ORGY, HOUSE BY THE CEMETERY, HOUSE ON THE EDGE OF THE PARK, I SPIT ON YOUR GRAVE, ISLAND OF DEATH, LAST HOUSE ON THE LEFT, LOVE CAMP 7, MADHOUSE, MARDI GRAS MASSACRE, NIGHTMARES IN A DAMAGED BRAIN, NIGHT OF THE BLOODY APES, NIGHT OF THE DEMON, SNUFF, S.S. EXPERIMENT CAMP, TENEBRAE, THE WEREWOLF AND THE YETI and ZOMBIE FLESH EATERS.

DEC 2ND: *Video Trade Weekly* says it seems certain that a Bill to dramatically change the scope of the Obscene Publications Act will be taken up during this session of Parliament, but video will not be the prime target. After intensive lobbying by Mary Whitehouse at Westminster, two MPs have announced that they intend to use their places in the ballot for private members' Bills for this purpose. Conservative Sir Nicholas Bonsor, sixth in the ballot, is seeking to introduce amendments to the Act very similar to those proposed by Mary Whitehouse, but Winston Churchill, having come second in the ballot, stands the best chance of changing the law. He tells the magazine that he is seeking all-party support for his measures, but concedes that the Video Recordings Act is doing some good: "The VRA was a very important piece of legislation and is now beginning to have a salutary effect on the availability of obscene video material. However, there remains cause for concern about the more extreme items which can still be obtained. I have met with Mrs Whitehouse and discussed her proposals and there is also a second set of proposed amendments which has been presented to me. As yet I have made no decision which set of ideas to adopt — it may be necessary to investigate a third option. Thus it is impossible to give any details as yet. However, it is not just video which continues to make obscene material available, but also television and publishing. Amendments to the Act must encompass all these media".

DEC 9TH: The trade press reports that Winston Churchill's private member's Bill, the "Obscene Publications Act (Amendments) Bill", has not taken up Mary Whitehouse's argument that the definition of obscenity is inadequate and should be changed. Instead he wants to concentrate on removing the exemption of television from the OPA and restrict soft-core porn to sex shops. Churchill's parliamentary secretary, Daphne Cave, says "Mr Churchill feels he will be more successful and produce quicker results if he goes along with the present definition of obscenity and pushes for restrictions on television and inpornographic magazines sales". Also, the bonus use of the VRA against video piracy has prompted the BVA to rethink its policy and recommend to members

THE SEDUCTION OF THE GULLIBLE

that new releases carry video classification certificates, like the ones used on cinema prints, accompanied by President Lord Harewood and director James Ferman's signatures, on the tapes. When the VRA was passing through Parliament, the BVA was successful in knocking out a proposal that distributors be legally required to show certificates on the actual tape prior to the showing of the film. Now the organisation has changed its mind because this will help sort out legitimate tapes from pirate ones.

DEC 16TH: In the trade press, James Ferman states that "5-10%" of video releases submitted to the Board for certification "will be too strong". An "80s perspective" will be brought to bear on older material, from the point of view of feminism, animal rights, etc. The Board are still holding out on a decision over THE EVIL DEAD, submitted on September 1st. No word either on THE EXORCIST, LAST TANGO IN PARIS or FRIDAY THE 13TH. CIC, which has the video rights to the FRIDAY THE 13TH sequels states "It wouldn't be prudent to put them out now". They're "waiting for grey areas to clear up".

1986

JANUARY. The cut version of ZOMBIE FLESH EATERS is taken off the "nasties" list.

JAN 17TH: Raids occur all over Scotland under Section 51 of the Civic Government (Scotland) Act. 20 dealers from Arbroath, Forfar and Angus are charged with stocking various "obscene videos", and face a maximum of 3 month in jail. This turn of events highlights differences in the Scottish and English legal systems – it has previously been thought that a twelve-month moratorium on OPA prosecutions until September 1st for films not appearing on the DPP's "nasties' list applied throughout the UK.

JAN 27TH: In Video Week, BVA director-general Norman Abbott warns that, e.g. JESUS OF NAZARETH and Bond movies will have to be withdrawn from video shops if Winston Churchill's Bill to amend the OPA, currently going through its second reading, is passed. The wording of two statements in particular are causing concern: 1) That an article would be adjudged obscene if it "depicts mutilation or vicious cruelty towards persons or animals" (on a rigid interpretation of this "depiction" test, JAWS would be regarded as treating animals in the same way as CANNIBAL HOLOCAUST, and JESUS OF NAZARETH's crucifixion scene would be regarded in the same light as any actual killing in a notional "snuff" movie) and 2) the statement that makes the amendment applicable to any "article published in a place to which persons under 18 years of age have access".

Also specifically prohibited would be the depiction of oral sex and cannibalism, among others. No account would be taken of context. A jury presented with a film or programme depicting one of the listed acts would be obliged to convict, with a three year prison sentence resulting for the defendant. The burden of proof would be shifted from the prosecution (which currently has to prove that nebulous "liability to deprave and corrupt") to the defence, overturning a cardinal point of British law. Abbott, who has been sitting in on the Bill's passage through Parliament, comments: "The Bill as it stands could have an absolutely catastrophic effect on a wide spectrum of films with 'PG, '15' or '18' certificates. It goes too far. The wording suggests that any film containing scenes of vicious cruelty would be obscene and, if the proposals went ahead, it could hit films like THE IPCRESS FILE, THE DEER HUNTER, MIDNIGHT EXPRESS and many more which would either have to be cut or withdrawn from video libraries because they are open to youngsters under 18".

FEB 1ST: The Churchill Bill passes its second reading in the Commons, with the BVA still insisting that a large number of mainstream titles are threatened with drastic cutting to remain marketable. But the Bill is criticised by junior Home Office minister David Mellor, who believes that TV and radio broadcasters, whom it seeks to bring under the OPA, are already subject to a more stringent code. The BVA note, with approval, two further statements by Mellor, which make it clear that the "laundry list" of prohibited scenes should be examined very closely, and that prohibition should relate only to "material supplied or published in such a way that it can be seen by children on the premises concerned'. Norman Abbott: "We are asking for counsel's opinions on the possibility that this wording, if so revised, might not apply to the contents of the tape, but merely the packaging. It could mean that the boxes will have to be cleaned up". Broadcasters are likely to retain their immunity from OPA prosecutions, but they may have to tighten up their voluntary code for dealing with sex and violence, which Abbott fears might influence the BBFC to be tougher on video than at present.

FEB 26TH: The "laundry list" of forbidden activities is dropped, but an amendment proposed by Churchill himself to exempt cinema and video from his Bill is slapped down by the direct intervention of David Mellor, who also scratches an attempt by William Cash, the pro-censorship Conservative MP for Stafford, to introduce a second list linking the Bill to the Video Recordings Act. Derek Mann of the Video Trade Association opines: "I think we certainly can't say we are out of the woods yet. My feeling is that the Bill is a monstrosity, whether or not it affects the video industry. It's an attack on the freedom of individuals, and we should do for our colleagues in the television in dustry what they failed to do for us with the Video Recordings Act". (The TV industry's response to these laudable sentiments? Independent Broadcasting Authority chief Lord Thomson moans that "professional broadcasters feel they are being made scape-goats for the sins of the video cassette trade").

The BVA's Norman Abbott urges all distributors, dealers and wholesalers to write to their MPs, "informing them that the video industry is already regulated by the Video Recordings Act and that further legislation is unnecessary and undesirable". He warns that: "this Bill is still a potential catastrophe for the video industry. Although the 'laundry list' of prohibited acts has now been dropped, it still contains wording that would ban certain cassettes down to 'PG' from high street libraries. It's so badly worded – especially in the clause that prohibits depictions of vicious cruelty to persons or animals that it could affect a third of all video releases. Winston Churchill does not intend it to have this effect but most of the Parliamentary committee currently discussing it want it to. However, all our problems would be solved if a Churchill amendment to exclude 'moving picture films and videos recordings within the meaning of the Video Recordings Act (1984)' is accepted. There's certainly no guarantee that it will be, though. The members of the committee ... have one objective in mind to clean up TV and prevent children from seeing or buying pornographic magazines. But if they let the Bill go through without our proposed amendments, what they will actually be doing is closing down art-galleries, decimating television, seriously damaging film and having a disastrous effect on video. It could be a case of the baby being thrown out with the bath-water. My only hope is a basic faith in Parliament, which usually gets it right in the end. There's a long way to go though".

MARCH. Early this month, the Churchill Bill is amended to exclude "videograms and other moving pictures" by a vote of 7 to 3 on its poorly-attended last day in committee. "The Bill has really now become a non-event" says Norman Abbott: "It now covers the shrink-wrapping of pornographic magazines in news-agents shops and extends the 'liable to deprave and corrupt' test under the OPA to TV and radio, where the BBC and IBA guide-lines are already much stronger than anything under the OPA. It's now all over bar the shouting. The Bill has been a waste of time ... little more than

THE SEDUCTION OF THE GULLIBLE

a gesture. It's been a storm in a tea-cup, and we can all now heave a sigh of relief".

MAR 10TH: The new "nasties" list is unchanged from last time. Police activity is dropping and has been for the last three months. Derek Mann, chairman of VTA, tells *Video Trade Weekly* : "The general feeling I get talking to police officers around the country is that as far as they're concerned, they're reducing the level of prosecutions for two reasons. The first is that they recognise that shops have cleared their shelves of this material and secondly, they see that the VRA will be there for them to use after September 1st this year when the first time-table period expires. Where the police do come across a glaring offence which they previously would have prosecuted under section 2, they are now tending to deal with it under Section 3, a simple destruction order. However Section 3 prosecutions, other than under these circumstances, are now not generally being carried out".

MAR 17TH: In *Video Week,* Norman Abbott calls for restrained video advertising: "While we are in the process of getting the least damaging legislation through Parliament, the appearance of an ad or even copy which depicts unnecessary violence could be provocative and our efforts to fight for the industry could suffer".

APR 14TH: (*Video Trade Weekly*) "PRE-ACT CERTIFICATES INVALID" "…back catalogues will have to be resubmitted to BBFC". "We had hoped to confirm certificates without the need for further examination …" explains James Ferman: "however, there have been some discrepancies in the past between material given interim classification and the actual programmes shipped to the trade". For this reason the BBFC is now insisting on seeing complete programmes for classification purposes with Ferman conceding that pre-Act re-submissions will "generally" be done free of charge. Norman Abbott, director general of the BVA, slams this as "completely ridiculous… it means that a film such as MARY POPPINS will have been examined three times, including its initial theatrical examination. However, the BBFC is unquestionably working within the parameters of its statutory authority". It is further revealed that when a film contains a strong scene which the BBFC are prepared to leave in, it may ask to inspect proposed art-work before awarding a certificate (Ferman: "… to ensure that scene is not used as the major selling point of the overall contents"). In line with new developments, CBS/Fox are preparing a new sleeve for Wes Craven's CHILLER, indicating that it's certificated '15' but the programme contains an '18' trailer for A NIGHTMARE ON ELM STREET.

Over 50% of 15-year olds have watched porn and so-called nasties according to a *Daily Mirror* survey. Conducted by Professor Neville Butler, Youthscan followed 15,000 children through childhood considering such issues as sex, leisure, drinking and smoking. Kids mostly claimed that they had seen the films in friends' homes.

APR 21ST: (*Video Week*) There are serious doubts about the September 1st VRA deadline being fulfilled. The BVA slams the BBFC for acting like "public guardians of morality" and accuses them of causing delay by refusing to confirm unofficial certificates they have awarded in preparation for the Video Recordings Act until they've inspected the cassettes again. Norman Abbott says this policy has heaped a further 7,000 titles onto the already awesome task and is patently unnecessary, as the videos have already been viewed. He contends that these certificates should just be rubber-stamped.

James Ferman counters that the BBFC wants to check shop copies for the addition of trailers or adverts without certificates. Abbott: "This is strictly not their business but the responsibility of the distributor. I think it's a pity that they won't trust the distributor to submit the necessary titles". Ferman insists that the Board is just being "meticulous" and that the delays are caused by distributors being slow to submit their tapes. "The industry owes it to the dealers not to leave them holding the baby" he warns: "It's the dealers who are going to be stung in September when criminal provisions begin to bite".

APR 25TH: The Churchill Bill fails to complete the report stage at its third reading after opponents "talk it down", staging a five-hour fillibuster.

APR 28TH: (*Video Week*) "FILM CENSOR IN HEATED SEMINAR ROW". James Ferman is called, to his face, "the most horrific influence on censorship in the last 30 years" by Michael DEATH WISH Winner, chairman of the Directors' Guild Censorship Committee, at a major London debate on film, video and TV censorship organised by the Association of Independent Producers. "I have been making films for some 30 years" storms Winner: "During that period, the moment of most increase in censorship and of the most major change in attitude towards what can and can't creatively be allowed was in 1975 when James Ferman was made film censor".

On the subject of VRA implementation, Palace's Nik Powell says: "It's quite a complex affair, for people who are not experts, to cope with. There is the added problem of having to certificate some 3-6,000 video titles, some 2,000 of which are almost un-traceable in terms of their original distributors and product details". Channel 4 chief Jeremy Isaacs, a member of the seminar audience, argues that Mary Whitehouse and her NVLA, one of the major forces behind Winston Churchill's TV control Bill, have "no case whatsoever" for TV censorship beyond that already auto-imposed by the IBA and BBC themselves. "She is trying to protect us from the real world. It is absolute baloney".

MAY 5TH: The trade press reveals how John Boorman graciously chose the Embassy Video launch party for his film THE EMERALD FOREST as the time to slam video as "the scourge of the entire industry". He continued "I find it a curious experience to attend my first video launch. It's a bit like proposing a toast at your own funeral". (Presumably he agreed to waive his rights to money deriving from the video release of his wretched movie, a flatulent re-hash of material more competently handled years previously by the likes of Ruggero Deodato, Umberto Lenzi and – God help us! – Jesus Franco, which stars his son Charlie – the kind of thing that gives nepotism a bad name! The aptly-named Boorman is forever whinging about how bad horror movies are, and he should know, having turned in that laughable waste of celluloid EXORCIST II: THE HERETIC – JM).

JUN 2ND: (*Video Week*) Anthony Chappell of British Home Video, Rode, Somerset, is accusing the government of breaking the European Convention on Human Rights by placing the BBFC under Home Office control and effectively introducing state censorship. Chappell, who last year made a successful submission to the European Commission on Human Rights over the execution of search and seize orders made the allegation at a hearing in the Court of Appeal, London, where he was refused leave to appeal over a fine for two videos seized in 1981, 3 years before the VRA. He alleges that the government has broken article 10 of the Convention by removing the Board's independent status when it introduced the VRA.

JUN 23RD: (*Video Trade Weekly*) The British government is currently opposing European Economic Community proposals which would prevent adult and violent films being beamed into homes with satellite dishes – contrary to its stance on video, it favours voluntary control here.

JUL 21ST: (*Video Week*) STAG SHOW GIRLS goes down in legal video history as the

THE SEDUCTION OF THE GULLIBLE

first video to use the BBFC appeals procedure set up under the VRA. Strand International Films convinced the 5-strong appeals committee panel on a majority decision that the film's certificate should be reduced from 'R18" to '18", thus saving it from the sex shop ghetto. James Ferman welcomed the hearing as "healthy" and called for more. Strand's marketing director Stephen Silver says this will stem the potential black market when the VRA Sept 1st deadline condemns the bulk of adult material as illegal.

Overwork of the BBFC as it heads towards that September 1st deadline might lead to increased classification fees. At the end of the calendar year 1985, the Board reported its first trading deficit as a self-financing body in over a decade, a post-tax loss of £13,567.

JUL 25TH: The press reports that Warner releases DEAL OF THE CENTURY, OF UNKNOWN ORIGIN, CRIMEBUSTERS and THE MAN WITH TWO BRAINS have been held up because they each contain an uncertified HEARTS AND ARMOUR trailer.

JUL 29-30TH: James Ferman warns the VTA convention in Birmingham that tabloid newspapers will be trying to catch dealers out in the act of renting '15' and 18' films to children, and that if they succeed, there will be renewed calls to make those categories of film unavailable on video. He predicts that the consequences of not sticking to the rules, quite apart from the £20,000 fine at stake, will be a "Puritan backlash" and more legislation: "The BBFC has got to please the police, the judges, the magistrates and the politicians in order that our decisions do not become challenged under the OPA. It will only take one or two decisions to go against us in court actions and it will throw the whole VRA into disrepute. If, after three years, the pressure groups can point out that it is not working properly, a new and unwelcome body may be brought in to classify video films". He concedes that the BBFC's finances have been dented by their task of classifying 3,750 videos by the deadline date of September, many of them at half price because they have already been granted "advisory" certificates up to two years ago. So far only one 'R18' cert has been refused on the grounds that the film contained scenes of non-consenting sex. No film containing sexual violence or sadism would be granted a certificate because it would almost certainly be found obscene under OPA. Ferman also comments that when a parent sends a child back to a library to return a '15' or 18' tape, it was not thought to be an offence, though this a legally grey area.

AUG 1ST: The professional Association of teachers conference in Manchester is told that children as young as eight are having their minds damaged by exposure to videos portraying brutal sex and violence. Teacher Sue McCaffrey tells delegates that 11-14 year-olds are now writing essays including "ghastly stories of victims being decapitated or mutilated... it is the young minds of children which are suffering. We must inform parents of the dangers to their children of exposure to such horrific material". The conference unanimously passes a motion deploring "the influence on children of news-papers, television and videos giving prominence to sex and violence".

SEP 29TH: *Video Business* reports how a police raid on a shop in London's Canning Town in October 1984 led to dealer Anthony Clayton-Roberts receiving a 12 month conditional discharge, a £120 fine and an order to pay costs of £50. Snaresbrook Crown Court heard he had four tapes locked in a safe in the shop – DRILLER KILLER, NIGHTMARES IN A DAMAGED BRAIN, SEXY ONES and THE VELVET EDGE. Clayton-Roberts told police he was unaware that he was breaking the law by renting the tapes out. Initially he denied four charges but during the trial he changed his plea to guilty over the sex films. Judge Mr Recorder Hitching said: "These films are banned for a reason, and these rules must be kept".

THE SEDUCTION OF THE GULLIBLE

OCTOBER. At the end of the month, John William Smith of The Video Library, Chichester Road, Copnor, Portsmouth, is cleared by a Portsmouth jury. His premises were raided in March 1984, with 157 tapes being seized, but it was not until exactly two years later that he was charged under Section 2 of the Obscene Publications Act, the charges relating to BLOOD RITES, FLESH FOR FRANKENSTEIN, THE FUNHOUSE, INFERNO, THE REVENGE OF THE BOGEY MAN and TENEBRAE. Six months later, a full 2 years after the initial raid, the case went to a three day trial. With Smith pleading not guilty on all charges, INFERNO, FUNHOUSE and REVENGE OF THE BOGEY MAN were dropped immediately from the case, with no evidence offered. Smith's not guilty pleas on TENEBRAE and BLOOD RITES (on a statutory defence) and FLESH FOR FRANKENSTEIN (on the grounds of "not obscene") were accepted by the jury, and defence costs awarded from central funds. VTA chairman Derek Mann testified in Smith's defence that he had already destroyed 150 titles from his stock before the police raid, fearing that they might be obscene. After the case, Smith declares: "To have the threat of jail hanging over me for all this time has been terrible for myself and my wife Margaret. I'm just glad it's all over, but I still feel sick about the case".

DEC 8TH: (*Video Week*) "THE CENSOR'S AXE FALLS UPON DISNEY". OLD YELLER is cut by 16 seconds, NIKKI – WILD DOG OF THE NORTH by 24, with the BBFC taking exception to the treatment of animals in these two films. Two THUNDERCATS cartoon videos are cut to get a 'U' certificate, by 58 seconds and 1 min 11 seconds respectively. John Brooker says: "Any pretence that the VRA is here just to save our toddlers from horror nasties and soft porn has surely gone right out of the window".

DEC 15TH: The trade press reports that John Roberts of J.R. Film Agency, Stafford, found guilty under Section 2 over CANNIBAL HOLOCAUST, LAST HOUSE ON THE LEFT and SNUFF, is thinking of appealing to the European Court of Human Rights. He pleaded not guilty on ANTHROPOPHAGOUS BEAST, BLOODY MOON, CANNIBAL HOLOCAUST, LAST HOUSE ON THE LEFT and NIGHTMARES IN A DAMAGED BRAIN, guilty on SNUFF. The defence argued that the tapes were not stocked in his shop and not used for gain. The jury did not believe the tapes were for his own use and found two others, apart from SNUFF, to be obscene. The rest were found to be not obscene (including NIGHTMARES IN A DAMAGED BRAIN, which must have been a great comfort to jailed distributor David Hamilton-Grant). Roberts was fined £100 each for the offending three (quite lenient when compared to the amounts exacted at some courts in the recent past) and £100 costs were awarded to the prosecution. Roberts claims the prosecuting barrister said, after the trial: "It's cost us £2,800 to bring this case to court".

1987

JAN 16TH: Today's second reading of the private member's Bill introduced by Conservative MP Gerald Howarth to change the Obscene Publications Act definition of obscenity from material "likely to deprave and corrupt" to material that "a reasonable person would find grossly offensive" is postponed until April 3rd, due to other business over-running. It's now felt that the Bill, which could have meant yet tougher video censorship, is unlikely to find time to get onto the statute books.

JAN 26TH: (*Video Trade Weekly*) "CAUGHT IN THE ACT". Some distributors are reportedly up to 50% short for phase 3 classification. With the next deadline five weeks away, dealers are still unsure as to what it's safe to keep on their shelves.

The BBFC says that a small number of titles have been refused a new certificate, but will not be more specific. Many are still to be viewed. Palace's THE BIG MEAT EATER and

THE SEDUCTION OF THE GULLIBLE

Vestron's MAKING OF MICHAEL JACKSON'S THRILLER are going up in certificate from '15' to '18'.

FEB 17TH: The trade press reports that the newly-formed Association of Major Dealers are boycotting Avatar's FAMILY AND HONOUR because it's sleeve bears the words "directed by the maker of I SPIT ON YOUR GRAVE". Avatar send out stickers to obliterate the offending reference. Obviously if the BBFC doesn't sanction a film, then it doesn't exist anymore... how apt that the VRA came onto the statute books in 1984!

MAR 7TH: *The Daily Mail* reports, under the headline "VAMPIRE FILM 'TURNED MAN INTO A KILLER' ", how a previously level-headed individual was driven to murder by watching FRIGHT NIGHT ... sure thing, you guys.

MAR 16TH: James Ferman warns in *Video Week* that the industry needs to clean up its act vis-a-vis packaging ("It is vital for the industry to self-regulate quickly in this matter"), his words coming hard on the heels of Gerald Howarth's revelation last week that packaging as well as content falls within his (now failing) plans to extend the OPA. The packaging issue came to the attention of the Home Office after that for an '18' title in a Watford shop, depicting a disembodied hand, caused a 15 year-old boy (yet another of those highly-strung mites) sleepless nights, leading to complaints from his parents and a Parliamentary question. Ferman and the BVA are both worried about Howarth's proposed "grossly offensive" definition of obscenity, and if it goes through they will be pressing for assurances that prosecutions cannot be taken against material classified under the Video Recordings Act without the consent of the DPP.

Ferman concedes the Board's difficulty in achieving total parity in classification standards, due to the increased number of examiners working to fulfil the VRA implementation schedule, but the general consensus is for more liberal treatment of consenting sex, hand-in-hand with increasingly strict treatment for rape and other sexual violence. The Board also faces the problem of classifying works such as THE EVIL DEAD, which has been acquitted on numerous occasions but still found obscene in a couple of cases. He predicts that Sam Raimi's film will eventually get a certificate, but only after more cuts. Though acknowledging the trade and industry's efforts to turn around the "jaded image" of video, he warns that "video is beginning to be plagued with problems. The sort of titles that haven't been around for the last three years have started showing up — there could be more 'nasties' on the horizon. Problems we hardly touched on a year ago are beginning to crop up".

APR 3RD: The Howarth Bill gets through its second reading on a large majority, exacerbating fears that the video industry will have to "clean up its act". Although Gerald Howarth concedes that his Bill still has a long way to go before it is likely to become law, the BVA's Parliamentary spokesman, Iain Muspratt, warns: "There is no room for complacency. It's very important that all video distributors follow the encouragement given by the BVA in making sure their promotion is extremely responsible".

MAY 3RD: As reported in *The Sunday Times* ("VIDEOS INSPIRE VIOLENT URGE FOR NASTY SIDE OF LIFE"), Australia's answer to the Parliamentary Group Video Enquiry (inspired by Mary Whitehouse's Antipodean lecture tours) publishes its contradictory findings: the enquiry reports that "sadistic enjoyment of violence" was found in 500 of the children surveyed, who wrote of specific scenes they "enjoyed so much they continually remembered them", but also that "more than half said they had unwanted memories of brutal violence and horror from which they were unable to free themselves". Theresponses themselves indicate the scepticism with which such evidence

THE SEDUCTION OF THE GULLIBLE

should be treated, e.g. one child's enthusiastic remembrance of the (non-existent) scene in FRIDAY THE 13TH "... where the girl chopped off her dad's head and used it as a birthday cake". Moving from the ridiculous to the sublime, another praised the moment in XTRO "when the alien ate the woman's head and kept on burping".

Also this month, a heavily advertised re-release of THE EVIL DEAD is scuppered due to Palace's inability to agree to draconian censorship cuts demanded by the BBFC.

AUG 3RD: The BBFC's Annual Report claims that the laissez-faire attitude of the police towards enforcement of the Video Recordings Act (only two prosecutions so far) may damage the industry: "The lack of proceedings during 1986 for the kind of offences the Act was specifically intended to catch is disquieting, to say the least, and the Board has been concerned by increasing evidence that there are unclassified works still being offered for supply in Britain, despite the fact that the classification deadline has passed. If the system of regulation which Parliament considered necessary is to be fully effective, it is essential that the Act make its mark at this early stage, since otherwise the illegitimate side of the video trade, which has been successfully curtailed since 1985, will once again expand, to the detriment of society and the reputation of the industry".

The report acknowledges the problem of classifying works which have been acquitted in some courts but found obscene in others, including of course THE EVIL DEAD, and notes a tailing off in the submission of "zombie-type" horror films. The Board's biggest concern is over the linkage of sex and violence, especially where the latter is directed towards women. Of the four films refused a certificate in 1986, three (HOUSE OF HOOK-ERS, CHAINED and PRECIOUS JEWELS) were on these grounds, while the fourth, TARGET MASSACRE, was not passed because of scenes in which a sniper lingered over views of couples making out before shooting them. Almost 10% of the titles screened by the Board were cut before being granted a certificate (438 out of 4,460), 290 from 952 in the '18' category, mainly for scenes that mixed sex with violence.

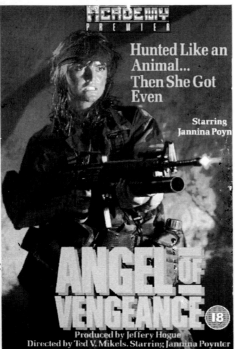

Hunted Like an Animal... Then She Got Even

Starring Jannina Poyn

ANGEL OF VENGEANCE

Produced by Jeffery Hogue
Directed by Ted V. Mikels. Starring Jannina Poynter

AUG 17TH: As reported in *Video Trade Weekly,* Academy Premier has pulled their release of Ted V. Mikels ANGEL OF VENGEANCE after the BBFC refused it a certificate. The film, in which a woman turns on her tormentors with assorted weaponry, is described by Mr Ferman as "an unremitting catalogue of brutal and sadistic violence and terror-isation for the purpose of entertainment without any critical context or justifica-tion". The Board's annual report emphasises concern over weapons scenes and welcomes government moves to bring cross-bows under stricter control. Mikels film is one of half-a-dozen titles refused a certificate this year on the grounds of violence, mostly directed towards women.

THE SEDUCTION OF THE GULLIBLE

AUG 19TH: Michael Ryan runs amok with a gun in Hungerford, wounding and killing several people before shooting himself. Despite the fact that Ryan did not own a video recorder, and by all accounts very rarely watched TV, blame is laid by the gutter press in predictable quarters, Ryan being dubbed a "Rambo" killer.

AUG 20TH: (*The Daily Star*) "THE TRAGIC PROOF"..."Hungerford provides it".

Meanwhile, various action / adventure-type movies are pulled from this and next week's TV schedules.

AUG 21ST: In *The Daily Telegraph*, Lesley Garner puts the blame for Hungerford on the availability of videos rather than the easy availability of fire-arms, and bemoans our "junk culture'. *The Sun* and *The News of the World*, who can usually be relied upon to treat such cases in sensationalist style, are surprisingly reticent, which is probably not entirely unconnected with the fact that they are currently running big promotions for the film LETHAL WEAPON.

AUG 26TH: At Newbury's Cannon cinema, the closest to the town of Hungerford, LETHAL WEAPON's run, which was to have begun on the 28th, is cancelled.

AUG 30TH: Evidence collected from 43 police forces in England and Wales fails to find any link between "pornography", including videos, and violent sex crimes. In a three-year survey of such crimes, over half the forces reported a total of 48 cases where criminals concerned had used pornography, but the report concludes: "In none of these was there any evidence that pornography had been the cause of the offences". Not batting an eye-lid, Mary Whitehouse declares: "This adds to our argument that the Obscene Publication laws need to be strengthened".

OCT 3RD: *The Daily Mirror* reports, under the headline "THE VIDEO STRANGLER", how a teenager in Nottingham strangled a seven year-old girl after watching Virgin's CLASS OF NUKE 'EM HIGH. "Killer copied film murder asserts *The Mirror*, describing NUKE 'EM as "a video nasty". Virgin's general manager William Campbell points out that the tape has a BBFC '18' certificate: "In no sense of the word could you say that the film is comparable with a video nasty", and indeed, Judge Justice Jupp, sentencing the youth, declined to take this ludicrous line.

OCT 26TH: The BVA warns of a possible new clamp-down on video, because the government is under the impression that the Video Recordings Act has failed, with only two prosecutions in two years, a result of the cost and difficulty to police in bringing such prosecutions. Norman Abbott says that Mrs Thatcher, in a recent meeting with representatives of the film, video and TV industries at 10 Downing Street, confirmed that new measures were under consideration. The BVA has taken a number of initiatives to make VRA enforcement easier, securing the agreement of the BBFC to waive the £50 fee payable by police for them to examine possibly illegal cassettes, offering police training on the details of the Act, and agreeing with anti-piracy body the Federation Against Copyright Theft (FACT) that its officers will from now on collect evidence for both VRA-infringing and piracy offences. Also under consideration is voluntary regulation of packaging, some of which, says the BVA "portrays the industry in a negative light".

NOV 16TH: *Video Trade Weekly* reports that video store proprietor and charity worker Paul Hunter, of Hunter Take Two Video Library in Bognor Regis, has been inundated with hate-mail following a recent publicity drive, reflecting the media's (completely groundless) linking of the Hungerford massacre to video.

THE SEDUCTION OF THE GULLIBLE

NOV 30TH: (*Video Business*) It has become clear that from December 1st the BBFC will be granting video certificates only to tapes for which the sleeve design has been vetted by the newly-formed Video Packages Review Committee (comprising representatives of the BBFC, the Advertising Standards Authority and the video distributors), after an initial inspection by a small internal BBFC committee. The Review Committee is asking distributors to incorporate its logo in their packaging. The indefatigable Norman Abbott explains that as the content of videos is toned down, some distributors are compensating with more sensationalist covers, and that self-regulation on this matter will hopefully avert more legislation: "The last thing we wanted was another law to regulate video". There are no hard and fast rules, but ostentatious weaponry is a no-no, especially in the wake of the Hungerford massacre ("Chain-sticks we eliminate totally" reveals a Review Committee member: "We never pass a chainstick").

1988

MAR 14TH: THE HOUSE BY THE CEMETERY is re-released on Elephant Video after having been granted a BBFC '18' video certificate on February 22nd. The certificate was awarded after over four minutes of cuts and the removal of a smear of blood from a knife on the pack-shot (presumably we are now to infer that Dr Freudstein is waving the thing around prior to buttering himself a slice of toast), the whole saga proving so taxing for Elephant supremo Barry Jacobs that he has sworn never to undertake such a release again.

Also this month, Tory MP Robert Jones, a Graham Bright wannabe, visits London's "Forbidden Planet" store and leaves with a copy of FANGORIA, which he shows to the Prime Minister. She describes it as "absolutely appalling and certainly not something that children should be allowed to see".

SEP 15TH: A Royal outburst over media violence at the opening of London's Museum Of the Moving Image: Prince Charles makes an impromptu attack on what he perceives as an "incessant menu of utterly gratuitous sex and violence" on cinema and TV. Singling out video, he rubbishes claims that there is no link between screen and real life violence as "palpable nonsense", heaping scorn on the "self-appointed, so-called experts" (those who live in glass palaces shouldn't throw stones! – JM) who maintain otherwise (but neglecting to outline the grounds of his own expertise on the subject). He expresses a hope that the Museum, as well as entertaining and educating, will help "to show people just how far good taste has diminished during the past 20 years". The Prince is obviously as ignorant of the Picasso dictum that "good taste" is "the chief enemy of creativity" as he is of the existence of the VRA. The Bishop of Peterborough opines that the Prince is "speaking for many parents", but BVA Director General Norman Abbott writes to Prince Charles, advising him that "the British video industry is now probably the cleanest in the world". He is also contacting the Press Council about a *Sunday Telegraph* article that described the video trade as "rotten" and the people in it "rotten to the core".

All this in the same week that Home Secretary Douglas Hurd, who has the power to

THE SEDUCTION OF THE GULLIBLE

issue directives to the BBFC (he can nullify its position as the statutory censoring body for video if he doesn't approve of its decisions, making him and subsequent Home Secretaries de facto state censors), attacks "designer violence" on video.

NOV 3RD: Within a month of coming into force, new powers given to trading standards Officers to deal with unrated videos are proving effective, Timothy Renton, Under-secretary of State at the Home Office tells the House of Commons. Renton reveals that the BBFC has issued 48 certificates of evidence that could lead to prosecutions and another 500 videos are being studied. Christopher Butler, Conservative MP for Warrington South, talks about "cowboys who deal with degrading filth".

1989

MAY 15: (*The Daily Mirror*) "PERILS OF A SPINE CHILLER". "Leading psychiatrist" Dr Lynn Drummond is quoted as claiming that "horror films can trigger off a rare mind disease". Apparently she's treated "several people who have been affected by films such as THE EXORCIST and THE OMEN". Dr Drummond (a consultant at St George's hospital in Tooting, South London) states that victims of something called "compulsive obsessive neurosis" can be "brainwashed by scenes of sex and blood-curdling violence", before coming to the perverse conclusion that these unfortunate wretches can only be cured by making them watch such films over and over again.

OCT 29TH: (*News Of The World*). "VIDEO FIEND GETS JAIL FOR KID ASSAULTS". "Factory worker Gary Longstone assaulted children after watching video nasties... (he) developed sexual fantasies involving young children after watching the films - then acted them out in real life" (so the guy wasn't a paedophile until he watched horror films... yeah, right! - JM).

DEC 3RD: VISIONS OF ECSTASY becomes the first film to be banned in Britain on the grounds of blasphemy. James Ferman justifies the ban, under the Video Recordings Act, on the grounds that the film "degraded Christ". Graham Bright says that this case vindicates the VRA: "It is a sick film involving violence and perversion. It is patently blasphemous and corrupting and should not be allowed on sale or to be viewed", though director Nigel Wingrove protests: "It is not about Christ ... he is part of the erotic imaginings of St Theresa". Michael Winner describes the film as "tame" in comparison to Scorsese's THE LAST TEMPTATION OF CHRIST.

DEC 11TH: *The Daily Express* sends children into video shops, hoping to elicit VRA infringements, but to their chagrin, dealers appear to be adhering to the law. The paper consoles itself by reporting that in the last six months, trading standards officers have clamped down, greatly increasing the number of VRA prosecutions.

DEC 15TH: The VISIONS OF ECSTASY ban is upheld.

1990

FEB 25TH: Former "video nasty" VISITING HOURS is screened on Rupert Murdoch's "Sky Movies" satellite TV channel, which has also recently shown INFERNO. Murdoch is of course the proprietor of *The Sun*, *The News of the World*, *The Times* and *The Sunday Times*, which did more than their fair share to stoke up "nasty" hysteria.

MAY. A heavily cut version of THE EVIL DEAD is finally re-released on sell-through in this month.

CHRONOLOGY: SEP 88 - MAY 90

THE SEDUCTION OF THE GULLIBLE

MAY 1ST: (*The Sun*) "I HEARD THE VOICE OF VIDEO MICHAEL". Robert "Satan" Sartin killed one man with a shot-gun and wounded 17 others at Monkseaton, Tyne and Wear, exactly a year ago. Yesterday, Newcastle Crown court heard that he is detained in a mental hospital, unfit to stand trial. Much is made of Sartin's obsession with the film HALLOWEEN, but as Home Office psychiatrist Dr Marion Swann points out: "He hears more than one voice, and one of them is Michael. Initially, he didn't know who this person was, but then he watched a video of HALLOWEEN and came to realise Michael was the voice he had been hearing". Michael Myers, of course, is never heard to speak in the HALLOWEEN movies, but the deranged Sartin, who displayed an obsession with Nazi tortures as a child and told school doctors that voices were urging him to kill his parents, cannot perhaps be blamed for failing to have noticed this. The media on the other hand, should have done so, but of course it's so much easier to blame video than to acknowledge how all the warning signs in this young man's case were so consistently and tragically ignored. The HALLOWEEN movies are described in *The Sun* as "so blood-thirsty they make the gruesome NIGHTMARE ON ELM STREET series look tame". A couple of pages later, a "Sky" screening of ELM STREET 2 is advertised.

MAY 2ND: *The Sun*, in a classic piece of reportage entitled "THE VIDEO CHILLERS UNLEASHING MAD KILLERS", perpetuates old myths and makes tenuous links, citing criminal cases supposedly inspired by films including CRIMES OF PASSION, FATAL ATTRACTION, JAGGED EDGE and FUZZ, also dragging up the gay bondage slaying that was inexplicably linked to ZOMBIE FLESH EATERS, plus a taxi-driver whose rape and stabbing of a neighbour is attributed to viewings of John Carpenter's THE THING, and Cincinnati mass-murderer Donald Harvey, whose slayings are supposedly based on PHANTASM. Harvey is quoted as saying that "reckless regard" (sic) for life in TV programmes gave him "a chilly thrill ... something akin to a climax when making love". Thanks for sharing these penetrating insights with us, Don...

JUL 9TH: Publicising owner Rupert Murdoch's satellite operation,*The News of the World* announces that "parents will be able to block out raunchy movies from their children using an amazing censor card". Funnily enough, they didn't care to argue, a few years previously, that VCR locks were the answer to "video nasties".

Towards the end of the month, police announce that they are investigating organised paedophile groups that have allegedly been video-taping the murder of children. By an astonishing leap of reasoning, Mary Whitehouse links these claims to the anodyne soft-core sex films allowed by the VRA, which of course she wants further bowdlerised.

JUL 28TH: *The Guardian* digs up the tired old SNUFF "controversy", conceding that "film experts believe the sequence is faked" (you don't have to be any kind of expert to work that out – JM) but quoting Tim Tate, author of CHILD PORNOGRAPHY: "SNUFF is alleged by paedophiles to be the first of a genre of child sex and torture films".

JUL 29TH: *The Sunday Times* concedes that SNUFF is a put-up job, but appears to mis-identify NIGHTMARES IN A DAMAGED BRAIN as a "snuff movie"

SEPTEMBER. CIC's re-issue of VIDEODROME, in its completely un-cut form, is allowed to carry on its cover the line: "Includes footage not previously available on Video in the UK", making rather a mockery of the Video Packaging Review Committee logo elsewhere on that sleeve, not to mention much of what has happened over the last several years.

Also this month, scores of children in Rochdale are removed from their homes and put into care after accusations of "Satanic sexual rituals". A growing suspicion soon

THE SEDUCTION OF THE GULLIBLE

develops that a miscarriage of justice has taken place, hysteria having been stoked by zealous evangelical Christian groups operating in the area. It also emerges that the five year-old retarded child who made the initial allegations might have made it all up after watching horror videos. Never ones to stop kicking a scape-goat when it's down, Britain's trash press turns this final revelation completely on its head, pushing the line that the alleged abuse really did take place, and it was inspired by ... aw c'mon, surely you don't need telling! THE EVIL DEAD, HOUSE and HOUSE 2, DUNGEONS AND DRAGONS, THE KINDRED, DRILLER KILLER, THE HOWLING and PROM NIGHT, along with something supposedly called KLAN, are cited as the guilty "nasties".

SEP 12TH: *Today* headline "THE EVIL LIVING". An editorial entitled "HORROR ON EVERY CORNER" blusters: "If the film and video industry cannot restrain itself from making horror movies that lead directly to child abuse, then it will have to be restrained by law". Children are described as being "at risk of degradation, humiliation, drugs and violence because some of the adults in their lives have taken to imitating the depravities they see on video. These videos are not the kind of sexy sleaze that can be got only through the under-ground porn trade. They are violent horror movies freely for sale or hire at every corner shop in Britain" (hyperbole, surely). "Horror is popular ... on some people it has little effect. But others are mesmerised by its images and copy them. From there it may only be a short step to bringing children in on the action". From this crazy conjecture, the editorial continues: "The government must set up an enquiry to establish just what the effects of these videos are on susceptible adults ..." (Having saved "vulnerable children" last time out, our moral guardians are now crusading on behalf of "susceptible adults" ... God help us all! – JM) "... Setting limits to what can be seen on our screens will not be easy" (those who have been reading this chronology will already have arrived, unaided, at that conclusion! – JM) "But it must be done or we will see Rochdale reproduced all over the country".

SEP 14TH: *Daily Mail* headline – "Seven years after they were banned...THE RETURN OF THE VIDEO NASTIES".

...which seemed a logical stopping-point in 1990 when I started shopping the first edition of this book around to prospective publishers – a lengthy, discouraging business, during which I was told that the whole subject of "nasties" was "old hat" But...

1992

APRIL: Mike Lee revives his Vipco label and starts re-issuing cut versions of such "nasties" as THE BEYOND, BLOODY MOON, THE BOGEYMAN, THE BURNING, DEATH TRAP, HOUSE BY THE CEMETERY, NIGHT OF THE BLOODY APES, NIGHT OF THE DEMON, THE SLAYER and ZOMBIE FLESH EATERS.

MAY 8TH: *Daily Star* – "SNUFFED OUT: cops swoop to seize 3,000 sick killer videos"

Daily Express: "VIDEO HAUL OF HORROR" "A nationwide network selling snuff videos of torture, mutilation and cannibalism has been smashed in a massive undercover operation. Trading standards officials who spent six months posing as dealers in the vile trade yesterday seized 3,000 tapes worth £150,000 ...campaigners against child abuse warn that 'snuff' movies where the victims are killed or 'snuffed out' during filming – are a growing menace".

Obviously it was the term "video nasty" that was "old hat". The plain fact that the VRA was in place and being enforced against suppliers of uncertificated tapes was not

THE SEDUCTION OF THE GULLIBLE

enough for the sensation-hungry media, their need for a new twist given added urgency by the resurgent spectre of recession. New scape-goats had to be found... or perhaps old ones would do, dressed up in preposterous new clothing by the engineers of moral panic. Unfortunately Peter Mawdsley, Liverpool's chief trading standards officer, wasn't playing ball: "Snuff films have been around for some time and I am not aware of anybody finding any evidence to date that these films do involve actual murders. But that is the allegation and that is the way that they are promoted. We will be checking the material and if any real or suspected snuff movies emerge, they will be handed to the police for investigation" (At the time of writing, in 1997, there is still no sign of any "snuff" prosecutions, so you can draw your own conclusion – JM).

The Express report concludes with the revelation that several people across the country are still being questioned and may face prosecution under the Video Recordings Act and possibly the Obscene Publications Act ... a bit of a slap on the wrist if these people were really dealing in "snuff movies", eh? Indeed, Mawdsley is quoted even more unequivocally in *Today* : "They are promoted as real and actual events, but having seen one, I do not believe they are"

1993

JAN 27TH: The BBFC demands 46 seconds of cuts from the video release of HENRY - PORTRAIT OF A SERIAL KILLER. James Ferman (who has gone on the record stating that he always wanted to be a film director) actually re-cuts the notorious "home invasion video" scene!

MARCH. At the end of this month, in the wake of concern over the murder of three year-old James Bulger in February (for which two ten year-olds have been charged), and consequent voicing of concern by various worthies, including the Prime Minister, the BBFC announces that it has commissioned the Policy Studies Institute to initiate the first independent research study for twenty years into the viewing habits of young offenders. The BBC, Independent Television Commission and Broadcasting Standards Council have all agreed to co-sponsor the research (But who's to draw up the report? Clifford Hill, where are you now?) A spokesman for the Department of National Heritage confirms that the issue of TV and video violence is "on the agenda for public debate ... it is never really off it".

APR 6TH: Resenting Peter Mawdsley's namby pamby insistence on proof and facts getting in the way of a good headline, the papers were gifted a rather more gullible trading standards official: *Daily Mail* – "JUNIOR HORROR SHOW. Snuff films on sale with Peter Pan at children's comic fair"... "'Snuff' videos showing scenes of murder, mutilation and cannibalism were on sale alongside Disney films at a children's comic fair ... they are believed to be among the most graphic of their kind yet seized in Britain. One, said Dr Mike Hilburn, chairman of Birmingham Trading Standards Committee, 'contained absolutely disgusting scenes of a man being hacked to death, decapitated and disembowelled'. He went on "I have never seen anything like this before, and I have no doubt that the scenes were genuine". Most graphic yet? Never seen anything like it? Sounds like boring old CANNIBAL HOLOCAUST to me, and – as everyone who hasn't spent the last ten years at the bottom of a lift shaft (like Dr Hilburn) should know by now – it is not, repeat NOT a snuff movie!

The Mail confirms that Ruggero Deodato's jungle opus is the film in question... "Trading Standards officers believe the video shows genuine footage of chanting, half-naked Amazon Indians butchering a white man depicted as a jungle explorer".

THE SEDUCTION OF THE GULLIBLE

The Daily Sport (for which there's some excuse, I suppose) embellished the story even more fancifully: "CANNIBAL HOLOCAUST showed a white man being hacked to death by a tribe of half-naked Amazonian Indians. The doomed 'actor' is thought to have been drugged before being decapitated and disembowelled with a jungle knife". "Other illegal nasties ..." continued *The Sport* " ... included HELLRAISER" (?!?)

AUG 17TH: (*Daily Star*) "NOW IRA SELL SNUFF VIDEOS" - "IRA godfathers are peddling vile snuff videos to raise cash for their murder campaigns. The sickening real-life films of children being tortured are aimed at British perverts. And the source of the videos is a pact between the Provisional IRA and former members of the Argentinean military junta. The movies were originally made by Argie death squads. Now the tapes have been smuggled to Europe and are being mass-produced by IRA back street dealers for sale in Britain. Three years ago, Scotland Yard mounted Operation Orchid, after it was feared that children had been abducted and slaughtered to make disgusting snuff movies. No tapes were found but the children's bodies are believed to have been buried in a secret grave in London's East End" (JM - No mention of the fact that the culprits for these murders had been brought to book, which would have necessitated acknowledging that they had no connection whatsoever to Gerry Adams or General Gualtieri. This incredible conspiracy theory, never substantiated but conveniently combining and blackening the names of several of *The Star*'s favourite bogeymen - even Colonel Gadaffi gets a name-check at one point - was run by that paper as it and its tabloid ilk continued to airily dismiss all accusations of British war crimes against Argentine conscripts during the Falklands War).

OCT 27TH: Today's *Times* leader, marking the death of Vincent Price, reminds us yet again that yes, the horror genre has indeed moved on since the days of Poe and Conan Doyle - "The traditional horror film did not encourage imitation. No member of its audience, however susceptible, was going to dress up in cobwebs and mummy-cloths and start making strange moaning noises behind the panelling before setting out on a new career as a mass strangler. The modern slasher and gang-rapist films ..:" ("gang-rapist films"? ... a genre I wasn't aware of - JM) "... with their explicit images of horror and violence, do not encourage a willing suspension of disbelief. They rape the imagination, and copy-cat crimes..." (evidence for the existence of which is piss-poor, at best -JM) "...suggest that they seriously endanger the vulnerable in their audience".

Also this month, Home Secretary Michael Howard assuages the wrath of Tory fund amentalist delegates to his party's annual conference with simplistic "law and order" rhetoric, promising a raft of correspondingly draconian measures in the upcoming Criminal Justice Bill.

NOV 24TH: After a 17-day trial at Preston Crown Court, two 11 year-old boys (Robert Thompson and Jon Venables) are convicted of murdering Liverpool toddler James Bulger. Trial judge Mr Justice Morland declares: "How it came about that two mentally normal boys aged ten and of average intelligence committed this terrible crime is hard for me to comprehend. It is not for me to pass judgement on their upbringings, but I suspect that exposure to violent video films may in part be an explanation"

NOV 25TH: The immediate fall-out of Justice Morland's comments is devastating for 24 year-old Yorkshire market trader Michael Reid (the man behind *The Daily Mail*'s immortal "SNUFF FILMS ON SALE WITH PETER PAN AT CHILDREN'S COMIC FAIR" headline). A victim of unfortunate timing, to say the least, Reid comes up before Birmingham magistrates with the judge's comments no doubt reverberating in their minds, and is hit with the highest fine yet under the Video Recordings Act - £19,250.

THE SEDUCTION OF THE GULLIBLE

NOV 25TH: With a fine sense of timing (especially as her autobiography QUITE CONTRARY is being launched), Mary Whitehouse announces that she is to resign as leader of the campaign to clean up British television, but not without putting the Bulger tragedy to predictable use: "How can we point the finger of shame at boys who have grown up in a world where sadism is seen as good for the box-office? People concerned about broadcasting standards... " (as if you couldn't guess - JM) "... should lobby their MPs for stricter obscenity laws".

NOV 25TH: *The Guardian* ("JUDGE'S REMARKS PROMPT MPS' HORROR VIDEO CURB CALL" reports that MPs are demanding restrictions on "masochistic (sic) and horror videos which show scenes of simulated or real-life murder and the mutilation of children" (!?! - JM) "Within minutes of the jury reaching guilty verdicts at Preston Crown Court, a Commons motion was tabled calling for a Home Office investigation into TV and video violence. Robert Wareing, Labour MP for West Derby, Liverpool, said: 'I would not want to put a license on all videos ...' (in fact for a full decade prior to this statement, all videos in the UK have had to be licensed - JM) '... which might offend some people, but those which are of a masochistic (sic) nature can undoubtedly do harm to certain people, andundoubtedly children should not be laid open to them'".

NOV 25TH: Under the headline "CRACK DOWN ON THE SICK VIDEOS THAT CAN TWIST YOUNG MINDS, SAY MPs", *The Daily Mail* reports how Liberal Democrat MP David Alton and Tory Michael Alison have tabled a motion in the Commons demanding an immediate investigation "into the role played by violent films in the psychological impulses that led to this murder", and demanding "tighter controls of violence on TV and through videos" Messrs Alton and Alison specifically cite the video CHILD'S PLAY 3 in connection with the Bulger case, stating that it "depicts a doll that turns into a child and which is subsequently killed by two boys on a ghost train. The depiction of murder, muggings and mutilation as entertainment is detrimental to the moral values of children exposed to violent films", they add.

In the same edition of *The Mail*, a piece headlined "FILM A JUDGE DAMNED - DID THIS GROTESQUE VIDEO INSPIRE A BOY TO MURDER?" propagates the myth that the Bulger trial judge had cited CHILD'S PLAY 3 while sentencing the two boy killers:"A horror film rented by the father of one of the killers could hold the key to James's savage slaughter. CHILD'S PLAY 3 bears such striking similarities to the killing that lawyers believed there might be a connection. The adult movie tells how a talking doll is possessed by evil and comes to life in a military academy where his face is splashed with blue paint during a war game. In a dreadful echo of the Bulger tragedy..." (Surely a foreshadowing, if anything - JM) "... he abducts the youngest cadet from the academy and tries to kill him under the wheels of a fairground ghost train. The video was the last one rented by Jon Venables's father before James was abducted, splashed with blue paint and killed on a railway line". Laurence Lee, the Venables family's solicitor, is quoted as saying: "Venables and his father are adamant that he did not watch CHILD'S PLAY 3 and I have no proof to the contrary. The boy has specifically told me he doesn't like horror movies".

The piece continues: "Police studied a list of more than 440 titles Mr Venables rented from various shops, but decided that none could be proved to have influenced his son" (So why this ridiculous piece? - JM) "Mr and Mrs Venables denied letting him watch anything other than children's films. But of the last 50 titles Mr Venables hired from one shop, the vast majority were far from being children's entertainment". (Why shouldn't they be? Is *The Mail* arguing that only kids' stuff should be available on video? Incredibly, this was indeed the way the anti-"nasties" campaign would progress - JM)

PAGE # 248

THE SEDUCTION OF THE GULLIBLE

NOV 25TH: (*The Sun*) "A GRIM WARNING OF THINGS TO COME". That intellectual giant Gary Bushell weighs in with the followin words of wisdom: "Liberal permissiveness is eating the fabric of our society. You want video nasties peddling stomach-churning filth? You got 'em. Western values? Who needs 'em!" When Bushell isn't blustering about decency and Western Values, he can be found gloating and cracking jokes over such incidents as the death of several transvestites in a sex cinema fire.

Elsewhere in the paper, the following attempt is made to pin down these putative parallels between CHILD'S PLAY 3 and the Bulger killing: "In the film, a boy entices the doll to chase him by calling it and running away - the same way Jon and fellow killer Robert Thompson lured James from his mother; the doll, named Chucky, has its face splattered with blue paint - James's killers stole three tins of blue paint which they threw in his face; Chucky has half its face sliced away by a scythe - the boys hit James on the head with a metal bar; the doll is taken to a rail track by a graveyard and attacked - the boys led James to his death on a railway line next to a cemetery; Chucky keeps getting up despite his injuries - James did the same when he was pelted with bricks". (Anyone attempting to substantiate David Alton's spurious citing of CHILD'S PLAY 3 in connection with this case is bound to come up with nothing better than the tenuous tripe covered in *The Sun*'s first five "points", but roping the unfortunate Bulger kid's desperate struggle to say alive into some kind of copy-cat scenario breaks new grounds in bad taste, even by this paper's notoriously shabby standards - JM)

The Sun continues that "A child psychologist... who asked not to be named" (how very odd: Guy Cumerbatch of Aston University, who takes an opposing view, has no such qualms about his findings being attributed to him - JM) has warned that some children who are "subjected to" horror films have difficulty telling fact from fantasy. David Alton, it is revealed, is urging Home Secretary Michael Howard to introduce stricter controls on TV and video violence, describing himself as "horrified" by the number of horror videos rented by Venables' father. "The idea that a child doesn't see these things when they are being freely shown in the home is so wrong. What happens when the father is out? We need to search our souls and ask ourselves what kind of world our children are growing up in. We are creating a brutal and violent ethos among too many. I think there is an undoubted link to violence on the TV and in videos" (He thinks it's undoubted? - JM) "Our homes have been penetrated by garbage. If you dress murder and rape as entertainment, how can a child know right from wrong?", he asks.

NOV 25TH: "CHILLING REPLAY OF DAD'S HORROR VIDEO" - *The Star* also has recourse to an anonymous lawyer (furtive bunch,huh?), and completely alters the tone of his comments by selective highlighting: "There are worrying similarities with this disturbing film. When I saw the film for the first time I was deeply affected by what I saw. But there is no evidence to suggest that the boys were in any way acting out scenes from the film".

NOV 25TH: "HORROR FILM LINK TO GRUESOME MURDER". *The Express* claims that "chilling similarities between a horror video and Jamie Bulger's terrible death were uncovered by detectives. They strongly suspect Venables, and perhaps his fellow killer, watched the film CHILD'S PLAY 3" (Not so - the police explicitly ruled out any such connection - JM) "No-one is suggesting this film made them do it", 'a lawyer' is quoted as saying (if only that were so - in fact this anonymous individual proceeds to have his cake and eat it by continuing: "some of the things they did to James may have been inspired by it - there are terrible parallels" - JM) "The prosecution decided against producing evidence indicating a possible a (sic) sexual attack on little James... but detectives privately admit that they suspect a sexual motive" concludes *The Express*.

THE SEDUCTION OF THE GULLIBLE

NOV 25TH: *The Mirror* reveals that Thompson and Venables had allegedly tried to abduct another two year-old boy, to throw under a car. "It would look like a road traffic accident" police Sergeant Phil Roberts is quoted as saying (and even David Alton would have had a hard job tying that to CHILD'S PLAY 3 - JM)

NOV 25TH: *Today* interviews a schoolmate of the Bulger killers. Michael Gee, as well as confirming their long track-record of arson and animal torture (classic early indicators of psychopathy), tells how Thompson had a long-standing plan to push a child under a bus at The New Strand shopping centre, Liverpool. This is what the boys originally tried to do with Jamie Bulger. They also tried to throw him in a canal before taking him to the railway track where he died, and these plan existed long before they could possibly have seen CHILD'S PLAY 3. Today also invokes the expertise of Peter Hill, Professor of child and adolescent psychology at St George's Hospital Medical school, London. "Showing a disturbed 10 year-old violent videos is dynamite" he contends: "That's the link for me" (now that's what I call making a rigorous scientific case! - JM)

Today's *Today* editorial: "It will never be known whether either of the murderers saw the film" (whether the connection exists or not, rest assured that *Today* and co are going to get all the mileage they can out of it - JM) "Police and defence lawyers insist it was a coincidence" (Yes, even those you'd expect to be grasping at any possible straws of mitigation - JM). Jon's mother Susan, 38, called the link between video nasties and the murder: 'rubbish... he was never allowed to watch adult films. The same applies to my other children. When they are in bed, that's when we will watch an 18 film'".

NOV 25TH: *The Liverpool Echo* publishes details of a report on Jon Venables by Dr Susan Bailey, a consultant forensic psychologist specialising in adolescents: "Venables recoiled from violent scenes in videos and his favourite film was THE GOONIES".

NOV 26TH: (*The Independent*) "VIDEO LINK TO BULGER MURDER DISPUTED" - "As accusations over the role of horror videos in violent crime mounted yesterday, senior Merseyside police discounted suggestions that they had influenced the murderers of James Bulger. The video furore surprised Merseyside senior detectives. One said: 'I don't know where the judge got that idea from. I couldn't believe it when I heard him. We went through something like 200 titles rented by the Venables family. There were some you or I wouldn't want to see, but nothing - no scene, or plot, or dialogue - where you could put your finger on the freeze button and say that influenced a boy to go out and commit murder'. Police were also told that a Roald Dahl story, 'The Swan', available in Liverpool schools and libraries, foretold the death. After the judge's comment on the possible influence of videos on the two young murderers, Detective Superintendent Albert Kirby said he had seen no evidence to suggest the boys had access to videos any worse than might be found in many homes. Despite strong pressure from MPs for action The Home Secretary responded cautiously to the statement by the Bulger trial judge, Michael Howard told the Commons yesterday that he would not 'rush into snap judgements'. David Maclean, Minister of State at the Home Office, said the judge's comments would be closely studied but police had found no evidence linking the case with 'video nasties'. Britain had the tightest European laws on videos: 'We cannot see any other way we can make the laws any tighter ... no matter how tightly Parliament may classify films, what you watch in your own home as viewers is the decision of parents and youngsters'". *The Independent* also reveals that, in the Commons, the Conservative MP Sir Ivan Lawrence, QC has called for action to curb "the constant diet of violence and depravity" fed to youngsters through television, videos and computer pornography. Sir Ivan, Chairman of the Home Affairs Select Committee, said it was becoming "daily more obvious" that this was a major reason for

THE SEDUCTION OF THE GULLIBLE

the rise in juvenile crime" "David Alton, Liberal Democrat MP for Liverpool, Mossley Hill, said people would be concerned that the video mentioned in the Bulger case, CHILD'S PLAY ..." (he means CHILD'S PLAY 3 ... and it wasn't mentioned in the trial - JM) "... had been scheduled for broadcast on SKY TV. 'Doesn't this demonstrate that the levels of violence which are transmitted by video and television have reached unsurpassed levels?' Mr Alton ... urged the Home Secretary to use forthcoming criminal justice legislation to deal with the portrayal of gratuitous violence. Mr Howard, echoing the Prime Minister, said he had great sympathy with Mr Alton's views. But before reaching any conclusions he wanted to reflect on the words of the trial judge and the police officer in charge of the case, and also on research being conducted by the BBFC" (JM - Presumably this is the point where Alton, knowing full well that impartial research would do his cause no good at all, decided to get together with Professor Elizabeth Newson, on whom much more later).

After reporting the above in characteristically level-headed style, *The Independent* contributes a surprisingly ill-informed editorial to the developing "debate" - "WE MUST PROTECT YOUNG MINDS"... "The uncanny resemblance" (to those who haven't bothered to watch the film and rely for their accounts on scummy tabloids ... how strange to find the honourable *Indie* in this category! - JM) "between the film CHILD'S PLAY 3 and the killing of James Bulger must be of concern. Some critics want greater control of 'video nasties'. They are right that a culture of gratuitous violence is being disseminated by means of videos. Although they are, surprisingly ..." (!) "... more tightly regulated than films shown in cinemas, inadequate parental supervision means that children gain easy access to grossly unsuitable material. But videos are only part of the problem: CHILD'S PLAY 3 has already been broadcast twice on satellite television and would have been screened again tonight but for the attention drawn to it by the murder of James Bulger". (*The Independent*'s line here, and that subsequently taken by others who should have known better, has no doubt been influenced by their current attempts to counter predatory pricing by competitors owned by Rupert Murdoch, who also owns BSkyB Television... satellite broadcasters of CHILD PLAY 3 - JM)

NOV 26TH: *The Guardian* proves more reliable than *The Independent*, though it too erroneously describes CHILD'S PLAY 3 as a video "referred to by the judge in the James Bulger murder trial". Canvassing the opinions of various pundits, it elicits the following views...

David Buckingham, Lecturer in Media Education at London's Institute of Education, currently researching what young people find upsetting on TV - "Something very horrible has happened; something very, very hard to explain. Video provides a nice, easy explanation. People are generating a very high level of anxiety in a case which is atypical. We're not talking about a crime wave; we're talking about something which happens very infrequently. A case like the Bulger murder is not something you can legislate against happening: banning videos won't prevent this sort of thing happening again".Tim Newburn, senior research fellow at the Policy Studies Institute - "I think the available evidence about violent films and behaviour is at best inconclusive. At the turn of the Century, there was great concern about violent images in Penny Dreadful comics. In the 1950s, panic that horror comics would lead to children copying the things they saw, led to the Children and Young Persons (Harmful Publications Act) 1959. Ten years ago, there was a huge panic about films such as DRILLER KILLER, which also led to a new law. There's been a recurrent moral panic about violent images which looks to a mythical golden age of tranquil behaviour".The Bishop of Worcester - "The two evil boys who killed Jamie Bulger should not be compared with other boys and government policy should not be made on the basis of one terrible case".

THE SEDUCTION OF THE GULLIBLE

Ken McArthur, senior vice-president of marketing at CIC Video, the distributors of CHILD'S PLAY 3 - "It is for video rental shops to decide whether to withdraw this legitimate release. Once the videos leave the store, the responsibility devolves onto the adult to make sure that those for whom the film is not suitable are not able to watch it"

The Guardian also reports: "SKY WITHDRAWS DEMON DOLL FILM FROM TONIGHT'S SCHEDULE". A BSkyB spokeswoman said: "We took the decision in the light of the judge's comments. We are a responsible and sensitive broadcaster and take such comments into account"

NOV 26TH: Unabashed by the revelation of its "Demon Doll" connection, The Sun mounts a lurid, full-colour front page splash headlined: "For the sake of all our kids ... BURN YOUR VIDEO NASTY" (Those with an attention span longer than two seconds might well ask "Why not 'burn your Sky satellite dish', too?"... see also The Mirror, 29/4/94 for proof of how The Sun was playing with fire in more ways than one by dispensing this advise - JM). The report continued by detailing how "a video chain boss yesterday torched his entire £10,000 stock of tapes linked to the James Bulger murder". Stoking up the witch-hunting hysteria, David Alton MP is quoted as praising The Sun's "campaign" and endorsing burning as "the answer to the 'gratuitous nastiness' of the video which may..." (!?!) "... have been seen by Jon Venables, one of the killers". That "video chain boss", identified as Imtiaz Ahmad, marketing director of Azad Video, says: "As soon as I saw the Sun report I ordered the shelves in our 80 stores cleared. I'm not going to have that kind of stuff in my shops". Azad, described as "Scotland's biggest chain", also has many branches in England. Indeed ...

NOV 26TH: (The Mirror) "The video shop boss who rented CHILD'S PLAY 3 to Jon Venables's father" (!) "said: 'It's staying on the shelves'. Azad video ..." (You remember, the folks who won't have that kind of stuff in their shops - JM) opened for business as usual with copies of CHILD'S PLAY 3 stacked among the dozens of horror films the store rents out. The Mirror asked Mrs Jackie Cullen whether she thought it might be tactful to withdraw the film, bearing in mind the judge's comments. She replied: 'There's no evidence that the children saw the film and the police say it had nothing to do with the murder. It's staying on the shelves'" (I think I prefer Mrs Cullen to her spineless Scottish counterpart Mr Ahmad - JM).

NOV 26TH: The Mirror castigates the Home Secretary for "dire short-sightedness". "It surely is simple to order that some films are not passed for viewing so children do not get a chance to see them". (JM .... which is exactly what already happens. But hang on, here comes the circulation war stuff...) "Yet such violence is not only available from the video shop. It is pumped into millions of homes virtually every night on satellite television. CHILD'S PLAY 2..." (CHILD'S PLAY 3, actually - JM) "... was to have been shown on Sky TV tonight. It has already been screened several times, as have dozens of other movies which children should not see".

NOV 26TH: Further sagacious comments from Mr Justice Morland: "It was a ghastly crime. It is unbelievable that it could have been perpetrated by 10 year-old boys. It could be argued that the exposure of children to family problems, television, newspapers, or videos played their part". ("Newspapers"? Funny how the press glossed over this particular pearl of judicial wisdom, huh? - JM)

NOV 26TH: The Star - "'SHIELD KIDS FROM THESE EVIL FILMS'" "'Keep this video nasty away from your kids!'. That was the reaction yesterday of Daily Star readers to the film that may have warped the minds of the killers of toddler James Bulger". The Star

THE SEDUCTION OF THE GULLIBLE

sits a cross-section of people down to watch CHILD'S PLAY 3. Comments include: "Having seen this, I am sure this is where the two boys who murdered James got their evil ideas from" (Administrator Natalie Miller, 19, of Enfield, Middlesex) and: "This should really be banned. We can't risk other children copying what these boys did" (ex-marine Neil Carroll from Liverpool, who apparently stopped viewing halfway through... if he didn't bother to watch the film's contentious ending, how did he know that the Bulger killing was a copy-cat affair? Tell it to the marines, Neil!)

NOV 26TH: "'MUM APED EVIL DOLL'" In an early report on the Suzanne Capper murder trial, *The Star* states that "a mum of three took on the role of a killer doll from a horror film as she injected a teenager with drugs just days before the girl was burned alive". No prizes for guessing the identity of this killer doll.

HORROR: Murder victim James Bulger, left — his killers had access to violent videos like these

NOV 26TH: (*The Star*) "WHY SICK VIDEOS *MUST* BE BANNED". David Alton states that "nasties" are the cause of "an epidemic of violence among children". "I strongly believe the easy availability of videos, often explaining highly explicit scenes of violence, help to explain the level of violence today compared with 15 years ago". (In fact for 15 years, violent videos have been far from "easily available", and if a decade of the toughest video censorship in a Western democracy has actually coincided with an increase in the incidence of violence in society, as Alton asserts, then surely that gives the lie to his whole argument - JM) "A video called CHILD'S PLAY 3 is an example. Would you want a video lying around your home that shows a doll coming to life, and then being attacked and mutilated? Common sense tells you that if you are exposed to something often enough it has an effect on you". (Note how the anti-intellectual calls for 'common sense' to take precedence over the weight of respectable scientific research become ever shriller in the aftermath of the Bulger case - JM) "Broadcasters should have to mark programmes with a 'V' if they contain violence. Each week they should have to publish the number of violent incidents they have broadcast. And horror videos and computer pornography should not be made available for sale or hire", Alton concludes.

NOV 26TH: (*Daily Mail*) Lynda Lee-Potter "We have a world where children are growing up virtually as savages. Through video shops they have recourse to scenes of evil and black magic. Whenever I have had to watch a sick video for professional journalistic reasons the images have stayed in my head for days. I have no doubt whatsoever of their destructive impact on disturbed young minds".

NOV 26TH: *Daily Mail* editorial - "WHEN AMORALITY BECOMES NORMALITY". "Mr Justice Morland suggested that violent films may have been part of the explanation of James's murder. But Detective Superintendent Albert Kirby, who lead the investigation, disagreed, while conceding that such videos are commonplace in homes around the country" (Not much or a "concession" if you don't think they are harmful - JM) "Whether or not this particular video influenced the killers is not the central point." (i.e. "we want to have our cake and eat it" - JM) "The point is that 'video nasties', being commonplace as the policeman rightly says ..." (Yep, they've actually recruited some-body who disagrees with them to back up their argument - JM) "... play a major part in conditioning young minds. That is common sense and not all the research in the world will disprove it. Heaven knows, many of the factors which contributed to the death of James Bulger are complex and difficult for the state to influence. But tougher video censorship is a simple move for a Government to make" (... and simplistic steps are the only ones *The Mail* understands - JM).

On this eventful day the death of Anthony CLOCKWORK ORANGE Burgess is announced, and *The Mail* sees fit to reproduce this quote from him: "Literary artists are always being treated as if they invented evil, but their true task, one of many, is to show that it existed long before they handled their first pen or word processor", without apparently realising its applicability to the "video nasty" furore going on elsewhere in the paper.

NOV 26TH: (*Daily Mail*) "A PSYCHIATRIST'S WARNING - KNIFE-EDGE CHILDREN CAN SO EASILY TURN INTO YOUNG SAVAGES". "Watching video nasties can be the 'break-ing point' for children prone to violence, child psychiatrist Professor John Pearce warned yesterday. Children of one parent families or of parents under stress were the most likely to watch violent films without supervision. Ironically, those children most at risk will watch most videos simply because of the way they live" (these dubious class pronouncements would be directly contradicted by the Policy Studies Institute's sub-sequent, authoritative findings - and isn't there more than a whiff of Clifford Hill's class-slanted, totally discredited VIDEO VIOLENCE AND CHILDREN report about them? - JM)

NOV 26TH: *The Times* ("CHILD'S PLAY - SCREEN SADISM IS IMMORAL WHETHER OR NOT IT CAUSES CRIME") deplores the fact that "where once this kind of material might have been regarded as a shameful private indulgence ..." ("Private" as in "in the home"? - JM) "... it is now freely available on every High street" (untrue - JM) "The speculation over whether (Venables) may have watched one particular film is ultimately of less significance than... members of a whole generation of children... growing up in a culture saturated by images of gratuitous cruelty and bestial violence. The demand for proof that watching depraved violence causes imitative crime is dangerously fallacious, both in this instance and in the wider debate about video sado-culture". (we just have to take *The Times*'s word for it - JM) "To claim that only some indisputable proof of a causal link could justify the curtailers of 'freedom of expression' is an evasion of an obvious truth: a society that accepts vividly enacted brutality is ipso facto making such acts conceivable, and even encouraging the belief that they are commonplace. This is not a matter for proof. It is self-evident". (No, it's *gibberish* ! if particular acts were not conceivable before the film-maker portrayed them, how did he ever conceive the idea of doingso in the first place? - JM) "Today's festering culture of video nastiness thrives in corners of Britain remote from the liberal drawing rooms where 'freedom of speech' is so uncritically defended" (yep, it's those dangerous working-class oiks again!)

Elsewhere in *The Times*, the balance of sanity is somewhat restored in a piece entitled "HORROR VIDEOS DO NOT TURN CHILDREN INTO HORRIFIC PEOPLE", in which Dr Guy Cumerbatch, senior lecturer in Applied Psychology at Aston University, who has been studying children and visual imagery for 20 years, points out that research carried out around the world has consistently failed to prove a conclusive link. He also insists that, by the age of 7, children can distinguish between fantasy and reality: "I'm quite sure these films will give your children bad nightmares, but horror films are designed to horrify, they do not make the children themselves horrific people".

NOV 27TH: (*The Guardian*) "BULGER JUDGE URGES DEBATE ON PARENTING AND VIDEOS". "Informed and worthwhile debate can take place for the public good in the case of grave crimes by young children", Mr Justice Morland is quoted as saying, adding that this could include exposure to violent video films "including possibly CHILD'S PLAY 3, which has some striking similarities to the manner of the attack on James Bulger". (Looks like the judge got his ideas about CHILD'S PLAY 3 from Alton and the newspapers rather than vice-versa, as is often otherwise presumed - JM).

NOV 27TH: (*The Sun*) "END FOR CHUCKY - VIDEO STORES RUSH TO BURN FILM LINKED WITH JAMES MURDER". "Store bosses (yesterday) emptied shelves of CHILD'S PLAY 3 - starring demon doll Chucky - and many copies went up in flames". (JM - Lots off shops took this publicity opportunity, and rumours persist that some of them burned photocopied covers in empty boxes, then sold off the tapes at vastly inflated prices, due to the interest being generated in this forgettable little film by the media's ludicrous attempts to link it to a real-life murder. Indeed, as is reported elsewhere in the paper...) "GHOULS IN LAST FLING". "Ghouls rushed yesterday to rent the few copies of CHILD'S PLAY 3 still being stocked by dealers defying public outrage. An assistant at Mr Video, in Sheffield, said sickeningly: 'The film's become very popular after the Bulger case. It's the best publicity a film could get.' At Blockbuster Video, Portswood, Southampton, a sales assistant said: 'There's been no shortage of people after it. It's all a bit sick'"

The impending Policy Studies Institute report is trailered as "a bid to link crime with screen violence". (Not so! In fact, when it became clear that the PSI report was coming to a diametrically opposed conclusion, *The Sun* dropped all mention of it, in favour of "research" that better suited its own prejudices - JM)

NOV 27TH: (*The Mirror*) "A spokesman from THE PSI said: 'Our survey shows this is a more complicated business than people think. They may be surprised by the results'".

NOV 28TH: (*The News Of The World*): "VILE VIDEO RING IS DESTROYED - BOY, 12, SOLD TORTURE FILMS": "A secret network selling vile videos of torture, mutilation and cannibalism has been smashed by trading standards officers after a two-year undercover operation" (i.e. they picked through classified ads in the most recent issue of fan magazines such as *Samhain* - JM). "One of the salesmen turned out to be a 12 year-old boy, who ran a mail order business in the grisly films from his bedroom. Now the sick masterminds behind much more gruesome films - such as CANNIBAL HOLOCAUST, HUMAN EXPERIMENTS and BLOODSUCKING FREAKS will face the courts. The videos were seized in raids on private homes in May and June last year. But it has taken many months to prepare the case because the subject matter was so vile, officers were only allowed to watch them in short bursts" (Why is watching scenes out of context always deemed dangerous for the average punter but beneficial for Trading Standards Officers? - JM). Liverpool's chief trading standards officer Peter Mawdsley

THE SEDUCTION OF THE GULLIBLE

embellishes this point: "They were seasoned officers who knew what to expect. But even they were shocked". That old journalistic standby, "an insider", reveals that: 'A lot of the dealing is done by word of mouth... the level of mutilation and torture and the graphic details put the price up". The report concludes with the bizarre observation that: "Some of the footage comes from film crews who follow ambulances to horrific road crashes and video the dead and injured victims".

NOV 28TH: The Scottish *Sunday Mail* hits rock bottom, running a piece entitled "CHILDREN OF HELL - DEADLY TRUTH BEHIND THOSE VIDEO NASTIES" in which it attributes the deaths of "Spook Kids" Heather O'Rourke (from intestinal disease) and Dominique Dunne (strangled by her boyfriend) to their appearances in the film POLTERGEIST: "If movie stars who make fantasy real can't cope with the aftermath, what chance have the children who watch it?" gibbers *Sunday Mail* hackette Fidelma Cook: "Aren't THEY being sucked into their TV screens just as surely as THE POLTERGEIST's angel?" Er, yeah... keep on taking the tablets, Fidelma!

NOV 28TH: (*Sunday Times*) "MPs SEEK BAN ON VIOLENT VIDEO FILMS". "Censors would have the power under (David Alton's) plan to award films a certificate of 'Not Suitable For Home Viewing'. MPs ... want the BBFC to bar from home viewing any material 'likely to cause gross offence to a reasonable person'." David Alton claims that "a head of steam has built up on this issue... present regulations are not enough. Under our proposal, people who want to watch the more horrific films can do so - but at the cinema. Our amendment would automatically have prevented SKY TV's broadcast of CHILD'S PLAY 3, which was pulled at the last minute". James Ferman demurs: 'I don't think these MPs realise how highly censored videos already are in this country. There are no wicked children in CHILD'S PLAY 3. It is a ghost story. Surely we are not going to ban ghost stories?'" The BBFC director also slams spurious links between the Bulger case and CHILD'S PLAY 3 as "totally in the minds of journalists". *The Mirror* didn't let him down...

NOV 29TH: *The Mirror* talk to CHILD'S PLAY 3 producer David Kirschner under the headline "DON'T BLAME ME FOR DEATH OF BABY JAMES": "Multi-millionaire Kirschner... had no idea that police investigating the horrific killing have drawn parallels between Jamie's execution and the final scenes of CHILD'S PLAY 3" (JM - This revelation must have come as a considerable surprise to those policemen too, since they have consistently ruled out any such connection). Elsewhere in the same edition, the Archbishop of Canterbury gives an obviously timely warning against "lapsing into moral panic" over the Bulger case.

DEC 1ST: (*The Mirror*) Downmarket "TV personality" and yellow press columnist Anne Diamond flexes her mighty intellect on the Bulger affair in a piece imaginatively entitled: "NASTY, MR KIRSCHNER": "'Don't blame me for James Bulger's murder', whines David Kirschner..." (Apparently disagreeing with Ms. Diamond = "whining" - JM), "... all the way from his beautiful Los Angles home, sitting alongside his wife and two daughters." (No doubt if Kirschner lived in a cardboard box his protestations would find more favour with Ms. Diamond, who is, incidentally, not noted for her own modest circumstances - JM) "Well, I have a message for Mr Kirschner ... the parents in this country are terrified. We're perplexed that two ten year-old boys could have killed James Bulger in such a way. Our gut tells us they must have seen your evil doll Chucky. They must have loved the film. And they must have seen it over and over again, because some of the things they did are almost exact copies of the screenplay" (JM - Not true! Nor am I convinced that the considered professional opinions of the massed police officers, lawyers, and social workers who insisted that these children had not watched

THE SEDUCTION OF THE GULLIBLE

Kirschner's film should be given less credence than the urgings of Ms Diamond's intestinal tract. As Dr Julian Petley would later write in the first issue of anti-censorship magazine *Scapegoat*: "No amount of wishful thinking or petulant foot-stamping will alter the fact that there is not a shred of evidence that the Bulger killers watched CHILD'S PLAY 3"). Desperately striving to eke out her word allocation, Diamond continues: "Why do so-called grown-up human beings make depraved video nasties? What ghastly, warped, depraved mind thinks up the plots, plans every sordid scene, lights the blood-strewn corpses to their best effect and mixes together the spin-chilling sound-effects?" (We thought you said you'd never seen one, Anne! - JM) Diamond ends on bizarre note: "This weekend, a woman in the Midlands said her child had seen the film, that he'd become possessed, and tried to kill the pet dog". Incredibly, she actually appears to believe that employing this anecdote strengthens rather than weakens her case!

DEC 2ND: *The Times'* letters page carries the following missive from the Video Standards Council's Merlyn Rees (President) and Iain Muspratt (Vice-President). "At no time during the (Bulger) trial did the prosecution or the defence indicate that video was at all relevant. Indeed, the police did exhaustively investigate whether there was a video connection and they have categorically and repeatedly stated that they found none. There is no evidence that either of the boys had ever watched CHILD'S PLAY 3 and the father of John Venables has specifically denied that his son had watched it. The hypothesis of a link has followed general comments on screen violence made by the trial judge, which was his personal opinion and was not based on the facts of the case. The video industry has always been very aware of its responsibilities and erred on the side of caution. It is subject to both the criminal law and voluntary controls that go far beyond anything required by law or practiced by all other media. It is also far more restricted than any other European country's and has statutory regulations that do not apply to terrestrial TV or satellite".

DEC 4TH: In the trade magazine *Video Home Entertainment*, dealers are warned by BVA vice-chairman Iain Muspratt: "The trade must be extra-vigilant with regard to enforcing age classifications", because the media will be looking to catch people out. In the same edition, CIC announces that it has withdrawn CHILD'S PLAY 3 from "live supply", and states that it "supports the BVA's view that the public should be continually educated in the definitions of the various classifications. However, the industry cannot assume responsibility for the role which parents should be playing to ensure that their children only have access to suitable entertainment products". James Ferman is quoted as saying: "The press have definitely been wrenching images out of context to mean something they don't mean in the film ... everybody wants an explanation, an excuse so they don't have to face the bitter truth, that there are families in this country living through hell, raising children who are not properly socialised... in the current climate, where people are worried about children dying, it's possible that anything would get through - but I think it would be very ill-judged".

The magazine also runs a profile on Liberal-Democrat MP David Alton, including the information that the Boundary Commission is likely to amalgamate his Mossley Hill Parliamentary seat with one of the die-hard Labour seats Walton, Riverside or Garston. Clearly, a man who needs to keep his face in the news. Alton (who would eventually concede defeat in his quest for a winnable seat and announce his decision not to stand as a parliamentary candidate in the next election) is quoted as saying that when he finally sat down and watched CHILD'S PLAY 3: "It was even worse than I expected" but *VHE* reproduces comments made on the film's release, by those very papers which now see it as the definition of depravity, e.g. "The horror is minimal - the best bits are the wisecracks" - (*Today*, 17/10/92) and "Yawn!" - (*The Sun*, 10/10/92).

THE SEDUCTION OF THE GULLIBLE

DEC 6TH: (*The Times*) Letters page - Andrew Sims and Peter Gray write, from St James's University Hospital: "We ... have ample evidence to show that children of all ages (watch adult videos). The viewer is encouraged to ... despise the victim as weak and inferior and to banish any feelings of guilt and remorse. Vulnerable people - children and those who are susceptible to suggestion through mental illness or frailty - need to be protected from this pernicious propaganda. The general public has no doubt that media violence produces violence in reality. Neither have TV advertisers any doubt that the media mould behaviour" (Yes, but connecting the complex issue of the possible effects of screen violence to advertising is like comparing chalk and cheese - JM). Sims and Gray continue: "We recommend that there should be a public and responsible evaluation of the facts" (So they would shortly associate themselves with the almost immediately discredited Newson report! - JM) "The vulnerable should be protected, even at the expense of censoring viewing", is their rather depressing and eminently predictable conclusion.

DEC 7TH: (*The Star*) "BULGER COPYCAT FEAR IN TORTURE ATTACK". "Two boys have been accused of torturing three little brothers on a railway line. The alleged attack by the youngsters, aged 10 and 11, came just five days after the end of the James Bulger murder trial". Detective Chief Inspector Bob Pattison is quoted as saying that 'the alleged offences occurred so very soon after the verdict in the Bulger inquiry that there is an obvious concern that there may have been an element of a copy cat link". (What now - "BURN YOU NEWSPAPER NASTIES"? Interestingly enough, a Mori opinion poll on violence in news coverage reveals at this time that the item which has provoked more viewer complaints than anything else is media coverage of the Bulger case - JM)

DEC 18TH: A *Daily Mail* piece entitled "EVIL THAT DEFIES BELIEF" is typical of the media's reporting of the conclusion to the Suzanne Capper torture / murder trial, with CHILD'S PLAY 3 now having to carry the can for the murderous antics of Manchester's drug-addled human dregs: "Last night evidence of the film's influence on Suzanne's torturers were mounting... one of the two women ringleaders apparently acted the part of Chucky, the evil-eyed doll which comes to life in the move series, as she repeatedly returned to the bedroom where Suzanne was being held captive to inflict more pain. The words 'I'm Chucky, wanna play?' - taken from a 'rave' music dance track - featuring the doll's catch phrase were recorded over and over on a 45-minute tape and pumped remorselessly into Suzanne's head through headphones" (In fact this murder had a lot more to do with the rave [= drug] scene than horror films- JM). "In one of the series of films, Chucky is destroyed by fire just as Suzanne was burnt" (Just about every act of violence that could happen to Chucky does happen to him over the course of the three films... does that mean he can be blamed for absolutely every act of violence that ever occurs? - JM) The Mail concedes that: "Detective Inspector Peter Wall suggested the link with the film was 'tenuous'".

DEC 24TH: *The Mirror* reports how the video release of the new Macauley Culkin film has been postponed from January until March at the earliest because the BBFC has not yet given it a rating. "In the film THE GOOD SON, Macauley switches from a cute-and-cuddly HOME ALONE boy ..." (in fact HOME ALONE is an incredibly violent film, without ever realistically portraying the consequences of such violence - JM) "... to an angel-faced villain. He kills his dog with a steel bolt, causes a Motorway pile-up, drops a railway bar on a railway track and corrupts his innocent young cousin. The 13 year-old star even utters the F-word" (How ridiculously fucking coy! - JM) Tory Sir Ivan Lawrence said: 'Children should certainly not be allowed to see it in the cinema ... and we should debate whether adults should either'". Other films whose video release would be postponed for long periods include RESERVOIR DOGS, BAD LIEUTENANT, TRUE ROMANCE,

THE SEDUCTION OF THE GULLIBLE

BEYOND BEDLAM, MENACE II SOCIETY, KICKBOXER - THE AGGRESSOR, MIKEY, SHOPPING and Michael Winner's DIRTY WEEKEND

1994

JANUARY. Towards the end of this month, the trash-press - and of course David Alton - get themselves in a self-righteous lather over the revelation that Mr Justice Morland has recommended the killers of James Bulger spend only 8 years in custody, although surely such leniency follows on logically from his comments (which the papers found so much to their liking) about the boys being somehow "made" to commit the crime by "video nasties".

JAN 14TH: As a "Satanic sex abuse ring" prosecution collapses in Bishop Auckland, *The Mirror* reports that alleged ringleader Vivienne Crosby "believes scenes from video nasties such as HELLRAISER might have triggered the youngsters' imaginations".

JAN 24TH: For arguing against her pro-censorship views on a TV discussion programme, the author of this volume is described by the National Viewers and Listeners Association's Joanna Bogle as "the kind of man who would have sent children down a coal-mine in Victorian times".

FEBRUARY. About this time, the Fred West mass-murder case is breaking. Yellow press hacks dispatched to "the House of Horrors" at 25 Cromwell Street in Gloucester, to discover what fiendish "nasties" drove West to his excesses, learn that he subsisted on a constant video diet of... Disney cartoons. In Exeter, John Gullidge, editor of the long-running horror fanzine *Samhain* (co-founded by the author of this volume) is the subject of harassment by local newspapers, which link his name to "video nasties" and "snuff movies", demanding that he be removed from the play-group at which he works as a part-time helper. Also, Prime Minister John Major's "Back to Basics" moral crusade, which has run hand-in-glove with the latest bout of "nasties" hysteria, is scuppered by the discovery of Stephen Milligan MP's body. This rising star of the Tory Party, a frequent pontificator on "family values" and moral decline, had masturbated himself to death while wearing women's underwear and a plastic bag over his head.

SNUFF MOVIE MOGULS AGED 15

Boys netted as cops swoop on evil video ring

● TWO boys of 15 were being quizzed by cops last night after the first "snuff" movies uncovered in Britain were seized in dawn swoops nationwide.

● The real killing videos were among 5,000 also showing rape, mutilation, torture, sex with animals and cannibalism. Twenty trader suspects were arrested for questioning during raids in 21 towns and cities.

FULL STORY: PAGE 10

THE SEDUCTION OF THE GULLIBLE

FEB 11TH: In a front page splash headed "SNUFF MOVIE MOGULS AGED 15", *The Daily Sport* claims that police have "smashed a nation-wide network selling vile horror videos. Many were 'snuff' movies, showing people murdered on camera. Others had shots of horrific road accidents. Documents revealed a network reaching to Australia and America".

FEB 11TH: (*The Mirror*) "VIDEO NASTIES HELD IN SWOOP..."" ... among them was the first 'snuff' video found in this country - an apparently genuine film of a woman being raped and beaten to death. It is believed to have been shot abroad. Trading standards officers went undercover to infiltrate the network, who import films from abroad and sell them at £120 a time. One investigator said: 'Some of this stuff is so sick you can't imagine it'. He said the haul was just 'the tip of the iceberg'".

Such hysterical misinformation is par for the course at *The Sport* and *The Mirror* (motto: "Honesty, Quality, Excellence") of course, but it's distressing to see supposedly "quality" broadsheets being swept along in the tide of hysteria...

FEB 11TH: (*The Guardian*) "DAWN-RAIL HAUL OF VIOLENT FILMS MAY INCLUDE 'SNUFF' VIDEOS". "Videos showing real killings - so called snuff movies - could be among thousands seized throughout the country yesterday in what was said to be the biggest operation of its kind. Lancashire's chief trading standards officer, Jim Potts, who co-ordinated the operation, said: 'My own opinion is that, sad to say, these videos show genuine killings ... it is clearly not acting and some of the scenes would not be possible if they were not real. We suspect they come from North or South America, where missing persons are more of a way of life'" (or "where life is cheap" ... just like it says on the sleeve of 'SNUFF', eh? The most worrying aspect of this whole fiasco is that when I rang Jim Potts, he denied that he had ever made these comments about "snuff movies" being bagged. Given these reports' tacit admissions that previous, similar scares have been unfounded, surely it's now time to snuff out forever this particularly odious piece of black propaganda against horror film aficionados - JM).

MARCH. Early this month, VISIONS OF ECSTASY director and Redemption Video main-man Nigel Wingrove wins an important victory at the European Court of Appeal, which rules that the BBFC has violated his freedom of expression by banning the film's video release, leaving the British government six weeks in which to find a friendly solution. Wingrove's lawyers believe that the government will have to abolish 800 year-old blasphemy laws, or wait another 12 months for the European Court to force a decision.

MAR 3RD: (*The Star*) "PORNO MAKES BOY, 13, A BEAST". Commenting on a case in which a youth had tried to rape a six year-old girl, while supposedly under the influence of computer pornography (which was at this time beginning to rival "nasties" as a focus of media anxieties), The Star quotes eccentric Tory MP Sir Teddy Taylor as 'fuming': "I want all porn banned... I'm very sceptical when people blame their actions on watching something on TV or computer screens". So if porn isn't to blame, why does he want it banned? Is it just that he's an old killjoy?

MAR 4TH: (*Today*) "KING MOVIE LED TO HORROR". "A schoolboy tried to cripple a classmate after seeing the Oscar-winning film MISERY, a court heard. The boy, then 16, attacked his sleeping pal's legs with a hammer in a copycat attack of the Stephen King blockbuster thriller".

MAR 22ND: Under the headline "CULT FILM DROVE MOB TO KILL", *The Star* pins the mob killing of "hero dad Les Reed" to blacksploitation epic JUICE ("It has a 15

THE SEDUCTION OF THE GULLIBLE

certificate and can be hired in any video shop across the country"), one of the killers having supposedly quoted a line from the film at the time of the attack. An editorial ("REAL HORROR") argues that: "Film makers make horror movies for only one reason: For profit". (But JUICE isn't a horror movie! - JM) "How many times have we heard that such movies have provoked terrible acts? Only recently a horror video was cited in the Jamie Bulger case. And yesterday another violent movie was said to be the inspiration for youths who kicked have-a-go hero Les Reed to death. Censorship is one thing. It would be wrong to ban free expression. But crazed violence, gratuitous horror is another. It's all very well to put age limits on movies, but who's trying to kid who? Everybody knows that kids can get hold of the very worst videos if they want - and they do. There's only one answer: Ban this horror, completely" (So ban all horror films because a killer mouthed some dialogue from a non-horror film ... words fail me! - JM)

APRIL. Pro-censorship academics rushed in to beat the more meaningful BBFC / Policy Studies Institute report to the news-stands, and their "research" ended up coming out on a date that was ironically appropriate for it ... All Fools' Day! - JM.

APR 1ST: *The Nottingham Evening Post* reports ("VIDEO NASTIES - EXPERT BACKS CALL FOR CONTROLS") that "Leading Nottingham psychologist" Professor Elizabeth Newson (head of Nottingham University's child psychology unit) has written to the Home Secretary claiming a causal link between violent video and real-life violence. Her letter includes the lines: "Many of us hold our liberal ideas of freedom of expression dear but now we begin to feel that we were naive in our failure to predict the extent of damaging material and its all too free availability to children. Most of us would prefer to rely on the discretion and responsibility of parents, both in controlling their children's viewing and in giving children clear models of their own distress in witnessing sadistic brutality. However, it is unhappily evident that many children cannot rely on their parents in this respect. By restricting such material from home viewing, society must take on a new responsibility in saving children from this as from other forms of child abuse". *The Post* also claims that co-signatories to the letter "include many of Britain's top paediatricians and child psychologists", and that it is "backed up by a dossier of evidence"... none of which it manages to reproduce.

APR 1ST: "PSYCHOLOGISTS' RETHINK BODES ILL FOR VIDEO NASTIES". *The Guardian* falls for Newson's nonsense, talking about "the startling admission yesterday by 25 leading child psychologists that they had underestimated the link between video and real-life violence". The paper summarises the Newson conclusions as follows: "Violence in the context of entertainment is dangerous because the viewer receives the implicit message that this is all good fun - something with which to while away one's leisure time. The child viewer receives distorted images of emotions that he has not yet experienced, so must accept - especially dangerous when love, sex and violence are equated. The ingenuity with which brutality is portrayed has escalated". Elizabeth Newson is quoted as saying: "It seems impossible to allow the situation to continue, and indeed escalate, as it now is" (Is this the voice of impartial, dispassionate science, or of somebody with a very definite social agenda? - JM).

APR 1ST: "VIDIOTS! - AT LAST, EXPERTS ADMIT: MOVIE NASTIES DO KILL"... "Britain's top psychologists finally admitted yesterday that *The Daily Mirror* got it right" crows *The Mirror*, which... "has been campaigning for a crackdown since the James Bulger murder case, linked to the CHILD'S PLAY 3 video, showed how TV horror can warp young minds" "Another expert", Professor Philip Graham, is quoted as saying: "On the balance of probability, we expect video nasties will affect children's minds" (There's nothing like a definitive scientific pronouncement - and that was nothing like one! - JM)

CHRONOLOGY: MAR 94 - APR 94

PAGE # 261

THE SEDUCTION OF THE GULLIBLE

"NOW BAN THEM" - in the same edition, *The Mirror* inaugurates yet another crusade to suppress "THE VIDEO NASTIES THAT SHAME BRITAIN... They are violent and they are sick. And they should be banned immediately. A homicidal doll called Chucky, a serial killer who suffocates children and a zombie who eats her boyfriend... these are just a few of the disgusting films that are invading British homes". The paper identifies "ten of the more graphic nasties that *The Mirror* has been campaigning against" (a list compiled after they had rung DARK SIDE editor Allan Bryce and asked him to reel off the titles of a few violent films that came to mind). After the expected tut-tutting over CHILD'S PLAY 3, the piece goes on to cite: "BRAINDEAD: Passed uncut by the BBFC, it showed a zombie baby having its head smashed against a swing and a massacre by lawnmower! FALLING DOWN: Disturbed Michael Douglas goes on the rampage through LA shooting anyone who gets in the way. A big hit in the cinema and on video". MAN BITES DOG, RETURN OF THE LIVING DEAD 3, HARD BOILED, HENRY and THE LAST BOY SCOUT are vilified, before *The Mirror* concludes its roll-call of shame with: "ROMPER STOMPER (Aussie skinheads lash out at Asians in CLOCKWORK ORANGE-style shocker), and THE SILENCE OF THE LAMBS. An Oscar winner in which Hannibal The Cannibal - chilling Anthony Hopkins - rips off his guard's face as he escapes from jail". (Just over the page though, *The Mirror* is happy to run a paid ad for the film KALIFORNIA, boasting the shout-lines "A GAME OF MURDER, EROTICISM AND PURE MENACE" and "A BRILLIANT EDGE-OF-THE-SEAT NIGHTMARE" - JM)

APR 1ST: (*The Star*) "VIDEO NASTIES: WE BOOBED SAY EXPERTS". "A chilling and horrifying link exists between video nasties and real-life violence, top psychologists admitted yesterday. The astonishing evidence ..." (What evidence? - JM) "... follows a campaign by Liberal MP David Alton to stop under-18s watching material at home likely to cause them psychological harm. As a prime example of the misery and tragedy it can cause, he has highlighted the case of murdered toddler Jamie Bulger and the gruesome link with the film CHILD'S PLAY 3".

APR 1ST: (*The Times*) "EXPERTS CONDEMN VIDEO NASTIES AS FORM OF CHILD ABUSE". Elizabeth Newson is quoted as saying that: "Those responsible for protecting children should not wait for the makers of video nasties to exercise restraint by setting their own standards" (an option that was taken away from them more than a decade previously - JM) and David Alton adds: "These video nasties are a form of child abuse. It is a matter for parents to decide what their children watch, but we cannot expect children to have total control over everything their children do and see".

APR 1ST: (*The Independent*) Steven Barnett, a media analyst at Goldsmith's College, London, says the Newson paper reflects a current fad among child behaviourists: "The trend at the moment is to say that's a link because that's what people want to hear. They ignore evidence that does not suit their theories".

APR 1ST: *Daily Telegraph* editorial: "VIOLENT CONNECTION". "It now appears there has been a trahison de clercs, betrayal by the experts, all along. Nearly the entire establishment ..." (What - 25 individuals? I know the Tories have been under-funding "the caring professions", but that's ridiculous! - JM) "... of one of the principle caring professions - psychologists and child-development specialists ..." (that's two, not one - JM) "... now admits it has been misleading us because it could not bring itself to tell the truth. Theletter to the Home Secretary published by 25 top psychologists is unequivocal, as is the research ..." (what research? - JM) "... by Dr Elizabeth Newsom" (You mean Newson ? - JM) "... which accompanies it. The latest revelation is a considerable triumph for David Alton. The scientific tide has turned decisively. The scene is at last set for a realistic debate on media censorship".

THE SEDUCTION OF THE GULLIBLE

APR 1ST: (*The Guardian*) "Yesterday's contribution from Elizabeth Newson, Professor of Development Psychology at Nottingham University's child development unit, was not the usual rent-a-quote in a debate where hard evidence is in notoriously short supply ..."
(JM - In fact "rent-a quote" is precisely what it turned out to be - note how all the way through the above both "penitent experts" and Alton have identified video horror with that most emotive of subjects - child abuse. A mere coincidence? The full extent of the April Fool gag that was being perpetrated only emerged when journos like yours truly called Professor Newson's Department of Development Psychology at Nottingham University to obtain a copy of her report and were told that they couldn't supply copies. Who could then? We were advised to contact the office of ... David Alton!)

APR 2ND: (*The Sun*) "VIDEO ALERT". "Anyone with an ounce of savvy has known it for ages. Video nasties are bad for children. At long last the so-called 'experts' have seen sense. Twenty-five of them issue a warning that horror and violence on TV can warp young minds. It's a bit late to help victims like James Bulger. But it's not too late for YOU to stop your kids watching sick films".

APR 2ND: "DOUBTS CAST ON CREDIBILITY OF REPORT SIGNED BY PSYCHOLOGISTS THAT LINKS CHILD CRIME TO FILMS". *The Independent* reports that the Home Secretary's resolve to resist demands for tighter controls on video (David Alton and Professor Elizabeth Newson want a "new" classification - Unsuitable for Home Consumption - for videos that are considered to contain "gratuitous violence") has been stiffened by the revelation that Newson wrote her highly publicised report to order for Alton. Professor John Morton, a leading psychologist and director of the Medical Research Council (not best pleased, perhaps, about being described as "naive" and "a traitor" - JM) slams the report as "unscientific", continuing: "This should not be taken as an independent report by psychologists. It is a commissioned piece by David Alton. Academically, it's just an opinion - a piece of polemic from a particular point of view". Indeed, Newson is condemned out of her own mouth when she is quoted as saying: "You can go on researching for ever. I thought it was important that this amendment should go through". Professor Newson is clearly some kind of "Cassandra in reverse" - she's talking rubbish, but everybody is listening to her! Meanwhile, the authoritative Policy Studies Institute report is to be given very short shrift... and not everybody got even that much attention: as Dr Julian Petley later writes in anti-censorship magazine *Scapegoat*. "... a document signed by 23 media academics (myself included), which questioned the whole basis of Newson's discussion paper and forcefully stated that her conclusions were completely out of kilter with most recent academic research on the media... was sent to all the same places as the Newson report - and totally ignored ".

APR 2ND: *The Guardian* reports that Michael Howard will not act until he has studied the PCI's upcoming report YOUNG OFFENDERS AND THE MEDIA, commissioned by the BBFC, the BBC and the Broadcasting Standards Council. Ann Hagell, co-author of the report, says that "any two children watching the same film react in different ways, so I do not see the sense in banning a film", adding that the ongoing revolution in communications technology would soon mean that such material could enter the home by myriad means. "Here was a chance (for Howard) to seize the initiative where this is widespread concern, political and academic" complains David Alton. "He gave the game away when he talked about the profits of the video industry". Clare Short, Labour MP for Ladywood says "it's time for some restrictions on the vile and brutalised images being poured out by mainstream videos aimed at children". Presumably - miraculously - she's unaware of the battery of long-established restrictions that already exist.

APR 2ND: *The Guardian* reveals that a consultant paediatric neurologist who signed the

THE SEDUCTION OF THE GULLIBLE

Newson report believes "there is no absolute scientific evidence proving a causal link between the effects of watching violent videos and committing violence". Dr Gwilym Hosking, consultant paediatric neurologist at Great Ormond Street hospital, has no doubt though that such a link exists, declaring himself unwilling "to wait a generation before anyone establishes the link". Other experts canvassed include Stephen Barnett, visiting lecturer at Goldsmith's College department of Communications ("They have changed their minds, because they have realised how accessible videos are. People have been doing horrific things for centuries"); Christopher Mottershead, general secretary of British Action for Children's Television: ("In the Bulger case the evidence was less than circumstantial. I think most people do regard the films as pure fantasy"); Michael Winner: ("Films and videos in England are more highly censored than in any other country in the free world and there are countries with far less censorship than we have and far lower crime rates. I do to believe that we are in danger of being stabbed by an eight year-old"); and Dr Guy Cumerbatch, leading media researcher ("The report is reckless. It has not demonstrated that there is any new evidence... It's almost on the level of the Mary Whitehouse argument - we have a more violent society since we have had television. It ignores all the other developments in society").

APR 2ND: (*The Times*) "EXPERT DISMISSES LINK WITH VIOLENCE". Dr Guy Cumerbatch, senior lecturer in applied psychology at Aston University, describes the Newson report as "naive and depressing", denying that there is any persuasive evidence linking media violence to its real-life counterpart in a simplistic "cause and effect" manner. Dismissing the report's "eminent signatories", he points out: "There is not a name there that has done research on the effects of the media or is from the media industry. What do they know about film?" Dr Cumerbatch, a Home Office advisor on this subject, insists: "The more we studied this link the more illusory it became. Obviously a 10 year-old watching a film meant for over-18s may be disturbed or upset but he is not going to become a cannibal or a killer as a result. The point of these films is to horrify people. They watch them because they are fascinated by the special effects".

APR 2ND: *The Telegraph* ploughs on with panegyrics to the discredited Professor Newson - "She believes all she has done is open the ears of academe to the anguished calls of a society seeking answers". "I am actually quite pessimistic, because I am not sure it is not too late" warns the Prof: " I feel we have a very large number of children who are already totally desensitised to violence. Now with the amazing rise of video shops..." (wrong - after the early '80s boom, video shops have been going bust at an ever-accelerating rate - JM) "... extreme violence is frighteningly commonplace and at its worst, children become so desensitised that they can commit crimes of the Jamie Bulger kind". We learn that "watching her grandchildren grow up has given her that little extra motivation in compiling her report" (so she had an axe to grind - JM) "What was so worrying for me", she continues: "was that I was asked to comment at the time of the Bulger case and felt I had nothing to say. I just felt despairing, but it is simply not good enough in the face of this to say 'I despair'". (I always thought that if you had nothing worthwhile to say, you shouldkeep your mouth shut. In fact Newson's comments here give further credence to those who've been arguing that people are casting around for any old explanation to make them feel better... certainly this is no basis for valid scientific enquiry - JM) Finally, Newson is quoted as saying that the Alton amendment to the Criminal Justice Bill "creating" (?!?) a restricted category for videos is "a first step" (?!?), but may be "too little, too late". ("First step"? Has she been trapped down a mine shaft for the last ten years or something? - JM)

APR 3RD: (*The Mail On Sunday*) "TORY REVOLT ON VIDEO NASTIES - HOWARD SET FOR DEFEAT BY BACKBENCHERS"... "Sir Ivan Lawrence, chairman of the Home Affairs

THE SEDUCTION OF THE GULLIBLE

Select Committee, (has) warned that between 300 and 400 MPs back tough controls - enough for measures suggested by Liberal Democrat MP David Alton to be made law". The Home Secretary is currently resisting the Alton as over-restrictive, in view of the fact that most British households do not include children but says that he will urge film censors to "take a tougher line in banning video nasties". Alton is castigating the BBFC for passing the likes of JUICE and CHILD'S PLAY 3 and quoted as saying that "a voluntary code is not enough" (Wasn't this battle already won, a decade ago? - JM)

APR 5TH: (*The Independent*) "BAD VIBES FROM THE SCREEN". "Raj Persaud - Clinical lecturer in psychiatry at the institute of Psychiatry, London" (and a regular contributor to the ever-popular "Richard & Judy" day-time TV show too - JM) is quoted as saying that "(In 1983) a study in the US journal *Psychological Reports* compiled 58 incidents of violence between 1970 and 1982, all of which were allegedly inspired by one movie - THE DEER HUNTER" (Pretty good going for a movie that only came out in 1978! - JM)

APR 7TH: (*The Guardian*) "SENSE AND CENSORSHIP": Richard Boston nails the Newson nonsense: "(Her report) is the opinion of one person. When she had written it, she sent it to a number of academics, not all of whose field of expertise was in child psychology or other allied relevant areas. 25 of them endorsed the report. How many did not? This whole hullabaloo has been set off by a document which proves not at all easy to get hold of, which hardly anyone has read and which is very low on substance. There's no original research in the paper... Professor Newson asks what is the 'different factor that has entered the lives of countless children and adolescents in recent years?' Her answer is 'this has to be recognised as the easy availability of gross images of violence on video'. What kind of evidence from an expert is 'This has to be ...'? Why shouldn't the different factor be Velcro, or the Rubik cube, or Mrs Thatcher, or cling-film, or Roland Rat? My own view is that nasties (video or otherwise) are the product of violence rather than its cause. To say otherwise, as do people like David Alton and Mary Whitehouse, is like suggesting that the wind is caused by trees shaking their branches".

APR 7TH: On the *Guardian* letters page, CRS Brown argues: "A dramatic escalation in the powers of The State should not be enacted on a tide of emotion. This country already has more rigorous censorship than other European nations. If true, the proposition that censorship reduces juvenile crime should be directly demonstrable by showing that the level of such crime in our country is already lower than that . Avedon Carol from Feminists Against Censorship adds: "Jamie Bulger was killed by two boys with a history of serious disturbances that were known to the authorities; they were not dealt with because of government cuts. Trying to distract us from dealing with the problems of children in trouble by promoting nonsense about 'video nasties' is the most morally reprehensible demonstration of social irresponsibility. That the present government wants us to ignore the damage done by their policies is unsurprising; that the Opposition parties and the media continue to fall for it so slavishly is downright shocking".

APR 7TH: Addressing a meeting of the pressure group Mothers Against Murder and Aggression (MAMA) in Liverpool, James Ferman states that "the rising tide of violent images available to children" leaves him "frightened for the future of Britain's youth". He talks of "a media-saturated nation" where technological advances are making it virtually impossible to effectively monitor children's viewing. But he rejects any alleged connection between CHILD'S PLAY 3 and the Bulger case and concluded that it was undesirable to totally eradicate violent imagery, because "in the interests of freedom of speech, we need to show adults the cost of violence".

APR 8TH: (*The Independent*) "JOBLESS LINK TO CRIME SUPPRESSED". "Senior Home

THE SEDUCTION OF THE GULLIBLE

Office officials have conceded that government economic policies have contributed to the rise in crime by failing to provide work for young people". But a report stating precisely this was deep-sixed. Better to blame "video nasties", huh?

At the end of this week *Empire* magazine publishes an opinion poll, eliciting predictably mixed responses from those polled: more than two thirds believe too much violence is screened, and 56% want violent films banned "to protect children", though 42% are against new legislation. Two-thirds think parents should take responsibility for their offspring's viewing, one in three feel it's down to the government, while a similar number feel the onus rests with film-makers. The magazine warns that Alton's proposed amendment to the Criminal Justice Bill will result in 18-rated classics such as RAGING BULL and THE GODFATHER being exiled to adult-only cinemas, the new "Unsuitable For Home Entertainment" classification making it illegal to have them in private homes. "I admit there will always be a market for this kind of undesirable material ...", comments Alton (What an elitist contradiction in terms) "... but occasionally society has to stand up and say: 'We don't want his sort of thing freely and easily available'". (Hey Dave - IT AIN'T! - JM). Elsewhere in this issue, James Ferman writes that the Bulger case "has shaken public confidence in one of the great sustaining myths of our time - the myth of childhood innocence", and that scapegoats were being sought. Despite the press's "rush to judgement", he points out, the Video Consultative Council "consisting of head teachers, local authority councillors, a child-care expert, a forensic psychologist, Justices of the Peace, researchers, representatives of the film, TV and video industries, and the former director of the National Society for the Prevention of Cruelty to Children", had unanimously declared CHILD'S PLAY 3 to be "irrelevant" to the Bulger case. Ferman also argues that the proposed new "not suitable for viewing in the home" category would add little to the powers that the BBFC already possesses, and that Alton's proposal for a restricted horror category analogous to R18 would consign such films to licensed sex shops: "We try to separate sex and violence, and would not endorse the supply of violent entertainment in an environment dedicated to sexual arousal".

APR 11TH: *The Times* reports ("CLASSICS CAUGHT IN BAN ON VIDEO NASTIES") that "home viewing of more than 9,000 films, many of them classics, is threatened... among the films that would be restricted to cinemas and private clubs are PSYCHO, SCHINDLER'S LIST, DANCES WITH WOLVES and THE JEWEL IN THE CROWN. (Michael Howard believes) that the amendment is impractical and unworkable and that the 220 MPs, including 80 Tories, who have signed it have not understood the implications". Tomorrow Howard will urge the BBFC to make greater use of their existing powers to cut and ban videos. "Mr Alton's amendment is so badly drafted it would rule out every-thing", claims James Ferman. Secreted away, at the bottom of all this, is news of the finally-published Policy Studies Institute report into the viewing habits of young offenders (anyone remember that?), which reveals that young offenders' viewing habits are virtually identical to those of their non-offending peers ("both groups prefer soap operas to video nasties") and concludes that Alton, Newson and co, are "on a doomed mission to find a simplistic solution to a complex problem".

Unfortunately *The Times*'s leader on this day ("SCREENING THE VIDEOS - BRITISH CHILDREN NEED PROTECTION FROM THE CORRUPTION OF VIOLENCE") chooses to totally disregard these PSI findings in favour of upholding Newson's discredited platitudes: "Unease has gone far beyond the level of tabloid hysteria ..." (True - it's spread to once-prestigious broadsheets now owned by the same yellow press baron - JM) "... or unsophisticated scare-mongering" (True again - this is pretty sophisticated scare-mongering, with all sorts of hidden agendas behind it - JM) "Expert opinion, led by the distinguished social scientist, Elizabeth Newson, has courageously recanted its

THE SEDUCTION OF THE GULLIBLE

THE SEDUCTION OF THE GULLIBLE

uncritical acceptance of the liberal anti-censorship orthodoxy." (In the UK?!? - JM) "Senior figures in child psychiatry and paediatric medicine now declare themselves convinced of what ordinary parents and teachers have long observed... adequate parental supervision can immunise children against most forms of corrupting influence. This may well be why European countries where family bonds are stronger and home life is more cohesive ..." (What - those scandalous Scandinavians and libertine Dutch? - JM) "... can afford to be more lax in their polices on film and video censorship" (The relatively low crime rates in countries with much more liberal censorship laws has long been a difficult one for advocates of more British censorship as an anti-crime measure to explain away - JM). "But their experience is quite irrelevant to Britain, where horror video addiction is part of a socially disadvantaged sink culture in which lack of parental supervision is endemic" (yep, we're still fighting that same old class war - JM).

APR 11TH: *The Guardian* acknowledges the release of the Policy Studies Institute report on YOUNG OFFENDERS AND THE MEDIA (largely ignored by the rest of the press on account of its conclusions, which are diametrically opposed to the Newson report) and its finding that the viewing habits of convicted young offenders are not significantly different from those of ordinary teenagers. "The report is the first serious research of its kind and is expected to show that both groups prefer soap opera such as HOME AND AWAY, EAST ENDERS and THE BILL to video nasties. It is also believed to conclude that the young offenders had less access to television and videos than other children". The paper contends that this will encourage the Home Secretary to deny government support to David Alton's proposed amendment to the Criminal Justice Bill, which "although well intentioned, would disenfranchise responsible parents and introduce a power for police to seize more than 9,000 video titles from people's homes". James Ferman is once again allowed to point out that the Bulger trial judge did not (as Alton keeps claiming) cite CHILD'S PLAY 3 in his summing up, and that "there was no evidence that either of the boy's killers had ever seen it".

APR 12TH: "VIDEO NASTY BLITZ". *The Mirror* reports that the Home Secretary is "wilting under pressure" (from itself and the public) to "crack down on violent videos in the home". Expected measures are said to include "tighter guidelines on censors' ratings for violent movies, power for the censor to stop the most horrific appearing on video at all..." (Does the reader really need reminding - as *The Mirror* clearly does - that the BBFC already has the power to ban whatever videos it wants, and frequently uses it? - JM) "... and tougher penalties for shopkeepers who supply outlawed tapes".

David Alton claims that the Video Recordings Act has fallen into disrepute "not only in Parliament. but more importantly among the public and parents especially. There's a feeling that far too many violent images are penetrating the minds of impressionable young children". *The Mirror* doesn't miss an opportunity to drag up the Bulger case, scandalously commenting: "James's young killers struck after watching it". Its grammar as shaky as its grip of the facts, the report continues: "MPs think the Alton proposals areriddled with faults but was the best way of spurring the government into action". Shadow Home Secretary Tony Blair describes the Alton amendment as "very vague, probably unworkable, and could give a future censor huge powers" (Like they don't already have them! - JM).

APR 12TH: *The Guardian* highlights just how differently things are done in the rest of Europe, which Britain is currently supposed to be forging closer ties with: "The debate raging over video film regulation belies the fact that Britain has the strictest rules in Europe on what can be seen on screen. Britain is one of the few countries where censors areprepared to cut mainstream American films. Elsewhere in Europe policies of videos and who sees them is at best sketchy". The report goes on to give such examples as: "In Britain the Bruce Willis thriller DIE HARD 2 was cut to allow for a 15 age restriction at the cinema, and two video versions were released, classified 15 and 18. In France the film was shown uncut to cinema goers of all ages and videos are not subject to scrutiny. In Greece there is no classification. Sweden's top film classification is 15, and in Holland and Denmark you can watch anything if you are over 16".

APR 12TH: *The Times* identifies the main implications of the Alton amendment as follows: "To change the criteria by which the BBFC define films likely to disturb children, to prevent them being made available to the general public. Some films could be put into a similar category as (sic) the 18R classification given to some pornographic films. This allows them to be shown only in licensed sex shops and clubs.
To make it a criminal offence for a film so classified to be rented, sold or distributed. Such films could not be put on general release.
To make it an offence for such films to be shown in any place where children under 18 are admitted, including private homes".

"The amendment..." according to this report: "... suggests that the category of films that should banned are those which include 'scenes of graphic violence likely to disturb young children' and films which include 'exceptionally disturbing scenes and inappropriate role models'". James Ferman points out that this could include "half the films made in the last quarter Century", and BVA director general Lavinia Carey warns that the public will not respond favourably to any withdrawal of their right to watch '15' and '18' films in their own homes.

APR 13TH: "CRACKDOWN ON VIOLENT VIDEO FILMS". *The Times* reports that Michael Howard last night averted an almost certain House of Commons defeat when he "bowed to parliamentary and public pressure to announce the toughest ever crackdown on violent videos... it will mean a ban in future on sadistic or graphically violent films such as CHILD'S PLAY 3 and JUICE. There will also be tougher penalties for distributors and retailers who break the law, including prison sentences. Mr Howard also held out the prospect that individual videos already circulating, such as CHILD'S PLAY 3, might be reclassified and withdrawn. He emphasised however that it would be impossible to reconsider the 24,000 films in existence".

David Alton has withdrawn his Criminal Justice Bill amendment in the wake of Howard's concession that the BBFC will now be obliged to consider whether a film is "likely to cause psychological harm" to children or "likely to present inappropriate role models". The Board will retain its discretion to pass violent but "artistically important films". Dealers in unclassified videos will face up to two years imprisonment, with six months for selling or hiring '18' titles to under-18's. A '12' classification for videos, something that already exists for cinema releases, is also being introduced by the BBFC. "The objectives we set out have been reached", says Mr Alton: "... a sensible accommodation has been reached". Labour's Tony Blair, who brokered the compromise, calls it "a very sensible way forward that will distinguish between gratuitously sadistic and violent videos and films like SCHINDLER'S LIST, which have a serious message".

Reactions include those of James Ferman ("From now on we are going to have to cut more and classify higher. Films that could previously have been 15 will be 18, and some of those that would have had an 18 certificate may not be given a video license at all"); BVA director Lavinia Carey ("Attention now needs to be focused on the illegal trade in unclassified videos at markets, car-boot sales and street corners. This trade is worth billions of pounds a year and needs to be stamped out"); and Elizabeth Newson ("It's

THE SEDUCTION OF THE GULLIBLE

too little, too late ... the government has not addressed the question of video games, or the effect of violent videos on adults"). Newson is also described as being "sceptical" about the PSI report that contradicted her views ("I'm sceptical"? ...What a thorough-going critique! - JM)

APR 13TH: *The Guardian*, editorial: "This week the Policy Studies Institute published scientific research examining the media habits of young offenders and ordinary school-children. There were very few differences, but one of the starkest was that one third of young offenders read *The Sun*. Is that now to be banned as an 'inappropriate role model'? See how slippery the slope can become?"

APR 13TH: Under the headline "BANNED - NOW CHUCKY CAN'T COME OUT TO PLAY", the late, unlamented *Today* newspaper gives a characteristically inaccurate appraisal of how the compromise amendment to the Criminal Justice Bill will affect the video industry. "The new laws will forbid horror films - like CHILD'S PLAY 3 - whose demonic doll Chucky was linked to the James Bulger murder - from being watched at home in future" (wrong - JM). "Similar videos will only be able to be seen in special clubs for over-18s. Horror videos will get 18R certificates - restricting them to licensed cinema clubs" (wrong! But *Today* does get the next bit right... even though it contradicts their headline! - JM) "The new rules will not be retrospective - meaning video nasties already passed by the censor will stay on the shelves". "A jubilant" David Alton is quoted as saying: "Introducing fines and imprisonment ..." (Wrong: they already exist - JM) "... will stop instances I know of when a six year-old was supplied with an 18 video by producing the family video card". Incredibly, in a moron-friendly graphic entitled "JUDGEMENT DAY"(!), Home Secretary Michael Howard's position is summed up as "INDECENT PROPOSAL", Alton's as "BASIC INSTINCT"!

APR 13TH: "BANNED THANKS TO YOUR *DAILY MIRROR*". Everyone's favourite crusading organ announces that "tough new laws will be brought in later this year to stop monsters like Chucky, the CHILD'S PLAY killer doll, warping young minds... the most nightmarish nasties will be swept from the shelves of Britain's video stores". David Alton - surprise, surprise - pops up to congratulate *The Mirror* on its anti-video vendetta and dangle the disquieting prospect that "violent videos already on sale could be banned along with new releases". On the same page, under the headline "CHUCKY'S PALS FACE CENSORS", the paper gives ludicrous potted synopses of "the ten worst videos that face a ban under the new crackdown" (I'm delighted to say that precisely none of them have been banned - JM)... "CHILD'S PLAY 3, JUICE, BODY MELT ('A husband is attacked by his wife's placenta'), HENRY, RETURN OF THE LIVING DEAD 3, BRAINDEAD ('Woman bitten by monkey develops a taste for raw meat'), HARD BOILED, DEATH WARMED UP, HOLLYWOOD HOOKERS' ('Prostitutes lure victims to chainsaw death') ..." (Incredibly, Fred Olen Ray's film was not allowed to be released in Britain with the word "chainsaw" in its title! - JM) "... THE HILLS HAVE EYES ('Savage cannibal punks')"...

Shamelessly, *The Mirror* continues: "some of these have played a direct role in three of the most horrific murder cases of the last year. Police were shocked by similarities between the killing of James Bulger and CHILD'S PLAY 3" (Wrong! - JM). As if this wasn't enough crap for one page, elsewhere on it "leading child psychologist Dr Ludwig Lowenstein" gives an enthusiastic thumbs-up to the latest tightening of the censorship screw "and reveals that top of his censorship hit-list are the movies NIGHTMARE ON ELM STREET, RESERVOIR DOGS, CHILD'S PLAY (sic), TEXAS CHAINSAW MASSACRE, FRIDAY THE 13TH, DRILLER KILLER and THE EXORCIST. (Well, Doc - of those seven, four are already banned on video and another only released with heavy cuts - JM).

APR 13TH: *The Daily Mail.* Lynda Lee Potter writes: "There are thousands of children in this country with fathers they never see and mothers who are lazy sluts. They are allowed to do what they want, when they want. They sniff glue on building sites, scavenge for food and until now, they were free to watch increasingly horrific videos. By 16 they are disturbed and dangerous".

APR 13TH: (*The Sun*) Editorial - "BAN NASTIES" "Every parent will welcome new laws to stop children seeing video nasties. There will be squeals of 'censorship', of course. So called experts will tell us there's no proof that violent films do children any harm. Well they sure as hell don't do any good. Remember what happened to little James Bulger, murdered by two boys who were suspected of watching horrific videos. Tell that to the experts". (But only if you want them to laugh in your face - JM)

A *Sight & Sound* editorial ("THE SENSIBLE PARTY)", comments on the compromise amendment: "It seems... that the amendment will not refer to already-certificated videos, (but) it will certainly be easier to exert informal pressure on distributors to 'voluntarily' withdraw unacceptable titles (let's say, NIGHTMARE ON ELM STREET) - and there is little doubt that the amendment will lead to the courts being used to challenge the BBFC's decisions", before proceeding to further Newson-nailing: "Swansea East MP Donald Anderson described the Newson paper in the Commons debate as 'that brave volte face on the part of so many distinguished scientists'. When journalists and academics got round to reading the paper, they found something different. The paper contained no new evidence, It was high on moral outrage and thin on argument. Newson's paper was not only unconvincing in itself. it was also not an experts' volte face. Neither Newson nor most of her signatories were in any way 'experts' on the effects of media. Those experts have by and large remained highly critical of her approach. Nor have most of Newson's signatories made any public pronouncements on the subject in the past. So we have no evidence that they ever believed anything other than what they now believe. Two of the signatories have, however, pronounced on the issue before. The already mentioned Professors Sims and Gray. Both were members of the Academic Working Party, described by its chairman Lord Nugent, as the 'informal group of parliamentarians and churchmen which came together in 1983 with the common wish to take action to protect children against injury from violent and obscene video tapes, which appeared to be circulating widely'. In 1985 Sims wrote that 'the video containing combinations of violence and sex is a potential mental and moral health hazard of a kind we have not experienced before'. Hardly a case of volte face here. But the press propagated the story, and the Labour Party, amongst others, bought it".

APR 14TH: "FILM CENSORS WILL BE MOST POWERFUL IN EUROPE". In the aftermath of the Alton/Blair amendment, *The Guardian* quotes Channel 4's Michael Grade to the effect that the BBFC is accumulating ever-increasing powers without being accountable to anybody, and reports on internal dissension within it over the extent of acceptable cutting and the status of films currently in video limbo, notably "THE EXORCIST". Apparently "accusations of autocratic management" will result in ten of the Board's 13 censors leaving at the end of the year, three of them insisting they've been sacked and barred from speaking publicly about their disagreements with Mr Ferman. The report concludes with an ominous prediction of increased rather than reduced controversy over video: "For the first time, censors will be under a statutory duty to take into account the likely psychological effects on children of a film and whether it presents an in-appropriate role model for them. That means, like all public bodies, its decisions can be challenged in the High Court under the judicial review process. Aggrieved parents or film-makers will be able to challenge their decisions in the court and, if successful, force the censors to reconsider them. It is clear that a new generation of obscenity cases is likely to make their way through the courts with the only restraint on its turning into a flood being the likely cost of mounting them".

APR 14TH: The tabloids' self-congratulation grinds to an embarrassed halt, as *The Mirror* reports ("HOWARD STALLS ON CHUCKY"): "Chaos loomed last night as Home Secretary Michael Howard stone-walled over banning the mind-bending Chucky the killer doll video. David Alton, who demanded the ban after months of a *Mirror* campaign, said: 'I'm very angry about this. there is no excuse for keeping this video on the shelves. I am incensed about CHILD'S PLAY 3 because of its influence in the death of Jamie Bulger'" (How low is this guy prepared to sink? - JM)

APR 16TH: "CLEAN UP TV OR ELSE". *Today* reports that Heritage Secretary Peter Brooke is summoning the heads of ITV and BBC to "a crunch meeting (over TV violence)... in the wake of the crackdown on video nasties". Apparently recent TV screenings of GOOD FELLAS and THE SHINING have been "causing concern". Accompanying this report, a photograph of Robert Englund made up as Freddie Krueger is hilariously captioned: "HALLOWEEN: a horror thriller featuring a child killer of six".

APR 17TH: "BRING BACK CENSORS"... *The News Of The World*'s Woodrow Wyatt ("The Voice Of Reason") rants: "Violent nasties ... we all know they breed imitative horrific rapes and other brutal crimes. There are thousands of filthy and sadistic videos on sale. They won't be destroyed. Nor will TV be stopped from showing films as bad or worse than any in the video shops. What's needed is a modernised revival of the discontinued British Board of Film Censors. Now there's only a feeble Board of British Film Classification, mainly manned by anti-censorship part-timers". (When the British Board of Film Censors changed its name to the British Board of Film Classification to obscure the fact that its powers had been hugely increased, they sure fooled this guy! - JM)

APR 18TH: "SICK VIDEOS HARM TWO MILLION KIDS". *The Mirror* reports another new survey, with the sensational claim that "Video Nasties have damaged a generation of primary school kids", adding for good measure: "More than two million kids between five to eleven are regularly glued to violent or pornographic videos". A teacher who talk part in the survey is quoted as saying that "some very young pupils are not sensitive to suffering and violence. They also have distorted views on sexual relations and know about sadistic sex". Another claims: "Some of the things pupils report having seen make me feel violently sick. Some children's eyes light up as they talk animatedly about murder and torture". Computer games are cited as another menace to the nation's youth.

APR 20TH: (*Today*) "BOY COPIES VIDEO NASTY". "A boy went on a Freddy-Kruger (sic) style rampage..." (what, appearing in people's dreams and stuff? - JM) "... after watching A NIGHTMARE ON ELM STREET, it was claimed yesterday. The 10 year-old clawed at the faces of classmates, copying the video nasty killer who rips victims with razor-sharp talons. Teacher Carol Shields of Hebburn, Tynside said: 'He has been exposed to violent videos and is exhibiting violent behaviour'".

APR 20TH: "VIDEO CRACKDOWN - BRITISH FILM IS FIRST VICTIM OF NEW RULES". *The Times* reports that "two of Britain's most promising young producers", Vadim Jean and Paul Brooks of LEON THE PIG FARMER fame have been denied a video certificate for their new picture, BEYOND BEDLAM, though last week an uncut version was granted an 'interim' 18 certificate. This was withdrawn on Monday due to the Alton/Blair amendment. James Ferman says: 'It was made quite clear in Parliament that too many videos are being seen by kids who are underage. We are acting in the spirit of that, and such films will be seen by management before they are issued with certificates'. Paul

THE SEDUCTION OF THE GULLIBLE

Brooks complains that: 'The new ruling is being interpreted hysterically. A certificate was granted as a routine mater by Mr Ferman's department, but he has absurdly recalled it". *The Times* concludes by revealing that Mr Brooks has re mortgaged his house to finance the new film, and that "without a video release, he will almost certainly lose his home".

APR 21ST: Demonstrating its shaky grasp of the facts, *The Mirror* reports, under the headline "OUT OF CONTROL - VIOLENT SAGA BEATS BAN ON NASTIES", that "BEYOND BEDLAM is so disturbing and horrific that it would have run a grave risk of falling foul of new video nasty laws. Its British makers... haven't taken that risk. Instead they have beaten the crackdown by applying for - and being granted - an 18 video certificate 6 months early".

APR 23RD: *The Star* runs a feature on BEYOND BEDLAM entitled "HOW DID THIS FILM NASTY SLIP THROUGH THE NET?" Losing your video certificate - as is actually acknowledged in the piece! - is surely an odd definition of "slipping through the net"! David Alton ("who last week won his long battle for a clamp on film porn") is quoted as "storming": "There's no subtlety in this type of film, which emerges from the dregs of the industry and leaves nothing to the imagination."

APR 29TH: (*The Mirror*) "2 MINUTES TO DEATH BY VIDEO - HIDDEN KILLER IN OUR HOMES". "Fire brigade chiefs who tested the fumes given off by a stack of blazing videos were horrified to discover that two lethal gasses were produced within two minutes - cyanide and carbon monoxide. Each is fatal when breathed in a confined space. A third gas given off by the tapes, chromium oxide, is a serious irritant. A cock-tail of all three breathed together make death a near certainty for anyone in the same room - or even the same house" (So much for "BURN YOUR VIDEO NASTIES!" - JM).

APR 30TH: (*The Star*) MELLOR WELLIED BY TV SHOW DRUNK. "A drunken yob attacked ex-minister David Mellor moments after he finished recording a TV programme - on VIOLENCE! The former National Heritage boss..." (and leading figure in guiding the VRA through Parliament - JM) "... was grabbed round the head and wrestled to the ground by the man, who shouted: 'David Mellor, you bastard. I'll f*****g kill you!' and 'You ricb bastard - you've never done a day's work in your life'".

MAY 8TH: In an expose on "nasties" dealer Tom Halloran, *The News Of The World* reveals how "Evil Halloran ... boasts that business has doubled since Home Secretary Michael Howard announced tough laws to protect children from video nasties ... and drove his wares underground: 'I'm storing up lots of the FACES OF DEATH videos', he said. 'They're really popular because its all blood and guts. I'm waiting to see what happens about this new legislation thing, because the price will go up'". Incredibly, *The News Of The World* appears to believe, or to want us to believe, that Mr Halloran would have had no problems openly selling FACES OF DEATH until a month ago!

JUN 25TH: (*The Sun*) "'SILENCE OF LAMBS' TREAT THEN PSYCHO KILLED MAN". "A mental patient asked for help because he though he might kill - then stabbed a man to death after staff let him watch horror video THE SILENCE OF THE LAMBS. David Usoro ... a religious maniac who calls himself Holy Trinity, admitted manslaughter on the grounds of diminished responsibility yesterday at Nottingham Crown Court, and was ordered to be detained at top security Rampton Hospital indefinitely". So it's not government under-funding of the health service that let down Usoro and his victim (note that this tragedy took place at a private hostel)... blame Hannibal The Cannibal!

JUN 26TH: "SEX SLASH HORROR OF O.J.'s BUTCHERED WIFE - PORN VIDEO CLUE

THE SEDUCTION OF THE GULLIBLE

TO MURDERS" *The Sunday Mirror* fearlessly reveals that before the killing of his wife and her friend, O.J. Simpson spent the evening watching a tape of THE GENESIS CHAMBER, "in which a scantily-clad girl is grabbed from behind by a knife-wielding man in a leather suit". "Experts believe this may have planted the seeds of murder in Simpson's mind" the paper reports, quoting psychiatrist Dr Carole Lieberman as saying: "It's possible the death of Nicole Simpson began in a hotel room when O.J. ordered GENESIS CHAMBER" (What - just when he *ordered* it? - JM).

Also this month, the compromise amendment to Section 4, Clause 4a of the Video Recordings Act is debated in the House of Lords, prior to its final reading in the House of Commons. The amendment states that: "(The BBFC) shall, in making any determination as to the suitability of a video work, have special regard to any harm that may be caused to potential viewers, or, through their behaviour, to society, in the manner in which the work deals with a) criminal behaviour b) illegal drugs c) violent behaviour or incidents d) horrific behaviour or incidents, or e) human sexual activity"

JUL 14TH: "'LET PARENTS HELP ROOT OUT THE EVIL VIDEOS'"... *The Daily Mail* reports a recommendation from the all-party Home Affairs Committee studying violent videos that "videos already on release could be called back for reassessment by the censor on the orders of parents". The paper cites "films such as CHILD'S PLAY 3 and JUICE, which have been linked to specific crimes" as "prime candidates for a recall".

JUL 14TH: "MPs URGE NEW CRACKDOWN ON VIDEO VIOLENCE". *The Daily Express* tells us more about that all-party Home Affairs Committee which, while accepting that research is inconclusive, now "supports the common-sense view that video violence (does) corrupt the young". Apparently this was after Elizabeth Newson told the committee that "these films suggest brute force is a prerequisite for manliness, that physical intimidation is irresistibly sexy, and that violence offers an effective solution to all human problems. Today's movies also advance the appalling idea that the most appropriate response to the suffering of others is sadistic laughter".

JUL 24TH: Anti-Criminal Justice Bill riots erupt in central London

JUL 31ST: "DOES PORN REALLY LEAD TO RAPE AND SEXUAL VIOLENCE?" (JM - No prizes for guessing that *The Sunday Express* answers in the affirmative) "NEW EVIDENCE THAT LINKS SEX CRIMES TO HORROR VIDEOS FUELS PSYCHOLOGISTS' DEBATE". "Horrific porn videos are blamed in the latest study into the causes of sex crime" according to this report, which continues: "Forensic psychologist Paul Britton, based at the Trent Regional Secure Unit, Leicester, believes the government should ban pornographic material" (so they're obviously defining the softer-than-soft erotica that is the only legally-available stuff in Britain as "horrific porn" - JM). Britton is quoted as saying: "I have even come across examples of gross mutilation of women's bodies which are the precise re-enactments of pornographic pictures that are used for masturbatory stimulus". Again, the idea that the British government should "ban" "pornography involving the gross mutilation of women's bodies", as though such material were now legally available, is just too ludicrous for words. But before we dismiss Britton's bizarre utterances as the rantings of a marginal eccentric, beneath our contempt, consider his leading part (as a "psychological profiler") in the hounding of Colin Stagg, a man tried for the Wimbledon Common murder of Rachel Nickel, and acquitted when the only evidence that could be produced against him was that he walked his dog on the common and admitted to (gasp!) enjoying sexual fantasies...

AUGUST. *The Radio Times* "Horror Special" (6-12th August) contains the following

THE SEDUCTION OF THE GULLIBLE

quote from former Hammer sex-pot Kate O'Mara: "I have nothing but loathing for video nasties - not that I've ever seen one".

AUG 18TH: (*The Star*) "FREDDIE MANIAC IN BLADE BLOODBATH". "A madman wearing Freddie Kreuger ..." (Try and spell it right, huh? - JM) "... blades launched a nightmare attack on two men at a petrol station in Cowgate, Newcastle-upon-Tyne". Despite the report's desperate attempts to hype a perceived horror film influence, it seem to have been martial arts weapons that were actually used.

SEP 5TH: After deliberating for three months, the BBFC inform Nigel Wingrove's Redemption Video that his proposed video release of Osvaldo de Oliveira's torrid "Women in Prison" effort, BARE BEHIND BARS has been refused a video certificate.

SEP 19TH: The BBFC inform Redemption that a drastically cut version of BARE BEHIND BARS has also been turned down for certification... "the film is irredeemable".

OCT 12TH: Having been denied video certificates for Jesus Franco's SADOMANIA and DEMONIAC (aka THE SADIST / RIPPER OF NOTRE DAME), Redemption Video announce their decision to challenge the BBFC's decision to withhold certification from BARE BEHIND BARS, at the Video Appeals Committee: "The film was submitted to the BBFC with some cuts... but was rejected on the grounds that it would deprave and corrupt those who watched it", runs a Redemption press release: "However the BBFC also applied a more stringent test set out in the Criminal Justice Bill, which is not yet law. This clearly shows that James Ferman and the BBFC are now applying a test when classifying videos which is more far reaching than anything in recent years".

Redemption Managing Director Nigel Wingrove: "The government that derided the nanny state seems to have overlooked the BBFC, who seem to think if you're too old to watch with mother, then watch what we watch or you can't watch at all". Paul Chinnery of Stephens Innocent, Redemption's solicitor, states: "This decision states that as a result of the BBFC's new approach to video classification, it will be much harder for many films to get a certificate. This will have a profound effect on creative freedom in the film and video industry. The BBFC has become a non-accountable arbiter of morals and taste and it should explain openly its new approach to the classification of videos rather than impose censorship behind the closed doors of number 3, Soho Square".

OCT 20TH: *The Mirror* reports concern over MIGHTY MORPHIN POWER RANGERS, after incidents in which playground hi-jinks have lead to injuries. Similar incidents supposedly contributed to the death of young Silje Redergard, leading to the programme being banned in Scandinavia (*The Mirror* neglects to mention that the ban was rescinded two days after it as imposed, after experts could find no connection). *Mirror* journalist Gill Swain expresses her anxiety that MIGHTY MORPHIN POWER RANGERS "looks so real" ("POWER RANGERS looks real "... is she on drugs?!? - JM).

NOVEMBER. Early this month, the Criminal Justice Bill becomes law as the Criminal Justice Act.

NOV 7TH: (*The Star*) "'BAN RIOTS VIDEO NASTY' RAGE MPs". A documentary entitled RIOT POLICE and classified 15 has drawn criticism from moaning minny Tories like Warren Hawksley, who complains: "I can't believe it is legal for anyone to publish or sell something which can be construed as inciting people to riot. I thought that was a criminal offence and, if it isn't, the government ought to look at making it so". Hey Warren... the Toxteth rioters featured on the tape weren't responding to future viewings of themselves on the tape (how could they be?), but to your government's policies!

NOV 10TH: "SAVAGE DOGS STAY MUZZLED". *The Mirror* describes Polygram Video chiefs as "furious" over the way Quentin Tarantino's RESERVOIR DOGS has been consigned to video limbo by the BBFC. "The film has been turned into a scapegoat" a Polygram spokesman complains: "We're so far behind the rest of the world it's unbelievable". *The Mirror* concedes that prohibition of this title has spawned a lucrative black market trade in pirate copies.

NOV 10TH: (*Today*) "A SPLATTER MOVIE TOO FAR".. "David Alton... has not seen (NATURAL BORN KILLERS) but following his successful campaign for new curbs on videos he is concerned about the prospect of it going on general release. 'I hope it won't be shown... it's as though film makers feel duty bound to produce something more shocking than has gone before'".

NOV 14TH: *The Sun* "exclusively" reports "KIDS SNAP UP £25 BOOTLEG KILLER VIDS - FILM BLAMED FOR MURDERS", getting its knickers in a knot about schoolkids apparently buying bootleg copies of Oliver Stone's NATURAL BORN KILLERS in the playground. The myth about this film being somehow "responsible" for "at least ten murders... in France and the U.S." is trotted out, and readers reminded that: "it's British launch was shelved last month after censors failed to agree it should be banned". A "furious mum" is quoted as saying: "It's outrageous that kids can buy copies of this horrific video at school".

DEC 1ST: (*The Star*) "DRAC MOVIE TURNED ME INTO VAMPIRE"... "A film nut stabbed his lover and drank her blood after watching the new horror blockbuster INTERVIEW WITH A VAMPIRE. Just the day before, the couple had been to see the horror film which is taking America by storm". The credulous *Star* repeats as gospel truth some of the "spooky on-set" stuff that the film's publicists' dreamed up and concludes with the hilarious observation that: "Chat show host Oprah Winfrey rushed out of a preview screening because she could not handle the horror".

DEC 21ST (*The Mirror*) "WHY MOVIES LIKE THIS MAKE A KILLING" As the hoo-hah over cinema certification of NATURAL BORN KILLERS continues, Philip Thomas - editor of (ever-meretricious) *Empire* magazine - is astonishingly quoted as saying: "Before NATURAL BORN KILLERS, the only things that seemed to worry British censors were violence against children and anything with martial arts weapons" (oh really, Phil?!?)

DEC 23RD: (*The Sun's* "Mega Guide" computer-game section). "SNAP UP THE BEAT 'EM UPS". "Gory beat 'em ups could soon be banned for all under-18s - with shop-keepers who flout the rules facing a spell in JAIL. Changes in legislation contained in the controversial Criminal Justice Bill could leave games classed as videos, which means that violent or pornographic titles will be BANNED. Existing games are currently exempt from the new rules (so better buy them up quick!)" How does this square with *The Sun's* well-known hard-line attitude towards videos, more narrowly defined? - JM.

DEC 27TH: Western fan "Cowboy" Bob Dixon is shot dead after waving a replica pistol at police in Golcar, West Yorkshire. There are no calls to ban DANCES WITH WOLVES.

1995

JAN 13TH: (*The Mirror*) "7 BOYS 'KILLED IN SNUFF HORROR'". "Detectives are investigating claims that a child-sex ring has murdered seven boys and disposed of their bodies with the help of a crooked undertaker. 'Snuff' movies are said to have been made of some killings with a home-movie camera. It is claimed that the paedophile ring murdered the youths, all Liverpool rent boys, aged 12 to 16, between 1989 and 1992. Investigations are continuing ..."

Also this month: BAD LIEUTENANT is certified '18' for video release, minus 106 seconds (chiefly of heroin injection and a nun being raped).

MAR 3RD: (*Daily Mail*) "TV FAILS TO TURN BACK THE TIDE OF VIOLENCE". "Watchdogs warned yesterday that 51% of programmes on the four main terrestrial channels last year included an act of violence, while 46% featured bad language". Ironically, in view of the incessant "anti-nasty" posturing of Rupert Murdoch's tabloids, four of his main satellite channels - Sky One, Sky Movies, The Movie Chanel and Sky Movies - top these figures: "87% of their programmes featured violence, and 76% bad language", according to a Broadcasting Standards Council report. On the same page, *The Mail* describes an outcry by "anti-pornography campaigners" against the poster for the Demi Moore / Michael Douglas picture DISCLOSURE (!)

MAR 14TH: "AGE OF THE ZOMBIE - CHILDREN WHO ARE PUSHED OVER THE EDGE BY VIDEO OR COMPUTER" "Violent video imagery could... in extreme cases (provide) the catalyst for killings similar to that of James Bulger" argues *The Daily Mail*, in the aftermath of Elizabeth Newson's address to The National Children's Bureau in London. "In Norway a young girl was kicked to death by three playmates. In Chicago, a five year-old was dropped from a high rise car park by two youngsters aged ten and 11" she says, placing the blame for these incidents in predictable quarters: "This has to be recognised as the easy availability to children of gross images of violence on video" (Why does it have to berecognised as this? Didn't Mary Bell and other notorious killer children commit their crimes decades before home video even existed? - JM)

KIDS GO CRAZY OVER DEATH FOR KICKS VID

■■ GEORGE HILL

A HORRIFIC American "snuff" movie showing TWENTY real-life killings is doing the rounds of Britain's schools.

Scores of kids have already seen the sickening video called The Face of Death.

The bloodlust murders shocked one 15-year-old girl so much she handed it to her parents in tears.

Now stunned MPs, child welfare campaigners and parents are demanding a clampdown on perverts who distribute the evil films.

Copies of the vile video are already being passed around by pupils at Manchester and Sheffield schools. It is narrated by a man in a white doctor's coat with a stethoscope around his neck who claims to be a neurologist.

Shock scenes in the documentary style film show.

● A man being DECAPITATED with a knife by Satanists in what is referred to as a training film.

● An Army EXECUTION in an Iron Curtain country where a man is roped to horses by the arms and legs and then ripped apart as the animals are ridden off in different directions.

● Footage claimed to be genuine of a woman serial KILLER in America being executed in the chair. Sparks shoot from her fingernails and she

ers plunging to their deaths when the elastic snaps and close-ups of mutilated road accident victims.

It also focuses on a Vietnamese family inspecting a litter of pups before slitting one open and cooking its entrails in a wok for their dinner.

Graves

that this tape is doing the rounds in our schools is extremely disturbing.

"The girl who told her parents about it was given the tape to watch by another pupil who was passing it on from someone else."

Clearly it had been seen by a number of other pupils at the school.

fear "snuff" movies have been made in Britain, but they have never uncovered enough evidence to bring anyone to trial.

The horrifying films arriving here from America from Europe in the Sex.

They are so called because victims, often young "snuffed out" after bein

HORRIFIED: Dennis Wrigley with the sickening video

Outrage as bloodlust 'snuff' movie hits Britain's schools

THE SEDUCTION OF THE GULLIBLE

APR 10TH: (*The Star*) "OUTRAGE AS BLOODLUST 'SNUFF' MOVIE HITS BRITAIN'S SCHOOLS - KIDS GO CRAZY OVER DEATH FOR KICKS VIDEO" "A horrific American 'snuff' movie showing TWENTY real-life killings is doing the rounds of Britain's schools". Cursory investigation of revealed that this "snuff movie", identified as "THE FACE OF DEATH" by Dennis Wrigley, leader of the Manchester based evangelical Christian group Maranatha, was actually FACES OF DEATH IV... does the reader really need telling that this tacky mondo offering is absolutely *not* a "snuff movie"? This fiasco merely the latest example of the falling *Star*'s apparent obsession with bizarre "snuff" conspiracies, didn't discourage the paper from the following piece of sensitive reporting...

APR 19TH: (*The Star*) "SNUFFED OUT BY EVIL PERVERTS". "A child sex ring murdered tragic bike boy Daniel Handley, police revealed last night. They fear he was snatched... abused in gay orgies and brutally murdered. The nine-year-old's agonising ordeal may have also been filmed by the evil monsters in a 'snuff' video. The sick videos get their name from the fact that victims are sexually attacked, tortured and beaten until their lives are 'snuffed' out. Gay perverts are known to make videos of their victims and the tape of his death" (Oh, so now we're sure it exists - JM) "... could hold vital clues to the identity of the killers. Cops know that if a tape was made..." (Then again, maybe not - JM) "... it will already be doing the rounds of other paedophile rings".

MAY 16TH: "MIRROR GETS BAN ON SICK VIDEO NASTY". The paper slaps itself on the back for "banning" (persuading Boots, W. H. Smith and Woolworth's not to stock) "Britain's most violent new video... THE ULTIMATE FIGHTING CHAMPIONSHIP II... the sleeve note boasts: 'Fractured bones, stitches, contusions, concussions, lacerations, haematomas, hyperextensions, torn ligaments, bruises and blood - it's all real'". Government officials are to investigate the award of an 18 certificate to this "shocking tape... the BBFC gave it tape the go-ahead after ordering cuts of only 6 minutes 31 seconds" ("only"?!? - JM). David Altonhasr his mandatory moan, and we are reminded that "(his) constituency is in Liverpool, where two boys killed toddler Jamie Bulger after one had watched (sic) the horrific video CHILD'S PLAY III" (other tabloids, equally censorious of "video nasties", continued to run ads for this tape - JM).

MAY 16TH: (*The Star*) "PORN FILM KILLS LAD". "Schoolboy Daniel Ruddy died while watching a raunchy porn video at his brother's home while baby-sitting". The unfortunate fifteen year-old epileptic actually died while throwing a fit, but when has *The Star* ever let good taste or respect for the dead get in the way of a good headline?

MAY 21ST: "ANGUISH OF CHILDREN IN A VIDEO NIGHTMARE - PARENTS LET EIGHT YEAR-OLDS WATCH SEX-AND-VIOLENCE FILMS". "Parents are allowing children as young as eight to watch extreme sex-and-violence films at home" reports *The Mail On Sunday*. "Some are being traumatised by the shocking scenes and end up having nightmares. And psychiatrists fear that many of them will be 'emotionally brutalised' by the experience... one in ten had viewed the disgusting, blood-sucking exploits of Hannibal Lecter in SILENCE OF THE LAMBS and almost the same number had watched sexually explicit BASIC INSTINCT". Dr Stephen Scott, consultant in child and adolescent psychiatry at London's Maudsley Hospital, is quoted as saying: "These films are likely to coarsen and brutalise the emotions of these children... we must change the threshold of violence. There's no need to show people bleeding with their heads blown off" (as a doctor, he should realise that it's difficult to blow a head off without at least some loss of blood - JM). David Alton, who wants special police units to enforce the law, complains: "I'm appalled that not one video shop has been prosecuted. We need policing on the ground to act as a deterrent against greedy individuals who don't care and need to be hit hard".

THE SEDUCTION OF THE GULLIBLE

JUN 10TH: "RESERVOIR DOGS KIDS LOCKED UP". *The Star* reports that "baby-faced raiders" Scott Richards, 14, and Richard Rothwell, 17, have been given 2 years youth custody for holding up stores with a replica gun. They "wanted to be like gangsters" after watching a tape of RESERVOIR DOGS. "Richards also stole his mother's purse, pointed a gun at her and yelled: 'Mum, you are dead, you bitch!'" Sounds like a problem caused by bad upbringing rather than video viewing. Indeed, both of these clowns were on amyl nitrate when they conceived and executed their stupid little heists.

The same day's *Mirror*, reporting on the same case ("RESERVOIR PUPPIES - TWO KIDS IN COPYCAT VIDEO RAID") mysteriously adds "The violent film was blamed for sparking a wave of killings in America" (Really? When? Methinks they're mixing up their RESERVOIR DOGS with their NATURAL BORN KILLERS! - JM)

JUN 14TH: Quentin Tarantino's RESERVOIR DOGS is finally released on video in the UK.

JUN 17TH: *The Sun* reports ("EXECUTIONS ON SICK VIDEO") that "a sick video showing films of 50 real executions hits High Street shops next week. It includes close-up shots of public lynchings, shootings and beheadings. A woman is shown being hacked to death and a blindfolded man gasps for breath for a minute after having his face blown apart by a firing squad". Anonymous "clean-up campaigners" are quoted as claiming that EXECUTIONS "panders to violence freaks and should be banned".

JUN 18TH: Under the unwieldy headline "BAN IT! *NEWS OF THE WORLD* EXPOSES SICK EXECUTION VIDEO THAT W. H. SMITH IS HAPPY TO SELL (IT SHOWS CLIPS OF REAL-LIFE KILLINGS), the paper targets one store in particular for stocking EXECUTIONS... "W. H. SMITH is stocking the stomach-churning collection alongside children's titles like POSTMAN PAT!" Co-producer David Herman defends the documentary by saying: "Anyone hoping to be entertained by this will be disappointed. It's grim and we want people to be shocked. I don't worry that young people might get to see it. I hope they do. I think it should be shown in schools, as it will promote debate" but David Alton calls for the tape to be banned and for James Ferman, who OK'd its 18 classification, to resign. "These videos must have a corrupting effect", he says: "The 18-certificate will mean nothing. Parents often don't know what kids are watching. I'm appalled that W. H. Smith might sell this. (They) used to be a family store. They must have lost their marbles". The store has announced that it is reconsidering its decision to retail EXECUTIONS, as they were erroneously informed that it had the backing of Amnesty International.

JUN 20TH: Inevitably... "STORE BANS VIDEO OF EXECUTIONS" (*The Mirror*)

JUN 22ND - 23RD: Redemption fail to convince the Video Appeals Committee to over-turn a BBFC ban on BARE BEHIND BARS. In the light of this decision, Nigel Wingrove reveals that plans to submit Bruno Mattei's VIOLENCE IN A WOMEN'S PRISON and Aldo Lado's LATE NIGHT TRAINS (aka NIGHT TRAIN MURDERS) have been dropped.

JUN 25TH: "WE'VE GOT YOU TAPED". *The News Of The World* sends underage youths into "some of the most trusted names on Britain's high street... family favourites like Virgin, Woolworth's, Boots and Tower Records" and finds that they are willing to sell her EXECUTIONS... sorry, to "peddle sex and violence to innocent kids". "Our under-cover child reporters went mostly unchallenged as they bought a vile collection of films showing rapes, murders and mutilations", concludes the paper's "shock investigation".

AUG 9TH: (*Daily Mail*) "SKY-HIGH VIOLENCE". A report from academics at Sheffield

THE SEDUCTION OF THE GULLIBLE

University, co-financed by the BBC and the Independent Television Commission, finds that one third of all the TV programmes they survived contained some violence, but ironically that satellite channels owned by Rupert Murdoch, also proprietor of several video-bashing tabloids, "were responsible for twice as much as terrestrial television". "Christopher Graffius, of the Movement for Christian Democracy" (David Alton's secretary, to boot - JM) ".. said 'The report turns the fire on satellite TV as a fall guy'". It was, of course, completely ignored by Murdoch's papers.

AUG 18TH: (*The Mirror*) "BASIC INSTINCT VIDEO MADE ME STAB SAILOR - MUM FELT ATTACK WAS A 'GOOD IDEA'". 41 year-old Vanessa Ballantyne of Portsmouth, "stirred by the violent images" according to The Mirror, picked up a sailor at random and stabbed him in the belly. He survived, she was banged up in a loony-bin, where she belonged, and the tabloids got their cheap headlines...
The Star - "BASIC INSTINCT TURNED WIFE INTO CRAZED KNIFE FIEND"
The Sun - "BASIC INSTINCT VIDEO MADE MUM A KNIFE MANIAC"

SEPTEMBER. In this month, Ray Brady's low-budget British production BOY MEETS GIRL is point-blank refused a video certificate by the BBFC.

SEP 24TH: Under the headline "VILE VIC'S TRADE IN TAPES OF TORTURE", *The News Of The World* exposes how "jobless builder Vic Swan is flogging some of the sickest porn videos ever seen in Britain... while claiming the dole, he rakes in cash from vile tapes showing gas chamber executions and concentration camp atrocities". Vile Vic is quoted as offering for sale "a film on people having sex with corpses" (presumably Jorg Buttgereit's NEKROMANTIC - JM), plus "videos showing cannibalism and animal abuse" (CANNIBAL FEROX / HOLOCAUST? - JM), as well as "S. S. EXPERIMENT CAMP and a load like that". Presumably Italian productions pirated from Dutch tapes, these latter items are mis-identified as "German and Dutch-made tapes" by *The News Of The World*, which then goes into imaginative overdrive by claiming that such items "are snapped up by neo-Nazi perverts". "Barrel-chested Swan, of Mitcham, Surrey" is also quoted as offering "a German torture and rape one which is the real thing... it's the bizzo!", enthuses barrel-chested Vile Vic.

OCT 29TH: "SEX AND VIOLENCE VIDEOS FACE BAN". *The News Of The World* trailers "a major government crackdown to be announced this week" in which, it claims, the classification of every video will be reviewed and many raised to '18', penalties will be upped to two years in jail and unlimited fines, video games will be brought under strict control, and "so-called educational videos, supplying filth disguised as instruction, will also be curbed". This clampdown is described as "a response to parental fears over the increasing availability of videos featuring soft porn and violence". The report describes how "Chucky, the horror doll in the Child's Play series, became a national bogeyman after he was linked to the James Bulger trial" and continues: "recent studies demonstrate (sic) videos DO have a lasting effect on children". Home Office minister Baroness Blatch says retailers will have two weeks to remove banned videos from their shelves".

NOV 7TH: (*The Mirror*) "PARK RAPIST, 14, GOT IDEA FROM PORN VIDEO". "A boy of 14 raped a 12 year-old girl (in Oldham, Greater Manchester) after watching a pornographic video. He later said: 'I got the idea from watching a video'. Police found the video, called PHYSICAL, hidden in the teenager's room along with balaclavas, knives and women's clothing". *The Sun* felt that PHYSICAL had given him more than an idea ("MASKED RAPIST AGED 14 - PORN FILM GAVE HIM EVIL URGE"). I know what I'd give him...

THE SEDUCTION OF THE GULLIBLE

1996

MAR 13TH: On the day that Lucio Fulci dies in Italy, paedophile Thomas Hamilton shoots up Dunblane Primary School in Scotland, killing sixteen children and one teacher. Without even taking time out to fabricate the kind of video link they concocted for the Hungerford massacre, the usual elements are soon howling for "restrictions on violent TV and video". Warner spinelessly announce that they are postponing the video release of NATURAL BORN KILLERS, a "postponement" that has now extended into an indefinite, self-imposed ban.

APR 8TH: Under the headline "MY PAL WAS KILLED BY HOLLYWOOD BLOOD LUST - AUTHOR BLAMES NATURAL BORN KILLERS FOR COPYCAT ATTACK", *The Sun* reports that best-selling author and lawyer John Grisham is blaming the murder of his friend Bill Savage on Oliver Stone's film, rather than the losers who actually committed it - Ben Darras and Sarah Edmondson (whom Grisham, incredibly, refers to as "Ben and Sarah"). He recommends that Stone be sued. Stone counters by complaining that he's being treated as a scapegoat and calling Grisham "a lawyer in search of a client". "Once grown and gone horribly wrong, these children must answer for their actions, not Hollywood directors" he concludes, reasonably enough.

APR 10TH: An inquest hears that 14-year-old Imtiaz Ahmed, obsessed with Disney's THE LION KING hanged himself, leaving a note that said: "I killed myself because I wanted to become a Lion King. Goodbye mum and dad, brothers and sisters, goodbye forever", together with a request that he should be buried with a tape of the film. His filofax contained the message: "I want to die, Allah. Please make me a Lion King". The media's failure to exploit this tragedy no doubt owed less to considerations of good taste (when has that ever stopped them?) than with the fact that the unfortunate kid was fixated on THE LION KING rather than, say, THE SILENCE OF THE LAMBS.

APR 28TH: *The Sunday Sport*, still embroidering a non-existent connection to the Bulger case, gets its soiled panties in a knot over THE GOOD SON finally being released on sell-through video. The supposedly retired Mrs Whitehouse gets to rant: "It is sick beyond measure. I would urge people to write to their MPs and demand that they take action". A lily-livered HMV spokesman proclaims: "We will not be promoting it at all. We recognise the circumstances and it is something we are sensitive to". Thankfully, Virgin Our Price take a more robust stand, asserting: "We believe that any link between the film THE GOOD SON and the James Bulger case is very tenuous". Indeed.

APR 28TH: Deranged surfer Martin Bryant shoots 35 people in the Australian state of Tasmania.

APR 29TH: Senior FBI mass murder consultant Dr Park Deitz claims that the Tasmanian massacre could have been "inspired" by media coverage of the Dunblane atrocity.

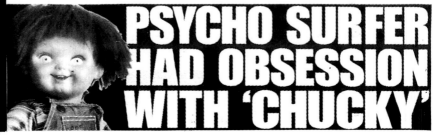

THE SEDUCTION OF THE GULLIBLE

MAY 3RD: Obviously smarting at Dr Deitz's conclusions, *The Mirror* lays blame for the Australian atrocity in more predictable quarters: "PSYCHO SURFER HAD OBSESSION WITH CHUCKY - HE LOVED KILLER DOLL" (Apparently *The Mirror* considered this angle more headline-worthy than Bryant's penchant for sex with animals!) "Bryant's former girlfriend, seventeen-year-old Jenetta Hoani gave an eerie glimpse into the twisted mind of the 28-year old surfer who killed 35 people in Tasmania on Sunday... 'He loved Chucky - he thought he was really cool. In the film...'" (CHILD'S PLAY 2, apparently - JM) "'... the doll comes to life and has to kill a boy so that it can be real. Then it goes around killing people. Chucky is really evil. He just laughs and carries on!'"

To confirm its opposition to violent entertainment, the centre pages of today's *Mirror* comprise a gung-ho guide to the SAS ("DEATH IS NATURE'S WAY OF SAYING YOU'VE FAILED SELECTION")... subsequent instalments feature "never before seen" shots of mangled Iranian corpses in the aftermath of the famous Embassy siege. Elsewhere in this issue, *The Mirror* reports The High Court's ruling that Home Secretary Michael Howard acted unlawfully when decreeing that Jamie Bulger's killers serve a minimum of 15 years behind bars. After all, they were "*made to do it* by a video", right?

MAY 7TH: *The Daily Mail* (...surprisingly late in jumping the bandwagon) "MOVIE CLAMPDOWN CALL AFTER TASMANIA HORROR - CHUCKY DOLL WAS KILLER'S INSPIRATION""Newly elected Liberal Prime Minister John Howard ... promised to press for tighter restrictions on violent videos and the broadcasting of horror films on TV. The demand for stricter controls on films came after it was revealed that schizophrenic Martin Bryant, who killed 34 (sic) people at the former prison colony at Port Arthur, was an avid fan of Chucky, the evil doll in the CHILD'S PLAY video films... Mr Howard said: 'It is hard to believe that the repetitive, mind-numbing violence sometimes seen on television does not have a deleterious effect on some people'."

Almost as an afterthought, *The Mail* adds that there will also be new restrictions on the availability of guns in Australia... you know, the things that actually killed those 34 (or was it 35?) people in Port Arthur, the kids in Dunblane, etc... etc... etc...

MAY 25TH *The Star* reports that Robert ("I HEARD THE VOICE OF MICHAEL MYERS") Sartin has been confined to a mental institution for life on account of his shooting rampage in Monkseaton, North Tyneside. "Cops found video tapes of the Hallowe'en (sic) series of movies... at his home... Myers was a psychopathic killer who donned an ice hockey mask" (Hang on... that was Jason from FRIDAY THE 13TH!)

JUL 5TH: (*The Star*) "KNIFE FRENZY OF A TEENAGE PREDATOR". Lincoln charmer Carol Cunningham dosed her daughter's boyfriend -14 year-old Ian McPhail - with LSD, then sent him next door to rob middle-aged Margaret Dennison, who miraculously survived near-decapitation after McPhail attacked her with a machete. McPhail described the visual disturbance he suffered due to the drug as "like a scene from PREDATOR... I saw all different colours". Naturally *The Star* ran this report next to a huge picture of Arnold Schwarzenegger, in a lame attempt to prop up its desperate "copy-cat" scenario.

AUG 26TH: Under the headline "PEEPSHOW OPS VIDEO IS SLAMMED", *The Star* reveals that "a 'video nasty' showing surgeons performing penis implants and other intimate ops was blasted by MPs and the British Medical Association last night. The stomach churner was filmed in British hospitals as a training aid for medics but goes on sale today for £12.99. Unsuspecting patients never knew it would be made public". David Donoghue, representing the makers of EVERYDAY OPERATIONS (previously responsible for EXECUTIONS) contends that no patient or hospital is identifiable, but

THE SEDUCTION OF THE GULLIBLE

Labour's consumer affairs spokesman Nigel Griffiths describes the video ("which shows gynaecological procedures, vasectomies and open heart surgery") as "a disgrace".

AUG 26TH: "BAN THE SALE OF NHS OP VIDEO NASTIES - FURY OVER 'SICK' FILM". *The Mirror* quotes Dr Vivian Nathanson, head of the British Medical Authority's ethics committee, as saying that EVERYDAY OPERATIONS ("which shows more than 20 ops in sickening detail") could "put patients off live-saving surgery... to make money from frightening people and perhaps stopping them from seeking treatment is clearly dis-tasteful... we urge people not to watch this video." David Donoghue, "who hopes to sell around 400,000 copies" describes the video as "educational", adding: "It is not cheap thrills. You can actually see what happens in hospitals. We live in a sanitised society where we are not allowed to see reality".

SEP 1ST: (*The Sunday Sport*) "IS THIS YOU UNDER THE KNIFE? FIRST EVER SHOTS FROM GRUESOME OPERATIONS VIDEO". "Horrifying" stills (repeated from The Mirror's AUGUST 26th report) include... ulp... the slicing of bunions!. *The Sport* reports that the release of EVERYDAY OPERATIONS has been postponed after the Department of Health won a High Court injunction, pending an investigation of "whether patients gave their permission for their explicit ops to be filmed" (What's an "explicit op", exactly? - JM), continuing: "Lawyers acting for film makers David Donoghue Associates (DDA) and its producers ICM Video, are fighting to have the ban lifted. They claim the video, due to hit the shelves a week ago, is 'in the public interest' and 'educational'. Father of four Mr Donaghue was involved in producing the highly controversial EXECUTIONS video last year, which featured death sentences being carried out. The movie made a profit of £300,000 in its first three days, despite being banned in some high street shops".

SEP 17TH: (*The Star*) "VID-OPS ON SALE IN SPRING". "Health Minister Gerald Malone had pledged earlier that such 'nasties' could never again be purchased by the general public... but David Donoghue, spokesman for IMC Videos, replied: 'It will be on sale in the spring, once the consent demanded by the British Board of Classification has been obtained'. Mr Donoghue also states that there is no public opposition to the video's release, and that the Department of Health has now conceded that the material is "valid". "How dare Mr Malone liken this educational film to a video nasty?" ask Mr Donoghue: "We demand an apology!"

NOVEMBER. Early this month, satellite channel Bravo runs a season of Italian horror movies, including DEMONS 1 and 2, and Lucio Fulci's THE BEYOND, HOUSE BY THE CEMETERY and ZOMBIE FLESH EATERS.

Halfway through the month, Prime Minister John Major has his eye firmly on the upcoming General Election...

NOV 6TH: (*The Sun*) "PM'S WAR ON VIDEO VIOLENCE"... "Violent videos and TV shows are the target of a new crackdown launched by Premier John Major last night. Film-makers and telly chiefs were warned to clean up their act - or face new laws. Ministers say those who profit from violence have a responsibility to ensure their shows do not damage society. They fear children exposed to bloodthirsty films can become evil thugs - like the youngsters who murdered little James Bulger after watching horror movie CHILD'S PLAY (sic). The government also wants less violence in kids' cartoons".

NOV 8TH: On TV discussion programme THE TIME, THE PLACE, the NVLA's Joanna Bogle - who once likened the author of this volume to a harsh Victorian industrialist (see JAN 24th, 1994) accuses him of "living in the 1950's"... that's progress, I guess!

THE SEDUCTION OF THE GULLIBLE

NOV 10TH: (*Sunday Sport*) "FURY AS CENSORS PASS BLOODIEST FILM EVER!" "A shocking film which features sickening scenes of a girl having a shotgun ABORTION have sparked new fury. The movie..." (Scooter McCrae's SHATTER DEAD - JM), "...so gruesome that it was seized by Customs as being obscene, is to go on sale as Prime Minister John Major launched a crackdown on video nasties". "I do not want to be seen as dictating to people what they should and shouldn't watch, but..." (of course there's a but) "... I find it very disturbing that films like SHATTER DEAD have even been made, let alone given a certificate by the BBFC", says Nigel Evans, Tory MP for Ribble Valley, before signing off with the nauseatingly condescending statement that he is "... not convinced that in today's society people can distinguish between fact and fiction".

NOV 10TH: (*News Of The World*) "HOW DID VILLAINS KNOW WHAT TO DO BEFORE TV?" asks Michael Winner, going on to argue that increasingly onerous censorship in the UK has been accompanied by a rocketing crime rate, whereas lax censorship abroad goes hand-in-hand with far more orderly societies. "We are quite capable of seeing TV and video that the rest of the world sees, without being namby-pambied, and remaining decent citizens. There is not some super-class of upper people who can see all this and not be affected and some sub-class - that's you and me - that can't because we'll go out and murder our neighbours", he concludes.

NOV 25TH: It is announced that by a vote of 7 to 2 the European court in Strasbourg has overturned the European Commission's ruling in favour of Nigel Wingrove and against the BBFC in the case of VISIONS OF ECSTASY. Wingrove had argued that the ban was a breach of his right of free expression under article 10 of the Convention of Human Rights, but the new judgement says that it fell within acceptable exceptions, which include protecting Christian feelings. Because the film could be offensive to believers, the ban was "neither arbitrary or excessive". The ruling is seen as a surprise, because the Court has previously tended to uphold the decisions of the Commission, which has more often than not meant finding against the British government.

DEC 1ST: Gun enthusiasts march in London against proposed tightening of gun controls in the wake of the Dunblane massacre. They blame the government for "caving in to media pressure", and claim that they are being used as scapegoats. Not that they're above using more familiar scapegoats themselves, their petition blaming "film, TV and video" for "encouraging gun misuse". Yeah, right...

Pandering to such hypocrisy, MPs like Frank Cook (Labour) and Sir Ivan Lawrence (Conservative), who bang on about the harmful effects on children of supposedly lax video laws, are at this time vocal in their opposition to any attempts to control the kind of firepower that actually slaughtered the Dunblane kids.

DEC 4TH: (*The Mirror*) "SICK! BAN THIS GORY HOSPITAL OPS VIDEO NASTY" "A sick video showing gory hospital emergency ops will hit High street shops next year. Last night the video - LIFE AND DEATH IN THE ER - sparked fury among MPs and medical experts who called for it to be banned". According to *The Mirror*, the tape comprises "a human heart being pulled out, a gaping facial bullet hole, stabbing victims and severed limbs...doctors are seen poking fingers into a hole between a gunshot victims' eyes... scenes are linked by still pictures of horrible injuries and ops". Margaret Ford, deputy director of the BBFC (who have cleared the tape for January release) says "You don't have to watch it if you don't wish to". Nigel Griffiths, opposition affairs spokesman, repeats his view that: "This sort of film should be banned. To say that this is educational is a sick joke", and a representative of the BMA condemns "sensationalist" videos watched for pleasure, not education".

THE SEDUCTION OF THE GULLIBLE

DEC 13TH: The Broadcasting Standards Council survey YOUNG PEOPLE AND THE MEDIA reports on the viewing habits of 10-16 year-olds. 81% of the youths questioned opined that their age-group did not need protecting, and 80% said that the BBFC did not represent their views. Although such findings would seem to run contrary to received wisdom, BSC chairman Lady Howe manages to put a more familiar spin on them by declaring: "The extent to which violence seems to be so much a feature of everyday as well as media life for young people has to be a worry for everyone".

DEC 13TH: Under the headline "TIME TO SACK THIS FEEBLE CENSOR", *The Daily Mail* goes for James Ferman's jugular. Opening up with xenophobia and personal abuse ("Though American by birth, he seems to see himself as the little Dutch boy, bravely inserting a finger into the dyke of Britain's official morality, while foreign filth cascades through in hundreds of other places"), *The Mail* proceeds to have its cake and eat it by working backwards from those proverbial "special circumstances" of home video viewing to a call for greater censorship in the cinemas ("Ferman admits that if ERASER is to gain an 18 certificate, it will have to be shorn of several more shots. In other words, he let through scenes of violence in the cinema which he knows would be unacceptable in the home"... note that David Cronenberg's CRASH is currently having a, er, rough ride getting a theatrical certificate - JM) and follows up with further twisted reasoning: ("I have seen the tiny cuts which Ferman made in action adventures... designed to remove evidence of the heroes enjoying their sadism... not only does much of the nastiest violence remain uncut, but the censors scissors actually render the heroes more likeable, because they are less obviously sadists. The unintended result is that audiences end up cheering the remaining violence even more, and that ultra-violent films which - uncut - would barely have been allowed an 18 certificate, are now finding a much wider audience among the young, thanks to a 15 or even a 12 certificate"). So Ferman is damned if he cuts, damned if he doesn't. I never thought I'd end up feeling sorry for the guy, but...

THE SEDUCTION OF THE GULLIBLE

If our censor finds much of this *Mail* piece confusing though, the conclusion is clear enough (albeit factually inaccurate): "If Ferman really wanted to take a tough line, he could. He could refuse to give certificates to ultra-violent films. The truth is that he has the power, but not the inclination" (yeah, right - JM). "It is time for him to go".

1997

JAN 19TH: (*The Sunday Mirror*) "STAGG CHOOSES TV TRIAL AS RACHEL'S BRUTAL MURDER IS RECREATED ON SCREEN". "A sleazy film-maker is trying to cash in on the brutal murder of Rachel Nickell... with the man cleared of killing her in the starring role. Barrie Goulding - who makes a fortune from sick videos of executions and operations - and business associate Christopher Berry-Dee plan to film a reconstruction of the Wimbledon Common slaying. And if Goulding's previous videos are anything to go by, the recon-struction will be savage and shocking".

JAN 26TH: "BANNED! *NEWS OF THE WORLD* STOPS VIDEO NASTY". "A porn film posing as 'educational' has been banned from High Street Stores after *The News Of The World* revealed its sleazy truth. HOOKERS - SEX FOR SALE is the latest vile production from film maker Barry Goulding, notorious for showing hangings in another sick video about state executions". The report goes on to reveal that W. H. Smith was stocking the video "after Goulding passed it off as a documentary" but stopped after *NOTW* investigators "uncovered the facts about its filth". "Outraged" Conservative MP Piers Merchant (shortly to come under scandalised tabloid scrutiny himself on account of his allegedly colourful love life) is quoted "slating" retailers who continue to stock the tape: "It is totally unsuitable for High Street Stores" he comments: "It is clearly designed to titillate rather than inform".

FEB 17TH: (*The Mirror*) "SNUFF MOVIES AT BROADMOOR" Next to a photo of one of the maximum security mental hospital's most notorious residents, Peter "Yorkshire Ripper" Sutcliffe, the paper reports that: "Sex-and-kill 'snuff' movies were among the hard core porn hoard discovered at Broadmoore... the videos were said to be among 100 vile and disgusting' movies found in a swoop... child sex offenders and killers are copying thesmuggled videos using their own recorders. Staff are now probing an alleged ring dealing in child porn".

APR 7TH: (*The Sun*) "COPS HUNT BRITISH SNUFF MOVIE FIEND". "A British sex pervert was being hunted last night over the suspected murders of up to five young boys for 'snuff movies'. The fiend and his pals allegedly killed the yougsters as they killed them during paedophile orgies in Holland. He was identified from a child porn film seized during a series of raids. Snuff movies were allegedly filmed by British paedophiles in Amsterdam during the late '80s. One British fiend told TV reporters the bodies of five young boys were dumped in a lake".

APR 21ST: (*The Sport* 'Horror Crime Exclusive') "PURE EVIL... BLOOD LUST OF HOOKER SNARED BY DEATH TAPE". "Vice girl Samantha Enoch knifed her sugar daddy lover to death after repeatedly watching horror film PSYCHO. Wealthy banker Habib Saliba, 47, was stabbed 26 times by the 20 year-old because she feared he would tell police about jewellery she stole from him. Enoch's sister, Michelle, claims that Samantha got ideas for the killing from watchinig horror films. Michelle, 18, said: 'She used to watch PSYCHO all the time and was obsessed with NIGHTMARE ON ELM STREET and HALLOWEEN. She was pure evil, and would watch the films on drugs'."

The report continues in a vein which indicates that Ms. Enoch might not exactly have been a model citizen long before she encountered horror videos, revealing that "the wild child killer also stabbed her mum in the face with a fork when she was two, started drinking vodka when she was three, had sex at 12 and became a hooker at 15, and bunked off from Norwood Girls' School to have sex with punters to pay for cocaine".

Just when you thought it was safe to assume that "alco-pops" had replaced "nasties" as the prime focus of national breast-beating....

AUG 18TH: The press starts agonising over research findings leaked by Birmingham University's Dr Kevin Browne, which will be presented to new Home Secretary Jack Straw in October. Entitled THE EFFECT OF VIDEO VIOLENCE ON YOUNG OFFENDERS, this two-year study has compared the reactions of violent and non-violent offenders with non-offenders to "violent or sexual incidents" on video. The study apparently suggests that violent offenders react differently to non-violent ones, with the former more likely to remember graphic details of what they have watched. The trash press seem to detect some kind of irony in these findings, given that Straw has supposedly been considering the possibility of putting more TV sets into prison cells to pacify inmates.

"STRAW TO CENSOR SCREEN VIOLENCE IN JAILS - YOUNG THUGS BARRED FROM VIDEO NASTIES" predicts *The Express*, heralding what it sees as "the first official link between crime and screen violence". The *Express* report continues: "Young offenders are set to be barred from watching violent videos in institutions. The crackdown... is designed to curb copycat crime. Ministers are concerned at the way films such as PULP FICTION... RESERVOIR DOGS... and NATURAL BORN KILLERS... appear to glamorise violence. There have been calls for tighter censorship in the wake of films such as CRASH, whose sado-masochistic scenes were branded ' beyond depravity'" ... by *The Express*, of course! Not content with quoting its own most recent hysterical outbursts, *The Express* proceeds to wheel out tried-and-trusted garbage about the Bulger case, i.e. "Robert Thompson and John Venables were said to have a fascination with the video CHILD'S PLAY 3"... though anyone who did ever say this was lying through their arse.

Needless to say, *The Mail* can't resist another wallow in the Bulger family's misery, either: "It was suggested during the trial that his killers were influenced by the video CHILD'S PLAY 3", its report "MOVIES "CAN MAKE YOUNG MORE VIOLENT... 'STUDY LINKS SCREEN SAVAGERY TO REAL-LIFE ATTACKS'" inaccurately rambles, before taking a huge leap in logic to sum up the new research's conclusion as "young violent offenders are more likely to be involved in assaults if they have seen disturbing films and videos". Elsewhere one Cornelia Oddie, deputy director of Family and Youth Concern, comments:"It takes an official report to make a scientific finding, but it is something parents have known for a long time". Tory MP Julian Brazier is allowed to chip in with the worst argument in the world (see appendix I) and contends that the new research "makes it imperative that the Home Secretary should revise film and video censorship, with a new management regime at the BBFC which better reflects public opinion". *The Mail* feels that he's about to get his wish: "Mr Straw is expected to act on the BBFC within the next few months. He is currently vetting possible replacements for the organisation's president".

The Telegraph agrees ("Mr Straw has already decided that, in future, the head of the BBFC will be selected by ministers, making the board more accountable to the government") in a report entitled "SEX AND VIOLENCE VIDEO BAN FOR YOUNG OFFENDERS". This is tack taken by most of the papers, though of course it took a tacky Murdoch organ to see the wider possible implications of these unremarkable "findings"...

THE SEDUCTION OF THE GULLIBLE

(*The Times*) "VIOLENCE ON VIDEO BRINGS PRESSURES FOR REGULATION" (Like there wasn't any already? - JM) "The Home Secretary is facing growing pressure to tighten up regulations considering the sale and distribution of videos in the sake of a new suggestion of links between violence on screen and the behaviour of offenders". Yes, along with those violent offenders, we're all going to have to suffer. Again.

THE END?

THE SEDUCTION OF THE GULLIBLE

THE WORST ARGUMENT IN THE WORLD...

... as formulated by Tory MP Julian Brazier: "People spend thousands of millions of pounds a year on advertising because they believe it can influence behaviour... it is naive to think screen violence does not".

But Julian, old bean... comparing films on video with commercials is like comparing chalk and cheese. Take Nick Kamen's famous "dropping your 501s in the launderette" ad, for example: if ads and videos affect people in the same way, and that way is "monkey see / monkey do", then instead of more people going out to buy pairs of Levis (as actually happened), the effect of this commercial would have been an epidemic of people de-bagging among the spin-driers. It didn't happen Julian, did it?

Now kindly go and boil your Right Honourable head, you prat...

THE SEDUCTION OF THE GULLIBLE

A list of films refused video certification by the BBFC in the period between September 1985 and October 1994 alone. Bear this in mind next time some moron MP or cynical gutter-press hack demands the "introduction" of powers to prevent certain titles being released on video in the UK...

ANGEL OF VENGEANCE (Ted V. Mikels); BACK IN ACTION; BARE BEHIND BARS; CALIGULA... THE UNTOLD STORY; CAGED WOMEN (later released in drastically cut version); THE CLASS OF 1984; A COMING OF ANGELS; CURFEW ; DEMONIAC (= THE RIPPER / SADIST OF NOTRE DAME); THE EVIL PROTECTOR (= BUTCHER, BAKER, NIGHTMARE MAKER); GAME OF SURVIVAL aka TENEMENT; HIDDEN RAGE aka PERFECT VICTIMS; HOT LINE; HOUSE OF HOOKERS; KICKBOXER 4 - THE AGGRESSOR; POSSESSION (UNTIL DEATH DO YOU PART); PRECIOUS JEWELS; PSYCHIC KILLER II (= ISLAND OF DEATH); SADO-MANIA; SAVAGE STREETS (later released in drastically cut version); SILENT NIGHT, DEADLY NIGHT PART 2; SLUMBER PARTY MASSACRE 2; SLUTS AND GODDESSES; THE STORY 'O' PART 2; TARGET MASSACRE; THE TRIP; THE VIOLATORS; VISIONS OF EVIL; VISIONS OF ECSTASY; WAR VICTIMS; WILD RIDERS

plus the bondage / corporal punishment shorts
A BRIEF ENCOUNTER; CHAINED; HEAD GIRL OF ST WINIFRED'S; SIXTEEN SPECIAL; SIXTH FORM AT ST WINIFRED'S; TIED AND TICKLED #4; TIED AND TICKLED #18; WARDEN'S END

In addition, the following have never been formally submitted because it remains an open secret that they stand absolutely no chance of gaining certification

DEATH WISH; THE EXORCIST; LEATHERFACE - THE TEXAS CHAINSAW MASSACRE PART 3; THE STRAW DOGS; THE TEXAS CHAINSAW MASSACRE; THE TEXAS CHAINSAW MASSACRE PART 2

ABOUT THE AUTHOR

JOHN MARTIN (seen here in a recent photograph) was born in Liverpool during 1959, the year that saw the introduction of both The Obscene Publications Act and The Mental Health Act. He's been trying to convince himself that all this was sheer coincidence ever since. Described as "a Marxist master of porn" for his sixth-form journalistic endeavours, Martin subsequently hit a downward career spiral. In 1986 he co-founded SAMHAIN, the first of the modern horror fanzines. 1993 saw the birth of his GIALLO PAGES, dedicated to Italian exploitation cinema. Martin has contributed to (among others) MAXIM, DARK SIDE, VIDEO WORLD, INFINITY, DEEP RED, EUROPEAN TRASH CINEMA, VIDEOOZE, CAMERA OBSCURA, STARBURST, FEAR and L'ECRAN FANTASTIQUE. The last three, though ostensibly "more professional" efforts than some of the others, all cheated him out of payment.

Martin considers it a minor miracle that he's managed to make a meagre living out of writing about obscure exploitation pictures, in a milieu dominated by such dis-honest distributors as Liverpool's WORLDS APART and Trevor Barley's ever-popular MEDIA PUBLICATIONS.

Martin currently lives in Nottingham with his wife Catherine, and an ever-expanding collection of rodents. He is determined to complete his long-threatened book about Lucio Fulci... one of these days.